IDENTITIES

IDENTITIES
Readings from Contemporary Culture

ANN RAIMES
Hunter College, City University of New York

HOUGHTON MIFFLIN COMPANY   Boston   Toronto

Geneva, Illinois   *Palo Alto*   *Princeton, New Jersey*

To my students in "Expository Writing," for being
involved and enthusiastic even in a required course.

Sponsoring editor: George Kane
Basic book editor: Martha Bustin
Senior project editor: Rosemary Winfield
Senior production/design coordinator: Jill Haber
Manufacturing coordinator: Florence Cadran
Marketing manager: Charles Cavaliere

Cover design: Len Massiglia
Cover Image: Alexandra Maldonado, The Stock Illustration Source, Inc.

Credits

Pages 501–503   Angelou, Maya. "Human Family." *I Shall Not Be Moved.* New York:
Random House, 1990, 4–5. Copyright © 1990 by Maya Angelou. Reprinted by
permission of Random House, Inc.

Acknowledgments are continued on pages 507–512, which constitute a continuation of the copyright page.

Printed in the U.S.A.

Library of Congress Catalog Card Number: 95-76979

ISBN: 0-395-70107-4

456789-B-99 98 97

Contents

❖

v

UNIT 3 Gender and Sexual Orientation 139

UNIT 4 Ethnic Affiliation and Class 201

UNIT 5 Family Ties 297

UNIT 8 **Nationality**   461

Alternative Table of Contents
Types of Writing and
Rhetorical Modes

❖

I. Types of Writing

LITERARY WRITING

SOCIOLOGICAL/SCIENTIFIC WRITING

WRITING SUPPORTED BY RESEARCH

WRITING SUPPORTED BY INTERVIEWS AND ETHNOGRAPHY

II. Rhetorical Modes

NARRATIVE

DESCRIPTION

ILLUSTRATION

DIVISION AND CLASSIFICATION

CAUSE AND EFFECT

ARGUMENT AND PERSUASION

Preface for Instructors

This anthology for first-year college writers presents a wide variety of carefully selected readings on the theme of identity and culture. Selections are organized around some of the basic dimensions of our multifaceted identities: name; gender and sexual orientation; age, appearance, and abilities; ethnic affiliation and class; family ties; education; beliefs and religion; and nationality. This theme of identity is uniquely suited to accomplishing the main goals of this book: helping students to develop college-level reading, thinking, and writing skills. Students have both knowledge of and curiosity about the subject of identity and are open to viewing it with new, more objective, critical and analytical perspectives. It is a subject that allows and facilitates a writer's growth from the strictly personal view to a view that encompasses larger issues and concerns of the wider world.

Many students today, no matter their age or backgrounds, have questions about who they are, who they are becoming in the course of their education, and how they fit and will fit into society's "big picture." And all students, by the time they arrive at college, have been shaped by family, experiences, and the culture at large. However, they may not have viewed these various forces analytically or considered the extent to which the culture itself is shaped by the diverse individuals who make it up, including themselves. The readings in this book encourage questioning—*What are the links between name and ancestry, between name and personal style? What do people like to be called, and why? Do we reinvent ourselves when we change a name, when we move away from our family or native country, when we get an education, or as we age? In what ways is identity fixed and in what ways is it fluid, fragile, and situational?*—and they encourage students to engage complex social and political issues, address matters of personal location to such issues, and elaborate critical reading skills through writing.

The readings in *Identities* have been assembled to provide fresh and varied points of view on such issues of becoming and belonging. Selections reflect our pluralistic, multicultural society. They are drawn from academic and popular sources, from a range of disciplines, and from the work of student and professional authors. Included are academic essays, journalism, autobiography, fiction, and poetry. The readings are current and accessible (most were written in the 1980s and 1990s), and they focus on contemporary life, which students are, in general, better equipped to analyze within the scope of a composition course. Most important, these readings are chosen to stimulate writing. Each gives students the opportunity to engage productively in discussion, research, and writing activities as they consider their own identities and others' across a range of situations. The readings are intriguing and relevant on an immediate, personal level, while leading outward to the study of interpersonal, cultural, and values-oriented issues.

Flexibility and coherence have been the watchwords from the beginning of the development of this anthology. The theme of identity links various issues together and gives a composition course an overarching framework, yet the theme allows teachers the discretion to shape the course according to their particular needs and interests. The eight units can be used in any order and in any combination, or straight through. Because of the interrelated nature of the material under the broad umbrella of identity, units build well one upon another, no matter in what order used. Ideas and voices reverberate from unit to unit in stimulating ways. Within each unit, selections encompass a range of difficulty levels and lengths, again to give flexibility.

Identities' pedagogical apparatus is designed to be straightforward and helpful, not intrusive. Its goal is to get students reading and thinking critically and writing with new sophistication and insight. To that end, the book's introduction takes students through basic strategies for critical reading and writing. Unit-opening quotations present several brief, thought-provoking perspectives. The unit introductions conclude with "Starting Points" questions for journal or freewriting that get students actively thinking about the upcoming topic. "Making Connections" questions at the ends of units point students toward ways the readings throughout the book interrelate and broaden the scope of topics to outside research. The readings themselves are followed by coherent pedagogy designed to (1) look at content and at syntactic, stylistic, or organizational features of the reading and (2) offer a range of writing assignments, some narrative and reflective, some analytical, argumentative, and contrastive. Throughout, the aim has been to keep in mind the context in which this reader will be used—the writing class—and to make the book's activities writing-centered.

Clearly, no single collection can address all the ramifications of the theme of identity. Identity can be shaped or defined by many factors, including occupation, hobbies, media, the environment, genetics, special talents such as music or art, involvement with alcohol or drugs, choice of heroes, psychological makeup, and so on, almost indefinitely. This book focuses on eight basic categories, which are starting points, not a definitive presentation of all that there is to say. This richness of topic leaves open many fruitful directions that you and your students can pursue in class or research work if desired. When students have little experience writing papers requiring critical literacy skills, the identity theme can be, again, flexible and coherent. It can also lead to revelations about how we fit together into a society and help students see themselves as valuable parts of a bigger picture.

The following are some of the features of *Identities* that help students to read, think, and write at a college level.

Features

- **Engaging Themes.** This reader focuses on questions of identity and culture in North America today. The cultural forces that shape identity are explored in eight thematic units: Name; Appearance, Age, and Abilities; Gender and Sexual Orientation; Ethnic Affiliation and Class; Family Ties; Education; Beliefs and Religion; Nationality. The readings in these units are rich with significant and relevant ideas and images.

- **Contemporary Authors and Selections.** Since nearly all of the selections were written in the 1980s and 1990s and address current topics, the issues and perspectives of the writers are stimulating and accessible. They challenge readers to think and express themselves in new and more sophisticated ways.

- **Diverse Authorship.** This book contains a diverse collection of authors writing within the United States and Canada. Some examples include the Hispanic writers Sandra Cisneros, Jimmy Santiago Baca, and Gloria Anzaldúa; the Native American writers Linda Hogan, Lesie Marmon Silko, and Louise Erdrich; the African American writers Henry Louis Gates, Jr., bell hooks, and Maya Angelou; and the Asian American writers Amy Tan, Richard Kim, and Jeffery Chan.

- **Varied Types of Selections.** A range of styles, purposes, and rhetorical modes are presented (see alternative tables of contents). Selections include literary writing, sociological/scientific writing, journalism, autobiography and personal writing, writing supported by outside sources, interviews and ethnography, cultural studies, student writing, short fiction, and poetry. The selections are also varied in length, with many shorter readings that can be used in class.

- **Inclusion of Student Writing.** Six full student essays are included, showing how student writers have tackled some of the issues raised in *Identities.* "Color Me a Clay," for example, by Carmelo Caylo, was written in response to reading other selections in the book.

- **Introduction to Reading and Writing.** The Introduction presents basic strategies for critical reading, including a sample selection with a student's annotations, and essential information about writing, including purpose, audience, and writing as a way of learning. In the Introduction and throughout the apparatus, this book encourages the careful, thoughtful reading that will translate into clearer, more effective papers.

- **Unit Openers to Present the Themes.** Each unit begins with a few thought-provoking **quotations.** For example, Unit 1, "Name," begins with quotations from Shakespeare ("What's in a name? That which we call a rose / By any other name would smell as sweet") and Madonna ("I sometimes think I was born to live up to my name. How could I be anything else but what I am having been named Madonna? I would have either ended up a nun or this"). The **introduction to the theme** discusses the theme and describes the selections. Finally, each thematic introduction ends with "Starting Points (for Journal or Freewriting)," a set of provocative questions about the theme.

- **Apparatus Focused on Writing.** The questions following each reading are divided into two sections: "Responding in Discussion or Writing" and "Writing Assignments." Throughout the book, questions that deal with aspects of a writer's style are labeled "Considerations of Style" and those that require outside sources are labeled "For Further Research." All questions aim at the development of critical reading skills and practical writing skills.

Ancillaries

- **Instructor Support.** An Instructor's Resource Manual is available to teachers who adopt *Identities*. Instructors using or considering using *Identities* may request a copy from a Houghton Mifflin sales representative.

- **A Compatible Handbook.** Instructors who use a handbook and reader together will be pleased to know that *Identities* and *Keys for Writers: A Brief Handbook* were conceived as books that can be used together (though they can also be used separately). Many of the examples in the handbook are drawn from selections in the reader; some of the student writing in the handbook is based on assignments in the reader; and so on. A full description of the connections between the two books, as well as a syllabus suggesting ways they can be used together, is found in the Instructor Support Packet for the handbook, *Keys for Writers*.

- **LitLinks: A Way to Bring the Internet into Composition Classes.** Houghton Mifflin has created an innovative, user-friendly way to make the wealth of information available on the Internet accessible and usable in composition courses. **LitLinks: On-line Resources for Writing Instructors and Students** lets instructors and students use the themes in *Identities* as entry points to the vast resources of the Internet. A class spending a week on the theme of "Family," for example, could pursue online exploration of that issue through LitLinks. LitLinks is a cluster of hypertext connections to sites on the World Wide Web. Between five and ten carefully chosen links are provided for each of the eight themes in *Identities*. For each link, users will see an on-screen description of what can be found at that site, as well as questions or activity ideas. To use LitLinks, you will need an Internet connection and a graphical browser such as

Netscape or Mosaic. You can access LitLinks directly at

http://www.hmco/hmco/college/english/LitLinks.html

Note: you must use upper-case "L"s in LitLinks. Or you can access LitLinks through the Houghton Mifflin College Division Homepage:

http://www.hmco.com

Help in using the World Wide Web is available on-screen, if necessary.

Acknowledgments

Special thanks go to colleagues at Hunter College who provided materials and insights on the topic of identities, particularly Louise DeSalvo, David Gordon, and Neal Tolchin; to Greta Wagle, who helped with biographical research; and to my other English department colleagues, who endured my distracted air over the course of writing this book. I am especially grateful, too, to the Hunter College students whose writing appears in this book—Mel Caylo, Marie Dallam, Polly Pui-Yee Lai, and Helen Skoratowicz—and to all the students in my first-year writing courses who tried out materials, filled out questionnaires, and offered advice and criticism. This book is dedicated to them.

As I worked through the drafts of this book, I was helped a great deal by the comments and suggestions of many knowledgeable and experienced writing instructors, who demonstrated how to be tough yet gracious, critical yet constructive in responding to a colleague's work. The reviewers confirmed my respect for the teaching of writing in this country by the care, thoroughness, broad knowledge, and perceptive insights of their responses and by their ability to connect issues of theory to classroom practice. I am grateful to all of the following:

Sylvia Charshoodian, Boston University
Jan Delasara, Metropolitan State College of Denver
Juan Delgado, California State University, San Bernadino
Joan Gilson, University of Missouri, Kansas City
John Heyda, Miami University
Ernest Johansson, Ohio University

William Jones, Rutgers University
Joseph LaBriola, Sinclair Community College
Ted Lardner, Cleveland State University
Dianne Luce, Midlands Technical College
Margaret Marshall, University of Pittsburgh
James McDonald, University of Southwestern Louisiana
Angelyn Mitchell, University of North Carolina, Wilmington
Michael G. Moran, The University of Georgia
Sarah-Hope Parmeter, University of California, Santa Cruz
John Reilly, Loyola Marymount University
Marti Singer, Georgia State University
Amy Ulmer, Pasadena City College
Ruth Ray, Wayne State University
Andrew Woolf, Northern Essex Community College

I have many people to thank at Houghton Mifflin, all of whom were, throughout the lengthy writing and revising process, warm, supportive, knowledgeable, responsive, and thoroughly professional. Particular thanks go to Susan Anker and Kristin Watts Peri, who first approached me with the project; George Kane, who took over as sponsoring editor and made many useful suggestions; Barbara Roth, who started me off on the right track; Sue Warne, who gave the book the benefit of her wisdom and experience; Bruce Cantley and Jennifer Roderick, who set up and kept track of reviews; Nandana Sen, who skillfully coordinated the production of the Instructor's Resource Manual; Elizabeth Huyck, who prepared the Instructor's Resource Manual; Rosemary Winfield, who skillfully saw the book through production; and, above all, Martha Bustin, development editor, whose contribution to this book has been enormous: giving advice, offering support, listening, hand-holding, rewriting, suggesting materials, and editing. I value her common sense and tact and find it hard to imagine what I will do when I no longer have to talk to her every day.

Finally, thanks go to my friends and family, who have been sorely and sadly neglected over the course of writing this book. Thanks to Anne Estern for arranging tennis games to keep me sane; to Roberta Bernstein, Viki Sand, Judy Bernstein, Bob Weintraub, Helen Rogan, Alfred Gingold, and Carl and Barbara Apstein for long telephone calls and wonderful get-togethers; to the many friends to whom I owe countless dinners and parties; as

always to Emily and Lucy Raimes for diverting me and never failing to make me laugh, even at deadline time; and to James
Raimes who, while suffering many inferior take-out meals and
weekends consumed with manuscripts, still managed to remain
loving and supportive.

Ann Raimes
Hunter College,
City University of New York

IDENTITIES

Introduction

❖

Shaping Identity and Culture

As we grow up and age, we often wrestle with trying to "find ourselves" and "discover who we are." We start off with what seems like a number of unchangeable givens in our individual identity: name, gender, appearance, and race, for instance; then we realize these are not fixed in the perceptions of others and we know we can continually reinvent ourselves. Our identities change to fit into various cultural communities as members of families, age groups, ethnic groups, or institutions like churches, colleges, and businesses. The process of shaping an identity does not occur in isolation; it is enriched when we learn to see, understand, and accept others and ourselves for what we are. As we make ourselves open to learn about others, about *us* and *them,* we learn where cultures intersect and what makes each one distinctive. We find bridges and boundaries. This connecting of ourselves to others—and distinguishing ourselves from others—is a valuable part of the shaping of identity and also of the process of education.

The authors represented in this collection explore some of the basic bridges and boundaries of identity. They try to provoke thought, feeling, and argument. They ask: What does it mean to be old or young; male or female; gay or straight; rich or poor; black, white, Jewish, Latino, or Asian; single, married, or divorced; and so on? They discuss the role of name, gender, appearance, age, abilities, and disabilities; consider how ethnic affiliation, family ties, education, and our belief systems shape a variety of identities within an individual; and assess perceptions of inheriting or claiming a nationality. The selections in this book present the writers' efforts to understand both the many components of their own identity and their contribution to the multicultural society

1

they live in. Just as they strive to understand their identities, all of us struggle to understand the tensions, conflicts, and resolutions that form our culture.

It is important to remember that the interaction between our culture—the shaping forces of the world and society around us—and ourselves is, in every respect, two-way. Our culture might shape and influence us, but it does not exist apart from us. Culture is not limited to the highbrow artistic world of painting, sculpture, classical music, and literature. It is much broader, referring to the customs, expectations, products, and way of life of the part of the world each of us happens to live in. This culture we can legitimately call *our* culture: It includes our homes, schools, occupations, religions, TV and popular songs, the people around us, and all the things we say and do—in fact, all the acts, activities, and artifacts of our everyday life. Collectively, we, in turn, help define and refine each community and culture we inhabit. These interactions, continually creative, are fueled by the interactive, creative processes of reading and writing.

Reading Critically

When we read, we open ourselves up to learning about others, and from them we learn new words and new worlds, along with new ways of thinking. We learn to challenge old beliefs and form new perspectives. Especially at the college level, reading is like entering conversations, hearing what people in various disciplines think about issues, and getting an ever-clearer sense of what the issues are.

Reading a text critically means taking action and responding dynamically to the ideas of others—unlike the often passive receptivity of watching TV or video. Reading critically means not just understanding the point the writer makes but probing how the writer's point of view is created and what circumstances give rise to it. It means assessing how the views are similar to or different from our own, and why. What is there on the page is something that you, the reader, interpret, and the background knowledge that you, the reader, bring to that text on the page helps with the interpretation. The meaning of the words is therefore not permanently fixed and stable, but emerges from a dynamic process of negotiation between the writer, the reader, and the words on the page.

Strategies for Critical Reading

The following strategies are useful for reading both the selections in this book and other assigned college texts. As you prepare to read, make sure you have a dictionary, notebook, pen, and pencil at hand. Do not underestimate the importance of a multistep reading process: previewing, reading, and then rereading. Often you must read something several times to understand it completely and have its points and ideas at your command.

Preview

Previewing something that you are about to read means looking through it first to get oriented. As you skim, look for information about:

- *The writer.* Learn about the writer from biographical notes in the text or from an encyclopedia or biographical dictionary.
- *Type of text.* Learn about the type of text (called the *genre*): Is it fiction, drama, or poetry? Or is it nonfiction, and if so, is it biography, autobiography, observation, explanation, or argument?
- *Source of publication.* Learn where the selection was published—in what kind of publication for what type of audience? Is it a newspaper editorial or letter, a magazine article, a literary essay, a chapter in a book, or an academic paper for a specialized audience? And when was it published? Answering such questions helps you put the work in context.

Examine and consider

- *The title, table of contents, and headings.* A title will often reveal a great deal about the subject matter and the author's approach to it. The table of contents will give you a sense of the work's scope. Headings will alert you to the overall structure of the piece and its main points.
- *Text signals.* Look over the text for key words in italics or boldface and for visuals. Examine the introduction and the conclusion, and look at the first sentence of each paragraph. For nonfiction, skimming will give you a sense of the content and organization of the whole piece.

Read and annotate

The most important skill to master in reading has to do with attitude:

Read with a purpose.   The purpose of the first reading is to understand the text and the writer's points. To do this, read with an open mind, for enjoyment. Read with an alert and engaged mind, with curiosity, and with patience.

Read actively.   Annotate the text as you read: Underline key words, phrases, or passages; circle words to look up later; write comments in the margin to link ideas or to raise your own questions; write a question mark next to passages that you do not understand at first; number the main points. If you prefer not to write in your text or if you are using a library book, make notes on a sheet of paper.

Reread

No one gets everything the first time through. Do yourself the favor of rereading. A piece that seemed boring or hard or not your style can become, upon thoughtful rereading, clear, memorable, and even exciting.

Reread with questions in mind.   Read any questions attached to a selection or read the question you will be writing about.

Reread analytically.   Note the main idea or thesis and details. Separate general and specific points, fact and opinion. Look up definitions of unfamiliar words. Identify striking sentences and language.

Challenge the writer.   Be bold in your responses. Examine how the writer draws conclusions and whether the evidence and the methods are valid. Evaluate the argument and how it is different from your point of view.

Write a summary.   Use your own words, with the book closed, to write a summary of the main ideas.

Sample annotated reading

The annotated selection that follows is one writer's response to "Knowing Oneself and Others" by Robert Ornstein. Note what the reader does: She underlines key words and key points, circles words and defines them, marks where definitions of important terms appear in the text, writes short summary points, notes examples, asks questions, and raises objections. Such an annotation provides a record of her interaction with the text; it enables her to refer to the passage and build on her response to the first reading.

❖

KNOWING ONESELF AND OTHERS

ROBERT ORNSTEIN

Robert Ornstein has a doctorate in psychology and is president of the Institute for the Study of Human Knowledge. He has written numerous books about the nature of consciousness and the functioning of the brain, including Multimind *(1986), from which this passage is drawn. Here Ornstein looks at some trends that have occurred as the study of the mind has progressed and suggests that in these trends one sees the human tendency to oversimplify.*

THERE IS A FAIRLY standard process of human discovery that we go through when we try to understand anything new. The explorers' first maps of exotic places like Africa showed a simple, undifferentiated continent. Only later, with much more research, did the complexity of the terrain become clear. An appreciation of the complexity and subtlety of painting, music, food, and ideas follows the same pattern. We have gone through the same process in understanding the nature of the human mind.

It has been about a hundred years since the beginnings of modern psychology and fifty or so years since the development of modern brain science. Meaningful

Compares study of mind to study of other fields

Lists key
questions

Def: uncer-
tainties,
possibilities

Def: "claims
there is"

Summarizes
Freud

Examples of
oversimplifi-
cation

Like who?

A person
who is
tense, impa-
tient and
aggressive

questions have been debated. Is our personality formed before the age of five? Are we in the grip of forces beyond our ken? Is our behavior determined by the contingencies of the situations or by our inherited predispositions. Is rationality possible to man? Are there transcendent faculties beyond the personal unconscious? Are we dominated by our unconscious? Is there an unconscious, anyway? At the core of many of our controversies—some intellectual, some philo-sophical, some personal—is an oversimplified under-standing of the nature of our mind.

The psychoanalytic viewpoint postulates a kind of undertow flowing deep within the mind, an unknow-able unconscious that can ultimately control our con-scious actions. The person, to Freud, is like a horse and a rider. The horse most often controls where the person goes, but the rider can say, "I wanted to go there anyway." Further, the person is divided into id, ego, and superego, all separate functions of mind, each with differing priorities and each seemingly in perpetual war with one another—especially the con-flict between our "old" animal self and the "new" con-scious rational parts.

Later adherents of psychoanalysis modified its view-point. Some felt that the ego or self was stronger and more capable than Freud did; some, like Jung, felt that we have access to a deeper pool of unconscious knowl-edge. Others believed that personality is primarily social or primarily in a quest for self-development and self-actualization. Each view pretty much ignored the others in an attempt to promote a grand design.

After the breakdown of the Freudian synthesis, the next step was the postulation of different general types of persons. A type is one with many consistent charac-teristics, such as those pointing to introversion or extroversion or the currently modish Type A. "Type" is a level of explanation that we feel comfortable with, as in "She's the very friendly type." But this simplification, too, is one of our illusions: the general type is just too general to hold up. People are not so consistent as to behave true to type. One person may be quite warm toward others at the office but may well be aloof in social relationships, another the reverse: which one is really the friendly type?

Can concept of typing still be useful, even if over-simplified?

People are certainly the most complex "objects" we ever perceive; they have different genetic predisposi-tions, different histories, and they seem different depending on our needs, interactions, personality, and perception. When two women are discussing the same man, one may say, "He's so domineering," the other, "He's so sweet." Because they have many separate and independent talents, different people seem to have a lot of identities within, and these change with different situations. Think back to Indiana Jones in *Raiders of the Lost Ark,* who was both a swashbuckling adventurer and a weak professor. None of us is simple.

Implication: multiple identities are normal and healthy as long as not carried to extreme.

The particular collection of talents, abilities, and capacities that each person possesses depends partly on birth and partly on experience. Our illusion is that each of us is somehow unified, with a single coherent purpose and action. Others present a smooth, seem-ingly consistent and unified surface as well. But it *is* an illusion.

The nature vs. nurture debate?

We are not a single person.

We are many.

As active readers, we take what we know and set it alongside what writers say about their lives and experiences and how they read their world. It follows, then, that we do not all read (and anno-tate) texts in the same way. And we certainly do not read to find the one "correct" interpretation—there is usually no such thing. When we read, we set up an interaction among the words on the page, the writer's meaning, and the background we as readers bring to the text. We compose meaning as we read from what we know about the world and from the words the writer has put on the page.

Reading what others write is not the only kind of reading we do. We also read the signs of the culture around us—advertise-ments, graffiti, art, cartoons, comics, TV shows—and we learn from them about the ideology and values of our culture. We read those signs with a critical eye, too, commenting on the ways that cigarette advertisements show healthy young people engaged in active outdoor sports—no coughing or emphysema!—or the ways women and minorities are depicted in TV soap operas.

Critical reading of media images or traditional print materials does not necessarily mean criticizing and attacking the message and the author. It means reading carefully, asking questions, making connections to our own knowledge and experience, and engaging in dialogue with the ideas we find, challenging them when they conflict with what we know and feel.

Your Purpose and Audience for a Piece of Writing

When what you write becomes a piece of reading material for somebody else, as it inevitably does as soon as you hand it over to a classmate, friend, professor, boss, or editor, you have to expect that it will now, in its turn, receive rigorous critical reading. In fact, a budding writer should not just expect criticism, but should actively seek it out and value the time and effort a reader puts in to reading and responding. All readers will bring their prior experience and their expectations (along with their biases!) to any written text, so you, too, have to expect that your readers will bring their own knowledge, biases, and experience to anything you write and that your texts might be read critically in more than one way.

As you approach a piece of writing, it is helpful to establish a clear picture of your purpose and audience. Asking the following questions will provide you with guidelines.

- What do I want to do?

  inform

  persuade

  record observations

  explain

  entertain or move

  stimulate

- What do I know about my reader(s)?

  What do they already know?

  What do they need to know, and how much do I have to summarize, describe, and explain?

Which terms do I need to define?

What are their cultural expectations as they pick up my text?

Can I get any samples of the type of writing they expect and value?

What Readers Expect

Although the many different purposes, audiences, and topics demand different patterns of organization, the following basic principles of readers' expectations will hold true across much of the college writing you will be asked to do:

- Readers expect to be able to identify a thesis. A thesis is your main, or guiding, idea, and it can be stated or implied, but it should be an opinion, not a fact. It should be an idea that you have figured out that you believe to be true. Readers expect that main idea to be clear and identifiable and to guide the direction of the piece of writing.

- Readers look for and enjoy reading specific details, such as examples, stories, descriptions, facts, statistics, definitions, classifications, comparisons, and contrasts. It is the details you use that make your work distinctive. Your details give readers the evidence that supports and develops your thesis and show why you hold that point of view.

- Readers expect your system of organization to be clear to them so they have no difficulty following your logic and line of reasoning. You as the writer should work much harder than your readers.

- Readers expect each paragraph to be well defined, mostly making one clear point linked unequivocally to the main idea of the whole piece of writing, with all its sentences smoothly connected and with clear links to the preceding and subsequent paragraphs.

Writing as a Way of Learning

Writing does more than simply report on what you have learned from others. Writing helps you discover ideas of your own. It can help shape who you are, how you think, and how you interact with your culture. When you write, you draw together yourself, your experiences, and your readers, creating a relationship among them. Some questions to consider as you work on a piece of writing are listed below.

1. Who will read what I write? Do I know what my readers expect?

2. What effect do I want to have on my readers? Do I want to enrich, entertain, energize, or enlighten them—or all of the above?

3. How can I get started? On second thought, don't even ask this question. Just do it. Scribble ideas down in any order without worrying about organization, spelling, and grammar. Use freewriting and brainstorming or any method that helps you put words on paper. Reading more to find out more about a subject can also be helpful if not done indefinitely as a means of procrastination.

4. How can I create order out of chaos? Some people like to write a draft and then make an outline of what they have written to see where more is needed. Others like to make a rough outline before they write a draft, as a set of guidelines. In any case, keep your mind on your thesis—developing an interesting one, altering it as necessary as you write, and using it to unify your essay. It is the point you want your readers to take away with them after reading.

5. What do I do with my first draft? Print it out, give it to others to read, set it aside for a while, then read it yourself to see if it fills the assignment and is clear and interesting. If you fall asleep while reading it, you probably need to go back to the drawing board. Usually, the best thing to do with a first draft is revise it. The worst thing to do is hand it in as a final draft.

6. What will breathe life into my paper? Not formulas and patterns of organization but insights from your own experience and reading, stories, incidents, accounts of other people's lives. If your paper is all about "everyone" and "all people" or "most people," it will need vigorous resuscitation to jolt it back to life. Include plenty of specific details and examples that will put you—the writer—firmly in your paper. Care about what you write; become engaged in the ideas, the argument, the details. It is ultimately this engagement that will bring a paper to life.

Before you hand in a paper, check your grammar and spelling. Use a handbook and a dictionary as an aid. Many word-processing programs provide a spelling checker and grammar checker. Use them, but read your paper yourself, too, to catch what the computer cannot.

Once you hand your paper over to a reader, your piece of writing will then be a piece of reading for someone else to read critically, interpret, understand, and react to. From it, your reader will learn about you, your views, your identity, and your culture. The cycle begins again.

Two of the most important questions we ask ourselves are "Who am I" and "Where do I fit in?" There are no easy answers to questions like these, and our answers might change according to time and situation. This book does not claim to offer a neat definition of identity or a precise psychological, historical, or social examination of the nature of self and society—if such things were even possible. Rather, the book sees questions like these as interesting and engaging at a personal level, yet also intellectually challenging for a college writing course.

Name

What's in a name? That which we call a rose
By any other name would smell as sweet.

—William Shakespeare, Romeo and Juliet, *II, ii, 43, 1597*

I sometimes think I was born to live up to my name. How could I be
anything else but what I am having been named Madonna? I
would either have ended up a nun or this.

—Madonna, Vanity Fair, *April 1991*

Name

❖

"Who's that?"
"That's Mel Caylo."
Often, a name carries the burden of announcing a person's identity, with no explanations attached. A name is what we use to identify ourselves to each other. That is why the task of having to give a name to a child is often perceived as complex, at least in cultures where tradition makes no impositions. Giving someone a name seems arrogant, almost like imposing an identity. Parents can spend hours—even days or weeks—on the task. Having a child almost inevitably becomes an occasion for thoughtful questioning of the links between a name and identity. Writer Chris Offutt pondered the significance of a name before the birth of his first child:

> The oldest recorded personal name is En-lil-ti, carved into a Sumerian tablet from 3300 B.C. "Rita" [his wife] is a Sanskrit word, meaning "brave" or "honest." My name [Christopher] means "bearer of Christ," a troublesome burden. When I was a child, Saint Christopher was removed from sainthood and I thought that meant he was bad, that I was impugned by his inadequacy. I decided to change my name but the family objected. Unbound by such fetters, a Hindu will choose a new name to mark significant personal change. Cherokee people may change their names several times to suit their personalities at different stages of life. I want a son's name to suit him so well he'll want it for life.
>
> —Chris Offutt, *The Same River Twice*

Offutt raises the issues of giving a name, choosing a new name, and perceiving a name as representative of a person's life. (He

15

and his wife finally chose the name *Sam* for their son.) The name our parents give us is the outward sign that identifies us. Chosen by our parents for a reason, it often signifies something of importance for them, or something of their tastes and styles. Yet we are not necessarily known by that name forever.

We can change a name legally when we marry, adopt a professional role, or align with or reject a specific ethnic group. Consider, for instance, African Americans who adopt African names to reflect their African ancestry or ties to the Muslim religion, Jews who change their names to conform to the Anglo standards of the dominant culture, and rap artists who change their names to stimulate pop culture. If we don't want to go as far as a legal name change, we often find other ways to reinvent ourselves, such as adopting an informal nickname.

The selections in this unit explore the links between an individual's name and ancestry; name changes, both voluntary and forced; and, broadening the scope, the importance of names for families and ethnic groups as well as individuals.

The unit begins with a piece of fiction from Sandra Cisneros's *The House on Mango Street,* in which the narrator explores how a name lets us look backward to generational ties in the family and to the resonance of a name for family history. In a personal reminiscence, Keith Gilyard reports on his own experiences associated with name, identity, and schooling. Student writer Carmelo Caylo describes how he came to be the only child in his family not given an Americanized name and what positive effects an unusual name can have.

Journalists Lance Morrow and Susan Ferraro go beyond the strictly personal realm to look at strange names and the reasons for women's name changes upon marriage. A historical account by Richard Kim describes the devastating effects of imposed name changes on individuals and families during wartime—what it means to have a name taken away and another substituted in its place. The link that Kim makes between individual name and ethnic ancestry is the subject of a scholarly analysis in which sociologist Mary C. Waters discusses how people use their names to provide affiliation with one of several ancestries, and Earl Shorris then extends the concept of the relationship between name and identity to the names given to ethnic groups, as he discusses the political power associated with the terms *Hispanic* and *Latino.* The unit ends with a poem by Linda Hogan celebrating her American Indian name as a sign of her ancestry. These selections reiterate in various ways the idea that a name is one of the most immediate indicators of our individual and cultural identities.

STARTING POINTS [FOR JOURNAL OR FREEWRITING]

Begin your consideration of the issue of naming as a sign of identity and culture by writing responses to the following questions about your own name. These responses could be included in a journal or in freewriting.

1. List the full names of the people in your family and their relationship to you. Comment on what your list of names tells about your family and family customs. Show the list to another student and discuss the comments each of you wrote.

2. How much do you feel your name suits you and is part of your identity? Would you ever change your name or have you ever changed it? Explain your answer.

3. Some writers, such as Lewis Carroll, Mark Twain, and George Eliot, have used pseudonyms to disguise their true identity. If you had to choose a pseudonym, what name would you choose and why?

4. Why do people get concerned about the names given to ethnic groups? What are the implications of using such terms as *colored, Negro, black,* or *African American?*

MY NAME

SANDRA CISNEROS

Sandra Cisneros, born in 1954 in Chicago, the daughter of a Mexican father and a Mexican American mother, is a poet and the author of the novels The House on Mango Street *(1989) and* Woman Hollering

Creek *(1991). This selection is the fourth chapter of* The House on Mango Street, *in which each chapter presents a vignette about growing up in the Hispanic area of Chicago. In the first three chapters, the narrator describes the run-down tenements of Mango Street, the hairstyles of each family member, and the "separate worlds" of the brothers and sisters in the family. Then she turns to herself and her name.*

IN ENGLISH MY NAME means hope. In Spanish it means too many letters. It means sadness, it means waiting. It is like the number nine. A muddy color. It is the Mexican records my father plays on Sunday mornings when he is shaving, songs like sobbing.

It was my great-grandmother's name and now it is mine. She was a horse woman too, born like me in the Chinese year of the horse—which is supposed to be bad luck if you're born female—but I think this is a Chinese lie because the Chinese, like the Mexicans, don't like their women strong.

My great-grandmother. I would've liked to have known her, a wild horse of a woman, so wild she wouldn't marry. Until my great-grandfather threw a sack over her head and carried her off. Just like that, as if she were a fancy chandelier. That's the way he did it.

And the story goes she never forgave him. She looked out the window her whole life, the way so many women sit their sadness on an elbow. I wonder if she made the best with what she got or was she sorry because she couldn't be all the things she wanted to be. Esperanza. I have inherited her name, but I don't want to inherit her place by the window.

At school they say my name funny as if the syllables were made out of tin and hurt the roof of your mouth. But in Spanish my name is made out of a softer something, like silver, not quite as thick as sister's name—Magdalena—which is uglier than mine. Magdalena who at least can come home and become Nenny. But I am always Esperanza.

I would like to baptize myself under a new name, a name more like the real me, the one nobody sees. Esperanza as Lisandra or Maritza or Zeze the X. Yes. Something like Zeze the X will do.

RESPONDING IN DISCUSSION OR WRITING

1. What kind of person do you think Esperanza is from this excerpt? How old is she, and what do you learn about her and her

family? Is she a character you think you would find appealing? Why or why not?

2. When Cisneros's narrator, Esperanza, says she doesn't want to inherit her great-grandmother's "place by the window," what do you think she means? What is she rejecting, and why?

3. *Considerations of Style.* Cisneros sometimes uses a sentence fragment (an incomplete sentence) purposefully, for stylistic effect. Where has she used fragments? What effect do you think she hopes to achieve with the fragments?

4. *Considerations of Style.* When Cisneros's narrator says of her great-grandmother that she is a "wild horse of a woman," she is using a comparison or a simile. What picture does she convey of her great-grandmother by comparing her to a wild horse? What kinds of behavior does this description make you think of? Imagine some stories about her great-grandmother's behavior. Then write some sentences about people you know in which you use a similar figure of speech, for example, "My friend's uncle is an enraged bull of a man" or "My best friend is like a delicate spring flower." Ask others to draw conclusions about the person's behavior, or gender if it is not stated, from your simile to test its effectiveness.

5. *Considerations of Style.* Cisneros's narrator uses a simile to make a comparison when she says, "At school they say my name funny as if the syllables were made out of tin." Try saying the name *Esperanza* in that way. How does this simile help you understand the way people say the narrator's name? Invent a sentence about how people pronounce your name, making a comparison: "People say my name as if . . ."

6. Why do families pass names on from generation to generation? Do you think it is a good idea to name children after parents and grandparents? Why or why not?

WRITING ASSIGNMENTS

1. What memories does your name hold for you? Write a short account (about the same length as Cisneros's chapter) of those memories and how, if at all, they have affected your attitude to your name. Try to let your reader experience how you felt at the time. Use details that put your reader in the scene as you describe setting, people, time, and the events that happened.

2. Explain to your reader how names are chosen and given in your family and explain, too, the role played by the traditions in the culture to which your family belongs. Back up any abstract explanation with stories or specific examples from your experience; for example, how was your cousin (or brother, sister, nephew, or other family member) named? What other options were considered?

3. *For Further Research.* Cisneros rejects part of her heritage when she says that though she has inherited her great-grandmother's name, she does not want to inherit "her place by the window." Choose one of your great-grandparents and tell a story about what life must have been like and explain which aspects of that life you would accept or reject and why. You might have to do family and library research for this assignment.

KEITH AND RAYMOND

KEITH GILYARD

Keith Gilyard, born in 1952, teaches at the University of Syracuse. He is the author of articles on poetry and race relations, American 40: Poems *(1993), and* Voices of the Self: A Study of Language Competence *(1991). The even-numbered chapters in* Voices of the Self *consist of autobiographical narrative and explore the writer's own schooling and his acquisition of standard English skills; the odd-numbered chapters deal with the more theoretical issues of language and schooling, particularly the development of language, self, and the ability to "switch codes" to fit specific situations. The following excerpt is from the fourth chapter.*

WE CAME TO CORONA when the garbage trucks still ran three or four times a week. But it wouldn't continue that way for long. The White evacuation, of mostly Irish and Italians, was nearly complete and all community services would eventually tail off leaving Blacks and blight hand in hand, wondering if they caused each other. Folks who stayed in Harlem, Brooklyn, or the Bronx would say we had moved out to Long Island. With a twenty-minute cab ride they thought we had reached outer suburbia. It wasn't nearly so great of course, but I could see how it seemed like a decent deal to families fleeing from tenements. Back then you could purchase a respectable two-family house for ten to fifteen thousand dollars, probably under the GI bill, rent out the top floor, and maybe see a comparatively rosy future. In our case we even got new furniture on credit. And we were on one of the nicest blocks in the neighborhood, tree-lined 34th Avenue, a block and a half east of Junction Boulevard. That was a street most aptly named for it served as a border between two neighborhoods, Corona and Jackson Heights, and between two worlds—a Black one and a White one. Junction Boulevard was often referred to as the Mason-Dixon line in Queens.

I was fairly pleased. The basement and backyard held good possibilities for hideaway and play, and there was a park right in the next block with seesaws, swings, the works. No Eighth Avenue. But not all that bad.

We were located virtually equidistant between P.S. 92 on 99th Street in Corona and P.S. 149 on 94th Street in Jackson Heights. They were both located on 34th Avenue and Sherry and I could spot them from in front of the house. We had no idea which way to go until our mother came outside with the baby carriage and headed east toward the dark-complexioned 92. I kept right on her heels, excited. We were turned away from that school, something about overcrowding and new zoning, and directed to 149. I kept on her heels, still excited, across the Mason-Dixon.

After Sherry and I were registered, the principal, Mr. Price, escorted us to class. His pants were too baggy and long. The back of the cuffs flapped up under his heels as he walked. We thought it was funny that he should want to ruin his pants that way, and all the way down the hall we fought the urge to burst out laughing. I didn't feel very humored, though, when he ushered me into Class 1-1 and exposed me to a room full of White kids. I trembled. I wanted to grab hold of one of Mr. Price's baggy trouser legs like it was a mother's apron, but I couldn't allow myself to show that much fear. I wished Sherry would come in but when I realized she wouldn't I wished the same shock on her wherever she went. Or worse. It's like they were trying to stare me back out of the room.

Goldstein. Rubin. Landau. Weiss. Cohen. I knew next to nothing about kids like that. Only saw them on the subway a couple of times and in the doctor's office downtown. My eyes frantically searched theirs, trying to find some sign I could translate into friendliness. There was one Black student, a girl in pigtails, and she stared as hard as anyone else. Mr. Price spoke at last.

"Hello class, this is Raymond Keith Gilyard." The name sud-   5
denly sounded important to me. "He's a fine enough young man, isn't he?" They answered in synchronized yesses. The principal continued. "What shall we call you, young Master Gilyard? Shall we call you Raymond or Keith?"

Nobody had ever called me Raymond before. Uptown it was always Keith or Keithy or Little Gil. Raymond was like a fifth wheel. A spare. And that's what I decided to make these people call me. *They cannot meet Keith now. I will put someone else together for them and he will be their classmate until further notice. That will be the first step in this particular survival plan.* Of course it wasn't thought out in those specific terms, but the instinct and action were there. And from that day on, through all my years in public school, all White folks had to call me Raymond.

The point was to have a plot. To keep a part of myself I could trust. A way to pull myself through. Be a Raymond, a brother, a son, a Keith, a son, a Raymond, a son, a brother. Keep juggling and save myself. So along with handwriting drills, simple addition, simple subtraction, and readings from the primer, I began getting familiar with these strange people around me. Peeping into their lives while trying to keep their strange pale noses out of mine. . . .

[In second grade,] I was the only Black in the one-level class because Saundra Meritt, whom I had grown to like during our time together in first grade, was placed in 2-3. Nowadays in public schools they may designate classes by room numbers like 2-301 or 2-315. There may be differences in performance levels among the classes but the students, at least the younger ones, may not be acutely aware of them. Probably better that way. But back in '59 I knew I was in with the so-called cream of my grade level. Even without the class numbers, the few dark faces I saw in each of the other classes made it easy to figure out what was going on. I had been "identified." I was, however, gaining more and more confidence in my role as student.

Along with Eddie Goldstein I became a class clown. We came up with the funniest quips and made the funniest faces. But we both wanted to be laughed with, not laughed at, so we scored highly on all our tests and raised our hands as vigorously as anyone else. I liked being able to play it either way. I also began expressing a certain physical dominance in the schoolyard, as I could outwrestle any of my classmates. This was as much due to aggression as to my skill. I could handle these people. And Mrs. Lehrman didn't hassle me much. She occasionally had to put my clowning in check, but her main beef seemed to be the way I would dot an *i*. I still hear her sometimes: They're just dots, Raymond. Not giant colored-in circles. Dots. Dots. Dots. Not anything so terribly important. If that was her major complaint against me I knew I had to be progressing satisfactorily. I even had an opportunity to show off for my father.

He showed up on one of those parents' observation days in a brown suit with a gray Ban-Lon shirt and a tan raincoat. When he came through the door all heads turned toward me. Then Linda Katz, as if she alone knew the scoop, tapped me on the shoulder from behind and whispered the obvious: "There goes your father, Raymond." Pops didn't bother to look my way, simply nodded to the teacher and strode swiftly to the back of the room where several other parents were already gathered.

We were working with the calendar. It was the fourteenth and Mrs. Lehrman wanted to know who could show her which date was exactly one week away. Hands shot up all around the room. Nearly everyone wanted to pounce on such an easy question, and I was among the most desperate. Waving my hand wildly and straining forward half out of my seat, squirming like I had to go to the bathroom or something, moaning, "Ooh ooh ooh Mrs. Lehrman, ooh!" She studied the contorted pleas on our faces, in our eyes. She hesitated as if she were trying to select a proper head of lettuce and then settled on Helen Rubin, who hadn't even raised her hand. Her mother was in the back, yet the girl still wasn't eager. It didn't seem fair she should be called on before I was.

I tried to attract my father's attention to let him know I knew the answer, but he was staring straight ahead. It was ironic because I had learned what I knew about the calendar from watching him run his finger down the left margin of the one in

10

our kitchen in order to count the Sundays. There just couldn't have been any easier question for me.

But Helen had it. She accepted the rubber-tipped pointer from the teacher and stuck it straight in the box marked 20. I couldn't believe she blew it like that. Hands shot up all over again, even more urgently, and Helen was told to sit down. I didn't bother raising my hand this time because I had become more interested in Helen's mother. She was wringing her hands. She lowered her head, then lifted it slowly and blew a thin stream of air from her mouth. I imagined her in a cartoon with steam spouting from her ears, forming a scowling mist over her graying head. I was still having fun with this vision as Bernie Cohen went up and pointed to 15. Eddie called him stupid and Bernie's father was in the back smiling. Fake. I could feel it. I turned my eyes back to Mrs. Rubin's anger.

"RAYMOND." I whirled to face the teacher. I was nervous because I thought she was going to reprimand me for not paying attention and it was certainly no time for that, but when she asked "Can you show us?" it took all the control I could muster to refrain from howling with laughter.

"I think I can show you, Mrs. Lehrman."

"Well let's hop to it then." She looked back at the group of observers and asked rhetorically, "We are having our little adventures today, aren't we?"

I fidgeted with my notebook, opened and shut my inkwell a few times, you know, appearing uncertain so I could build the suspense. I slowly rose to my feet, very deliberately tucked in my shirt, and hitched my trousers. Show time. I took the pointer from Mrs. Lehrman, switched it from hand to hand, tapped the floor with the rubber tip a couple of times, and picked out that glorious 21.

"Thank you, Raymond" said Mrs. Lehrman in relief. She smiled and I poked out my chest and headed for my seat. Cast a glance at Pops. He wasn't one for the big grin, but his faint nod of approval let me know he was pleased.

It would have been better still if Pops could have caught my act a few weeks later when Mrs. Lehrman asked if anyone knew the difference between a house and a home. No one else in the class even attempted an answer. The perfect stage for me. I mean getting called on and supplying the correct response was exciting

enough, but you knew there were other young knights who could
have handled the question. To dominate the floor completely,
however, was to be top royalty. And there I was, the king.

"A house can be anywhere you live with walls and ceilings and   20
floors. But it's not a home until there is love." This answer seemed
to really excite the teacher.

"That is well put, Raymond. Very, very interesting." I sat down
as my classmates stared in amazement, probably wondering where
I picked up this information. I wouldn't tell them I had learned it
in Sunday School. And I was really somewhat amazed myself that
not a single one of them could answer that question. I began to
wonder more seriously about what these Jews were learning in
those synagogues and those one-afternoon-a-week Hebrew School
classes. What were the few Catholics, who got out early on
Wednesdays for religious instruction, learning over at Blessed
Sacrament?

I felt I was coming along nicely. Sang "America the Beautiful"
and "My Country, 'Tis of Thee" as loudly as anyone. Recited the
pledge of allegiance at a time when it was mandatory to do so.
Related strongly to "Jack and the Beanstalk" and felt great admira-
tion for both Androcles and the lion. Thought Miles Standish was
a hero for fighting Indians and beheading Wituwamat. Respected
wig-wearing, silver dollar-slinging George Washington, Honest
Abe, and President Eisenhower. Showed the proper concern
for the Cold War, was glad Red China was denied entry to the
U.N., and was properly upset when a spying Francis Gary Powers
was shot down from the Russian skies. Smooth sailing on into
3-1. . . .

I was on course even steadier than ever. Spelling tests. Book
reports. Multiplication. Division. History. Astronomy. Current
events. Mr. Price came on the loudspeaker to request we give a
moment of silence for U.N. Secretary-General Hammarskjöld,
who died in a plane crash while on the way to take care of some
business in the Congo. Kennedy was in, took our class decisively,
and we were in the era of manned space flights. We jammed the
auditorium to listen to the radio broadcast of Alan B. Shepard's
joy ride aboard the Freedom 7. I clapped in tune with everyone
else. Yes sir. Raymond was doing fine.

Keith was developing well also. Found my first best friend,
Lonnie Blair, while I was walking down 97th Street on the way to

the store. He was in front of his house throwing pebbles up onto his own roof. He held the bunch in his left hand and plucked and tossed them with his right. He was a skinny, close-cropped young boy, very much like myself. When he noticed me approaching, he dropped the pebbles right where he stood and came up straight to my face.

"Hey boy, what's your name?"   25

"My name Keith."

"Oh yeah?"

"Yeah. What's your name?"

"Ain't none a your damn business. That's what the hell it is."

"Well mine ain't none a yours then."   30

"Is too 'cause you just told me your name stupid."

"I did not."

"Did so."

"What I say?"

"Said your name was Keith, dummy. Can't remember what you   35
just said?"

"I was just foolin you."

"You wasn't foolin me, Keith. You can't."

He did have me on that one and I didn't like it one bit. I stepped around him and continued on my way. He kept following, paused to pick up a rock and hurl it up on a neighbor's roof, then pulled alongside.

"You know I seen you before in school."

"So I seen you too."   40

"Yeah, Keith, but I seen you first 'cause I always see people first before they see me. Where you use to live at?"

"I come from Harlem."

"Harlem? I heard about that place. That means you 'pose to be tough or somethin? You ain't as tough as people from Brooklyn."

"That's where you from?"

"Yeah, Keith, that's where I'm from!"   45

"So that don't make you so tough."

"Tougher than you."

"No you not."

"Yes I am, Keith. What if I did somethin to you? What would you do?"

"Do somethin back to you."   50

"Like what?"

"You'll see. I'm use ta fightin. I been in gang fights."

"Aw man, get outa here. You ain been in no gang fights."

"I have so. Where you think I got this scar from?" I put a hand up to the left side of my face to really draw his attention to it. I closed in on him, but kept enough distance so that out of the corner of my eye I could watch his reaction. He really appreciated that scar. I had an edge on him, had him leaning toward belief.

"How that happen?"   55

"I told you I was in a gang fight. I got cut with a butcher knife. You don't know about stuff like that. You too little."

"I'm just as big as you" he said defiantly.

"Yeah but you couldn't get out like I could. When everybody in my house was sleepin I use to sneak out at midnight. That's when the big people had the gang fights. I was the only kid they let in. This big man cut me and I was bleeding a lot but my side got him."

"Did they kill him?" he asked eagerly.

"Yeah they killed him. What you think?"   60

"Well they 'pose to anyway. I was in gang fights too you know."

"Where's your scar then?"

"You don't have to have one."

"Yes you do. If you was in one you have to have a scar. If you was in a *real* one."

I knew I scored heavily with that tale, so did he, and we had set up a pretty good basis for a friendship. Neither one of us was going to be bullied. . . .

RESPONDING IN DISCUSSION OR WRITING

1. Much of the story Gilyard tells about school focuses on race: on black and white neighborhoods and black and white students in school. When you were in elementary school (ages six through ten), what was your experience of racial difference?

2. *Considerations of Style.* When Gilyard writes about developing Keith and forming a friendship with Lonnie Blair, how is the language different from the language used by Gilyard, the author of the book, and Raymond, the student in school? Consider how your own language changes in different contexts.

3. The passage omitted at the end of paragraph 22 begins: "Where I punched Susan Goldberg straight in her eye." It fills

four pages. What do you imagine happens in these pages? What
do you imagine Susan Goldberg's story is?

4. What does Gilyard mean when he says, "The point was to have
a plot" (paragraph 7)? What is the plot, and why does he think it
is necessary? What does it say about the society he lives in and the
way he perceives it?

5. Explore what you see as the answer to the question Raymond is
asked about the difference between a house and a home. Is your
response different from Raymond's? What is your reaction to
Raymond's response?

WRITING ASSIGNMENTS

1. Respond to Gilyard's essay by writing a response to the issue of
having different names represent different identities. Here are
some questions to consider: Have you ever felt you have two different identities, one inside school and one outside school? If so,
what was the difference, and what caused you to form the separate
identities? How do you respond to Gilyard's two names, Keith and
Raymond? What different identities do they represent? What do
you make of the fact that as an academic and author he now calls
himself Keith?

2. *For Further Research.* Interview three to five people and ask
them about their reactions to their names when they were children. Find out if they have stories to tell about their names. If
they do, try to find common threads in their reactions and stories
and draw conclusions from your small sample about what a name
means to a child.

❖

COLOR ME A CLAY

CARMELO CAYLO

*Carmelo Caylo, born in 1969 in New York City, wrote this essay after he
had read some of the selections in this chapter. He was at the time a student in a required course in writing for college freshmen. He passed it and*

*has graduated, majoring in media studies. He plans to go to graduate
school in journalism.*

YOU'RE PROBABLY WONDERING, "WHAT kind of title is that?" Well, if
you rearrange the letters, you'll spell out my name. "Color Me a
Clay" is actually an anagram of my name. In fact, so is this silly
phrase, "Calm Early Coo." I sometimes like to fool around with
letters and numbers, rearranging them into weird combinations
from their more conventional configurations. But this is not an
essay about anagrams, it's an essay about names.

I am the eldest child of Carmelito Caylo ("Loyal Coat Crime")
and Carmenchita Caylo ("China Clam Care Toy"). Obviously, you
can see where my name is derived from. Oddly enough, my
father's name is the junior version and my name is the senior version. My younger brother is named Theodore Caylo ("The Coy
Door Ale"). Both of my parents are first generation Filipinos, so
with my brother they strayed from the usual Spanish names that
Filipinos tend to have and instead chose a Greek inspired one.
(The story goes that at the time my parents were very good friends
with a Greek couple, and they often told of stories where children
with names that had their roots in Greek went on to become
great successes.) My younger sister, the baby of the family, is
named Kimberlee Caylo ("Climb a Yoke Reel"), also not Spanish
influenced. Her name was inspired by my mom's obstetrician/
gynecologist, Dr. Kimberly Cohen. (My parents changed the
spelling of the last syllable to give it an Asian touch, or so they say.
I think that they actually misspelled it on the birth certificate.) My
mom says that she was moved by her doctor's great personality
and her courage in facing the adversity that stemmed from the
prejudice she received from the males in her profession.

Only with me did my parents choose to use a Spanish name.
They tell me that they did so out of reverence for their heritage.
My father's parents were named Balbino Caylo ("Coin a Ball
Boy") and Jesusa Caylo ("Cajole Say Us"). My mother's parents
were named Jose Ferrer ("For Jeerers") and Pilar Ferrer ("Rarer
Pilfer"). As you can see, all had Spanish names, as do many
Filipinos because of the era in our history when we were ruled by
the Spaniards. It was not an accident that my brother and sister
do not have traditional names. My parents reasoned that one
child with a Spanish name is enough. Any subsequent children

would have "Americanized" names. ("When in America, do as Americans do," they say.) Despite this, the culture of our race is not lost upon us. My siblings and I still feel a sense of nationalistic pride towards the Philippines, and, although none of us are fluent in our native tongue, we feel right at home when we go back to visit.

I am not bitter that I was the only child not given an American name. I have learned to Americanize it by having my peers call me Mel instead. I did not always like my name, however. Growing up with a name like mine resulted in incessant teasing from my classmates. I was a rather roly-poly kid, so my name was often rhymed with food names. I was tagged things like "Marshmallow," "Jello Melo," "Melo Yellow," "Melo Fellow," "Caramello," "Watermelon," and "Melody," which, unfortunately for me, was the brand name of the pudding we were served in the cafeteria. Over the years I learned to accept the teasing and laugh along with it. In fact, the teasing helped me to realize that mine is not a common name, and that made me feel sort of special. I kept telling myself that all the other kids were jealous of my name, and that's why they teased me. For me, a fat little kid who lacked any self-esteem whatsoever, my name was my salvation.

That time in my life made me learn to be proud of my name.   5 Even now, although I go by a nickname, I make sure that people know what my real name is first: Mole Car, I mean Carmelo.

RESPONDING IN DISCUSSION OR WRITING

1. What did you expect when you read the title of this essay? What were your feelings when you found out what it meant?

2. What do you think Caylo's purposes were in writing this piece? Which of the following common purposes for writing seem to apply here—to record observations and experiences, to explain a point, to draw generalizations from personal experience, to inform, entertain, or persuade? What in Caylo's piece of writing determines your reply?

3. *Considerations of Style.* How would you categorize the tone of Caylo's essay: Is it formal, semiformal, or informal (conversational)? Which features in the writing determine your response?

4. If you were to give this student writer advice about revising this essay, what would it be?

5. What do you think Caylo does best in this essay? Which part or parts of the essay do you like best, and why?

6. Caylo made anagrams from names by using exactly the same letters to form new words. Try making an anagram out of your own name. How many can you come up with?

WRITING ASSIGNMENTS

1. Caylo's essay introduces themes other than names: family heritage, role models, sexist prejudice, preservation of culture, the cruelties of children, and the trials of growing up as a "roly-poly kid." Take one of these themes and use your own experience to tell a lighthearted story, but one that makes a clear statement about your theme. Combine personal observation with analytical thinking as you draw conclusions about people's behavior and attitudes.

2. Write a response in letter form to Carmelo Caylo telling him your reactions to his essay. If his account leads you to think about your own life, tell him where that happens and tell the story of what it makes you recall. With the letter format, you need to decide on how formal and informal you will be. You do not know Caylo personally, yet he is a fellow student, taking a writing course. Write this as if Caylo were going to read it and reply.

THE STRANGE BURDEN OF A NAME

LANCE MORROW

Lance Morrow, born in 1939, is a journalist and a regular contributor to Time *magazine. He won the national Magazine Award in 1981. His books include* The Chief: A Memoir of Fathers and Sons *(1985),* America: A Rediscovery *(1987), and* Fishing in the Tiber *(1988). This article was published as the end-piece essay in* Time *on March 8, 1993.*

A NAME IS SOMETIMES a ridiculous fate. For example, a man afflicted with the name of Kill Sin Pimple lived in Sussex, in 1609. In the spring of that year, the record shows, Kill Sin served on a jury with his Puritan neighbors, including Fly Debate Roberts, More Fruit Fowler, God Reward Smart, Be Faithful Joiner and Fight the Good Fight of Faith White. Poor men. At birth, their parents had turned them into religious bumper stickers.

Names may carry strange freights—perverse jokes, weird energies of inflicted embarrassment. Another 17th century Puritan child was condemned to bear the name of Flie Fornication Andrewes. Of course, it is also possible that Andrewes sailed along, calling himself by a jaunty, executive "F.F. Andrewes." Even the most humiliating name can sometimes be painted over or escaped altogether. Initials are invaluable: H.R. (Bob) Haldeman, of the Nixon White House, deftly suppressed Harry Robbins: "Harry Haldeman" might not have worked for him.

Names have an intricate life of their own. Where married women and power are concerned, the issue becomes poignant. The official elongation of the name of Hillary Rodham Clinton suggests some of the effects achieved when customs of naming drift into the dangerous atmospheres of politics and feminism.

The history of "Hillary Rodham Clinton" goes back in time, like a novel: at birth, Bill Clinton was William Jefferson Blythe, his father being a young salesman named William Jefferson Blythe 3rd, who died in a car accident before Bill was born. In a story now familiar, the 15-year-old future President legally changed his name to Bill Clinton in order to affirm family solidarity with his mother and stepfather, Roger Clinton. In 1975, when Bill Clinton got married, his new wife chose to keep the name Hillary Rodham. But five years later, Clinton was defeated in a run for re-election as Arkansas Governor, at which point, to assert a more conventional family image, Hillary Rodham started calling herself Hillary Clinton. But she was not exactly taking Bill's name either, since "Clinton" had not originally been Bill's. Bill was once removed from his own birth name, so now Hillary was, in a sense, twice removed.

A name may announce something—or conceal something. In some societies, the Arab or Chinese, for example, a beautiful child may be called by a depreciating name—"Dog," "Stupid," "Ugly," say—in order to ward off the evil eye. Hillary Rodham knew that in some parts of the political wilds, she attracted the evil eye to the 1992 Democratic ticket. So during her demure, cookie-baker phase, she was emphatically "Hillary Clinton," mute, nodding adorer and helpmate of Bill. She half-concealed herself in "Hillary Clinton" until the coast was clear. With the Inauguration, the formal, formidable triple name has lumbered into place like a convoy of armored cars: Hillary Rodham Clinton.

The name problem for married women is a clumsy mess. Married women have four or more choices. 1) Keep the last name they were given at birth. 2) Take the husband's last name. 3) Use three names, as in Hillary Rodham Clinton; or, as women did in the '70s, join the wife's birth name and the husband's birth name with a hyphen—a practice that in the third generation down the road would produce geometrically expanded multiple-hyphenated nightmares. 4) Use the unmarried name in most matters professional, and use the husband's name in at least some matters personal and domestic. Most men, if they were to wake up one morning and find themselves transformed into married women, would (rather huffily) choose Option No. 1.

Variations: one woman who has been married three times and divorced three times uses all four available last names, changing them as if she were changing outfits, according to mood or season. More commonly it happens that a woman has made her professional reputation, in her 20s and 30s, while using the name of her first husband, then gets divorced and possibly remarried, but remains stuck with the first husband's name in the middle of her three-name procession.

Names possess a peculiar indelible power—subversive, evocative, satirical, by turns. The name is an aura, a costume. Dickens knew how names proclaim character—although anyone named Lance is bound to hope that that is not always true. Democrats used to have fun with "George Herbert Walker Bush." The full inventory of the pedigree, formally decanted, produced a piled-on, Connecticut preppie–Little Lord Fauntleroy effect that went nicely with the populist crack that Bush "was born on third base and thought he had hit a triple."

How many names does a decent person need? For ordinary getting around, two, as a bird requires two wings. More than two, as a rule, is overweight. Only God should use fewer than two.

The words with which people and things are named have a changeful magic. Some cultures invent different names for people in different stages of life. In Chinese tradition a boy of school age would be given a "book name," to be used in arranging marriages and other official matters. A boy's book name might be "Worthy Prince" or "Spring Dragon" or "Celestial Emolument." (Does a father say, "Hello, have you met my boy, Celestial Emolument?")

Hillary Rodham Clinton may find her name changing still further as her White House power evolves. Perhaps by next year, she will be known as "H.R. Clinton." Maybe the year after that, she will be "H.R. (Bob) Clinton."

RESPONDING IN DISCUSSION OR WRITING

1. Morrow makes the strong claim that a name can be "a ridiculous fate." How does he support that claim of "ridiculous"? How does he show the reader what he means? Do you find his examples that a name can be a ridiculous fate convincing?

2. Look at the first sentence of each paragraph in Morrow's essay. Which ones announce the paragraph's topic and lead to the development of the paragraph with examples and illustrations? What happens when you read only the first sentence of each paragraph?

3. *Considerations of Style.*   Write down adjectives that convey the tone of Morrow's article. Discuss with others what list of four adjectives would convey the best impression of this article to somebody who had not read it.

4. Morrow comments that "only God should use fewer than two" names. Think of examples of people who use only one name. What is the effect of using only one name?

5. What would you recommend for the name of the wife of the President of the United States: her husband's last name (Jacqueline Kennedy, Hillary Clinton), her own given name (Jacqueline Bouvier, Hillary Rodham), or a combination of the two (Jacqueline Bouvier Kennedy, Hillary Rodham Clinton)? What are your reasons for your choice? How might each name be perceived by the electorate? What different image does each convey?

6. *For Further Research.*   Morrow says that most men, put into the position of married women, would choose to keep their own name. Survey ten men and see if your results match Morrow's predictions. What are the implications of your findings?

WRITING ASSIGNMENTS

1. Argue for or against Morrow's comment that "the name problem for married women is a clumsy mess." First, you need to understand and explain Morrow's argument and how he supports it. Consider, too, the opposing view that the choice of a name in marriage could be seen as an advantage for women—an opportunity to say something about themselves in relation to family and social customs. Take a specific stance on the issue. Include the strongest arguments and supporting details you can find.

2. *For Further Research.* Use classroom interviews with other students, interviews outside class, library research, or a combination of all three approaches to investigate the giving or changing of names in two different cultures and compare and contrast the customs. Explore and explain how people's options are related to issues of social power, family structure, and male and female roles in the culture.

NAME DROPPER

SUSAN FERRARO

Susan Ferraro is a journalist who writes book reviews and articles on various topics, including health, women's issues, and business. She is also the author of Remembrance of Things Fast *(1990). The following article appeared as the "Hers" column in* The New York Times Magazine *on May 2, 1993.*

THE PLACE WAS A busy restaurant, the occasion one of those necessary, nervy first meetings with someone new—in this instance, an editor—who might be able to throw some work my way. As we settled ourselves, my companion lowered her menu and peered at me intently. "You're not what I expected," she said abruptly.

"I thought you'd have dark hair, brown eyes, look more
Italian. . . ."

"I use my married name," I said.

"Your husband's name?" Surprise pushed puzzlement off her
face and reverberated through her voice. "But most writers today,
women that is. . . . Why?"

"It scans better," I said firmly. "Ferraro has more rhythm than
Flynn."

It scans better? As evasions go, that might be more credible than   5
saying the dog ate the family tree, but not much. Yet as even the
redoubtable Hillary Rodham Clinton found, this name game of
labels and love, of personhood and passion and patronymics, is
too tricky to sort out over a menu.

When people ask (and they do, all the time) why I don't use my
"own" name, part of me wants to shout back: "My name is what I
say it is." But I feel a twinge of guilt too. For many, many women
my age—who grew up in the 60's and 70's and embraced
feminism with the same fervor that the 18th century embraced
democracy—keeping the name they were born with after marriage is a powerful way of announcing that they define themselves,
that they have their own history, that they are no man's chattel. I
felt a little as if I'd turned my back on these female warriors,
almost as if I'd betrayed feminism itself.

And I'd done it, in part, for the usual sappy, deliciously irrational and not politically correct reason that makes Valentine's
Day big business. I was in love. I wanted to shout our association
from the rooftops and everywhere else—introductions, letter-
heads, legal documents, tax forms.

I also confess that something about marrying this man put me
back in touch—for a blessedly brief moment—with my inner adolescent. I'd been the kid with the flat chest, hair that curled on
alternate sides like New York City parking regulations, and an
absurdly short Irish nose. As my contemporaries made clear in a
hundred different ways, they had boyfriends and I had hangnails.
Pleasant it was to imagine attending a high-school reunion with
proof positive on my name tag that someone loved me.

But I never did attend a reunion. I have used the "Mrs." only
when traveling with my husband on *his* business and once, years
ago, to get rid of a willful young stud at a bus stop. "Just tell me

your name," he insisted, circling like a wild man. "Mrs. Ferraro," I
said, and watched him disappear. It was not ideologically honest
to indicate that I was unavailable because another man had
put his mark on me; I should have ignored him, called a cop
or flipped him to the sidewalk in a slick karate move. But he
scared me.

Changing my name meant defining myself as an adult, choosing my own label. Taking a new name was about growing up. It
was about how, much as I loved him, I stopped being Daddy's little girl.

Don't get me wrong. My father, a West Coast newsman, was the
best father he could be. He was funny and smart, sentimental
about his baby girl, sometimes sarcastic, and a raconteur who
knew everything about politics. He had flinty Montana eyes, and
at 5 feet 6 inches tall he loomed through my childhood as a man
of the public world and the quiet peripheries where deals got
done.

He gave me outlandish presents, and he loved me even when
we clashed, and we did, fearsomely; he was there when I hurt, and
he actually cried for me once. To him, all women, including his
daughter, were a mystery—and that was how he liked them. As
long as I bore his name, some part of me was always Bill Flynn's
girl, a sixth grader with scabby knees, a teenager whose hair
curled on alternate sides, a writer who might or might not be as
good as her dad.

There didn't seem much difference to me, politically, which
name I used. A woman who marries can keep the last name she
was born with, but it remains a kind of patronymic inherited from
a father or, if mother was remarkably independent, grandfather.
Short of taking a wholly new name, maybe a woman's first name
that can double as a last name (Ms. Hillary?), there is no way out.

Not that formidable women haven't tried. I know one who used
her husband's name in the 60's, then dropped it when feminism
bloomed and assumed the last name of a female relative several
generations back whom she admired. But it was still that relative's
father's name and—as fate would have it—it happened to be a
last name, like Henry or Joseph, that is a man's first name too.

Some women stick a hyphen emphatically between their "own"
last name and their husband's. But it's still her father's name

joined to her husband's, and if it survives at all it probably will be his name, not hers, that the grandchildren inherit. A friend, a respected feminist, kept her name when she married but suddenly took her husband's after the birth of their daughter (to whom they had given his name). "I could not have a different name than hers," she said. The need to be a family unit, officially, is powerful and not a bad idea.

When my father grew old, he was able to be proud of me as a writer, not just as his daughter. But as my byline began to appear, his grew less frequent and then disappeared altogether. It was terrible, a death before death, and then he really did die. If I'd kept his name, would he have felt his own decline less sharply? Might it have seemed that some part of him was still alive in the business he loved best?

Probably not. His old age and decline were excruciatingly personal; he lived his own life, as he taught me to live mine. He was from another generation, too, in some ways much more distant from me than I am from the young brides today who are once again, in droves, taking their husband's names. My father never once, in 20 years of addressing letters to me, got the vowels in my married name arranged in the right order, but he accepted that name as a matter of course. His name was given to a baby girl; we both knew that I made my own as an adult.

Looking back, I'm glad that I chose names when I married. It pulled some doors closed and blew others open. I needed to be something other than a newsman's daughter who wanted to be just as good as her old man. As an adult woman, I am responsible for my own life and label. My name is what I say it is: My choice. Me.

I'm also glad that my father never realized that I shed his name for a reason instead of a custom.

RESPONDING IN DISCUSSION OR WRITING

1. Ferraro's editor expects Ferraro to "look more Italian." Describe occasions in which someone has made incorrect assumptions about you because of your name. What are the results of the practice of linking name with background and appearance?

2. What did changing her name mean for Ferraro? What does the decision reflect about her attitude to her past and to her new role and status? How do you react to her decision?

3. How do you think Ferraro's father would have reacted if he had known her reason for changing her name? Why do you think Ferraro talks so much about her father in this article?

4. *Considerations of Style.*   Ferraro introduces this article by telling a personal story describing an event that happened to her. How does the opening story function for you, the reader?

5. *Considerations of Style.*   Ferraro uses comparisons and contrasts to come up with surprising expressions such as "They had boyfriends and I had hangnails." What other comments in the selection had a surprising quality? Note any pattern among them that may emerge.

6. Whom do you think Ferraro considered as the audience for this piece of writing? Why?

WRITING ASSIGNMENTS

1. Ferraro tells the story of a woman who changed her name to her husband's only after she had a child. She comments on this approvingly, saying, "The need to be a family unit, officially, is powerful and not a bad idea." Explain how you feel about Ferraro's opinion. Make sure your readers know where you stand on the issue of name change; give the reasons for your opinion and provide support through anecdotes and examples, as Ferraro does.

2. When two people get married, names often become a problem and people turn to a variety of solutions. Describe some of the solutions they find, give examples, and explain the advantages and disadvantages of each. Which course of action seems to you to be the most acceptable and why? Illustrate your arguments with specific examples.

LOST NAMES

RICHARD E. KIM

Richard E. Kim was born in Korea in 1932, immigrated to the United States after World War II ended, and lives in Massachusetts. He has taught at various universities, including the University of Massachusetts and San Diego State University. The book from which this excerpt is taken, Lost Names, *is subtitled* Scenes from a Korean Boyhood. *It was published in 1970. This excerpt describes an incident during the Japanese invasion and occupation of Korea in World War II (1939–45), when the Japanese took over the schools and language instruction and insisted on the local residents adopting Japanese names.*

WHEN I ARRIVE AT the school, our teacher is already in our classroom. He is a young Japanese, a recent graduate of a college in Tokyo. He is twenty-four years old, soft-spoken, and rather gentle with the children. He is lean, in fact, so lean that we give him a nickname the moment he is assigned to our class: Chopstick. Always pale-faced and looking in poor health, he likes to recite Japanese poetry in class, though we hardly understand it.

I set about making the fire in the stove, with the help of several of my friends, who will later toss a coin to see who gets the "second place." The air in the classroom is freezing and, through my cotton socks, I can feel the icy chill of the wooden floor. It is unusual for our teacher to be in the classroom before the bell rings, so all the children are silent, hunched over their desks, rubbing their feet furtively to keep them warm. The teacher is sitting on his chair, behind the lectern on the platform, quietly looking at us. When I have the fire going at last, I shovel in some coal on top of the pine cones crackling inside the blazing stove. The stove sits in the middle of a square, tin floorboard in the center of the class. It is like a small island. I sit at a desk next to it, checking it regularly or adding more water to a tea kettle sizzling on top of it.

The bell rings, and we sit up straight, hushed.

The teacher stands up, looking at a piece of paper in his bony hand. He keeps silent for a long time, looking out the windows. It is almost like a blizzard outside—the wind roaring and howling, the snow whipping down, slanting at nearly a forty-five–degree angle. The snow is so heavy and thick that I can barely make out the other buildings across the frozen pond.

"Well," he says.

And I bid the children rise from their chairs, and, when they do, I command them to bow to our teacher. We all bow our heads to him; then we sit down.

"Today," he says, without looking at us, holding up the piece of paper in front of him, "I must have your new names. I have the new names of most of you in this class, but the principal tells me that some of you have not yet registered your names. I shall call your old names, and those who are called will be excused from the class immediately, so that they can go home and return with their new names, which have been properly registered with the proper authorities in town. Do you understand what I am saying?"

Without waiting for our reaction, and still without looking at us, he calls out several names. My name is called.

"You may be excused," he says, crunching the piece of paper into a ball in his fist. "Report back as soon as you can."

He gets down from the platform and says, "The rest of you will remain quiet and go over your homework." With that announcement, he abruptly turns away from us and walks out of the room.

I put my shoes on outside the classroom and, brushing aside the questions from the bewildered children, I start running away from the school as fast as I can in the blinding snow and choking, icy wind, running and skidding and stumbling in the deep snow. My new name, my old name, my true name, my not-true name? I am plunging and slogging through the snow, thinking, "I am going to lose my name; I am going to lose my name; we are all going to lose our names." . . .

My grandmother says, "Leave the boy home. He will catch cold."

My father says, "No, Mother. I want him to come with me. I want him to see it and remember it." My father is wearing a Korean man's clothes: white pantaloon-like trousers, with the bottoms tied around his ankles, a long-sleeved white jacket, a blue vest, and a gray topcoat. My father is seldom seen in our native clothes, except when he has to attend a wedding or a funeral. He is wearing a black armband on the left sleeve of his gray topcoat. He is not wearing a hat.

"Have some hot soup before you go," says my grandmother.

"No, thank you, Mother," says my father, holding my hand. "Stay with Father and keep an eye on him." 15

My grandmother nods. "It is the end of the world," she mutters angrily. "Damn them! damn them!"

"Come on," says my father to me.

Outside, by the west gate, four of my father's friends are waiting for us. They are dressed like my father—all wearing black armbands on the left sleeves of their gray topcoats. I bow to them, but no one says a word either to me or to anyone else. On the small stone bridge outside the gate, they pause for a moment, whispering among themselves. The stream is frozen and covered thick with snow. Passers-by bow to the group. The four men—my father's friends—are the bookstore owner, an elder of our Presbyterian church, a doctor, and a farmer who also has an apple orchard. The snow is slashing down on us, and my ears are cold, even with ear muffs on. Snowflakes get inside my collar, making me shiver. We walk down the street; my father is in the middle of the group, holding my hand. I slip on an icy patch and stumble, and the bookstore owner helps me up and holds my hand. In the snow-covered open-air market place, which is closed down during the winter, the wind howls even more strongly, shrieking through the electric wires and telephone poles. The snow is beating down so hard that I have to bow my head and face sideways, but the men are walking straight up, occasionally returning, in silence, the bows from the other men on the street. We go past the town hall, past the Japanese department store and shops, and through the main street, where most of the shops are—the bakery, the barber shop, the watch shop, the restaurant, the clothing store, the bicycle shop, the grain store, the pharmacy, the doctor's office, the dentist's office, the hardware store, the bank, the grocery store . . . and the townspeople are looking out from their shops and offices—some bowing to us, some waving at us—and, as we continue down the main street, we are followed by other people, and more and more people join us as we come near the end of the main street. My father and the bookstore owner are still holding my hands, and I have to try hard to keep up with the men, though they are walking very slowly. At the end of the main street, we come to an intersection and turn to the right. It is an uphill road, and the snow-laden wind whips down from the top of the hill, almost blowing me off my feet, and I feel the men's hands tighten their grips on mine. At the top of the hill, there is a small Methodist church and, across from it, the police station. We struggle up the snow-packed hill, by the long stone wall of the police station, and enter its main gate. Inside, on the station grounds, in the deep snow, a long line of people barely moves along. We walk over the crackling snow and stand at the end of the line. We exchange bows with the people standing in line. No one says anything—I, my father, the bookstore owner, the doctor, the farmer, the elder of our church, and all those people who have preceded or followed us . . .

I am freezing with cold. I stamp my feet, crushing the icy snow on the ground. Without a word, the bookstore owner opens the front of his topcoat and pulls me inside and covers me up, except for my face, which is snuggled against the back of my father. He turns, looks at me, and fixes my ear muffs. He neither says a word to me nor smiles at me. I know when to keep quiet.

The line, hardly advancing, gets longer and longer. New people   20
are lined up even outside the station grounds.

Someone comes to us. Someone from the front of the line. He is a young Korean man. He bows to my father. "Please, sir," he says, "come and take my place."

My father shakes his head. "I will wait for my turn here. Thank you anyway."

He stands silent for a moment.

"It is all right," my father says. "Go back to your place."

He bows to my father once more and says, before he returns to   25
the front of the line, "I am dying of shame, sir"; then, his words nearly lost in the howling snow, "I don't know what I can do."

A little while later, a Japanese policeman comes toward us. When he comes near to us, I can tell that he is an inspector. He is wearing a black cape. I see his long saber peering out of the bottom of his cape. I can hear the clank the saber makes against his black leather riding boots. He salutes my father. He has a long turned-up mustache. "It is an honor," he says to my father, "to see you in person here. You could have sent one of your servants."

My father is silent.

"Please come with me," says the Inspector. "I can't have you lined up out here like a common person. Please."

"I will wait for my turn, just like everyone else," says my father. "They have been here longer than I have."

"Come with me," insists the Inspector. "Please." 30

Afraid and, to my shame, trembling, I look up at my father.

My father looks at the Inspector and then at his friends.

Other people are watching us.

I feel the hands of the bookstore owner tighten on my shoulders.

"If you insist," says my father. 35

The Inspector looks down at me. "You must be freezing," he says. His white-gloved hand reaches out for my snow-covered hair.

I duck my head inside the topcoat of the bookstore owner.

"Bring the boy with you, by all means," says the Inspector.

I hear my father's boots crunching on the snow. I free myself out of the bookstore owner's hands and nearly bump into the back of my father.

He takes my hand. "Come with me." 40

The Inspector walks beside my father. His black cape is billowing in the wind and snow, flapping and flapping—and his saber jingling and clanking. We walk toward the front door of the granite station building. As we pass by the people in the line, they bow to my father silently. My father's head is bowed, and, without looking at the people, he goes slowly, holding my hand.

The Inspector opens the front door and holds it for us. A Korean detective inside the building quickly bows to my father. "You really didn't have to come in person, sir," he says in Korean. "I would have been glad to have registered your new name for you if I had known you were coming in person. In this cold."

We are inside the station. Other people in the line are admitted inside one at a time. The air is steamy and warm. The hallway is swarming with black-uniformed policemen, all wearing sabers. The wooden floor is slushy with melting snow.

The Inspector ushers us into a large room immediately to the right of the hallway by the door. There are two big tables, each with a policeman sitting behind. At each table, by the side of the Japanese policeman, a Korean detective sits on a chair, apparently interpreting for those Koreans who cannot understand Japanese.

The Korean detective who met us at the door brings a chair 45 from the back of the room. He offers it to my father.

My father does not sit down.

The Inspector tells the detective to bring some tea.

One of the men sitting at one of the tables facing the Japanese policeman cannot speak Japanese and has to have the words interpreted. The man is old; he helps out in the open-air market place on market days, doing odd jobs.

The Japanese policeman, dipping a pen in an inkwell, does not lift his face from a large ledger on the table when he says to the Korean detective by his side, "Tell the old man we will pick out a name for him if he can't make up his mind."

The Korean detective picks up a sheet of paper and shows it to the old man, translating the policeman's words.

The old man shakes his head, looking at the paper, which contains a long list of names. "Anything," he mumbles. "It doesn't matter."

The Korean detective does not translate those words. Instead, he puts his finger on one of the names and says, "How about this one, old man?"

The old man says, "It doesn't matter which. No one's going to call me by that name anyway—or by any other name."

"Then, this will be recorded as your new name." The Korean detective tells the policeman the old man's "new" name—a Japanese name.

"All right," says the policeman. He writes the name in the ledger. "What about his family members?"

The Inspector comes back into the room, accompanied by another Japanese policeman. I know him. He is the Chief of Police.

My father exchanges bows with the Chief of Police.

The Chief of Police says, "Such inclement weather, and you honor us by being here in person. Is this your son?"

I edge nearer to my father.

The Chief of Police, a short man with bushy eyebrows and large eyes behind dark brown tortoise-shell glasses, looks at the Inspector and says, "Well, I trust the Inspector here will take care of your matter as speedily as he can. Anything, anytime I can be of any help or service, please call on me. I am, indeed, honored by your presence here in person."

My father and he exchange bows again. The Chief of Police goes out of the room, his black leather riding boots jangling and dragging his spurs on the wet floor.

My father takes out a piece of paper from his vest pocket. He hands it to the Inspector. "I assume," he says, "this is what you want, Inspector. I hope you will be pleased."

The Inspector looks at the paper. "Yes, yes," he says. "Iwamoto. . . . Ah—it is a very fine name, sir. It does justice to your person. It reminds me of your house by the mountain and, also, of your orchard, with all those rocky mountains around it. I will have it registered. You needn't wait for the certificate, needless to say. I will have someone bring it to your house later."

"Iwamoto" . . . "Iwamoto." I mouth the name. Our new name. My new name. "Iwa"—rock. "Moto"—root . . . base . . . foundation. "Rock-Foundation." So this is our "new" surname, our Japanese "family" name.

"Come," my father says to me.   65

The Korean detective leads us out, with the Inspector by my side. At the front door, which the detective holds open, the Inspector gives my father a salute. "I thank you, sir, for taking the trouble to come in person."

We step out into the cold. The snow is turning into a blizzard. The long line of people is still standing outside, hunched and huddled, rubbing their ears and faces, stamping their feet in the snow. My father pauses for a moment on the steps, one arm around my shoulders, and says:

"Look."

Afraid, bewildered, and cold, I look up at his face and see tears in his eyes.

"Take a good look at all of this," he whispers. "Remember it.   70
Don't ever forget this day."

I look at all those people lined up, from the steps all the way to the gate and outside. I feel a tug at my hand, and I follow him down the steps. We walk by the people slowly, my father not speaking. They bow to him, some removing their hats. My father, bowing back, approaches the group of his friends still in line. In silence, they shake hands.

Then, we move on along the line of people standing in the snow. Some shake hands with my father; most of them merely bow, without words. We are outside the gate. There, too, a long line has formed and is still forming, all the way down the hill, past the gray stucco Methodist church . . . and I am thinking, "We lost our names; I lost my name; and these people are all going to lose their names, too, when they walk into the police station, into that half-empty large hall, when a 'new' name, a Japanese name, is entered in the big ledger with a pen dipped into a dark blue inkwell. . . ."

"What does our new name mean, sir?" I ask my father when we are down the hill and on the main street.

"Foundation of Rock," he says, shielding my face from the bitter-cold snow with his hand. ". . . on this rock I will build my church. . . ."

I do not understand him.

"It is from the Bible," he says.

By twelve o'clock, all the children in our class have new names. As soon as each class submits to the principal a complete list of all the new names, the class is sent out of the school to go to the Japanese shrine to pay its respects to the gods of the Empire and make its report to the Emperor—to announce that we now have Japanese names. At least once a week, each class is required to go to the shrine for an hour of meditation and prayer for the victory and prosperity of the Empire. It was our class's turn the day before, and we "prayed" for the victory and safety of the German *Luftwaffe* pilots who are bombing England in—as I shall learn years later to call it—the Battle of Britain.

Every town and every village now has a shrine—a miniature copy of the "main" shrine somewhere in Japan, where all the souls of the dead soldiers, for example, are supposed to go to rest. The shrine in our town is a small, wooden structure with a gable roof and several flights of stone steps built halfway up the mountain behind our house. The shrine is tended by a middle-aged Japanese Shinto priest, a bald-headed little man with a fat wife, who happens to live in a house that is next to ours, though carefully separated from ours by a bamboo fence.

The snow is coming down hard as we struggle up the narrow, icy path in file. Whenever there is a strong wind, the heavily laden pines shower down on us swarms of little icicles and snow. My bare hands are freezing, my bare ears are numb, and my feet are wet and cold with snow that slips inside my boots. Everyone's cheeks are red and raw from the icy wind. We gasp our way up the mountain. There is a small plaza at the foot of the stone steps, and the wind at the clearing is unbearable. The lashing, biting wind shrieks and whines all around us. The town below is invisible—lost in the blizzard, smothered by the raging snow. At the command of our teacher, I have to coax the children to gather and stand in formation. Then we kneel down in the snow, with our heads bowed. The teacher tells the priest, who has come down the steps from the shrine up above, that we are all there to report to the gods and the Emperor our new names. The priest, dressed in a purple-and-white priest's garment, wears a small sort of hat on his bald head. The teacher gives him the list of our new names. The priest reads the names one by one, slowly, bowing his head to the shrine above with each name. Then the priest chants something in a singsong voice, and, when he finishes the chanting, we all bow, now standing up. Snow clings to my pants, and my hands are wet from the snow. We look like a group of snowmen, covered as we are from top to bottom with the snow. At last we are dismissed by the priest, who goes back up the stone steps into the shrine, back to the sanctuary of his gods and the spirit of the Emperor that resides in it. Years later, when, at last, our Liberation comes, we raid the shrine, which is then already wrecked and has been set on fire by the townspeople, and, there, in the inner sanctuary, we discover a small wooden box; in it, we find, wrapped in rice paper, two wooden sticks to which we have been bowing and praying all those years—the sticks from a tree on the "sacred" grounds of the "main" shrine in Japan. . . .

Our teacher dismisses the class for the day. The children, no longer in formation, scramble down the mountain path, without a word and without a sound. The teacher wants me to come with him. I follow him down the path in silence. I skid once on the way down and roll over, plunging into a deep pile of snow. He offers his hand and helps me up on my feet. His bare hand clasps my bare hand. He leads me down the mountain on the path, which forks at the foothill, one path going toward the school and the other going into the town, past our house. He takes the path that goes by our house. He is still holding my hand. I do not know how to disengage my hand from his. I do not want to be seen letting him hold my hand, but he grips it firmly and strides toward our house. We pass the Shinto priest's Japanese-style wooden house. We are at the east gate of our house.

Someone must have seen us coming down the path and told my father, because we find my father at the gate waiting for us. He has not changed his clothes.

My father and the teacher exchange bows.

I slip away from the teacher and stand by my father.

"No school this afternoon?" says my father to no one in particular.

I shake my head.

The teacher says, in Japanese, "Too much has happened to the children today already; so I sent them home for the day."

My father simply nods his head.

"I hope you don't mind my bringing him home," says my teacher, casting a quick glance at me.

"Not at all."

A moment of silence follows, all of us standing there in the pouring snow by the gate. I am wondering if my father will invite the teacher in, but he is quiet and shows no hint of asking the young Japanese in.

Then, the teacher gestures abruptly, as if to touch my face. "I am sorry," he says.

My father gives him a slight bow of his head.

"Even the British wouldn't have thought of doing this sort of primitive thing in India," says the Japanese.

I am at a loss, trying to comprehend what he says and means.

". . . inflicting on you this humiliation . . ." he is saying. ". . . unthinkable for one Asian people to another Asian people, especially we Asians who should have a greater respect for our ancestors. . . ."

"The whole world is going mad, sir," says my father quietly, "going back into another dark age. Japan is no exception."

My teacher nods. "As one Asian to another, sir, I am deeply ashamed."

"I am ashamed, too, sir," says my father, "perhaps for a reason different from yours."

My teacher, without a word, bows to my father, turns round, and disappears into the blinding snow.

"It is a small beginning," says my father, as he has said before about my Korean teacher, who is now somewhere in Manchuria. He gives me a hug. "I am ashamed to look in your eyes," he says—another one of those mysterious things he likes to say. "Someday, your generation will have to forgive us." I don't know what he is talking about, but the scene and the atmosphere of the moment, in the roaring wind and with the snow gone berserk, make me feel dramatic.

"We will forgive you, Father," say I, magnanimously.

His arm tightens around my shoulders. "Come on," he says, leading me into the house. "We have one more place to go to. Your grandfather and I are going out to the cemetery. Would you like to come?"

I nod. I am, suddenly, too overwhelmed and awed by enigmas beyond my child's understanding to speak.

"I hope our ancestors will be as forgiving as you are," he says. "It is a time of mourning."

And, only then, do I understand the meaning of the black armband on his sleeve and on those of his friends. . . .

Today, I lost my name. Today, we all lost our names.
February 11, 1940.

RESPONDING IN DISCUSSION OR WRITING

1. Kim refers to a nickname of "Chopstick." What nicknames do you and your friends and family members have, and how did those names come about?

2. When the Japanese teacher takes the boy home, what is it that he wants to communicate to the boy's father? Are his comments expected or not? Why or why not? What are the different reasons for father and teacher feeling "ashamed" (paragraphs 97, 98)?

3. Why do you think the boy's father says, "Someday, your generation will have to forgive us" (paragraph 100)? What other events or situations can you think of in which a father might say this to a child, when a whole generation will need to forgive the previous generation?

4. *Considerations of Style.* Kim uses the present tense for this narrative. Why do you think he has chosen that tense even though he is writing about an incident that happened in February 1940? What effect does the author achieve by mentioning the date only at the end of the chapter?

5. The boy's walk with his father to register their name is described in great detail (paragraph 18): the weather, the shops, the people, the landmarks along the way. What is the effect of such a detailed description? Why do you think Kim includes all these specific details? What emotional reactions does he want his readers to have to his story?

WRITING ASSIGNMENTS

1. Consider the issue of the gap between the generations and the feeling of guilt in this story: "I am ashamed to look in your eyes" (paragraph 100). Is the legacy of shame and guilt one that is frequently handed down from one generation to the next? Or do you view the legacy in more positive terms?

2. *For Further Research.* The date takes on an important role in Kim's chapter, occupying a significant place, right at the end of the chapter. Research the historical background of Kim's story, setting it in a broader context of events at that time. Consult newspapers, almanacs, and histories of World War II to write an account of what was happening in February 1940.

❖

NAMES AND CHOICE OF ANCESTRY

MARY C. WATERS

Mary C. Waters, a professor of sociology at Harvard University, has also taught at the University of California, Berkeley. While there, she interviewed sixty third- and fourth-generation white people of ethnic background in the suburbs of San Jose and Philadelphia; on the 1980 census form, all of them had indicated one or more ancestry groups with which they most identified (the response of "American" was discouraged on the form). This excerpt from her book Ethnic Options: Choosing Identities in America *(1990) comes from a section headed "The Choice of Ancestry," in which Waters shows how her interviewees from mixed ancestral backgrounds "use surname and looks to decide which of their ancestries to identify with." This selection comes from the first part, the discussion of surname.*

PEOPLE ARE QUITE AWARE of the ways in which others use surnames to label them, and mention of others using their surnames to identify them was a common theme in the interviews. Often people mentioned their surnames when I asked them if it was a common experience for people to ask or comment about their ethnic backgrounds. Cindy Betz is an example: "As soon as they see my last name, they ask me what nationality I am. That is usually the clincher. If I go into a bank, they say, 'How do you pronounce that? What nationality is that?' So I think that is probably why at work, [when] a lot of people see my name, they say, 'What is that?'"

For those whose self-identification corresponds to their ethnic surname, the response of others to the surname may reinforce their pride in their ethnic identification. For example, Tom Scotto:

> *Q:* Is it a common occurrence for people to ask or comment on your ancestry?
>
> *A:* Yes, of course. In fact when you meet someone new, lots of times they will comment on my last name. It's Sicilian. They'll say, "Oh, you are Sicilian!" Then sometimes they will make a crack about the Mafia. In my shop people will come in and they will make a comment about the fact that I am Italian. When I worked in the phone company or when I was in the Navy guys would tease me about being Italian. It is OK, it is just meant good-naturedly. It is a way of getting to know you. I would know if they meant something bad by it.

When asked whether it was common for others to ask about or comment on their ethnic ancestry, most respondents replied that it was not very common in their day-to-day lives. Most, however, could remember the last time someone had asked, and almost always the stranger or acquaintance had asked about the respondent's surname. Most respondents were very aware of what their name symbolized to others and were accustomed to either saying, "Yes, you guessed correctly" or correcting the wrong impression.

Mike Gold was more concerned about why people commonly asked him about his last name, not because he suspected that they would guess that he was English, Scottish, and French, but because he was sure that they were trying to discover whether he was Jewish or not: "A lot of times when I am on the phone with somebody and they ask my name, they ask me how to spell it because they want to know if it is spelled Gould instead of just Gold, which I think means they want to know whether I am a Jew or not."

In fact, Gold's concern reflects the fact that while almost everyone is aware of the extent to which surnames are used to determine ethnic ancestry, everyone also knows what unreliable
indicators surnames are. There are three factors that undermine
the reliability of surnames as a predictor of ancestry: intermarriage, name changes, and changing sensitivity in society to types
of surnames. Each of these is considered below.

Intermarriage. The first problem in using surnames to ethnically
identify people is intermarriage. A surname commonly indicates
only the paternal side of the ancestral line. Children are usually
given their fathers' surnames and wives generally take those of
their husbands, so that it is in fact relatively difficult to trace one's
origins through the maternal line.

When husband and wife are from the same ethnic group, the
husband's name is a valid marker of the ethnicity for the whole
family. If your maiden name is Gallucci and your married name is
Pontucci, those judging your ethnicity from your surname will
come to the same conclusion whichever you use. However, in the
case of marriage across ethnicities, the surname becomes an
unreliable marker of ethnic ancestry because it only gives information on one side of the family. Yet since it is still widely used
in our society to determine ethnicity, it has a strong effect on self-
identification. People know that others use their surnames to
assign them to particular ancestries and sometimes self-identify
correspondingly.

The effect of intermarriage on the accuracy of labeling via surname is evident in the remarks made by Sean O'Brien about his
wife. Proud of his Irish heritage, he joked about the fact that he
never would have dated or married his wife if her father had been
Italian and her mother Irish, giving her an Italian surname, rather
than the way that it was: an Irish father, Italian mother, and Irish
surname: "I tease Christine . . . She is half Irish and half Italian
and her maiden name is Fitzpatrick. That's the only reason I
asked her out because she had an Irish last name. If her last name
had been Italian, I probably never would have asked her out."

A similar story was told by Bonnie Ostrowski, a 50-year-old
housewife, whose immigrant parents were quite insistent that she
date only Polish boys. Her future husband was Polish, German,
Scottish, and Irish, but had a Polish last name, which allowed her

to date him even though he was not "pure" Polish: "The only person I ever was serious about was my husband and his name was right . . . even if he was German, Scottish, and Irish, he was Polish!" Bonnie thought it quite ironic that people guessed her to be Polish based on her husband's last name, when she was in fact more Polish than he was.

Married women are often mistakenly assigned the ethnicity [10] associated with their surnames, which are actually their husband's surnames. This can have different consequences, depending on the type and level of ethnic identity of the women involved. Some women who were very strongly ethnically identified had some of that identity muted by a less identifiable surname. For instance, Judy Gray Gilligan, who grew up going to Serbian summer camps and observing many Serbian customs, feels very close to her Serbian roots and is proud of her Serbian heritage. Yet when I asked her if she felt Serbian sometimes and American at other times, she replied: "Well, because my last name has been Gray for the last twenty years, I think of myself as an American. I think the only time that the Serbian enters it is when I am at a Serbian function or I am among my family and they expect me to be Serbian, and then my identity shifts a bit."

Elaine Williams, a 32-year-old office worker, is of wholly Italian background, but married a man of English background with the last name of Williams. Since she no longer has an Italian last name, fewer people ask her about her background:

> *Q:* Is it a common occurrence for people to ask or comment on your ethnic background?
> *A:* No, not now that my name is not Italian. Because apparently I do not look real Italian. But before I was married, when people would learn my name, they would say, "Oh, you are Italian." And, if they were too, then we would discuss being Italian together. But I don't find that as much now.

On the other hand, sometimes a name change as the result of being married gives a woman who had no particularly strong ethnic background the chance to be considered "ethnic" by others. Liz Field, a 35-year-old weaver, who is now divorced, but had an Italian last name when she was married, observed:

I had more fun with my name when it was DeCinci. People were always saying, "How do you spell that?" and "Are you Italian?" Some people just assumed I was Italian . . . an old Italian woman who was a friend's grandmother tried to prove to me that I was Italian . . . she was absolutely positive . . .

Name Changes. The second problem with using a surname as an indication of ancestry is that it may have been changed. There is a long history of surname changes in the United States. Many immigrants had their names changed for them by immigration or other officials. Other immigrants or their children changed their names on purpose to make them sound less ethnic.

Many of the people I interviewed had names that had been changed at some point by their ancestors. For instance, the Albert family knew that their name had once been Alberti. Bob Albert's grandfather had changed it when he first immigrated to Louisiana from Sicily. Bob Albert thinks it was changed in order to escape discrimination:

> My grandfather's name was Alberti. For one reason or another he dropped the *i* from the name, so our name was Albert. It has been that way ever since, so my dad was born Albert. I kind of presume that maybe it was for business reasons because down in Louisiana there were a lot of French people and maybe he wanted to be in business and maybe he wanted to make them think that he was French rather than Italian.
>
> [15]

Janet Albert Parro, his 28-year-old daughter, was convinced that because her name had been changed, she had been spared a great deal of teasing in elementary school. She recounted many stories of children with complicated Italian names who were ridiculed by other children. "I had a girlfriend, her last name was Poppilissio. That made the kids hysterical . . . But I didn't have an Italian last name." Janet was in effect "passing" as non-Italian while the other children were making fun of those with Italian last names.

Knowledge of Surnames. The third way in which the use of surnames to determine ethnic identity can lead to error involves misidentification with the wrong ethnic group. The association of a particular surname with a particular ethnic group is the result of a learning process. As children grow up, they learn what is considered a typical Irish or Italian or Dutch name. They also learn through individual experience to associate the surnames of people they know with the ancestry they know the other person identifies with. This learning process admits of many potential errors and misidentifications, which may well vary by ethnic group.

Two respondents described this type of confusion. Lisa Paulo, a 24-year-old bank teller, was sure that hers was a well-known Portuguese surname. She reported, however, that others often thought it was Italian. Janet Albert Parro reported the same type of error with her husband's Spanish last name—an ironic twist, since Janet herself had escaped identification as Italian when she was young because her father's family had changed their name from Alberti to Albert. Many other people also said they were often misidentified as Irish or Italian, two of the most common and widely recognized groups. Bonnie Ostrowski reported that a paper boy had once tried to make her name Irish by billing a Mrs. O'Strowski.

Even when people use surnames to figure out their *own* ancestry, they are at risk of making a mistake based on misidentifying other surnames. For example, Rose Peters:

> *Q:* What would you put on the census form?
>
> *A:* Italian and Irish. That is not really complete. I can give you a list, but that would have been my answer.
>
> *Q:* What else is there?
>
> *A:* Welsh, English, and Lithuanian. I just found this out recently. I was raised thinking I was half Italian and half Irish.
>
> *Q:* How did you find out?
>
> *A:* Well, in 1981 I guess I took a sociology course and the teacher assigned us to find out about our last names. I based it on my maiden name and I thought it was Irish and I went home and told my father and he got in this big huff and said, "No, it's Welsh." All this time I thought it was all Irish.

The ways in which people came to misidentify names are varied. In many cases it may be that a name actually does originate in another ethnic group, which the individual does not think his or her ancestors are from. Perhaps generations ago on the paternal side, Lisa Paulo's ancestor was an Italian who went to Portugal. Or possibly because the Portuguese are a much less numerous group in the United States, there is a lack of knowledge of the structure of their names among the general public. Since they look and sound similar, people generally lump together Portuguese and Italian names.

RESPONDING IN DISCUSSION OR WRITING

1. Waters uses the terms *options* and *choosing* in the title of her book about ethnic identity. To what extent do you think she is justified in perceiving ethnic identification as a choice or option? Would you agree with her that it is a choice? Or do you feel that ethnicity is something we are born with? How can the two differing perceptions affect the way we perceive ourselves and others?

2. In this selection, Waters makes the point that surnames are not always reliable predictors of ancestry. What support does she offer for that point, and how does she organize that support? Do you find her support convincing?

3. *Considerations of Style.* How does Waters organize the findings of her research and present them in a logical way? How are text sections linked so that the reader knows how each section refers to the unit's main idea?

4. Describe an incident in which ethnic identification, comments about ancestry, or names as indicators of ancestry played an important role in your eyes. Are there any differences between your reaction to the incident when it occurred and your recollection of it now?

5. Waters tells us many stories of the ways in which people respond to other people's last names. What feelings and reactions do you usually have when you meet someone whose name indicates the same ancestry as yours? Do you ever ask about ancestry because it is not obvious to you from a person's name?

6. *Considerations of Style.* Waters's book, the source of this excerpt, is an academic research study, published by a university press. It contains statistical tables, documentation of sources, footnotes, and an extensive bibliography. What was your experience like in reading it? How readable and engaging did you find it? Explain what it is about the text that leads you to your answer.

WRITING ASSIGNMENTS

1. Waters mentions how a girl with a name changed from *Alberti* to *Albert* was in fact "'passing' as non-Italian" (paragraph 15). In what other ways does the concept of "passing" reveal itself in everyday life? Discuss occasions when people might try to "pass" as somebody different, for example, in terms of abilities, age, gender, education, class, nationality, or race. Explain why you think people try to pass and adopt a role and new identity. Make connections to other readings in this unit that address the notion of "passing."

2. *For Further Research.* Find five to ten people who identify themselves as connected to an ethnic group (not in your own family). Conduct your own survey and find out how they would answer the 1980 census question "What is your ancestry?" Note the following instructions for the census taker that accompanied this question:

> Print the ancestry group with which the person *identifies.* Ancestry (or origin or descent) may be viewed as the nationality group, the lineage, or the country in which the person or the person's parents or ancestors were born before their arrival in the United States. Persons who are of more than one origin and who cannot identify with a single group should print their multiple ancestry (for example, German-Irish).
>
> Be specific; for example, if ancestry is "Indian," specify whether American Indian, Asian Indian, or West Indian. Distinguish Cape Verdean from Portuguese, and French Canadian from Canadian.
>
> A religious group should not be reported as a person's ancestry.

Source: Bureau of the Census 1980.

Write an essay in which you draw conclusions from what your respondents say, and relate those conclusions to the ones Waters offers.

❖

LATINO, SÍ. HISPANIC, NO

EARL SHORRIS

Earl Shorris, born in 1936, is a journalist who writes frequently about the American scene. His most recent book is A Nation of Salesmen *(1994), which is about the way selling affects America's social, political, and moral life. Other books include* Scenes from Corporate Life: The Politics of Middle Management *(1981) and* Latinos: A Biography of the People *(1992). He is a contributing editor for* Harper's *magazine, and he also writes for the* New York Times. *The following article was published in the* New York Times *on October 28, 1992. In it, Shorris discusses the significance of names given not just to individuals but to entire ethnic groups.*

WHEN THE KING OF Spain was asked last year what name he used for those people in the U.S. who were related to him by language, he is reported to have said, with regal certainty, "Hispanic."

Ricardo Gutiérrez, a salesman from the east side of Los Angeles, faced with the same question, answered with equal certainty, "Latino."

Although Mr. Gutiérrez would seem to have superior knowledge of cultural issues in the U.S., many people and institutions, including the Census Bureau, side with the King. I am not one of them.

Of course, there are those who think that the King and the salesman are wrong. They oppose the use of any single word to describe all of the King's linguistic relatives—a lawyer whose family came from Puerto Rico, a waiter who emigrated from Spain, a Quiché Indian farmworker from Guatemala, a poet from the Dominican Republic and a taxi driver from Colombia.

They raise a serious issue. The use of a single word to name a group including people as disparate as Mexicans and Cubans conflates the cultures. And whatever conflates cultures destroys them. 5

Nevertheless, there will have to be a name, for political power in a democratic society requires numbers, and only by agglomeration does the group become large enough to have an important voice in national politics. Agreement on one encompassing name is therefore vital. And possible, for any set that can be defined can be named. Which brings up another problem.

The group cannot be defined racially, because it includes people whose ancestors came from Asia to settle in the Western Hemisphere thousands of years ago, as well as people from Europe, the Iberian Peninsula and Africa. Religion won't do either. The group comprises Roman Catholics, many Protestant denominations, Jews and people who still have deep connections to Mixtec, Nahua and other native American religious rites and beliefs.

Economically, the group ranges from the chairman of the Coca-Cola Company to undocumented farmworkers who sleep in burrows dug into the ground in the hills east of Oceanside, Calif.

Nothing is left to define the linguistic relatives of the King but the language itself. There must be some connection to the Spanish language, if not in use, then in memory. If the language was not acquired from Roman soldiers who landed in Spain 2,000 years ago, then it was acquired from Spanish soldiers who landed in the Western Hemisphere 500 years ago.

During preparations for the 1980 U.S. Census, several names for the group were discussed. Latino won out, according to people who took part in the discussions, but at the last minute someone said it was too close to Ladino, an ancient language of Spain, now spoken by only a few Spanish Jews. Hispanic was chosen instead.

Since then, Hispanic and Latino have taken on political, social and even geographic meaning. Latino is used in California. In Florida, Hispanic is preferred by Cubans no matter what political, social or educational views they hold. Hispanic is used more often than Latino in Texas but neither word is used much; Mexican, Mexican-American and Chicano dominate there. Chicago, which has a mixture of people from the Caribbean and the mainland, has adopted Latino. In New York City, both names are used, depending largely on one's politics.

Hispanic belongs to those in power; it is the choice of establishments, exiles, social climbers and kings. Latino has been adopted by almost everyone else. Latino and Hispanic are the left and right, commoner and king of names. Democrats are generally Latinos, Republicans are Hispanics. Many Anglos, people who oppose bilingual education and those who support English-only laws prefer Hispanic, which is an English word meaning, "pertaining to ancient Spain."

But neither politics nor economics should determine the choice of a name. Language defines the group, provides it with history and home; language should also determine its name— Latino. The vowels of Latino are a serenade, Hispanic ends like broken glass. Latino/Latina has gender, which is Spanish, as against Hispanic, which follows English rules. Perhaps the course of democracy and assimilation dictates that someday this linguistic connection to culture must die, but there is no hurry; we need not be assassins now.

RESPONDING IN DISCUSSION OR WRITING

1. Shorris says that "political power in a democratic society requires numbers." What do you think he means by that, and what other examples can you think of to support his statement? When we think of minorities in a society as having smaller numbers than the majority, what does that say about political power?

2. *Considerations of Style.* Two brief anecdotes introduce the topic of the names given to Spanish speakers. How effective are the anecdotes? Does it make any difference which one he tells first?

3. At what point in the article do you learn precisely what Shorris's point of view is on the issue of names? Why does he reject compromise on the issue of choosing a name?

4. *Considerations of Style.* Writers of short articles like this one have to structure their finished product carefully. How does Shorris meet the constraints of the form: Where does he state his thesis in this article? How much space does he devote to supporting it, and what support does he offer?

5. Write down the names that are often used for the ethnic group that you belong to. Make a distinction between formal terms, slang terms, and derogatory terms. Look the words up in a dictionary that contains etymology (that is, the derivations of words) and

examples, and find out the history and connotations of the words.

6. How important do you think it is to pay attention to the names of various ethnic groups? Does it matter what people are called? Are ethnic names important? If so, why do they change so often?

WRITING ASSIGNMENTS

1. Shorris says that "neither politics nor economics should determine the choice of a name." Write an essay explaining why you think Shorris made that statement and reacting to the statement. Do you agree with it? What should, in your view, determine the choice of a name for an ethnic group?

2. Shorris's article in the *New York Times* produced the following two published letters of response.

> To the Editor:
> Earl Shorris (Op-Ed, Oct. 28) argues that the term Latino is better than Hispanic because "Latino/Latina has gender, which is Spanish, as against Hispanic, which follows English rules." If the original language determines the name of a group, we must stop using all English names for ethnic groups such as Chinese-Americans, Haitian-Americans and Japanese-Americans.
>
> Hispanics use that term in its English form only when speaking English. Otherwise they say Hispano or Latino, both of which are consistent with the spoken language.
>
> Mr. Shorris confirms that Hispanic is the preferred usage in Florida and Texas, and that both terms are used in New York. He should know both terms were used long before the Census Bureau picked up Hispanic for demographic statistical purposes.
>
> Despite wide usage of the term, Mr. Shorris asserts that "Hispanic belongs to those in power." That is a contradiction, unless he is stating that power (whatever he means by it) is held only by Hispanics (or Latinos) in Florida, Texas and New York.
>
> He asserts also: "The use of a single word to name a group including people as disparate as Mexicans and Cubans conflates the cultures. And whatever conflates cultures destroys them."
>
> Nevertheless he rushes headlong to advocate the name Latino as a substitute for Hispanic because, in his words, Hispanic does not sound "like a serenade." This sounds stereotypical and maybe even a little offensive.

A better argument would be that Latino is a more inclusive term: my Brazilian and Haitian friends refer to themselves as Latino, although certainly not Hispanic. Thus, although all Hispanics are Latinos, not all Latinos are Hispanic.

Indeed, Italians and French may call themselves Latinos, probably with more justification than hundreds of thousands of Latinos in the United States who hardly speak Spanish or any other Latin-based language, and who are further removed from their Latin roots than their parents or grandparents.

I suggest that both terms are acceptable because millions of people use them in self-reference and as a badge of pride. Thus, both terms reflect a sense of identity with Spanish or Latin roots. Yet, neither term is accurate because they both exclude the indigenous population of Latin America, as well as Africans, Asians and countless other non-Latin European populations. If Hispanic is an imposed official term, so is Latino, since it was the French who imposed that name on the southern continent of our hemisphere.

So, take your pick. But implying political connotations to our choices is doing a disservice to our need for unity and socioeconomic empowerment. Implying that one term is elitist and the other is correct is an elitist assumption. Remember, there are Hispanic as well as non-Hispanic Latinos in our nations. All are victims of an imposed colonial system that sets each against all. Let us stop bickering about these two externally imposed terms and let's get on with education, achievement and cultural growth.

Héctor Vélez Guadalupe
Associate Prof. of Sociology
Ithaca College
Ithaca, N.Y., Oct. 29, 1992

•

To the Editor:

Earl Shorris (Op-Ed, Oct. 28) displays the power of language to communicate and obfuscate. The terms Latino and Hispanic refer to peoples who for almost half a millennium have been called something else: mestizo, mulatto, ladino. Paradoxically, there are no Hispanics or Latinos in Latin America; in no country but this do census or social practices acknowledge such ethnicities.

In the United States, the terms have served to deflect the impact of racism and, subtly, to insure its survival. Since the 1944 "Caucasian Resolution" in Texas, which declared Mexican-Americans white in a rigidly segregated society, Anglo-Americans have attempted to fit newcomers from the south into an existing racial scheme. The use of cultural terms with vague Mediterranean affinities suits this purpose at present.

Sadly, 500 years after the landing of Columbus, such terms serve to obliterate the indigenous and African elements that have formed the majority of the peoples of the Caribbean and of Mesoamerica.

I.K. Sundiata
Chmn., African and Afro-American Studies, Brandeis University
Waltham, Mass., Nov. 6, 1992

Write a letter to the editor responding to one or both of the letters, making it clear whether you agree with the writer(s) or not and why. A letter to a newspaper editor will have a formal, though not stuffy, tone; the aim is often to take someone to task, to make a point, and to try to get others to understand your point and agree with you. Do not attack the letter writers personally. Concentrate on discussing the ideas they express and providing good evidence as to why you support or refute those ideas.

❖

SONG FOR MY NAME

LINDA HOGAN

Linda Hogan, born in 1947, is an American Chickasaw Indian. She has taught creative writing and American Indian literature at colleges in Colorado and Oklahoma. She is the author of several books of poems, a novel, Mean Spirit *(1990), and numerous poems and short stories in nearly fifty magazines. She won an American Book Award in 1986 for* Seeing through the Sun. *The following poem was published in her volume* Calling Myself Home *(1978).*

> Before sunrise
> think of brushing out an old woman's
> dark braids.
> Think of your hands,
> fingertips on the soft hair.   5

If you have this name,
your grandfather's dark hands
lead horses toward the wagon
and a cloud of dust follows,
ghost of silence.   10

That name is full of women
with black hair
and men with eyes like night.
It means no money
tomorrow.   15

Such a name my mother loves
while she works gently
in the small house.
She is a white dove
and in her own land   20
the mornings are pale,
birds sing into the white curtains
and show off their soft breasts.

If you have a name like this,
there's never enough water.   25
There is too much heat.
When lightning strikes, rain
refuses to follow.
It's my name,
that of a woman living   30
between the white moon
and the red sun, waiting to leave.
It's the name that goes with me
back to earth
no one else can touch.   35

RESPONDING IN DISCUSSION OR WRITING

1. What kind of feeling remains with you after you finish reading
(and rereading) this poem? What do you think causes that feeling?

2. What images does Hogan conjure up for you to contemplate as
you read? What messages do those images convey, and how do
they connect to the idea of her name?

3. *Considerations of Style.* How do the form, style, and purpose of this poem about a name differ from the prose selections in this unit?

4. *Considerations of Style.* How often and where does the poet use the word *name*? What purpose does the repetition serve for you, the reader?

5. Write a few words that summarize what each stanza in Hogan's poem says. Then write what you think the whole poem is about and go back to the poem's lines to show how they convey the meaning.

6. What audience do you think Hogan had in mind for this poem? What guides your answer?

WRITING ASSIGNMENTS

1. Write a poem, short article, or very short story with the title "Song for My Name."

2. *For Further Research.* Linda Hogan's tribal affiliation is with the Chickasaw. Through library research using books, articles in journals and small press publications, indexes, and electronic databases, find out what you can about the tribe and its customs. (Ask a librarian for help if you need it.) Write an essay in which you describe the Chickasaws in relation to one of the following: their history, language, location, present circumstances, or customs.

Making Connections: Name

1. Some of the readings in this unit deal with names of individuals, some with names of ethnic groups. What have the selections you have read told you about the connections between the acts of naming individuals and ethnic groups? Are there both similarities and differences? Write an essay in which you examine not only the giving of names to individuals and ethnic groups but the ways in which those names are received.

2. Both Cisneros and Gilyard write about changing their name. In what ways are their reasons for changing their name similar and different? What conclusions can you draw about the issues that concerned them at that time and the life they led?

3. Ferraro and Waters discuss the connections people make between name and ethnic affiliation. Both discuss the ways people view their name and heritage. Put yourself in the position of Waters. Write a formal letter from her to Ferraro, responding to the ideas in Ferraro's article, with reference to the ideas expressed in Waters's piece. Both writers make references to self-identification and to how others identify them, so consider how they approach these topics.

4. In the years 1880–1920, when immigrants arrived in the United States at Ellis Island in large numbers, they were often given new names. After doing library and interview research, write an essay in which you report on how names were assigned and how the recipients of new names reacted.

5. Reread the stories told by Kim (about forced national subjugation) and Waters (about voluntary immigration) and consider the importance of names and name changes in the different political situations. Write an essay in which you point out how reactions to name changes may differ and why. You might also want to use illustrations from other readings and from your own experience.

6. In an informative essay, describe the changes in the names given to an ethnic group other than Hispanic/Latino, for example, Asian or African American. Use library research to find out when changes occurred and discuss the possible causes and effects of the changes.

7. Do you see a name more as a burden that people inherit or a chance to make choices—about defining ancestry or choosing a direction with a name change? Write an essay in which you discuss the reasons for your opinions, and supply examples and incidents from your experience and from the readings in this unit.

8. The following article appeared in the *New York Times* on March 19, 1993. Write a letter to the *New York Times* in which you (a) discuss reasons why a government might feel the need to make laws about the kinds of names parents can and cannot choose and (b) discuss your response to the article.

A BOY NAMED BEERHALL

Remember "A Boy Named Sue," the Johnny Cash song about a child who grew up punching people who laughed at his name? Not likely in Germany, where parents are forbidden by law to choose names that blur gender or otherwise "endanger the well-being of the child." Names that didn't make the cut in 1992 were recently cited in an annual survey.

Among the rejected were *Bierstübl* ("beerhall"), *Störenfried* ("disturber of the peace") and *Whoopy* (for the actress Whoopi Goldberg), because it is a stage name and too closely akin to the phrase "making whoopee."

According to The Week in Germany, published by the German Information Center, riskier names aren't altogether out of the question. It cites "a case in Munich, in which parents were able to persuade a judge to allow them to name their child 'Cougar.'" What would the judge have thought when the musician Frank Zappa named his son Dweezil and his daughter Moon Unit?

—*New York Times*, 19 March 1993

Appearance, Age, and Abilities

It is only shallow people who do not judge by appearances. The true mystery of the world is the visible, not the invisible.

—OSCAR WILDE, The Picture of Dorian Gray, *chapter 1, 1891*

"Beauty is truth, truth beauty,"—that is all
Ye know on earth, and all ye need to know.

—JOHN KEATS, Ode on a Grecian Urn, *1820*

Appearance, Age, and Abilities

❖

Our name announces us to others, and when we then appear in person, our physical appearance tells even more about who we are. At first meeting, people can discern what we look like, roughly how old we are, and maybe, to some degree, what abilities and disabilities we have. They also learn about our tastes and preferences by looking at the way we dress and wear our hair. Appearance, age, and abilities play a large role, too, in how we view our own identity. Any factors that set us apart, from physical differences to genius, can cause feelings of pride, or, at times, alienation. Susan Athey, a twenty-four-year-old economist, offered a faculty position at about two dozen prestigious universities, recalls a boy writing on her math book in sixth grade, "You're cute. Too bad you're a brain." Her response was to try to fit in by getting bad grades.

In the academic, social, and work worlds, our age and personal presence often affect how other people respond to us. Will we be pleasantly accepted, coldly rejected, or receive a range of responses between these extremes? How people respond to us, of course, varies; it is subjective. The right height, weight, looks, clothes, carriage, way of speaking, thinking, and so on cannot be easily or neatly measured. A great range exists; a great range is accepted. Our physical and mental characteristics, however, affect not only how we impress others, but how we behave and react to others. Imagine the potentially different reactions of a fifteen-year-old and a fifty-year-old to a large and rowdy outdoor music concert. One might emphasize the riotous fun of the event, the variety of the participants, and great performers, while the other might dwell on drugs, violence, and the state of the toilets.

We are daily bombarded with images that seem intolerant of age, imperfection, and variety. The media—newspapers, magazines, TV, music, movies—often present in their productions and advertisements a world in which youth, health, and physical beauty are valued. How do these images affect our views of ourselves and others? If the people driving the snappy sports cars are young and glamorous and we are not young or not glamorous, then we are left outside the perfect world on the page or screen. We might feel, the sponsors and advertisers hope, that buying a fancy sports car (or a certain kind of soap, a video or CD, a pair of sneakers, or whatever) will make us appear younger and more glamorous to others, will make us feel like insiders in our culture, not outsiders.

The authors collected in this unit grapple with the issue of identity relative to physical appearance, age, and abilities. What constitutes physical beauty? Bruce Bower reports on the surprising results of a psychological study. From bell hooks (the author does not capitalize her name) we hear about hair: how and why African American women straighten their hair, with hooks moving from personal family memories and cross-generational interactions to how appearance for her has become connected to much larger questions of race, politics, and gender. The next two selections deal with incidents from childhood. Alice Walker writes of a disfiguring childhood injury and how she adapted to it; Leonard Kriegel recounts incidents involving a signed baseball that speak to the way polio affected both his childhood and his love of baseball. The issues of the generations also concern Emily Raimes, a high school senior at the time of writing; in her essay, she tells of building connections and friendships with people much older than herself. Nicolette Toussaint writes on overcoming isolation from a different perspective; she describes the problems of being deaf and of people seeing only her disability instead of her many abilities.

Dealing with changes in physical and mental health forms the topic of the next two selections. The clinical neurologist Oliver Sacks describes a patient with Korsakov's disease whose behavior leads him to consider how our inner narratives help us maintain a sense of identity and a sense of self. Louise Erdrich's short story

"The Red Convertible" examines the effect war can have on a person's identity. Finally, dealing with physical and mental changes that are part of the natural cycle of growing up, Audre Lorde's poem presents images of the impact of adolescence.

STARTING POINTS [FOR JOURNAL OR FREEWRITING]

Begin your own consideration of how you see your physical appearance, age, and special abilities or disabilities as playing a role in the shaping of identity by writing responses to the following questions.

1. Up until now, which age has been for you the best and which the worst? How much of a role did external events play in how you feel about those ages?

2. How important do you think physical attractiveness is to feelings of satisfaction in life and to success? What features to you are the marks of physical attractiveness for men and women?

3. What are the connotations attached to each of the following words: handicapped, disabled, crippled, physically different, differently abled, physically challenged? Do you have what you or anyone else might call a disability? How many people do you know with disabilities? How much have the disabilities affected the course of their lives?

4. Which of your physical characteristics are you most satisfied with, and which are you least satisfied with? Why? What do the feelings of your family, friends, peers, and people in general have to do with your feelings of satisfaction? What roles have those physical characteristics played in your daily life?

5. From your own experience and that of your peers, how would you characterize (a) adolescence and (b) old age? What are the main emotions and conflicts that you associate with those times in a person's life?

❖

AVERAGE ATTRACTIONS

B R U C E   B O W E R

Bruce Bower is a contributing editor for Science News *in the field of behavioral sciences. This article, which appeared in* Science News *in 1990, reports on a study that tries to determine what constitutes physical beauty.*

HERE SHE COMES, MISS America. Her demeanor exudes poise, her figure curves gracefully, her face is incredibly average.

That's right, average. And no, the computer did not jumble the judges' votes, at least not according to Judith H. Langlois of the University of Texas at Austin and Lori A. Roggman of the University of Arkansas at Fayetteville. These two psychologists have provided a scientific answer to a question that has puzzled philosophers for centuries: What constitutes physical beauty? Their surprising answer: The most attractive people are not blessed with rare physical qualities others can only dream about. A knockout face possesses features that approximate the mathematical average of all faces in a particular population.

In other words, Miss America's face is an extremely typical example of all faces, constituting what psychologists call a facial "prototype." Strictly speaking, her beauty is average. And the same goes for handsome male faces.

"This is a very exciting principle," says psychologist Ellen S. Berscheid of the University of Minnesota in Minneapolis. "We can get an empirical handle on facial beauty now."

Until seeing Langlois and Roggman's data, Berscheid, like most other investigators of physical attraction, contended that physical beauty was unmeasurable. Good looks were assumed to be perceived as a unified whole, a kind of "gestalt face" that could not be broken down or averaged in the laboratory. "We thought it was impossible to determine whether, say, Cary Grant's ears or

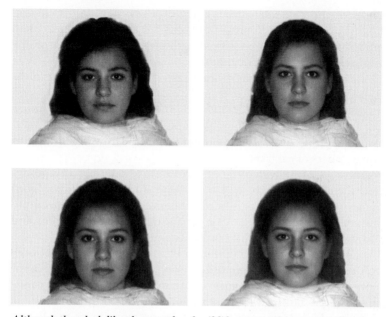

Although these look like photographs of real-life women, they are actually computer-generated composite faces. The top left image consists of four faces; the top right consists of eight faces; the bottom left combines sixteen faces; the bottom right comprises thirty-two faces. When asked to rank faces like these, college students rated the bottom two composites as most attractive, even compared with the individual faces that made up the composites.

Elizabeth Taylor's nose are attractive in an absolute sense," Berscheid remarks.

If Berscheid's about-face foreshadows a widespread adoption of the notion that attractive faces are average, the implications will extend beyond rating the raw beauty of movie stars. For instance, an analysis of groups of children's faces at different ages might provide surgeons with reliable guideposts for reconstructing craniofacial deformities resulting from accidents or inborn defects, Langlois says. Craniofacial surgeons currently operate with no standardized, age-based criteria for reshaping a disfigured face, she adds.

For now, the theory of "average beauty" rests on an intriguing facial analysis of 96 male and 96 female college students. Mug shots of the students—predominantly Caucasian, but including some Hispanics and Asians—were scanned by a video lens hooked up to a computer that converted each picture into a matrix of tiny digital units with numerical values.

Langlois and Roggman divided each group into three sets of 32 faces. In each set, the computer randomly chose two faces and mathematically averaged their digitized values. It then transformed this information into a composite face of the two individuals. Composite faces were then generated for four, eight, 16 and 32 members of each set.

Each set of individual faces and its corresponding composites was then judged by at least 65 college students, including both males and females. The students rated composite faces as more attractive than virtually any of the individual faces, Langlois and Roggman report in the March *Psychological Science.*

Student judges attributed the most striking physical superiority to the 16- and 32-face composites. Composites made from eight or fewer faces did not receive attractiveness ratings significantly greater, in a statistical sense, than individual ratings.

Not only does the averaging of 16 or more faces produce a highly attractive composite image; it also seems to produce a prototypical face. The 16- and 32-face composites in each set looked very similar to each other, and also looked similar to the corresponding composites in the other two same-sex sets, the researchers note. It did not matter that some composites were randomly generated from individual faces rated more unattractive than attractive, while other composites consisted of a majority of faces judged as attractive.

Although a composite of a different racial group—say, 32 Asian faces—would surely look different from a predominantly Caucasian composite, Langlois predicts that both Asian and non-Asian judges would rate a composite Asian face as very attractive.

"We don't claim to have simulated what the human mind does," Langlois says. "Our digitized images only approximate the averaging process that is assumed to occur when humans form mental prototypes [of an attractive face]."

The finding helps explain numerous recent observations that both infants as young as 2 months old and adults perceive the same faces as attractive, regardless of the racial or cultural background of the person viewing a face (SN:5/16/87, p. 310). In the

January *Developmental Psychology,* Langlois and her co-workers report that 1-year-olds are happier, less withdrawn and more likely to play with a female stranger judged as attractive by adults than with an equally unfamiliar female rated unattractive. The same infants play significantly longer with a doll possessing an attractive face as judged by adults than with a doll whose face is unattractive to adults.

Faces serve as a critical source of social information, especially for babies, who may prefer an attractive or prototypical face because it is easier to classify as a face, Langlois suggests. In fact, she says, evolutionary pressures over the past several million years may have endowed humans with a built-in "beauty-detecting" mechanism that averages facial features. According to this scenario—which is admittedly difficult to test—humans have evolved to respond most strongly to the most prototypical faces, which most readily yield social information through such facial expressions as happiness or disgust.

On the other hand, people may acquire preferences for attractive faces early in infancy, when the ability to sort diverse stimuli into meaningful categories organized around prototypes is apparently already in place. For example, 6-month-olds respond most strongly to basic vowel sounds—the long "e" in the word "peep," for example—that adults perceive as the best examples of particular vowels. This suggests that specific speech sounds serve as "perceptual anchors" from infancy onward (SN: 7/15/89, p. 37).

Whatever the case, the principle that averageness is a critical element of attractiveness probably applies to as many as nine out of 10 people whose countenances are considered alluring, Berscheid says. Most exceptions may be individuals in the public eye, such as movie stars, whose appeal sometimes lies largely in perceptions indirectly linked to facial beauty, such as glamour and fame.

Langlois agrees, citing Cher as one such exception. Cher's facial features are clearly not average, but many people view her as attractive, Langlois says. Opinions about Cher's facial beauty are undoubtedly affected by her expressions in photographs, the youthfulness of her face, her glamorous image and numerous media reports describing her younger boyfriends, the Texas psychologist points out.

For similar reasons, raters might judge a sample of movie stars as more attractive than student composites, Langlois asserts. Further research is needed to investigate attractiveness factors that lie beyond the bounds of an absolute measure of beauty, she says.

In the meantime, those of us who muddle by without Cary   20
Grant's ears or Elizabeth Taylor's nose can find solace in the suggestion that attractive faces are, in fact, only average.

And even Cher can take comfort. Neither Langlois nor anyone else has the faintest idea how to quantify charisma.

RESPONDING IN DISCUSSION OR WRITING

1. What would you list as the characteristics that make up physical beauty? Make one list for men and one for women.

2. *For Further Research.*   Find magazine or newspaper pictures of people you consider physically beautiful and label the features that to you constitute beauty. Would you consider that the features depict averageness?

3. *Considerations of Style.*   What is surprising about the essay's first paragraph, and how does the surprise prepare you for the writer's thesis?

4. How do you react to the fact that the 192 faces analyzed for the study were mainly Caucasian? Does that affect the way you view the results? How do you react to the researchers' hypothesis in paragraph 12 that composites of other races would be rated as attractive?

5. In paragraph 18, Langlois cites the actress Cher as an exception to the general principle that averageness is a crucial element of what makes someone seem attractive. What other well-known people would you list as exceptions to this principle?

WRITING ASSIGNMENTS

1. Respond to the observation that "faces serve as a critical source of social information" (paragraph 15). What kind of social information does a face reveal?

2. Consider how connected your appearance is to your own feeling of identity. If you could redesign your own physical appearance, what changes would you make and why? What effects would those changes be likely to produce?

❖

STRAIGHTENING OUR HAIR

BELL HOOKS

The author, bell hooks, who spells her name without any capital letters, took her great-grandmother's name. She was born Gloria Watkins in 1952 and is a university teacher, poet, and essayist. She frequently writes about literature and art and issues of gender, race, and class. Her best-known books are Talking Back: Thinking Feminist, Thinking Black *(1989) and* Sisters of the Yam: Black Women and Self Recovery *(1993). She is Professor of English at City College of New York. This article appeared in* Z Magazine *in 1988.*

On SATURDAY MORNINGS WE would gather in the kitchen to get our hair fixed, that is straightened. Smells of burning grease and hair, mingled with the scent of our freshly washed bodies, with collard greens cooking on the stove, with fried fish. We did not go to the hairdresser. Mama fixed our hair. Six daughters—there was no way we could have afforded hairdressers. In those days, this process of straightening black women's hair with a hot comb (invented by Madame C.J. Waler) was not connected in my mind with the effort to look white, to live out standards of beauty set by white supremacy. It was connected solely with rites of initiation into womanhood. To arrive at that point where one's hair could be straightened was to move from being perceived as child (whose hair could be neatly combed and braided) to being almost a woman. It was this moment of transition my sisters and I longed for.

Hair pressing was a ritual of black women's culture—of intimacy. It was an exclusive moment when black women (even those who did not know one another well) might meet at home or in the beauty parlor to talk with one another, to listen to the talk. It was as important a world as that of the male barber shop—mysterious, secret. It was a world where the images constructed as barriers between one's self and the world were briefly let go, before they were made again. It was a moment of creativity, a moment of change.

I wanted this change even though I had been told all my life that I was one of the "lucky" ones because I had been born with "good hair"—hair that was fine, almost straight—not good enough but still good. Hair that had no nappy edges, no "kitchen," that area close to the neck that the hot comb could not reach. This "good hair" meant nothing to me when it stood as a barrier to my entering this secret black woman world. I was overjoyed when mama finally agreed that I could join the Saturday ritual, no longer looking on but patiently waiting my turn. I have written of this ritual: "For each of us getting our hair pressed is an important ritual. It is not a sign of our longing to be white. There are no white people in our intimate world. It is a sign of our desire to be women. It is a gesture that says we are approaching womanhood . . . Before we reach the appropriate age we wear braids, plaits that are symbols of our innocence, our youth, our childhood. Then, we are comforted by the parting hands that comb and braid, comforted by the intimacy and bliss. There is a deeper intimacy in the kitchen on Saturdays when hair is pressed, when fish is fried, when sodas are passed around, when soul music drifts over the talk. It is a time without men. It is a time when we work as women to meet each other's needs, to make each other feel good inside, a time of laughter and outrageous talk."

Since the world we lived in was racially segregated, it was easy to overlook the relationship between white supremacy and our obsession with hair. Even though black women with straight hair were perceived to be more beautiful than those with thick, frizzy hair, it was not overtly related to a notion that white women were a more appealing female group or that their straight hair set a beauty standard black women were struggling to live out. While this was probably the ideological framework from which the process of straightening black women's hair emerged, it was expanded so that it became a real space of black woman bonding through ritualized, shared experience. The beauty parlor was a space of consciousness raising, a space where black women shared life stories—hardship, trials, gossip; a place where one could be comforted and one's spirit renewed. It was for some women a place of rest where one did not need to meet the demands of children or men. It was the one hour some folk would spend "off

their feet," a soothing, restful time of meditation and silence.
These positive empowering implications of the ritual of hair pressing mediate but do not change negative implications. They exist
alongside all that is negative.

Within white supremacist capitalist patriarchy, the social and
political context in which the custom of black folks straightening
our hair emerges, it represents an imitation of the dominant
white group's appearance and often indicates internalized racism,
self-hatred, and/or low self-esteem. During the 1960s black people who actively worked to critique, challenge, and change white
racism pointed to the way in which black people's obsession with
straight hair reflected a colonized mentality. It was at this time
that the natural hairdo, the "afro," became fashionable as a sign
of cultural resistance to racist oppression and as a celebration of
blackness. Naturals were equated with political militancy. Many
young black folks found just how much political value was placed
on straightened hair as a sign of respectability and conformity to
societal expectations when they ceased to straighten their hair.
When black liberation struggles did not lead to revolutionary
change in society the focus on the political relationship between
appearance and complicity with white racism ceased and folks
who had once sported afros began to straighten their hair.

In keeping with the move to suppress black consciousness and
efforts to be self-defining, white corporations began to acknowledge black people and most especially black women as potential
consumers of products they could provide, including hair-care
products. Permanents specially designed for black women elimi-
nated the need for hair pressing and the hot comb. They not only
cost more but they also took much of the economy and profit out
of black communities, out of the pockets of black women who
had previously reaped the material benefits (see Manning
Marable's *How Capitalism Underdeveloped Black America,* South End
Press). Gone was the context of ritual, of black woman bonding.
Seated under noisy hair dryers black women lost a space for dialogue, for creative talk.

Stripped of the positive binding rituals that traditionally surrounded the experience, black women straightening our hair
seemed more and more to be exclusively a signifier of white
supremacist oppression and exploitation. It was clearly a process
that was about black women changing their appearance to imitate

white people's looks. This need to look as much like white people as possible, to look safe, is related to a desire to succeed in the white world. Before desegregation black people could worry less about what white folks thought about their hair. In a discussion with black women about beauty at Spelman College, students talked about the importance of wearing straight hair when seeking jobs. They were convinced and probably rightly so that their chances of finding good jobs would be enhanced if they had straight hair. When asked to elaborate they focused on the connection between radical politics and natural hairdos, whether natural or braided. One woman wearing a short natural told of purchasing a straight wig for her job search. No one in the discussion felt black women were free to wear our hair in natural styles without reflecting on the possible negative consequences. Often older black adults, especially parents, respond quite negatively to natural hairdos. I shared with the group that when I arrived home with my hair in braids shortly after accepting my job at Yale my parents told me I looked disgusting.

Despite many changes in racial politics, black women continue to obsess about their hair, and straightening hair continues to be serious business. It continues to tap into the insecurity black women feel about our value in this white supremacist society. Talking with groups of women at various college campuses and with black women in our communities there seems to be general consensus that our obsession with hair in general reflects continued struggles with self-esteem and self-actualization. We talk about the extent to which black women perceive our hair as the enemy, as a problem we must solve, a territory we must conquer. Above all it is a part of our black female body that must be controlled. Most of us were not raised in environments where we learned to regard our hair as sensual or beautiful in an unprocessed state. Many of us talk about situations where white people ask to touch our hair when it is unprocessed then show surprise that the texture is soft or feels good. In the eyes of many white folks and other non-black folks, the natural afro looks like steel wool or a helmet. Responses to natural hairstyles worn by black women usually reveal the extent to which our natural hair is perceived in white supremacist culture as not only ugly but frightening. We also internalize that fear. The extent to which we are comfortable with our hair usually reflects on our overall feelings about our bodies. In our black women's support group, *Sisters of the Yam,* we talk about the ways we don't like our bodies, especially our hair. I suggested to the group that we regard our hair as though it is not part of our body but something quite separate— again a territory to be controlled. To me it was important for us to link this need to control with sexuality, with sexual repression. Curious about what black women who had hot-combed or had permanents felt about the relationship between straightened hair and sexual practice I asked whether people worried about their hairdo, whether they feared partners touching their hair. Straightened hair has always seemed to me to call attention to the desire for hair to stay in place. Not surprisingly many black women responded that they felt uncomfortable if too much attention was focused on their hair, if it seemed to be too messy. Those of us who have liberated our hair and let it go in whatever direction it seems fit often receive negative comments.

Looking at photographs of myself and my sisters when we had straightened hair in high school I noticed how much older we looked than when our hair was not processed. It is ironic that we live in a culture that places so much emphasis on women looking young, yet black women are encouraged to change our hair in ways that make us appear older. This past semester we read Toni Morrison's *The Bluest Eye* in a black women's fiction class. I ask students to write autobiographical statements which reflect their thoughts about the connection between race and physical beauty. A vast majority of black women wrote about their hair. When I asked individual women outside class why they continued to straighten their hair, many asserted that naturals don't look good on them, or that they required too much work. Emily, a favorite student with very short hair, always straightened it and I would tease and challenge her. She explained to me convincingly that a natural hairdo would look horrible with her face, that she did not have the appropriate forehead or bone structure. Later she shared that during spring break she had gone to the beauty parlor to have her perm and as she sat there waiting, thinking about class reading and discussion, it came to her that she was really frightened that no one else would think she was attractive if she did not straighten her hair. She acknowledged that this fear was rooted in feelings of low self-esteem. She decided to make a change. Her new look surprised her because it was so appealing.

We talked afterwards about her earlier denial and justification for wearing straightened hair. We talked about the way it hurts to realize connection between racist oppression and the arguments we use to convince ourselves and others that we are not beautiful or acceptable as we are.

In numerous discussions with black women about hair one of the strongest factors that prevent black women from wearing unprocessed hairstyles is the fear of losing other people's approval and regard. Heterosexual black women talked about the extent to which black men respond more favorably to women with straight or straightened hair. Lesbian women point to the fact that many of them do not straighten their hair, raising the question of whether or not this gesture is fundamentally linked to heterosexism and a longing for male approval. I recall visiting a woman friend and her black male companion in New York years ago and having an intense discussion about hair. He took it upon himself to share with me that I could be a fine sister if I would do something about my hair (secretly I thought mama must have hired him). What I remember is his shock when I calmly and happily asserted that I like the touch and feel of unprocessed hair.

When students read about race and physical beauty, several black women describe periods of childhood when they were overcome with longing for straight hair as it was so associated with desirability, with being loved. Few women had received affirmation from family, friends, or lovers when choosing not to straighten their hair and we have many stories to tell about advice we receive from everyone, including total strangers, urging to understand how much more attractive we would be if we would fix (straighten) our hair. When I interviewed for my job at Yale, white female advisers who had never before commented on my hair encouraged me not to wear braids or a large natural to the interview. Although they did not say straighten your hair, they were suggesting that I change my hairstyle so that it would most resemble theirs, so that it would indicate a certain conformity. I wore braids and no one seemed to notice. When I was offered the job I did not ask if it mattered whether or not I wore braids. I tell this story to my students so that they will know by this one experience that we do not always need to surrender our power to be self-defining to succeed in an endeavor. Yet I have found the issue of hairstyle comes up again and again with students when I give lectures. At one conference on black women and leadership I walked into a packed auditorium, my hair unprocessed wild and all over the place. The vast majority of black women seated there had straightened hair. Many of them looked at me with hostile contemptuous stares. I felt as though I was being judged on the spot as someone out on the fringe, an undesirable. Such judgments are made particularly about black women in the United States who choose to wear dreadlocks. They are seen and rightly so as the total antithesis of straightening one's hair, as a political statement. Often black women express contempt for those of us who choose this look.

Ironically, just as the natural unprocessed hair of black women is the subject of disregard and disdain we are witnessing return of the long dyed, blonde look. In their writing my black women students described wearing yellow mops on their heads as children to pretend they had long blonde hair. Recently black women singers who are working to appeal to white audiences, to be seen as crossovers, use hair implanting and hair weaving to have long straight hair. There seems to be a definite connection between a black female entertainer's popularity with white audiences and the degree to which she works to appear white, or to embody aspects of white style. Tina Turner and Aretha Franklin were trend setters; both dyed their hair blonde. In everyday life we see more and more black women using chemicals to be blonde. At one of my talks focusing on the social construction of black female identity within a sexist and racist society, a black woman came to me at the end of the discussion and shared that her seven-year-old daughter was obsessed with blonde hair, so much so that she had made a wig to imitate long blonde curls. This mother wanted to know what she was doing wrong in her parenting. She asserted that their home was a place where blackness was affirmed and celebrated. Yet she had not considered that her processed straightened hair was a message to her daughter that black women are not acceptable unless we alter our appearance or hair texture. Recently I talked with one of my younger sisters about her hair. She uses bright colored dyes, various shades of red. Her skin is very dark. She has a broad nose and short hair. For her these choices of straightened dyed hair were directly related to feelings of low self-esteem. She does not like her features and feels that the hairstyle transforms her. My perception was that her choice of red straightened hair actually called attention to the features she was trying to mask. When she commented that this look receives more attention and compliments, I suggested that the positive feedback might be a direct response to her own projection of a higher level of self-satisfaction. Folk may be responding to that and not her altered looks. We talked about the messages she is sending her dark-skinned daughters—that they will be most attractive if they straighten their hair.

A number of black women have argued that straightened hair is not necessarily a signifier of low self-esteem. They argue that it is a survival strategy; it is easier to function in this society with straightened hair. There are fewer hassles. Or as some folk stated, straightened hair is easier to manage, takes less time. When I responded to this argument in our discussion at Spelman by suggesting that perhaps the unwillingness to spend time on ourselves, caring for our bodies, is also a reflection of a sense that this is not important or that we do not deserve such care. In this group and others, black women talked about being raised in households where spending too much time on appearance was ridiculed or considered vanity. Irrespective of the way individual black women choose to do their hair, it is evident that the extent to which we suffer from racist and sexist oppression and exploitation affects the degree to which we feel capable of both self-love and asserting an autonomous presence that is acceptable and pleasing to ourselves. Individual preferences (whether rooted in self-hate or not) cannot negate the reality that our collective obsession with straightening black hair reflects the psychology of oppression and the impact of racist colonization. Together racism and sexism daily reinforce to all black females via the media, advertising, etc. that we will not be considered beautiful or desirable if we do not change ourselves, especially our hair. We cannot resist this socialization if we deny that white supremacy informs our efforts to construct self and identity.

Without organized struggles like the ones that happened in the 1960s and early 1970s, individual black women must struggle alone to acquire the critical consciousness that would enable us to examine issues of race and beauty, our personal choices, from a political standpoint. There are times when I think of straightening my hair just to change my style, just for fun. Then I remind myself that even though such a gesture could be simply playful on my part, an individual expression of desire, I know that such a gesture would carry other implications beyond my control. The reality is: straightened hair is linked historically and currently to a system of racial domination that impresses upon black people, and especially black women, that we are not acceptable as we are, that we are not beautiful. To make such a gesture as an expression of individual freedom and choice would make me complicit with a politic of domination that hurts us. It is easy to surrender this freedom. It is more important that black women resist racism and sexism in every way; that every aspect of our self-representation be a fierce resistance, a radical celebration of our care and respect for ourselves.

Even though I have not had straightened hair for a long time, 15 this did not mean that I am able to really enjoy or appreciate my hair in its natural state. For years I still considered it a problem. (It wasn't naturally nappy enough to make a decent interesting afro. It was too thin.) These complaints expressed my continued dissatisfaction. True liberation of my hair came when I stopped trying to control it in any state and just accepted it as it is. It has been only in recent years that I have ceased to worry about what other people would say about my hair. It has been only in recent years that I could feel consistent pleasure washing, combing, and caring for my hair. These feelings remind me of the pleasure and comfort I felt as a child sitting between my mother's legs feeling the warmth of her body and being as she combed and braided my hair. In a culture of domination, one that is essentially anti-intimacy, we must struggle daily to remain in touch with ourselves and our bodies, with one another. Especially black women and men, as it is our bodies that have been so often devalued, burdened, wounded in alienated labor. Celebrating our bodies, we participate in a liberatory struggle that frees mind and heart.

RESPONDING IN DISCUSSION OR WRITING

1. *Considerations of Style.* Hooks begins her article with a story from her past, then expands the narrative to include generalizations about the culture in which she was growing up and how it reflected the assumptions of race, gender, and class that were current at the time. What function does the beginning story serve

and how does it relate to the more general discussion of race, gender, and class that follows it?

2. In paragraph 11, hooks discusses incidents involving a job search. Do you think hooks was right to ignore well-meaning advice about how to wear her hair? How important do you think appearance is in a job interview? What would you choose to wear to a job interview and why?

3. In paragraph 8, hooks makes a connection between the "need to control" our appearance with "sexual repression." Why do you think she makes that connection? Can you think of incidents and examples that support or refute her idea?

4. What connections does hooks make between "white supremacist capitalist patriarchy" (paragraph 5) and hair straightening? How do you respond to the connections she makes? Do you agree with them or not?

5. In presenting oneself to others, how important do you think a hairstyle is to a person's sense of identity and image?

6. What rituals existed in your family that were connected with rites of initiation into manhood or womanhood? Consider family activities that mark the passage into adulthood, like hooks's memory of family gatherings to straighten their hair, not formal cultural rituals such as religious services.

WRITING ASSIGNMENTS

1. In paragraph 9, hooks tells us that she asks her students to write "autobiographical statements which reflect their thoughts about the connection between race and physical beauty." Write your own statement on this topic as if you were a student in hooks's class.

2. *For Further Research.* On a day when you are among a lot of people (for instance, in a crowded classroom, in a cafeteria, on public transportation, in an auditorium), write notes about at least six different types of hairstyles that you see. Then reflect on your observations and write an account of what you saw, classifying the styles you saw into types, comparing, or contrasting the styles. Comment also on your reactions to these hairstyles and the assumptions you make about the people wearing them.

❖

BEAUTY: WHEN THE OTHER DANCER IS THE SELF

ALICE WALKER

*Alice Walker, born in Georgia in 1944, is an African American writer
who has won many prestigious awards for her essays and fiction, including the Pulitzer Prize, which she won in 1983 for her novel* The Color
Purple, *which was made into a motion picture. The essay "Beauty: When
the Other Dancer Is the Self" appears in* In Search of Our Mothers'
Gardens, *a collection of essays published in 1983.*

IT IS A BRIGHT summer day in 1947. My father, a fat, funny man
with beautiful eyes and a subversive wit, is trying to decide which
of his eight children he will take with him to the county fair. My
mother, of course, will not go. She is knocked out from getting
most of us ready: I hold my neck stiff against the pressure of her
knuckles as she hastily completes the braiding and then beribbon-
ing of my hair.

My father is the driver for the rich old white lady up the road.
Her name is Miss Mey. She owns all the land for miles around, as
well as the house in which we live. All I remember about her is
that she once offered to pay my mother thirty-five cents for cleaning her house, raking up piles of her magnolia leaves, and washing her family's clothes, and that my mother—she of no money,
eight children, and a chronic earache—refused it. But I do not
think of this in 1947. I am two and a half years old. I want to go
everywhere my daddy goes. I am excited at the prospect of riding
in a car. Someone has told me fairs are fun. That there is room in
the car for only three of us doesn't faze me at all. Whirling happily in my starchy frock, showing off my biscuit-polished patent-
leather shoes and lavender socks, tossing my head in a way that
makes my ribbons bounce, I stand, hands on hips, before my
father. "Take me, Daddy," I say with assurance; "I'm the prettiest!"

Later, it does not surprise me to find myself in Miss Mey's shiny
black car, sharing the back seat with the other lucky ones. Does

not surprise me that I thoroughly enjoy the fair. At home that night I tell the unlucky ones all I can remember about the merry-go-round, the man who eats live chickens, and the teddy bears, until they say: that's enough, baby Alice. Shut up now, and go to sleep.

It is Easter Sunday, 1950. I am dressed in a green, flocked, scalloped-hem dress (handmade by my adoring sister, Ruth) that has its own smooth satin petticoat and tiny hot-pink roses tucked into each scallop. My shoes, new T-strap patent leather, again highly biscuit-polished. I am six years old and have learned one of the longest Easter speeches to be heard that day, totally unlike the speech I said when I was two: "Easter lilies / pure and white / blossom in / the morning light." When I rise to give my speech I do so on a great wave of love and pride and expectation. People in the church stop rustling their new crinolines. They seem to hold their breath. I can tell they admire my dress, but it is my spirit, bordering on sassiness (womanishness), they secretly applaud.

"That girl's a little *mess*," they whisper to each other, pleased.   5

Naturally I say my speech without stammer or pause, unlike those who stutter, stammer, or, worst of all, forget. This is before the word "beautiful" exists in people's vocabulary, but "Oh, isn't she the *cutest* thing!" frequently floats my way. "And got so much sense!" they gratefully add . . . for which thoughtful addition I thank them to this day.

It was great fun being cute. But then, one day, it ended.

I am eight years old and a tomboy. I have a cowboy hat, cowboy boots, checkered shirt and pants, all red. My playmates are my brothers, two and four years older than I. Their colors are black and green, the only difference in the way we are dressed. On Saturday nights we all go to the picture show, even my mother; Westerns are her favorite kind of movie. Back home, "on the ranch," we pretend we are Tom Mix, Hopalong Cassidy, Lash LaRue (we've even named one of our dogs Lash LaRue); we chase each other for hours rustling cattle, being outlaws, delivering damsels from distress. Then my parents decide to buy my brothers guns. These are not "real" guns. They shoot "BBs," copper pellets my brothers say will kill birds. Because I am a girl, I do not get a gun. Instantly I am relegated to the position of Indian. Now there appears a great distance between us. They shoot and shoot at everything with their new guns. I try to keep up with my bow and arrows.

One day while I am standing on top of our makeshift "garage"—pieces of tin nailed across some poles—holding my bow and arrow and looking out toward the fields, I feel an incredible blow in my right eye. I look down just in time to see my brother lower his gun.

Both brothers rush to my side. My eye stings, and I cover it with my hand. "If you tell," they say, "we will get a whipping. You don't want that to happen, do you?" I do not. "Here is a piece of wire," says the older brother, picking it up from the roof; "say you stepped on one end of it and the other flew up and hit you." The pain is beginning to start. "Yes," I say. "Yes, I will say that is what happened." If I do not say this is what happened, I know my brothers will find ways to make me wish I had. But now I will say anything that gets me to my mother.

Confronted by our parents we stick to the lie agreed upon. They place me on a bench on the porch and I close my left eye while they examine the right. There is a tree growing from underneath the porch that climbs past the railing to the roof. It is the last thing my right eye sees. I watch as its trunk, its branches, and then its leaves are blotted out by the rising blood.

I am in shock. First there is intense fever, which my father tries to break using lily leaves bound around my head. Then there are chills: my mother tries to get me to eat soup. Eventually, I do not know how, my parents learn what has happened. A week after the "accident" they take me to see a doctor. "Why did you wait so long to come?" he asks, looking into my eye and shaking his head. "Eyes are sympathetic," he says. "If one is blind, the other will likely become blind too."

This comment of the doctor's terrifies me. But it is really how I look that bothers me most. Where the BB pellet struck there is a glob of whitish scar tissue, a hideous cataract, on my eye. Now when I stare at people—a favorite pastime, up to now—they will stare back. Not at the "cute" little girl, but at her scar. For six years I do not stare at anyone, because I do not raise my head.

Years later, in the throes of a mid-life crisis, I ask my mother and sister whether I changed after the "accident." "No," they say, puzzled. "What do you mean?"

What do I mean?   15

I am eight, and, for the first time, doing poorly in school, where I have been something of a whiz since I was four. We have just moved to the place where the "accident" occurred. We do not know any of the people around us because this is a different county. The only time I see the friends I knew is when we go back to our old church. The new school is the former state penitentiary. It is a large stone building, cold and drafty, crammed to overflowing with boisterous, ill-disciplined children. On the third floor there is a huge circular imprint of some partition that has been torn out.

"What used to be here?" I ask a sullen girl next to me on our way past it to lunch.

"The electric chair," says she.

At night I have nightmares about the electric chair, and about all the people reputedly "fried" in it. I am afraid of the school, where all the students seem to be budding criminals.

"What's the matter with your eye?" they ask, critically.   20

When I don't answer (I cannot decide whether it was an "accident" or not), they shove me, insist on a fight.

My brother, the one who created the story about the wire, comes to my rescue. But then brags so much about "protecting" me, I become sick.

After months of torture at the school, my parents decide to send me back to our old community, to my old school. I live with my grandparents and the teacher they board. But there is no room for Phoebe, my cat. By the time my grandparents decide there *is* room, and I ask for my cat, she cannot be found. Miss Yarborough, the boarding teacher, takes me under her wing, and begins to teach me to play the piano. But soon she marries an African—a "prince," she says—and is whisked away to his continent.

At my old school there is at least one teacher who loves me. She is the teacher who "knew me before I was born" and bought my first baby clothes. It is she who makes life bearable. It is her presence that finally helps me turn on the one child at the school who continually calls me "one-eyed bitch." One day I simply grab him by his coat and beat him until I am satisfied. It is my teacher who tells me my mother is ill.

My mother is lying in bed in the middle of the day, something I have never seen. She is in too much pain to speak. She has an abscess in her ear. I stand looking down on her, knowing that if she dies, I cannot live. She is being treated with warm oils and hot bricks held against her cheek. Finally a doctor comes. But I must go back to my grandparents' house. The weeks pass but I am hardly aware of it. All I know is that my mother might die, my father is not so jolly, my brothers still have their guns, and I am the one sent away from home. 25

"You did not change," they say.

Did I imagine the anguish of never looking up?

I am twelve. When relatives come to visit I hide in my room. My cousin Brenda, just my age, whose father works in the post office and whose mother is a nurse, comes to find me. "Hello," she says. And then she asks, looking at my recent school picture, which I did not want taken, and on which the "glob," as I think of it, is clearly visible, "You still can't see out of that eye?"

"No," I say, and flop back on the bed over my book.

That night, as I do almost every night, I abuse my eye. I rant and rave at it, in front of the mirror. I plead with it to clear up before morning. I tell it I hate and despise it. I do not pray for sight. I pray for beauty. 30

"You did not change," they say.

I am fourteen and baby-sitting for my brother Bill, who lives in Boston. He is my favorite brother and there is a strong bond between us. Understanding my feelings of shame and ugliness he and his wife take me to a local hospital, where the "glob" is removed by a doctor named O. Henry. There is still a small bluish crater where the scar tissue was, but the ugly white stuff is gone. Almost immediately I become a different person from the girl who does not raise her head. Or so I think. Now that I've raised my head I win the boyfriend of my dreams. Now that I've raised my head I have plenty of friends. Now that I've raised my head classwork comes from my lips as faultlessly as Easter speeches did, and I leave high school as valedictorian, most popular student, and *queen,* hardly believing my luck. Ironically, the girl who was voted most beautiful in our class (and was) was later shot twice through the chest by a male companion, using a "real" gun, while she was pregnant. But that's another story in itself. Or is it?

"You did not change," they say.

It is now thirty years since the "accident." A beautiful journalist comes to visit and to interview me. She is going to write a cover story for her magazine that focuses on my latest book. "Decide how you want to look on the cover," she says. "Glamorous, or whatever."

Never mind "glamorous," it is the "whatever" that I hear. Suddenly all I can think of is whether I will get enough sleep the night before the photography session: if I don't, my eye will be tired and wander, as blind eyes will.   35

At night in bed with my lover I think up reasons why I should not appear on the cover of a magazine. "My meanest critics will say I've sold out," I say. "My family will now realize I write scandalous books."

"But what's the real reason you don't want to do this?" he asks.

"Because in all probability," I say in a rush, "my eye won't be straight."

"It will be straight enough," he says. Then, "Besides, I thought you'd made your peace with that."

And I suddenly remember that I have.   40

I remember:

I am talking to my brother Jimmy, asking if he remembers anything unusual about the day I was shot. He does not know I consider that day the last time my father, with his sweet home remedy of cool lily leaves, chose me, and that I suffered and raged inside because of this. "Well," he says, "all I remember is standing by the side of the highway with Daddy, trying to flag down a car. A white man stopped, but when Daddy said he needed somebody to take his little girl to the doctor, he drove off."

I remember:

I am in the desert for the first time. I fall totally in love with it. I am so overwhelmed by its beauty, I confront for the first time, consciously, the meaning of the doctor's words years ago: "Eyes are sympathetic. If one is blind, the other will likely become blind too." I realize I have dashed about the world madly, looking at this, looking at that, storing up images against the fading of the light. *But I might have missed seeing the desert!* The shock of that possibility—and gratitude for over twenty-five years of sight—sends me literally to my knees. Poem after poem comes—which is perhaps how poets pray.

ON SIGHT

I am so thankful I have seen
The Desert
And the creatures in the desert
And the desert Itself.

The desert has its own moon
Which I have seen
With my own eye.
There is no flag on it.

Trees of the desert have arms
All of which are always up
That is because the moon is up
The sun is up
Also the sky
The stars
Clouds
None with flags.

If there *were* flags, I doubt
the trees would point.
Would you?

But mostly, I remember this: 45

I am twenty-seven, and my baby daughter is almost three. Since her birth I have worried about her discovery that her mother's eyes are different from other people's. Will she be embarrassed? I think. What will she say? Every day she watches a television program called "Big Blue Marble." It begins with a picture of the earth as it appears from the moon. It is bluish, a little battered-looking, but full of light, with whitish clouds swirling around it. Every time I see it I weep with love, as if it is a picture of Grandma's house. One day when I am putting Rebecca down for her nap, she suddenly focuses on my eye. Something inside me cringes, gets ready to try to protect myself. All children are cruel about physical differences, I know from experience, and that they don't always mean to be is another matter. I assume Rebecca will be the same.

But no-o-o-o. She studies my face intently as we stand, her inside and me outside her crib. She even holds my face maternally between her dimpled little hands. Then, looking every bit as serious and lawyerlike as her father, she says, as if it may just possibly have slipped my attention: "Mommy, there's a *world* in your eye." (As in, "Don't be alarmed, or do anything crazy.") And then, gently, but with great interest: "Mommy, where did you *get* that world in your eye?"

For the most part, the pain left then. (So what, if my brothers grew up to buy even more powerful pellet guns for their sons and to carry real guns themselves. So what, if a young "Morehouse man" once nearly fell off the steps of Trevor Arnett Library because he thought my eyes were blue.) Crying and laughing I ran to the bathroom, while Rebecca mumbled and sang herself off to sleep. Yes indeed, I realized, looking into the mirror. There *was* a world in my eye. And I saw that it was possible to love it: that in fact, for all it had taught me of shame and anger and inner vision, I *did* love it. Even to see it drifting out of orbit in boredom, or rolling up out of fatigue, not to mention floating back at attention in excitement (bearing witness, a friend has called it), deeply suitable to my personality, and even characteristic of me.

That night I dream I am dancing to Stevie Wonder's song "Always" (the name of the song is really "As," but I hear it as "Always"). As I dance, whirling and joyous, happier than I've ever been in my life, another bright-faced dancer joins me. We dance and kiss each other and hold each other through the night. The other dancer has obviously come through all right, as I have done. She is beautiful, whole and free. And she is also me.

RESPONDING IN DISCUSSION OR WRITING

1. What does the essay's title lead you to expect the essay to be about? At what point were you able to relate the title to the ideas in the essay? What can you say about the dancer and the theme of self and identity that runs through the readings in this unit?

2. *Considerations of Style.*   What reactions do you have to Walker's use of present and past tenses, particularly her use of the present tense even when describing past time: "It is Easter Sunday, 1950"? In what ways does her use of tenses enhance or complicate her narrative?

3. In paragraph 44, Walker describes her feelings upon first seeing the desert. Have you had any similar experiences of seeing something for the first time and appreciating its beauty?

4. *Considerations of Style.*   The sentence "You did not change" occurs a few times in Walker's narrative. Why do you think she decided to repeat the sentence? What effect was she hoping for?

5. Is there anything in your experience that could make you recall happy memories and then say, as Walker does, "But then, one day, it ended" (paragraph 7)?

6. What role does the issue of race play in this essay? Does the issue add to or detract from the way you react to the story about the accident and its aftermath?

WRITING ASSIGNMENTS

1. Walker tells about an event that changed how she felt about her appearance and her whole self. Tell about a time when something happened to you that changed how you felt about yourself. Let your reader know what happened and how you felt about it. Give details about time and place and all the people involved. At some point in your essay, include a brief summary of Walker's essay—using your own words—that includes the main points she makes; then compare and contrast your own experience to hers so that your reader knows how you see her experience in relation to your own.

2. Do you think that Walker has presented accurately the effect a childhood injury can have on a person's life, or are the effects of such an injury underplayed or overplayed? Is she too self-conscious about her appearance, or does appearance always have a profound effect on how other people see us and react to us and how we feel about ourselves? Express your opinion on these issues and relate incidents, stories, and examples that provide evidence for why you hold that opinion.

❖

SUMMER DREAMS

LEONARD KRIEGEL

Leonard Kriegel, born in 1933, was a polio victim during his childhood and has used crutches ever since. He is a teacher and prolific writer of critical works (Edmund Wilson, *1971), fiction* (Quitting Time, *1982), and nonfiction* (Falling into Life, *1991). This personal essay was published in* Sewanee Review *in 1991.*

ON THE DAY THEY clinched the American League pennant at the end of September 1945, every member of the Detroit Tigers baseball team signed an official league ball to be sent to me in the upstate hospital where I was learning to live without the use of my legs, a result of the crippling aftereffects of polio. A few weeks earlier my Uncle Morris had gone to Yankee Stadium to watch the Tigers play the Yankees. At that time it was much easier for fans to speak to the ballplayers, particularly to bullpen pitchers who would loll in the sun until the call came to warm up. My uncle had spoken of "my nephew's condition" to one of the pitchers taking in the sun in the Tiger bullpen. The Yankees were going nowhere during that final summer of wartime baseball, but the Tigers were locked in an exciting pennant race with the Washington Senators. If the Tigers went on to win the pennant, my uncle was assured by the Tiger pitcher (for reasons I cannot to this day fathom, he refused to tell me which pitcher it was) a baseball would be signed, sealed, and sent to me at the hospital.

For my uncle that baseball was a present to his sick nephew; for the Tiger pitcher, now perhaps dead, it was probably a way of placating the baseball gods and ensuring a pennant. But for me that ball was an object of worship. No Percival or Galahad, purifying body and soul as he prepared to quest for the Holy Grail, could have touched his god with the naked adoration with which I held that autographed ball in my hand.

Like every other boy in that hospital ward, each of us crippled by polio or arthritis or a mysterious bone disease called osteo-myelitis, I was ordinarily generous with my personal possessions. We boys shared books and comics and model airplanes as we shared pain and fear. But, from the moment I removed it from its brown paper wrapper, that autographed baseball was set apart from the casual bartering of ward life. I kept it wrapped in cello-phane in the top drawer of the night table next to my bed. While I was willing to show it to any boy who asked to see it, I alone had the right to touch it. Their adoration was to come from the eyes alone—mine embraced fingers and eyes.

Not even my closest friends in the ward challenged my flagrant selfishness. That autographed baseball was somehow understood to be my personal talisman—and its promise was that my passion for the game would miraculously make me whole again. Those of my friends who shared my love of baseball must have sensed, as I did, that the Tigers of 1945 were a most proper icon for a crip-pled twelve-year-old boy to worship. A team composed both of wartime misfits and splendid players, they had ridden the power-ful bat of the great Hank Greenberg—released from five years of army service early in August—and the talented arm of the splen-did lefthander, Hal Newhouser, to take the pennant race from a stubborn Washington team by a game and a half.

The names on that ball constituted a litany of redemption for   5
me. I still vividly remember the soothing effect silently reciting those names had as I removed the ball from its resting place in the nightstand drawer in the dark of night, enfolded by my close identification with Hank Greenberg (like me, a big righthanded Bronxite of Eastern European Jewish immigrant parentage), infused with the stubborn onomatopoeic burliness of Stubby Overmire's name, fascinated by the tongue-in-cheek excess of the name Dizzy Trout, and inspired by the blocklike power of the big Cherokee Indian first baseman, Rudy York.

As a Dodger fan I would rather have met Pete Reiser than Hank Greenberg. But even at twelve I understood that my worship of that baseball had nothing to do with the individual players and lit-tle to do with the fact that the ball arrived in the ward the day after the Tigers defeated the Chicago Cubs in a thrilling if slop-pily played World Series. Nor was it the subtlety of baseball as a game that made me touch that ball with the reverence a medieval mendicant must have felt as he touched the yellowed bones of a saint.

That ball simply embodied the idea of physical grace for me—a grace ripped from my life by a virus more than a year earlier. I used to think that polio had merely reinforced my natural street skepticism. I was, after all, a child of a city where even five-year-olds prided themselves on their ability to accept the way things were. At twelve, I felt I should be able to face the prospects before me without illusion. Only I couldn't. Nor were any of the other boys in the ward, whether country-reared or city-bred, prepared to accept being crippled as a permanent condition. Even a twelve-year-old boy has to learn to work his way into the reality of absence. My lifeless legs might fail to respond to the ministrations of physical therapists, but in my mind I was still destined to play major league baseball.

Those names I recited perpetuated my illusion of becoming whole again. The great Greenberg had survived a year of tank warfare in Europe. Prince Hal Newhouser pitched not only with exceptional skill but with a heart murmur serious enough to keep him out of the service. Doc Cramer treated my illusions and Skeeter Webb stung my still-potent aspirations and Jimmy Outlaw testified to the legitimacy of believing that a devious dreamer could play the role of cooperative patient.

When I returned to the city in August of 1946, I carried that autographed baseball with me. My books and comics and board games and model airplanes were left in the ward, to be distributed as the spoils of departure are usually distributed in hospitals and jails, random bequests as quixotic as disease mandated.

But once I settled again in the apartment in the Bronx, where I lived with my mother and father and younger brother, the talismanic appeal of that ball shrivelled. No longer did I recite those names etched across the gradually yellowing horsehide and feel myself graced by prospective redemption.

Not that I consciously faced the prospects of living out my life as a cripple. If anything, removed from a world in which everyone had been crippled, I felt the stigma of my situation even more. But I discovered my imagination was capable of choosing other avenues of fantasy, and I learned to march in fantasized triumphs to the beat of different drummers. At the corner candy store I purchased pulp magazines on which I gorged my craving for adventure and fantasy. On dead schoolday afternoons, when my normal friends were deciphering geometric codes and chemical balances in high-school classrooms, I might tune into some afternoon soap opera on the radio that probed the question of whether a woman could find romance after thirty-five. Long before I discovered Hemingway and Farrell and Wright and Mailer, I sought romance in "historical" novels written by Thomas B. Costain and Frank Yerby and Rafael Sabatini. And when I needed athletic fantasies, the voice of Red Barber describing the intricacies of Dodger baseball made illusion more vivid, more specific, than reciting the names printed on an autographed baseball could ever be.

But the game of baseball retained an imaginative purity I could not find elsewhere—not in pulp magazines, not in radio soap operas, not in technicolor popular fiction. Once I learned to maneuver up and down subway stairs and to walk long distances on braces and crutches that came to seem as natural as shirt and pants, I would take the IND line's D train to Yankee Stadium to watch a game in which perfection and subtlety had struck a singular balance. By the time I was fifteen, I recognized that not only would I never play baseball again but that I would never again walk without braces strapped to my legs and crutches stabbing into my arms. And yet such knowledge was accepted by my rational mind alone. My imaginative life sent me roaming through greener fields. The result was a fantasized schizophrenia. Even as I forced myself to push on braces and crutches through streets that threatened to hold me back, I performed at bat and in the field with grace and skill, an adolescent dreamer, a ballplayer in whose passionate longing fantasy and reality were one and the same.

No matter how strong my fantasies about again playing baseball became, my view of the game grew less romantic. Lovers become husbands and fans become students of the game. And both the knowledge and the specific intimacies which they bring to what they are dedicated grow as if they possessed a life other than the life of the dreamer who calls them into existence.

And so I would drift back to catch a fly ball while listening to the soft southern timbres of Red Barber's voice or dance on my fantasy legs off third base, tutored by Jackie Robinson, threatening to steal home and bring the crowd in Ebbetts Field to its feet. Yet, even as I dreamed of glories beyond the death of my legs, I forced myself to concentrate on the task of rehabilitating myself. If I consciously chose to embrace fantasies of playing baseball with a dreamer's skills, I unconsciously understood that the real me possessed a very damaged body and that my chances of survival in this world depended on how well I could learn to force that body to respond to my true needs.

I don't suppose the split between my imagination and the reality facing me was very different from what normal adolescents had to live with. Desire outstrips performance for most sixteen- and seventeen-year-olds—and their fields of dreams lack even the icon ready to the touch I possessed. What they had was simply a more available normalcy. They knew what was expected of them, and if their talents had failed to withstand the inevitable recognition age brings and they were forced to accept their limitations as athletes, they could still turn their attention to acceptable destinies. For me, on the other hand, illusion grew stronger and stronger precisely because there was so little beyond illusion.

I could only try to ignore the realities I could not control. If the majors beckoned in imagination, braces and crutches could be ignored. Crippled and bound to prostheses, I nonetheless remained a ballplayer in my dreams. A simple enough declaration—and a fantasy fed not merely through those dreams but through expecting that inevitable day when braces and crutches would peel away, like the outer skin of an onion, and I would step through time and circumstance to recapture a boy's skill and prowess full-blown.

True to the power of illusion, I forced myself to save my weekly fifty-cent allowance until I had enough money to purchase a first baseman's mitt. I treasured that mitt, not as I treasured the autographed ball, but because it fed my illusions in the most prosaic manner. I oiled it lovingly, tying its clawlike halves around a baseball so that it would hold a shape designed to make me a fielder who possessed a sure glove.

I would lean against one of the cars parked on the street we lived on and have a catch with my younger brother, Abe, or else with one of my friends. My brother and my friends were patient with me. They guarded my illusions because their own had died.

None of them would ever play major-league baseball either, and if they had been called upon to serve as guardians of time's passing for me, well, then, they would serve with grace and charity.

"Let's have a catch!" That was, after all, what I was doing—having a catch. It never occurred to me then to wonder whether my brother or my friends were dreaming similar dreams to my own as they tossed a baseball from one side of the creosote-smelling August street to the other. Did they, as I did, in the second or two they held the ball and fingered its red-stitched seams, see themselves dancing off third base, preparing to steal home to Jackie Robinson's rhythms? Did they fantasize crowds as thick as fields of ripe wheat watching their every move? Did they transform reality into this almost unbearable passion for a boy's game? Was this how they, too, chose to view an adolescent's dream of fulfillment?

I have never asked my brother these questions. Nor did I, forty years back, ask them of my friends who helped feed my fantasies of wholeness by tossing a baseball with me back and forth across the street. But I can still call up the blessings having a catch offered me. There are rituals by which we feed the motions of the spirit. And I remember day after summer day leaning against a parked car, the clawlike first baseman's mitt on my left hand, my right crutch propped like a door jamb between shoulder and asphalt so that I could hold my balance. I watch the ball thrown from the other side of the street and wait until the very last moment before I snatch at it the way I had seen the graceful Yankee first-baseman, George McQuinn, snatch balls from the air. And all the time, an imaginary play-by-play reverberates in my head, keyed to the sharp smack of the baseball hitting leather.

The experience of so intense an imaginary life can easily be codified, fitted to Erickson's idea of the seven stages of man or to any number of other theories of psychological compensation or to Freud's insistence on the dominance of Eros or Becker's insistence on the stronger dominance of death. I prefer to note that among the gifts imagination bestows is the ability to avoid a too-early confrontation with one's prospective fate. For me throwing that baseball from one side of the street to the other was sufficient in itself. My fantasized talents were real enough in my mind to stave off the debts I would, sooner or later, be forced to acknowledge.

That was the way I played baseball, propped like a carefully balanced rock against a parked car as thousands cheered in my
mind. And I loved the game even more than I had loved it before
I was struck by polio. But, as I look back, I loved even more the
time it provided me for the gradual acceptance of the idea that
the physical grace I had lost had been lost forever. In a curious
way a game I would engage in a passionate romance with for my
entire life was most real to me, most vividly alive, as the fantasies it
generated helped keep an untenable reality at bay.

Of all sports baseball is most resistant to time. One worships its
simple lines in some part of the mind at war with the very idea of
time. Or perhaps it simply tempers our sense of time passing by
affirming the way we once were. This essay was itself generated by
an obituary I read while eating breakfast a few days ago. Roger
(Doc) Cramer, who played in the major leagues for twenty years
and who had 2705 hits to his credit, had died over the weekend at
the age of eighty-five. Maybe Doc Cramer was not a genuinely
great player, but he could do everything—hit, field, run, bunt,
move a runner over—with style and grace. Throughout his long
major-league career he was what used to be called a ballplayer's
ballplayer. Better still, Doc Cramer's name was on that baseball I
held so worshipfully in my hands forty-five years ago.

I have long since put an end to all hero worship. At least, I
think I have. But, if I close my eyes, I can still see that ball, the sig-
natures running into each other until I imagine a circle of names,
with no beginning and no end, promising to bring me back to
that time of my trial and the beginnings of my imagination's fulfillment. I think of how that ball helped me stave off recognitions
that had to be held off until I was truly ready for them. And I find
myself wishing that I could say Thank you to Doc Cramer and to
Hank Greenberg and to Skeeter Webb and to Rudy York and to
Stubby Overmire (who, for some reason or other, I have decided
was the mysterious bullpen pitcher who pledged that baseball to
my uncle) and to all those other dead players who kissed my need
when I was a twelve-year-old boy living in a hospital ward.

A sentimental wish, no doubt, not tough enough for an
America in which baseball cards which no longer smell of bubble
gum are sold for sums that would pay a present-day utility
infielder's salary for an entire week. I am not a man for so headily
entrepreneurial a time. And I shouldn't have been surprised this
afternoon when I told the story of my autographed baseball to a

colleague twenty years my junior and, his voice tinged by excitement, I heard him blurt out: "My god, do you know what that ball would be worth if you had it today?" And then: "What did you do with it?"

How do I tell him that what I did with it was to feed my illusions for one last necessary time? For that was the ultimate gift that autographed baseball, talisman of my difficult years, offered me. For one final moment it helped me again hear cheering in my head when I needed that cheering. Without my asking for it, the day would soon arrive when I would have no choice but to accept the prospects before me and recognize that I had better build a life as best I could because I was certainly never going to play ball again. That autographed baseball was a casualty of my need for illusion. It missed its time of marketability when it was sacrificed to its owner's need for dreams.

One sunny weekday afternoon I leaned against a parked car, propped in my ready-to-play position as my friend Frankie threw a baseball from one side of the street to the other. I had been having a difficult time in the field all afternoon, just as any major leaguer has days when he should have stayed in bed. The ball we were playing with had long since lost its cover, and it had been taped and retaped with that cheap, sticky black bandaging New York City electricians supposedly swore by.

Once again Frankie threw and once again I snatched at the ball, the tens of thousands of fans cluttering my mind beginning to get on me with catcalls and boos. But this turned out to be one snatch too many. The ball didn't fall to the ground this time. It simply hit my glove and, tape sticking to the mitt's webbing, unraveled, collapsing in a mass of dust and string at my brace-bound feet. Frankie rushed across the street and stared at the disintegrated mass. He reached down, distastefully touching it as he might have touched a dead pigeon.

"That's it," Frankie said. "No more ball."

"I have a ball upstairs," I said, pulling a key from my pants pocket. "In the closet next to my bed."

Frankie went upstairs to my apartment and found the ball. He had seen it before, but he said nothing about the names etched across its yellowing leather skin. He knew, of course, who those heroes were. But we were having a catch and his priorities, like mine, were not yet glued to what modern-day Americans like to view as investment capital. Besides, Frankie and I were still

American innocents. No sportswriter ever tagged Doc Cramer with a name like Charley Hustle, just as no one ventured to guess what the worth of his signature might ultimately become.

Still there is a kind of justice even to memories of failed investments. Once we began to play with that autographed ball, I felt renewed surety in my glove. I couldn't miss what Frankie threw— as long as I could reach it. Unfortunately, even as the tens of thousands of onlookers in my head cheered my remarkable turnaround, my friend Frankie experienced a spell of wildness that made it easier for him to hit the brick wall of the apartment building behind me or the curbstones to my left and right than to hit my unerring mitt. One by one, the names on the ball disappeared, chalked and cut and scuffed into oblivion by granite and brick and creosote. That baseball autographed by the entire Detroit Tigers team on the day they clinched the pennant in 1945 would never again feed my illusions. For one last time it had rescued me from a bad day. And the cheering fans who rose as if one in my head to offer me the kind of ovation Stan the Man Musial received in Ebbetts Field after he had beaten my beloved Dodgers into submission were voicing their approval of how that autographed baseball, that icon, had for the last time snatched victory from potential disaster. There are, it turns out, different kinds of futures markets. And all sorts of marketability. In the final analysis the bargain was mine—both to make and to keep.

RESPONDING IN DISCUSSION OR WRITING

1. Why did baseball mean so much to Kriegel in 1945? After he left the hospital, in what ways do you think he used his imagination to help compensate for what his body could no longer do? In what other ways might people use their imaginations to help compensate for what they cannot do?

2. Kriegel says that the ball "embodied the idea of physical grace" for him. Do any objects embody that idea for you? If so, which ones and why?

3. Have you or someone you know ever experienced a split between imagination and reality? Do you think Kriegel's decision to buy a baseball mitt was a foolish one, considering his physical condition?

4. Was the ending of Kriegel's story unexpected for you? In what other ways could it have ended?

5. When you were a child, did you have a possession that was for you "an object of worship" as Kriegel's autographed baseball was for him? If so, what was it and why was it special? Or even if something was not an object of worship, what would you say was your favorite possession in your childhood and why?

WRITING ASSIGNMENTS

1. Briefly summarize the events in Kriegel's life that revolve around the autographed baseball, and then explain why Kriegel says, "That autographed baseball was a casualty of my need for illusion" (paragraph 26). Discuss how general you think the "need for illusion" is for everyone, and include stories and examples that show how other people have and fulfill such a need. What role do dreams and illusions play in shaping our identity?

2. *For Further Research.*   Kriegel wrote (in 1969) an article called "Uncle Tom and Tiny Tim: Reflections on the Cripple as Negro"; the title sets up a connection between the minority status of disability and ethnicity. Find the essay in a library, read it, and discuss the connections Kriegel makes between physical ability and race. Does reading Kriegel's second article affect the way you read and respond to "Summer Dreams"?

❖

MAKING OLD FRIENDS

EMILY RAIMES

Emily Raimes, born in 1971 in New York City, was a senior in high school when she wrote and published this account of a summer job in an old people's nursing home. She has worked as an assistant editor in a publishing company and is now living in Beijing, China. Her essay was published in New York Woman *in December 1988.*

MOST OF MY FRIENDS spend their summer vacations traveling around Europe or the States or taking high-paying jobs. And in the past I've done the same. The summer of 1988, however, was completely different. It was the summer before my senior year of high school, and I knew it might be my last chance to be in the city before going off to college. A friend from school told me about a program called the City Volunteers Corps. She said it was difficult but worthwhile. Since I'd been looking for something to do that would benefit people besides myself, I signed up.

I was sent to a week-long training session in upstate New York with the other members of the corps. None of us knew whether we'd be assigned to a human-services or physical project when we returned to the city. The list of possible jobs ranged from painting a house in Harlem to working with homeless children, and the training was meant to prepare us for any work experience we might end up in. We were put into teams of fifteen and spent the week listening to lectures, running group discussions and working on physical projects such as blazing trails and getting everyone in the team to climb over a wooden wall. That week was so tough, both mentally and physically, that I returned to the city ready for anything. I was assigned to a Manhattan nursing home.

It was an ugly, yellow brick home, and almost all the residents were very sick or, as the staff put it, confused. Most of the patients were in wheelchairs, and my duty was to keep them company and help them in any way I could. At first I found it hard. Aside from visiting a grandmother in England, I'd had very little contact with older people and was nervous around them. I knew that talking to them would be very different from talking to people my own age, and I didn't really expect to be able to understand or get close to any of them. In the beginning it seemed they were all crazy. There was the woman who gave me thirty cents and told me to get myself an ice cream; the woman who wouldn't let me touch her because, unlike most of the staff, I wasn't black; the woman who had me make three trips to the store for the right kind of cottage cheese; the man who tried to kiss me; and the woman who wanted me to read the Bible to her and then go to church with her and be converted. But the more I talked to the residents, the closer I became to them, two in particular.

Mrs. Noonan (the patients' names have been changed) is eighty-nine and has seven children. She came to the nursing home for a short stay, but while there she fell out of the narrow bed, broke her hip and is now in a wheelchair—and probably the home—for good. As a result, she is bitter about both the place she lives and her life in general. She has no friends in the home and doesn't like the people her own age or any of the regular staff. She says she feels like a prisoner. Her only friends are the volunteers, who like her because her sarcastic remarks can be very funny. Mrs. Noonan is starting to lose her memory and she knows it, which makes her even more bitter. One day she told me that she had spoken to one of her daughters that morning. When I asked her which one, she thought for a long time, looked at me in despair and said, "If it takes me so long to remember my own daughter's name, I must really be getting stupid, like all the rest of the people in this place."

Mrs. Noonan liked me because I listened to her talk about her childhood and her family. She didn't like to talk about the present unless she was making fun of the other residents on the floor—"that woman over there has the brains of an apple"—but she did like to talk about when she was young and had a big house in Brooklyn. Almost every day she would wait for me to come to her room. I would take her downstairs to the coffee shop and she would buy ice cream or a Coca-Cola. She said I made her feel younger. She wanted me to spend all my time with her, and sometimes, when I had to leave her to talk to someone else, she became upset and demanded that I come back in ten minutes. When I first met Mrs. Noonan, she was always complaining and didn't seem to either know or care what year it was, but after a while she became more interested in her surroundings and would ask me what day it was and what the weather was like or even how my subway trip had been that morning.

And then there was Rita Feller. Rita is one of the confused ones. She's lost most of her memory, except what has to do with her childhood. She often can't remember something that happened two minutes ago. I never learned her age or anything about her family. Every time I asked her she gave me a different answer. She never remembered my name, although I told her almost every day, but she did remember who I was. She would talk about the differences between us, comparing our hands, our clothes and our hair. She could talk for hours about my hair, which is curly while hers is straight, and she often tried to trick me into saying that I had a perm.

One morning Rita greeted me by saying, "Last night when you weren't here I got so lonely I started to cry." She has no friends in the home, and almost nobody takes her seriously. The staff think she's crazy. After a few weeks of talking to her, though, I realized that Rita knew very well what she was talking about—she just couldn't say it right. When she forgets a word, she just chooses another one that may or may not fit, making it hard to understand her. Once I realized that she used pronouns randomly, used the word *material* to refer to almost any object, the word *house* to refer to a person or personal space and the word *maternity* for almost any word she can't remember, her nonsense turned into sense. So when she said to me, "When he was at her house he saw all of her material," I figured out that she meant, "When you were in my room you saw all of my belongings." She had shown me the photographs, pamphlets and clothes that truly were the only things she owned.

Although Rita was lonely, she was usually happy, and she loved to laugh. She wasn't bitter at all, perhaps because she couldn't remember things. If I asked Mrs. Noonan whether she had slept well, she would grumble and say, "Terrible!" Then she would laugh and deliver her sarcastic punch line: "How could I sleep with my idiot of a roommate mumbling all night?" But if I asked Rita the same question, she would smile and say, "Wonderful, thank you!"

I grew to look forward to the very different smiles of my two friends, so much so that every time I walked over to Mrs. Noonan and Rita in the morning and their faces lit up, I forgot the nervous feelings I'd had about older people. They're both still at the nursing home, and I'm back in school. I'd like to visit them, but I'm not sure they'd remember me.

RESPONDING IN DISCUSSION OR WRITING

1. What summer jobs or other jobs have you had and what lessons did you learn from them about the working world, life, and yourself?

2. How much contact have you had with people much older than yourself? What can you say about that contact? Was it rewarding or not?

3. How might Mrs. Noonan at her most sarcastic describe your college teachers and your college?

4. Rita Feller wasn't talking nonsense; she was using words systematically to fit another meaning. Devise a system of language of your own that someone else will need to work out. Say or write a few sentences using your system and see how quickly someone can find out what you mean.

5. Describe how you see yourself at age sixty or seventy. What will you be doing, what will you look like, and where will you be living? How different do you think your life will be from your parents' lives or the lives of other members of your family?

6. What connections can you make between aging and identity? In what ways might aging change a person's identity—both for the person and for those around him or her?

WRITING ASSIGNMENTS

1. Write Raimes's story from the point of view of either Mrs. Noonan or Rita Feller. Use the first person (*I*) and describe the nursing home, events, and the arrival of the young student from the point of view of the older resident. You are not expected to invent all new stories here. Rather, take the incidents that Raimes describes and think about them from someone else's viewpoint. How might an older person describe the events differently from the way Raimes presents them?

2. Write an essay in which you explore what you see as the main challenges of growing old. Suggest what people can do to meet the challenges. Let your reader know the evidence you have for your ideas by giving examples of people you know or have read about.

HEARING THE SWEETEST SONGS

NICOLETTE TOUSSAINT

Nicolette Toussaint is a writer and painter who lives in San Francisco. This article appeared in Newsweek *in May 1994.*

Every year when i was a child, a man brought a big, black, squeaking machine to school. When he discovered I couldn't hear all his peeps and squeaks, he would get very excited. The nurse would draw a chart with a deep canyon in it. Then I would listen to the squeaks two or three times, while the adults—who were all acting very, very nice—would watch me raise my hand. Sometimes I couldn't tell whether I heard the squeaks or just imagined them, but I liked being the center of attention.

My parents said I lost my hearing to pneumonia as a baby; but I knew I hadn't *lost* anything. None of my parts had dropped off. Nothing had changed: if I wanted to listen to Beethoven, I could put my head between the speakers and turn the dial up to 7, I could hear jets at the airport a block away. I could hear my mom when she was in the same room—if I wanted to. I could even hear my cat purr if I put my good ear right on top of him.

I wasn't aware of *not* hearing until I began to wear a hearing aid at the age of 30. It shattered my peace: shoes creaking, papers crackling, pencils tapping, phones ringing, refrigerators humming, people cracking knuckles, clearing throats and blowing noses! Cars, bikes, dogs, cats, kids all seemed to appear from nowhere and fly right at me.

I was constantly startled, unnerved, agitated—exhausted. I felt as though inquisitorial Nazis in an old World War II film were burning the side of my head with a merciless white spotlight. Under that onslaught, I had to break down and confess: I couldn't hear. Suddenly, I began to discover many things I couldn't do.

I couldn't identify sounds. One afternoon, while lying on my side watching a football game on TV, I kept hearing a noise that sounded like my cat playing with a flexible-spring doorstop. I checked, but the cat was asleep. Finally, I happened to lift my head as the noise occurred. Heard through my good ear, the metallic buzz turned out to be the referee's whistle.

I couldn't tell where sounds came from. I couldn't find my phone under the blizzard of papers on my desk. The more it rang, the deeper I dug, I shoveled mounds of paper onto the floor and finally had to track it down by following the cord from the wall.

When I lived alone, I felt helpless because I couldn't hear alarm clocks, vulnerable because I couldn't hear the front door open and frightened because I wouldn't hear a burglar until it was too late.

Then one day I missed a job interview because of the phone. I had gotten off the subway 20 minutes early, eager and dressed to the nines. But the address I had written down didn't exist! I must have misheard it: I searched the street, becoming overheated, late and frantic, knowing that if I confessed that I couldn't hear on the phone, I would make my odds of getting hired even worse.

For the first time, I felt unequal, disadvantaged and disabled. Now that I had something to compare, I knew that I *had* lost something; not just my hearing, but my independence and my sense of wholeness. I had always hated to be seen as inferior, so I never mentioned my lack of hearing. Unlike a wheelchair or a white cane, my disability doesn't announce itself. For most of my life, I chose to pass as abled, and I thought I did it quite well.

But after I got the hearing aid, a business friend said, "You know, Nicolette, you think you get away with not hearing, but you don't. Sometimes in meetings you answer the wrong question. People don't know you can't hear, so they think you're daydreaming, eccentric, stupid—or just plain rude. It would be better to just tell them." 10

I wondered about that then, and I still do. If I tell, I risk being seen as *un*able rather than *dis*abled. Sometimes, when I say I can't hear, the waiter will turn to my companion and say, "What does she want?" as though I have lost my power of speech.

If I tell, people may see *only* my disability. Once someone is labeled "deaf," "crippled," "mute" or "aged," that's too often all they are. I'm a writer, a painter, a slapdash housekeeper, a gardener who grows wondrous roses; my hearing is just part of the whole. It's a tender part, and you should handle it with care. But like most people with a disability, I don't mind if you ask about it.

In fact, you should ask, because it's an important part of me, something my friends see as part of my character. My friend Anne always rests a hand on my elbow in parking lots, since several times, drivers who assume that I hear them have nearly run me over. When I hold my head at a certain angle, my husband, Mason, will say, "It's a plane" or "It's a siren." And my mother loves to laugh about the things I *thought* I heard: last week I was told that "the Minotaurs in the garden are getting out of hand." I imagined capering bullmen and I was disappointed to learn that all we had in the garden were overgrown "baby tears."

Not hearing can be funny, or frustrating. And once in a while, it can be the cause of something truly transcendent. One morning at the shore I was listening to the ocean when Mason said, "Hear the bird?" What bird? I listened hard until I heard a faint, unbird-like, croaking sound. If he hadn't mentioned it, I would never have noticed it. As I listened, slowly I began to hear—or perhaps imagine—a distant song. Did I *really* hear it? Or just hear in my heart when he shared with me? I don't care. Songs imagined are as sweet as songs heard, and songs shared are sweeter still.

That sharing is what I want for all of us. We're all just temporar-   15
ily abled, and every one of us, if we live long enough, will become disabled in some way. Those of us who have gotten there first can tell you how to cope with phones and alarm clocks. About ways of holding a book, opening a door and leaning on a crutch all at the same time. And what it's like to give up in despair on Thursday, then begin all over again on Friday, because there's no other choice—and because the roses are beginning to bud in the garden.

These are conversations we all should have, and it's not that hard to begin. Just let me see your lips when you speak. Stay in the same room. Don't shout. And ask what you want to know.

RESPONDING IN DISCUSSION OR WRITING

1. Many people wear glasses or hearing aids. What experiences have you had with someone who has a hearing or a visual disabil-ity? What was the person's attitude to the disability? What was yours? What adjustments did you make?

2. *Considerations of Style.*   What is the effect of Toussaint's begin-ning her article with a story about her childhood? What other options could she have used to begin her one-page article?

3. Toussaint gives a lot of examples of the sounds she began to hear when she first wore a hearing aid, such as the sound of "papers crackling." Block your ears for a few minutes and then list which sounds you notice that you usually take for granted.

4. Toussaint gives examples of how not hearing well affected her. Make a list of the problems that a person with sight loss would encounter and how that person could deal with the problems. Also list the problems that others might have in dealing with the disability.

5. Toussaint says, "We're all just temporarily abled." How could you illustrate that from what you have seen, read, or experienced?

WRITING ASSIGNMENTS

1. Toussaint describes never mentioning her lack of hearing. Do you think that people should immediately alert those around them to a disability? What are the consequences of doing so or not doing so? Write an essay in which you explore how others might react in both cases. What advice would you give Toussaint on this issue?

2. Most people have a peculiarity they would like people not to notice, or something they feel makes them "disabled" rather than "unable," for example, a visual impairment, a learning disability, a physical or motor problem, a speech impediment. Write about what you see as your peculiarity or disability. Explain how it affects you and others around you, whether you tell people about it or not, and whether you, like Toussaint, welcome people asking you about it.

❖

A MATTER OF IDENTITY

OLIVER SACKS

Oliver Sacks, born in London in 1933, is Professor of Clinical Psychology at the Albert Einstein College of Medicine. He writes about his patients as they attempt to cope with disorders of the neurological system. His early book, Awakenings *(1974), has been made into a film starring Robin Williams and Robert De Niro. His most recent work is* An Anthropologist on Mars *(1995). The* New York Times Book Review *has called Sacks "one of the greatest clinical writers of the twentieth century." The following essay appears in a book of his essays,* The Man Who Mistook His Wife for a Hat *(1985). Sacks writes in the first person, describing incidents from the point of view of the clinical neurologist.*

"WHAT'LL IT BE TODAY?" he says, rubbing his hands. "Half a pound of Virginia, a nice piece of Nova?"

(Evidently he saw me as a customer—he would often pick up the phone on the ward, and say "Thompson's Delicatessen.")

"Oh Mr Thompson!" I exclaim, "and who do you think I am?"

"Good heavens, the light's bad—I took you for a customer. As if it isn't my old friend Tom Pitkins . . . Me and Tom" (he whispers in an aside to the nurse) "was always going to the races together."

"Mr Thompson, you are mistaken again."   5

"So I am," he rejoins, not put out for a moment. "Why would you be wearing a white coat if you were Tom? You're Hymie, the kosher butcher next door. No bloodstains on your coat though. Business bad today? You'll look like a slaughterhouse by the end of the week!"

Feeling a bit swept away myself in this whirlpool of identities, I finger the stethoscope dangling from my neck.

"A stethoscope!" he exploded. "And you pretending to be Hymie! You mechanics are all starting to fancy yourselves as doctors, what with your white coats and stethoscopes—as if you need a stethoscope to listen to a car! So, you're my old friend Manners from the Mobil station up the block, come in to get your baloney-and-rye . . ."

William Thompson rubbed his hands again, in his salesman-grocer's gesture, and looked for the counter. Not finding it, he looked at me strangely again.

"Where am I?" he said, with a sudden scared look. "I thought I   10
was in my shop, doctor. My mind must have wandered . . . You'll be wanting my shirt off, to sound me as usual?"

"No, not the usual. I'm *not* your usual doctor."

"Indeed you're not. I could see that straightaway!" You're not my usual chest-thumping doctor. And, by God, you've a beard! You look like Sigmund Freud—have I gone bonkers, round the bend?"

"No, Mr Thompson. Not round the bend. Just a little trouble with your memory—difficulties remembering and recognising people."

"My memory has been playing me some tricks," he admitted. "Sometimes I make mistakes—I take somebody for somebody else . . . What'll it be now—Nova or Virginia?"

So it would happen, with variations, every time—with improvi-   15

sations, always prompt, often funny, sometimes brilliant, and ultimately tragic. Mr Thompson would identify me—misidentify,
pseudo-identify me—as a dozen different people in the course of
five minutes. He would whirl, fluently, from one guess, one
hypothesis, one belief, to the next, without any appearance of
uncertainty at any point—he never knew who I was, or what and
where *he* was, an ex-grocer, with severe Korsakov's, in a neurological institution.

He remembered nothing for more than a few seconds. He was
continually disoriented. Abysses of amnesia continually opened
beneath him, but he would bridge them, nimbly, by fluent confabulations and fictions of all kinds. For him they were not fictions,
but how he suddenly saw, or interpreted, the world. Its radical
flux and incoherence could not be tolerated, acknowledged,
for an instant—there was, instead, this strange, delirious, quasi-
coherence, as Mr Thompson, with his ceaseless, unconscious,
quick-fire inventions continually improvised a world around
him—an Arabian Nights world, a phantasmagoria, a dream, of
ever-changing people, figures, situations—continual, kaleido-
scopic mutations and transformations. For Mr Thompson, however, it was not a tissue of ever-changing, evanescent fancies and
illusion, but a wholly normal, stable and factual world. So far as *he*
was concerned, there was nothing the matter.

On one occasion, Mr Thompson went for a trip, identifying
himself at the front desk as "the Revd. William Thompson," order-
ing a taxi, and taking off for the day. The taxi-driver, whom we
later spoke to, said he had never had so fascinating a passenger,
for Mr Thompson told him one story after another, amazing personal stories full of fantastic adventures. "He seemed to have been
everywhere, done everything, met everyone. I could hardly believe
so much was possible in a single life," he said. "It is not exactly a
single life," we answered. "It is all very curious—a matter of
identity."

Jimmy G., another Korsakov's patient [whom Sacks has
described at length], had long since *cooled down* from his acute
Korsakov's syndrome, and seemed to have settled into a state of
permanent lostness (or, perhaps, a permanent now-seeming
dream or reminiscence of the past). But Mr Thompson, only just
out of hospital—his Korsakov's had exploded just three weeks
before, when he developed a high fever, raved, and ceased to

recognize all his family—was still on the boil, was still in an almost frenzied confabulatory delirium (of the sort sometimes called "Korsakov's psychosis," though it is not really a psychosis at all), continually creating a world and self, to replace what was continually being forgotten and lost. Such a frenzy may call forth quite brilliant powers of invention and fancy—a veritable confabulatory genius—for such a patient *must literally make himself (and his world) up every moment.* We have, each of us, a life-story, an inner narrative—whose continuity, whose sense, *is* our lives. It might be said that each of us constructs and lives, a "narrative," and that this narrative *is* us, our identities.

If we wish to know about a man, we ask "what is his story—his real, inmost story?"—for each of us *is* a biography, a story. Each of us *is* a singular narrative, which is constructed, continually, unconsciously, by, through, and in us—through our perceptions, our feelings, our thoughts, our actions; and, not least, our discourse, our spoken narrations. Biologically, physiologically, we are not so different from each other; historically, as narratives—we are each of us unique.

To be ourselves we must *have* ourselves—possess, if need be repossess, our life-stories. We must "recollect" ourselves, recollect the inner drama, the narrative, of ourselves. A man *needs* such a narrative, a continuous inner narrative, to maintain his identity, his self. [20]

This narrative need, perhaps, is the clue to Mr Thompson's desperate tale-telling, his verbosity. Deprived of continuity, of a quiet, continuous, inner narrative, he is driven to a sort of narrational frenzy—hence his ceaseless tales, his confabulations, his mythomania. Unable to maintain a genuine narrative or continuity, unable to maintain a genuine inner world, he is driven to the proliferation of pseudo-narratives, in a pseudo-continuity, pseudoworlds peopled by pseudo-people, phantoms.

What is it *like* for Mr Thompson? Superficially, he comes over as an ebullient comic. People say "He's a riot." And there *is* much that is farcical in such a situation, which might form the basis of a comic novel. It *is* comic, but not just comic—it is terrible as well. For here is a man who, in some sense, is desperate, in a frenzy. The world keeps disappearing, losing meaning, vanishing—and he must seek meaning, *make* meaning, in a desperate way, continually inventing, throwing bridges of meaning over abysses of meaninglessness, the chaos that yawns continually beneath him.

But does Mr Thompson himself know this, feel this? After finding him "a riot," "a laugh," "loads of fun," people are disquieted, even terrified, by something in him. "He never stops," they say. "He's like a man in a race, a man trying to catch something which always eludes him." And, indeed, he can never stop running, for the breach in memory, in existence, in meaning, is never healed, but has to be bridged, to be "patched," every second. And the bridges, the patches, for all their brilliance, fail to work—because they *are* confabulations, fictions, which cannot do service for reality, while also failing to correspond with reality. Does Mr Thompson feel *this*? Or, again, what *is* his "feeling of reality"? Is he in a torment all the while—the torment of a man lost in unreality, struggling to rescue himself, but sinking himself, by ceaseless inventions, illusions, themselves quite unreal? It is certain that he is not at ease—there is a tense, taut look on his face all the while, as of a man under ceaseless inner pressure; and occasionally, not too often, or masked if present, a look of open, naked, pathetic bewilderment. What saves Mr Thompson in a sense, and in another sense damns him, *is* the forced or defensive superficiality of his life: the way in which it is, in effect, reduced to a surface, brilliant, shimmering, iridescent, ever-changing, but for all that a surface, a mass of illusions, a delirium, without depth.

And with this, no feeling *that* he has lost feeling (for the feeling he has lost), no feeling *that* he has lost the depths, that unfathomable, mysterious, myriad-levelled depth which somehow defines identity or reality. This strikes everyone who has been in contact with him for any time—that under his fluency, even his frenzy, is a strange loss of feeling—that feeling, or judgment, which distinguishes between "real" and "unreal," "true" and "untrue" (one cannot speak of "lies" here, only of "non-truth"), important and trivial, relevant or irrelevant. What comes out, torrentially, in his ceaseless confabulation, has, finally, a peculiar quality of indifference . . . as if it didn't really matter what he said, or what anyone else did or said; as if nothing really mattered any more.

A striking example of this was presented one afternoon, when William Thompson, jabbering away, of all sorts of people who were improvised on the spot, said: "And there goes my younger brother, Bob, past the window," in the same, excited, but even and indifferent tone, as the rest of his monologue. I was dumbfounded when, a minute later, a man peeked round the door, and

said: "I'm Bob, I'm his younger brother—I think he saw me passing by the window." Nothing in William's tone or manner—nothing in his exuberant, but unvarying and indifferent, style of
monologue—had prepared me for the possibility of . . . reality.
William spoke of his brother, who *was* real, in precisely the same
tone, or lack of tone, in which he spoke of the unreal—and now,
suddenly, out of the phantoms, a real figure appeared! Further,
he did not treat his younger brother as "real"—did not display
any real emotion, was not in the least oriented or delivered from
his delirium—but, on the contrary, instantly treated his brother *as*
unreal, effacing him, losing him, in a further whirl of delirium—
utterly different from the rare but profoundly moving times when
Jimmie G. [in Chapter Two] met *his* brother, and while with him
was unlost. This was intensely disconcerting to poor Bob—who
said "I'm Bob, not Rob, not Dob," to no avail whatever. In the
midst of confabulations—perhaps some strand of memory, of
remembered kinship, or identity, was still holding, (or came back
for an instant)—William spoke of his *elder* brother, George, using
his invariable present indicative tense.

"But George died nineteen years ago!" said Bob, aghast.

"Aye, George is always the joker!" William quipped, apparently
ignoring, or indifferent to, Bob's comment and went on blather-
ing of George in his excited, dead way, insensitive to truth, to reality, to propriety, to everything—insensitive too to the manifest
distress of the living brother before him.

It was this which convinced me, above everything, that there
was some ultimate and total loss of inner reality, of feeling and
meaning, of soul, in William—and led me to ask the Sisters, as I
had asked them of Jimmie G. "Do you think William *has* a soul?
Or has he been pithed, scooped-out, de-souled, by disease?"

This time, however, they looked worried by my question, as if
something of the sort were already in their minds: they could not
say "Judge for yourself. See Willie in Chapel," because his wise-
cracking, his confabulations continued even there. There is an
utter pathos, a sad *sense* of lostness, with Jimmie G. which one
does not feel, or feel directly, with the effervescent Mr Thompson.
Jimmie has *moods*, and a sort of brooding (or, at least, yearning)
sadness, a depth, a soul, which does not seem to be present in Mr
Thompson. Doubtless, as the Sisters said, he had a soul, an
immortal soul, in the theological sense; could be seen, and loved,

as an individual by the Almighty; but, they agreed, something very disquieting had happened to him, to his spirit, his character, in the ordinary, human sense.

It is *because* Jimmie is "lost" that he *can* be redeemed or found, at least for a while, in the mode of a genuine emotional relation. Jimmie is in despair, a quiet despair (to use or adapt Kierkegaard's term), and therefore he has the possibility of salvation, of touching base, the ground of reality, the feeling and meaning he has lost, but still recognises, still yearns for . . .

But for William—with his brilliant, brassy surface, the unending joke which he substitutes for the world (which if it covers over a desperation, is a desperation he does not feel); for William with his manifest indifference to relation and reality caught in an unending verbosity, there may be nothing "redeeming" at all—his confabulations, his apparitions, his frantic search for meanings, being the ultimate barrier *to* any meaning.

Paradoxically, then, William's great gift—for confabulation— which has been called out to leap continually over the ever-opening abyss of amnesia—William's great gift is also his damnation. If only he could be *quiet*, one feels, for an instant; if only he could stop the ceaseless chatter and jabber; if only he could relinquish the deceiving surface of illusions—then (ah then!) reality might seep in; something genuine, something deep, something true, something felt, could enter his soul.

For it is not memory which is the final, "existential" casualty here (although his memory *is* wholly devastated); it is not memory only which has been so altered in him, but some ultimate capacity for feeling which is gone; and this is the sense in which he is "de-souled."

Luria speaks of such indifference as "equalisation"—and sometimes seems to see it as the ultimate pathology, the final destroyer of any world, any self. It exerted, I think, a horrified fascination on him, as well as constituting an ultimate therapeutic challenge. He was drawn back to this theme again and again—sometimes in relation to Korsakov's and memory, as in *The Neuropsychology of Memory*, more often in relation to frontal-lobe syndromes, especially in *Human Brain and Psychological Processes,* which contains several full-length case-histories of such patients, fully comparable in their terrible coherence and impact to "the man with a shattered world"—comparable, and, in a way, more terrible still, because they depict patients who do not realise that anything has befallen them, patients who have lost their own reality, without knowing it, patients who may not suffer, but be the most God-forsaken of all. Zazetsky (in *The Man with a Shattered World*) is constantly described as a *fighter,* always (even passionately) conscious of his state, and always fighting "with the tenacity of the damned" to recover the use of his damaged brain. But William . . . is so damned he does not know he is damned, for it is not just a faculty, or some faculties, which are damaged, but the very citadel, the self, the soul itself. William is "lost," in this sense, far more than Jimmie—for all his brio; one never feels, or rarely feels, that there is *a person* remaining, whereas in Jimmie there is plainly a real, moral being, even if disconnected most of the time. In Jimmie, at least, re-connection is *possible*—the therapeutic challenge can be summed up as "Only connect."

Our efforts to "re-connect" William all fail—even increase his confabulatory pressure. But when we abdicate our efforts, and let him be, he sometimes wanders out into the quiet and undemanding garden which surrounds the Home, and there, in his quietness, he recovers his own quiet. The presence of others, other people, excite and rattle him, force him into an endless, frenzied, social chatter, a veritable delirium of identity-making and -seeking; the presence of plants, a quiet garden, the non-human order, making no social or human demands upon him, allow this identity-delirium to relax, to subside; and by their quiet, non-human self-sufficiency and completeness allow him a rare quietness and self-sufficiency of his own, by offering (beneath, or beyond, all merely human identities and relations) a deep wordless communion with Nature itself, and with this the restored sense of being in the world, being real. 35

RESPONDING IN DISCUSSION OR WRITING

1. How do you react to William Thompson's interpretations? Do you find them, for instance, amusing, odd, frightening, or something else? Would people react differently to him in a hospital and in everyday life?

2. *For Further Research.*   From Sacks's essay, what would you infer about the symptoms of Korsakov's disease? Refer to a medical

encyclopedia to find out what you can about the characteristics and causes of the disease.

3. *Considerations of Style.*   Sacks uses a great deal of direct quotation of conversation in this essay. How would the effect on the reader be different if he had used reported speech (such as "Thompson asked me if I wanted ham or Nova") instead of direct speech?

4. What do you think Sacks means when he says that "each of us *is* a biography, a story." What leads him to make this point? And how does he relate it to William Thompson's behavior?

5. Sacks describes Thompson's situation as comic and terrible. What justification does he give for using both descriptions?

6. How do you react to Sacks's assessment that Thompson is "desouled," has lost his "ultimate capacity for feeling," and is less capable of being redeemed than Jimmie?

WRITING ASSIGNMENTS

1. Think about and discuss with others the following passage in Sacks's essay: "We have, each of us, a life-story, an inner narrative—whose continuity, whose sense, *is* our lives. It might be said that each of us constructs and lives a narrative, and that this narrative *is* us, our identities." In an essay with this passage as the focus, relate the passage to William Thompson and then consider how you construct and live the narrative of your own life. How much of who you are comes from what you inherit (from genes, from family) and how much from what you do to construct the story of your life? Make connections between how this reading and other readings in the first two units address the issue of "identity as narrative."

2. To what extent do you think people are driven, as Sacks says, to a "narrative need," to the need to tell stories? Are dreams and daydreams part of our need to construct narratives? Write an essay in which you express your own point of view and give examples of the ways in which people might avoid or demonstrate such a "narrative need."

THE RED CONVERTIBLE

LOUISE ERDRICH

This short story by Louise Erdrich tells about brothers on a Native American reservation, one of whom fought in the Vietnam War and was forever mentally scarred by the experience. Erdrich herself, born in 1954, grew up on a reservation in North Dakota. Part German American, part Chippewa, she now lives in New Hampshire with her writer husband and six children. As well as writing short stories and poetry, Erdrich has written novels, including The Beet Queen *(1986) and* Tracks *(1988), and a nonfiction work,* Blue Jay's Dance *(1995). This story about Lyman Lamartine is from connected stories in her first novel,* Love Medicine *(1984), which is about two families.*

I WAS THE FIRST one to drive a convertible on my reservation. And of course it was red, a red Olds. I owned that car along with my brother Henry Junior. We owned it together until his boots filled with water on a windy night and he bought out my share. Now Henry owns the whole car, and his younger brother Lyman (that's myself), Lyman walks everywhere he goes.

How did I earn enough money to buy my share in the first place? My one talent was I could always make money. I had a touch for it, unusual in a Chippewa. From the first I was different that way, and everyone recognized it. It was the only kid they let in the American Legion Hall to shine shoes, for example, and one Christmas I sold spiritual bouquets for the mission door to door. The nuns let me keep a percentage. Once I started, it seemed the more money I made the easier the money came. Everyone encouraged it. When I was fifteen I got a job washing dishes at the Joliet Café, and that was where my first big break happened.

It wasn't long before I was promoted to busing tables, and then the short-order cook quit and I was hired to take her place. No sooner than you know it I was managing the Joliet. The rest is history. I went on managing. I soon became part owner, and of course there was no stopping me then. It wasn't long before the whole thing was mine.

After I'd owned the Joliet for one year, it blew over in the worst tornado ever seen around here. The whole operation was smashed to bits. A total loss. The fryalator was up in a tree, the grill torn in half like it was paper. I was only sixteen. I had it all in my mother's name, and I lost it quick, but before I lost it I had every one of my relatives, and their relatives, to dinner, and I also bought that red Olds I mentioned, along with Henry.

The first time we saw it! I'll tell you when we first saw it. We had gotten a ride up to Winnipeg, and both of us had money. Don't ask me why, because we never mentioned a car or anything, we just had all our money. Mine was cash, a big bankroll from the Joliet's insurance. Henry had two checks—a week's extra pay for being laid off, and his regular check from the Jewel Bearing Plant.

We were walking down Portage anyway, seeing the sights, when we saw it. There it was, parked, large as life. Really as *if* it was alive. I thought of the word *repose,* because the car wasn't simply stopped, parked, or whatever. That car reposed, calm and gleaming, a FOR SALE sign in its left front window. Then, before we had thought it over at all, the car belonged to us and our pockets were empty. We had just enough money for gas back home.

We went places in that car, me and Henry. We took off driving all one whole summer. We started off toward the Little Knife River and Mandaree in Fort Berthold and then we found ourselves down in Wakpala somehow, and then suddenly we were over in Montana on the Rocky Boy, and yet the summer was not even half over. Some people hang on to details when they travel, but we didn't let them bother us and just lived our everyday lives here to there.

I do remember this one place with willows. I remember I laid under those trees and it was comfortable. So comfortable. The branches bent down all around me like a tent or a stable. And quiet, it was quiet, even though there was a powwow close enough so I could see it going on. The air was not too still, not too windy either. When the dust rises up and hangs in the air around the dancers like that, I feel good. Henry was asleep with his arms thrown wide. Later on, he woke up and we started driving again. We were somewhere in Montana, or maybe on the Blood

Reserve—it could have been anywhere. Anyway it was where we met the girl.

All her hair was in buns around her ears, that's the first thing I noticed about her. She was posed alongside the road with her arm out, so we stopped. That girl was short, so short her lumber shirt looked comical on her, like a nightgown. She had jeans on and fancy moccasins and she carried a little suitcase.

"Hop on in," says Henry. So she climbs in between us.   10

"We'll take you home," I says. "Where do you live?"

"Chicken," she says.

"Where the hell's that?" I ask her.

"Alaska."

"Okay," says Henry, and we drive.   15

We got up there and never wanted to leave. The sun doesn't truly set there in summer, and the night is more a soft dusk. You might doze off, sometimes, but before you know it you're up again, like an animal in nature. You never feel like you have to sleep hard or put away the world. And things would grow up there. One day just dirt or moss, the next day flowers and long grass. The girl's name was Susy. Her family really took to us. They fed us and put us up. We had our own tent to live in by their house, and the kids would be in and out of there all day and night. They couldn't get over me and Henry being brothers, we looked so different. We told them we knew we had the same mother, anyway.

One night Susy came in to visit us. We sat around in the tent talking of this and that. The season was changing. It was getting darker by that time, and the cold was even getting just a little mean. I told her it was time for us to go. She stood up on a chair.

"You never seen my hair," Susy said.

That was true. She was standing on a chair, but still, when she unclipped her buns the hair reached all the way to the ground. Our eyes opened. You couldn't tell how much hair she had when it was rolled up so neatly. Then my brother Henry did something funny. He went up to the chair and said, "Jump on my shoulders." So she did that, and her hair reached down past his waist, and he started twirling, this way and that, so her hair was flung out from side to side.

"I always wondered what it was like to have long pretty hair," 20
Henry says. Well we laughed. It was a funny sight, the way he did
it. The next morning we got up and took leave of those people.

On to greener pastures, as they say. It was down through Spokane
and across Idaho then Montana and very soon we were racing the
weather right along under the Canadian border through
Columbus, Des Lacs, and then we were in Bottineau County and
soon home. We'd made most of the trip, that summer, without
putting up the car hood at all. We got home just in time, it turned
out, for the army to remember Henry had signed up to join it.

I don't wonder that the army was so glad to get my brother that
they turned him into a Marine. He was built like a brick outhouse
anyway. We liked to tease him that they really wanted him for his
Indian nose. He had a nose big and sharp as a hatchet, like the
nose on Red Tomahawk, the Indian who killed Sitting Bull, whose
profile is on signs all along the North Dakota highways. Henry
went off to training camp, came home once during Christmas,
then the next thing you know we got an overseas letter from him.
It was 1970, and he said he was stationed up in the northern hill
country. Whereabouts I did not know. He wasn't such a hot letter
writer, and only got off two before the enemy caught him. I could
never keep it straight, which direction those good Vietnam soldiers were from.

I wrote him back several times, even though I didn't know if
those letters would get through. I kept him informed all about the
car. Most of the time I had it up on blocks in the yard or half
taken apart, because that long trip did a hard job on it under
the hood.

I always had good luck with numbers, and never worried about
the draft myself. I never even had to think about what my number
was. But Henry was never lucky in the same way as me. It was at
least three years before Henry came home. By then I guess the
whole war was solved in the government's mind, but for him it
would keep on going. In those years I'd put his car into almost
perfect shape. I always thought of it as his car while he was gone,
even though when he left he said, "Now it's yours," and threw me
his key.

"Thanks for the extra key," I'd said. "I'll put it up in your 25
drawer just in case I need it." He laughed.

When he came home, though, Henry was very different, and I'll say this: the change was no good. You could hardly expect him to change for the better, I know. But he was quiet, so quiet, and never comfortable sitting still anywhere but always up and moving around. I thought back to times we'd sat still for whole afternoons, never moving a muscle, just shifting our weight along the ground, talking to whoever sat with us, watching things. He'd always had a joke, then, too, and now you couldn't get him to laugh, or when he did it was more the sound of a man choking, a sound that stopped up the throats of other people around him. They got to leaving him alone most of the time, and I didn't blame them. It was a fact: Henry was jumpy and mean.

I'd bought a color TV set for my mom and the rest of us while Henry was away. Money still came very easy. I was sorry I'd ever bought it though, because of Henry. I was also sorry I'd bought color, because with black-and-white the pictures seem older and farther away. But what are you going to do? He sat in front of it, watching it, and that was the only time he was completely still. But it was the kind of stillness that you see in a rabbit when it freezes and before it will bolt. He was not easy. He sat in his chair gripping the armrests with all his might, as if the chair itself was moving at a high speed and if he let go at all he would rocket forward and maybe crash right through the set.

Once I was in the room watching TV with Henry and I heard his teeth click at something. I looked over, and he'd bitten through his lip. Blood was going down his chin. I tell you right then I wanted to smash that tube to pieces. I went over to it but Henry must have known what I was up to. He rushed from his chair and shoved me out of the way, against the wall. I told myself he didn't know what he was doing.

My mom came in, turned the set off real quiet, and told us she had made something for supper. So we went and sat down. There was still blood going down Henry's chin, but he didn't notice it and no one said anything, even though every time he took a bite of his bread his blood fell onto it until he was eating his own blood mixed in with the food.

While Henry was not around we talked about what was going to happen to him. There were no Indian doctors on the reservation, and my mom couldn't come around to trusting the old man,

Moses Pillager, because he courted her long ago and was jealous of her husbands. He might take revenge through her son. We were afraid that if we brought Henry to a regular hospital they would keep him.

"They don't fix them in those places," Mom said; "they just give them drugs."

"We wouldn't get him there in the first place," I agreed, "so let's just forget about it."

Then I thought about the car.

Henry had not even looked at the car since he'd gotten home, though like I said, it was in tip-top condition and ready to drive. I thought the car might bring the old Henry back somehow. So I bided my time and waited for my chance to interest him in the vehicle.

One night Henry was off somewhere. I took myself a hammer. I 35 went out to that car and I did a number on its underside. Whacked it up. Bent the tail pipe double. Ripped the muffler loose. By the time I was done with the car it looked worse than any typical Indian car that has been driven all its life on reservation roads, which they always say are like government promises— full of holes. It just about hurt me, I'll tell you that! I threw dirt in the carburetor and I ripped all the electric tape off the seats. I made it look just as beat up as I could. Then I sat back and waited for Henry to find it.

Still, it took him over a month. That was all right, because it was just getting warm enough, not melting, but warm enough to work outside.

"Lyman," he says, walking in one day, "that red car looks like shit."

"Well it's old," I says. "You got to expect that."

"No way!" says Henry. "That car's a classic! But you went and ran the piss right out of it, Lyman, and you know it don't deserve that. I kept that car in A-one shape. You don't remember. You're too young. But when I left, that car was running like a watch. Now I don't even know if I can get it to start again, let alone get it anywhere near its old condition."

"Well you try," I said, like I was getting mad, "but I say it's a 40 piece of junk."

Then I walked out before he could realize I knew he'd strung together more than six words at once.

After that I thought he'd freeze himself to death working on that car. He was out there all day, and at night he rigged up a little lamp, ran a cord out the window, and had himself some light to see by while he worked. He was better than he had been before, but that's still not saying much. It was easier for him to do the things the rest of us did. He ate more slowly and didn't jump up and down during the meal to get this or that or look out the window. I put my hand in the back of the TV set, I admit, and fiddled around with it good, so that it was almost impossible now to get a clear picture. He didn't look at it very often anyway. He was always out with that car or going off to get parts for it. By the time it was really melting outside, he had it fixed.

I had been feeling down in the dumps about Henry around this time. We had always been together before. Henry and Lyman. But he was such a loner now that I didn't know how to take it. So I jumped at the chance one day when Henry seemed friendly. It's not that he smiled or anything. He just said, "Let's take that old shitbox for a spin." Just the way he said it made me think he could be coming around.

We went out to the car. It was spring. The sun was shining very bright. My only sister, Bonita, who was just eleven years old, came out and made us stand together for a picture. Henry leaned his elbow on the red car's windshield, and he took his other arm and put it over my shoulder, very carefully, as though it was heavy for him to lift and he didn't want to bring the weight down all at once.

"Smile," Bonita said, and he did.   45

That picture. I never look at it anymore. A few months ago, I don't know why, I got his picture out and tacked it on the wall. I felt good about Henry at the time, close to him. I felt good having his picture on the wall, until one night when I was looking at television. I was a little drunk and stoned. I looked up at the wall and Henry was staring at me. I don't know what it was, but his smile had changed, or maybe it was gone. All I know is I couldn't stay in the same room with that picture. I was shaking. I got up, closed the door, and went into the kitchen. A little later my friend Ray came over and we both went back into that room. We put the picture in a brown bag, folded the bag over and over tightly, then put it way back in a closet.

I still see that picture now, as if it tugs at me, whenever I pass that closet door. The picture is very clear in my mind. It was so sunny that day Henry had to squint against the glare. Or maybe the camera Bonita held flashed like a mirror, blinding him, before she snapped the picture. My face is right out in the sun, big and round. But he might have drawn back, because the shadows on his face are deep as holes. There are two shadows curved like little hooks around the ends of his smile, as if to frame it and try to keep it there—that one, first smile that looked like it might have hurt his face. He has his field jacket on and the worn-in clothes he'd come back in and kept wearing ever since. After Bonita took the picture, she went into the house and we got into the car. There was a full cooler in the trunk. We started off, east, toward Pembina and the Red River because Henry said he wanted to see the high water.

The trip over there was beautiful. When everything starts changing, drying up, clearing off, you feel like your whole life is starting. Henry felt it, too. The top was down and the car hummed like a top. He'd really put it back in shape, even the tape on the seats was very carefully put down and glued back in layers. It's not that he smiled again or even joked, but his face looked to me as if it was clear, more peaceful. It looked as though he wasn't thinking of anything in particular except the bare fields and windbreaks and houses we were passing.

The river was high and full of winter trash when we got there. The sun was still out, but it was colder by the river. There were still little clumps of dirty snow here and there on the banks. The water hadn't gone over the banks yet, but it would, you could tell. It was just at its limit, hard swollen, glossy like an old gray scar. We made ourselves a fire, and we sat down and watched the current go. As I watched it I felt something squeezing inside me and tightening and trying to let go all at the same time. I knew I was not just feeling it myself; I knew I was feeling what Henry was going through at that moment. Except that I couldn't stand it, the closing and opening. I jumped to my feet. I took Henry by the shoulders and I started shaking him. "Wake up," I says, "wake up, wake up, wake up!" I didn't know what had come over me. I sat down beside him again.

His face was totally white and hard. Then it broke, like stones   50
break all of a sudden when water boils up inside them.

"I know it," he says. "I know it. I can't help it. It's no use."

We start talking. He said he knew what I'd done with the car. It
was obvious it had been whacked out of shape and not just
neglected. He said he wanted to give the car to me for good now,
it was no use. He said he'd fixed it just to give it back and I should
take it.

"No way," I says. "I don't want it."

"That's okay," he says, "you take it."

"I don't want it, though," I says back to him, and then to   55
emphasize, just to emphasize, you understand, I touch his shoulder. He slaps my hand off.

"Take that car," he says.

"No," I say. "Make me," I say, and then he grabs my jacket and
rips the arm loose. That jacket is a class act, suede with tags and
zippers. I push Henry backwards, off the log. He jumps up and
bowls me over. We go down in a clinch and come up swinging
hard, for all we're worth, with our fists. He socks my jaw so hard I
feel like it swings loose. Then I'm at his rib cage and land a good
one under his chin so his head snaps back. He's dazzled. He looks
at me and I look at him and then his eyes are full of tears and
blood and at first I think he's crying. But no, he's laughing. "Ha!
Ha!" he says. "Ha! Ha! Take good care of it."

"Okay," I says. "Okay, no problem. Ha! Ha!"

I can't help it, and I start laughing, too. My face feels fat and
strange, and after a while I get a beer from the cooler in the
trunk, and when I hand it to Henry he takes his shirt and wipes
my germs off. "Hoof-and-mouth disease," he says. For some reason this cracks me up, and so we're really laughing for a while,
and then we drink all the rest of the beers one by one and throw
them in the river and see how far, how fast, the current takes
them before they fill up and sink.

"You want to go on back?" I ask after a while. "Maybe we could   60
snag a couple nice Kashpaw girls."

He says nothing. But I can tell his mood is turning again.

"They're all crazy, the girls up here, every damn one of them."

"You're crazy too," I say, to jolly him up. "Crazy Lamartine
boys!"

He looks as though he will take this wrong at first. His face twists, then clears, and he jumps up on his feet. "That's right!" he says. "Crazier 'n hell. Crazy Indians!"

I think it's the old Henry again. He throws off his jacket and starts springing his legs up from the knees like a fancy dancer. He's down doing something between a grass dance and a bunny hop, no kind of dance I ever saw before, but neither has anyone else on all this green growing earth. He's wild. He wants to pitch whoopee! He's up and at me and all over. All this time I'm laughing so hard, so hard my belly is getting tied up in a knot.

"Got to cool me off!" he shouts all of a sudden. Then he runs over to the river and jumps in.

There's boards and other things in the current. It's so high. No sound comes from the river after the splash he makes, so I run right over. I look around. It's getting dark. I see he's halfway across the water already, and I know he didn't swim there but the current took him. It's far. I hear his voice, though, very clearly across it.

"My boots are filling," he says.

He says this in a normal voice, like he just noticed and he doesn't know what to think of it. Then he's gone. A branch comes by. Another branch. And I go in.

By the time I get out of the river, off the snag I pulled myself onto, the sun is down. I walk back to the car, turn on the high beams, and drive it up the bank. I put it in first gear and then I take my foot off the clutch. I get out, close the door, and watch it plow softly into the water. The headlights reach in as they go down, searching, still lighted even after the water swirls over the back end. I wait. The wires short out. It is all finally dark. And then there is only the water, the sound of it going and running and going and running and running.

RESPONDING IN DISCUSSION OR WRITING

1. What does the first paragraph of the story lead you to expect, and how does it relate to the ending? When you first read "Now Henry owns the whole car," what interpretation do you give the

statement? What do you think the narrator's intent is in this first paragraph?

2. *Considerations of Style.* How would you characterize the tone of the writing in the story: formal, informal, conversational, stiff? What makes you answer the way you do? What effect does the tone have on you as a reader?

3. *Considerations of Style.* Erdrich frequently uses a series of short sentences, as in paragraphs 10 through 15. What is the effect of these short sentences? Would it have been a good idea for Erdrich to have combined the sentences to make longer sentences? Why or why not?

4. The story is about two brothers growing up on an Indian reservation. How important is the theme of ethnic identity to the story? Could the same story have been written about brothers from a small town in Pennsylvania?

5. The typographical setting splits the story up into ten parts, each one separated from the others with a space. What is the focus of each part? Do you think the separation into parts is significant in any way for the reader—does it make a difference to the act of reading?

6. What type of car would you like to buy? Why? Which features are important for you? Or do you see a car simply as a means of getting from A to B?

WRITING ASSIGNMENTS

1. In Erdrich's story, track down all the references to Henry's army experiences and discuss in an essay what role they play in the story. Consider how central his Vietnam service is to the story as a whole.

2. The picture that Bonita took is the topic of two sections of the story (paragraphs 42–47). Consider the picture's importance in the story. What does it add? Would the story suffer if Erdrich had omitted this episode? Write an essay in which you discuss the role the picture plays. Let your reader know how the picture fits into the story and how significant you think it is to the story's development.

❖

HANGING FIRE

AUDRE LORDE

Audre Lorde (1934–1992), an African American poet born in New York City, is the author of several books of poetry and essays in which she explores, among other themes, issues of racial and sexual orientation. Her acclaim as a poet made her a prominent spokesperson for feminists and lesbians. She taught writing at the City University of New York from 1968 until her death from cancer in 1992; her book The Cancer Journals *(1980) describes her early experience with the illness.*

I am fourteen
and my skin has betrayed me
the boy I cannot live without
still sucks his thumb
in secret   5
how come my knees are
always so ashy
what if I die
before morning
and momma's in the bedroom   10
with the door closed.

I have to learn how to dance
in time for the next party
my room is too small for me
suppose I die before graduation   15
they will sing sad melodies
but finally
tell the truth about me
There is nothing I want to do
and too much   20
that has to be done

and momma's in the bedroom
with the door closed.

Nobody even stops to think
about my side of it   25
I should have been on Math Team
my marks were better than his
why do I have to be
the one
wearing braces   30
I have nothing to wear tomorrow
will I live long enough
to grow up
and momma's in the bedroom
with the door closed.   35

RESPONDING IN DISCUSSION OR WRITING

1. What memories do you have of being fourteen years old? Is the person you were then recognizable to you now?

2. What meaning do you give to the poem's title?

3. *Considerations of Style.*   Each stanza of the poem ends with the refrain "with the door closed." What do you make of that refrain? Why is it given such prominence?

4. How do you relate to the incidents and feelings that Lorde's poem describes? Do you feel they connect to your experience as an adolescent?

5. Which lines in the poem have more resonance for you than any others? What makes those lines have special meaning for you?

WRITING ASSIGNMENTS

1. Describe each of the points Lorde makes about adolescence and discuss whether you think they are important ones for most adolescents you know or have known. What kind of picture of adolescence does Lorde paint?

2. Write a poem or a short piece of prose that shows another side of adolescence—a more positive one—from the one Lorde depicts.

Making Connections:
Appearance, Age, and Abilities

1. Alice Walker and bell hooks present very different perspectives on the African American experience of growing up. Write an essay in which you explore those differences and consider which of the two essays connects more closely to your experience and why.

2. A lot of people see obesity as a disability. They worry about their weight. They diet, exercise, go to health clubs, and take pills in an effort to lose weight. Do research on prejudice in the workplace against heavy people or on what seems to be the best way to maintain a steady weight. Write your results in an essay that presents a clear thesis.

3. Both Leonard Kriegel and Nicolette Toussaint find ways of reconciling themselves with their disabilities. Write an essay in which you describe and assess the approaches of the two writers to their physical condition. How similar or dissimilar do you think their approaches are?

4. An article by sociologist Irving Kenneth Zola ("Self, Identity, and the Naming Question," *Social Science and Medicine* 36 [1993]: 167–173) discusses the similarities between ethnic minorities and women as being that each can claim pride: "Black is beautiful"; "Sisterhood is powerful." But, Zola asks, "What about those with a chronic illness or disability? Could they yell, 'Long live cancer!' or proclaim, 'I'm glad I had polio.'" Write an essay in which you refer to some of the readings in this unit to discuss Zola's contention that for the sick or disabled "the traditional reversing of the stigma will not so easily provide a basis for a common positive identity."

5. Sacks says that "each of us constructs, and lives, a narrative and that this narrative *is* us, our identities." Apply this dictum to the life of Henry Lamartine in Louise Erdrich's short story and write an essay in which you consider his behavior from Sacks's viewpoint.

6. Kriegel, Walker, Lorde, and Raimes write about childhood, adolescence, and old age. In an essay, discuss the relationship between young and old people and suggest ways in which you think young people could be more responsive to the needs of the old.

7. Examine some eyecatching advertisements in four current magazines specifically aimed at an audience of either men or women. Write an essay in which you classify the types of advertisements you find, and draw conclusions about the types of ideal forms of appearance they present. Consider the following: What does it mean to be beautiful or handsome? Where are the models photographed? What are they wearing? Which hairstyles are the most popular? What messages do the advertisements send about gender roles and the importance of appearance?

8. Do research to find out what forms of assistance are available for college students who have a vision or hearing disability. Also discover what literature your college publishes to help students with disabilities and advise their teachers and classmates. Then write a brief guide for students who have vision or hearing impairments.

9. The story by Erdrich tells about the change in a Vietnam veteran when he returned home after the war. Do research to find out what disabling symptoms Vietnam War veterans have experienced and what discussions exist about the causes, treatment, and cures. You could also refer to the selection by Harold Bryant in Unit 7, in which he describes his experiences in Vietnam and after the war.

10. Some people stand out because their intellectual or physical abilities are superior to their peers'. The selection by Gilyard in the first unit touches on how he was distinguished from many of his peers by being placed in the top-level class in school. Do research to find articles about someone who is outstanding, for example, Ludwig van Beethoven, Joan of Arc, Albert Einstein, Richard Feynman, Babe Ruth, Stephen Hawking, Georgia O'Keeffe, John Lennon, Martina Navratilova, and Michael Jordan, in order to find out what qualities made them outstanding and how they dealt with that difference.

Gender and Sexual Orientation

Men and women, women and men. It will never work.

—ERICA JONG, Fear of Flying, *chapter 16, 1973.*

What is most beautiful in virile men is something feminine: what is most beautiful in feminine women is something masculine.

—SUSAN SONTAG, Against Interpretation, *"Notes on 'Camp'," Note 9, 1964.*

Gender and
Sexual Orientation

❖

IN THE 1970s PEOPLE were telling each other a story that went like this:

> In a dreadful car accident, a father and his six-year-old son were badly hurt when a truck collided with their car. They were taken unconscious into a nearby hospital and immediately surrounded by doctors and nurses. As the surgeons arrived to operate to try to save their lives, one of the surgeons looked at the little boy and cried out: "Oh, no, that's my son."

This story was an enigma to some of us. How could that be, we asked? Then, gradually, realization dawned. The surgeon was, of course, a woman, the boy's mother. It took us time to get the point of the story because we were accustomed to thinking of women as housewives, not surgeons. We had constructed expectations and roles for gender. We still do.

Our gender is clear at birth: "It's a boy!" or "It's a girl!" we shout. Forming a gender *identity,* however, is a long and complicated process. The roles associated with each gender are culturally determined and always in flux. They are part of what we adopt and adapt to in a culture. Furthermore, expectations of masculinity and femininity are different across cultures and across decades and centuries. They can vary from family to family and from region to region. The culture we live in determines to a large extent family roles, romantic and sexual relationships, matters of influence and power, and the treatment of men and women in the workplace and in society at large.

With changing standards of male and female roles also go changing attitudes to sexual orientation. In some cultures,

141

homosexuality and lesbianism are taboo; in others, they are accepted. Despite the many inarguable ways gay people contribute to society and the arts, debates still rage in various parts of North America about whether homosexuals should be allowed to marry, pay joint taxes, adopt children, raise a family, teach young children, and serve in the military.

The following quotations and clichés say a great deal about the attitudes toward the gender roles perceived in Western culture:

Frailty, thy name is woman. (William Shakespeare)

A woman's place is in the home.

Boys shouldn't cry.

Girls shouldn't fight.

Women are the gentle sex.

Pink for a little girl, blue for a boy.

A man's gotta do what he's gotta do. (Joan Didion summarizing John Wayne's attitude)

Real men don't eat quiche. (Title of a book by Bruce Feirstein)

The most important things a woman can do are marrying a nice man and cooking nice food. (Julia Child)

My advice to the women of America is to raise more hell and fewer dahlias. (William Allen White)

Psychologist Sigmund Freud summed up these attitudes when he said, "Anatomy is destiny."

"Anatomy is destiny"—but is it? Films such as *Some Like It Hot, Victor/Victoria, Tootsie, The Crying Game, Orlando,* and *Mrs. Doubtfire* have explored a variety of situations in which one sex passes for the opposite sex, motivated by sexual and erotic reasons, economic causes (the need to find a job), and social and familial factors (to be close to children and family). To what degree is a person defined by his or her gender? What can be learned by considering the roles and assumptions of the opposite sex? The writers of the selections in this unit all grapple with the question of how gender and sexual orientation shape identity. The unit begins with two pieces that address gender differences: a short story, or fantasy, by Lois Gould about raising a child with no regard to gender, and an examination by linguist Deborah

Tannen of men's and women's speech and behavior patterns. Two magazine articles, by Alan Buczynski and Bernice Kanner, address the topic of men's attitudes: their ways of bonding at work and the ways advertisers equate the idea of "masculine" with "strong." Sexual orientation is the topic of the next three essays: Rosemary Mahoney describes the confusions that arise when gender identity is not immediately and visibly apparent, Carolyn Heilbrun brings some historical and European perspective to the gender issue with her description of the woman writer George Sand, a woman who took a man's name and wore men's clothes, and Steven Epstein looks at gay politics as related to the issue of ethnic identity. Ruth Sidel uses interviews to construct a picture of a new type of woman who wants to compete in a male-dominated world. The chapter ends with a poem by Erica Jong that examines a woman's role.

STARTING POINTS [FOR JOURNAL OR FREEWRITING]

Begin considering the connections you can make among gender, sexual orientation, identity, and culture by writing responses to the following questions.

1. When you were growing up, what differences did you notice in the ways boys and girls were treated?

2. What differences have you noticed in the way men and women talk, for example, in the way they express themselves when lost, angry, or seeking or offering advice?

3. In what ways are men and women treated differently in different parts of society or in different cultures, and do the differences lead to inequalities? In what ways do the differences apply to homosexual men and women?

4. What values does North American society attach to the jobs traditionally performed by men and women?

X: A FABULOUS CHILD'S STORY

LOIS GOULD

Lois Gould is a novelist and journalist who often writes on controversial feminist issues. She is the author of Such Good Friends *(1970),* Necessary Objects *(1972),* La Presidenta *(1981), and* A Sea-Change *(1976), an adult fairy tale, which describes gender roles and sexual identity changes as a woman goes through a gender metamorphosis. The following fictional work was published as a children's book in 1978.*

ONCE UPON A TIME, a Baby named X was born. It was named X so that nobody could tell whether it was a boy or a girl.

Its parents could tell, of course, but they couldn't tell anybody else. They couldn't even tell Baby X—at least not until much, much later.

You see, it was all part of a very important Secret Scientific Xperiment, known officially as Project Baby X.

This Xperiment was going to cost Xactly 23 billion dollars and 72 cents. Which might seem like a lot for one Baby, even if it was an important Secret Scientific Xperimental Baby.

But when you remember the cost of strained carrots, stuffed bunnies, booster shots, 28 shiny quarters from the tooth fairy . . . you begin to see how it adds up.

Long before Baby X was born, the smartest scientists had to work out the secret details of the Xperiment, and to write the *Official Instruction Manual,* in secret code, for Baby X's parents, whoever they were.

These parents had to be selected very carefully. Thousands of people volunteered to take thousands of tests, with thousands of tricky questions.

Almost everybody failed because, it turned out, almost everybody wanted a boy or a girl, and not a Baby X at all.

Also, almost everybody thought a Baby X would be more trouble than a boy or a girl. (They were right, too.)

There were families with grandparents named Milton and
Agatha, who wanted the baby named Milton or Agatha instead of
X, even if it *was* an X.

There were aunts who wanted to knit tiny dresses and uncles
who wanted to send tiny baseball mitts.

Worst of all, there were families with other children who
couldn't be trusted to keep a Secret. Not if they knew the Secret
was worth 23 billion dollars and 72 cents—and all you had to
do was take one little peek at Baby X in the bathtub to know what
it was.

Finally, the scientists found the Joneses, who really wanted to
raise an X more than any other kind of baby—no matter how
much trouble it was.

The Joneses promised to take turns holding X, feeding X, and
singing X to sleep.

And they promised never to hire any baby-sitters. The scientists
knew that a baby-sitter would probably peek at X in the bathtub, too.

The day the Joneses brought their baby home, lots of friends
and relatives came to see it. And the first thing they asked was
what kind of a baby X was.

When the Joneses said, "It's an X!" nobody knew what to say.

They couldn't say, "Look at her cute little dimples!"

On the other hand, they couldn't say, "Look at his husky little
biceps!"

And they didn't feel right about saying just plain "kitchy-coo."

The relatives all felt embarrassed about having an X in the
family.

"People will think there's something wrong with it!" they whispered.

"Nonsense!" the Joneses said cheerfully. "What could possibly
be wrong with this perfectly adorable X?"

Clearly, nothing at all was wrong. Nevertheless, the cousins who
had sent a tiny football helmet would not come and visit any
more. And the neighbors who sent a pink-flowered romper suit
pulled their shades down when the Joneses passed their house.

The *Official Instruction Manual* had warned the new parents that
this would happen, so they didn't fret about it. Besides, they were
too busy learning how to bring up Baby X.

Ms. and Mr. Jones had to be Xtra careful. If they kept bouncing
it up in the air and saying how *strong* and *active* it was, they'd be

treating it more like a boy than an X. But if all they did was cuddle it and kiss it and tell it how *sweet* and *dainty* it was, they'd be treating it more like a girl than an X.

On page 1654 of the *Official Instruction Manual*, the scientists prescribed: "plenty of bouncing and plenty of cuddling, *both*. X ought to be strong and sweet and active. Forget about *dainty* altogether."

There were other problems, too. Toys, for instance. And clothes. On his first shopping trip, Mr. Jones told the store clerk, "I need some things for a new baby." The clerk smiled and said, "Well, now, is it a boy or a girl?" "It's an X," Mr. Jones said, smiling back. But the clerk got all red in the face and said huffily, "In *that* case, I'm afraid I can't help you, sir."

Mr. Jones wandered the aisles trying to find what X needed. But everything was in sections marked BOYS or GIRLS: "Boys' Pajamas" and "Girls' Underwear" and "Boys' Fire Engines" and "Girls' Housekeeping Sets." Mr. Jones went home without buying anything for X.

That night he and Ms. Jones consulted page 2326 of the *Official Instruction Manual*. It said firmly: "Buy plenty of everything!" 30

So they bought all kinds of toys. A boy doll that made pee-pee and cried "Pa-Pa." And a girl doll that talked in three languages and said, "I am the Pres-i-dent of Gen-er-al Mo-tors."

They bought a storybook about a brave princess who rescued a handsome prince from his tower, and another one about a sister and brother who grew up to be a baseball star and a ballet star, and you had to guess which.

The head scientists of Project Baby X checked all their purchases and told them to keep up the good work. They also reminded the Joneses to see page 4629 of the *Manual*, where it said, "Never make Baby X feel *embarrassed* or *ashamed* about what it wants to play with. And if X gets dirty climbing rocks, never say, 'Nice little Xes don't get dirty climbing rocks.'"

Likewise, it said, "If X falls down and cries, never say, 'Brave little Xes don't cry.' Because, of course, nice little Xes *do* get dirty, and brave little Xes *do* cry. No matter how dirty X gets, or how hard it cries, don't worry. It's all part of the Xperiment."

Whenever the Joneses pushed Baby X's stroller in the park, 35 smiling strangers would come over and coo: "Is that a boy or a girl?" The Joneses would smile back and say, "It's an X." The strangers would stop smiling then and often snarl something nasty—as if the Joneses had said something nasty to *them*.

Once a little girl grabbed X's shovel in the sandbox, and zonked X on the head with it. "Now, now, Tracy," the mother began to scold, "little girls mustn't hit little—" and she turned to ask X, "Are you a little boy or a little girl, dear?"

Mr. Jones, who was sitting near the sandbox, held his breath and crossed his fingers.

X smiled politely, even though X's head had never been zonked so hard in its life. "I'm a little X," said X.

"You're a *what?*" the lady exclaimed angrily. "You're a little b-r-a-t, you mean!"

"But little girls mustn't hit little Xes, either!" said X, retrieving the shovel with another polite smile. "What good's hitting, anyway?"

X's father finally X-haled, uncrossed his fingers, and grinned.

And at their next secret Project Baby X meeting, the scientists grinned, too. Baby X was doing fine.

But then it was time for X to start school. The Joneses were really worried about this, because school was even more full of rules for boys and girls, and there were no rules for Xes.

Teachers would tell boys to form a line, and girls to form another line.

There would be boys' games and girls' games, and boys' secrets and girls' secrets.

The school library would have a list of recommended books for girls, and a different list for boys.

There would even be a bathroom marked BOYS and another one marked GIRLS.

Pretty soon boys and girls would hardly talk to each other. What would happen to poor little X?

The Joneses spent weeks consulting their *Instruction Manual*.

There were 249 and one-half pages of advice under "First Day of School." Then they were all summoned to an Urgent Xtra Special Conference with the smart scientists of Project Baby X.

The scientists had to make sure that X's mother had taught X how to throw and catch a ball properly, and that X's father had been sure to teach X what to serve at a doll's tea party.

X had to know how to shoot marbles and jump rope and, most of all, what to say when the Other Children asked whether X was a Boy or a Girl.

Finally, X was ready.

X's teacher had promised that the class could line up alphabetically, instead of forming separate lines for boys and girls. And X had permission to use the principal's bathroom, because it wasn't marked anything except BATHROOM. But nobody could help X with the biggest problem of all—Other Children.

Nobody in X's class had ever known an X. Nobody had even heard grown-ups say, "Some of my best friends are Xes." 55

What would other children think? Would they make Xist jokes? Or would they make friends?

You couldn't tell what X was by its clothes. Overalls don't even button right to left, like girls' clothes, or left to right, like boys' clothes.

And did X have a girl's short haircut or a boy's long haircut?

As for the games X liked, either X played ball very well for a girl, or else played house very well for a boy.

The children tried to find out by asking X tricky questions, like, 60 "Who's your favorite sports star?" X had two favorite sports stars: a girl jockey named Robyn Smith and a boy archery champion named Robin Hood.

Then they asked, "What's your favorite TV show?" And X said: "Lassie," which stars a girl dog played by a boy dog.

When X said its favorite toy was a doll, everyone decided that X must be a girl. But then X said the doll was really a robot, and that X had computerized it, and that it was programmed to bake fudge and then clean up the kitchen.

After X told them that, they gave up guessing what X was. All they knew was they'd sure like to see X's doll.

After school, X wanted to play with the other children. "How about shooting baskets in the gym?" X asked the girls. But all they did was make faces and giggle behind X's back.

"Boy, is *he* weird," whispered Jim to Joe. 65

"How about weaving some baskets in the arts and crafts room?" X asked the boys. But they all made faces and giggled behind X's back, too.

"Boy, is *she* weird," whispered Susie to Peggy.

That night, Ms. and Mr. Jones asked X how things had gone at school. X tried to smile, but there were two big tears in its eyes. "The lessons are okay," X began, "but . . ."

"But?" said Ms. Jones.

"The Other Children hate me," X whispered.

"Hate you?" said Mr. Jones.

X nodded, which made the two big tears roll down and splash on its overalls.

Once more, the Joneses reached for their *Instruction Manual.* Under "Other Children," it said:

"What did you Xpect? Other Children have to obey silly boy-girl rules, because their parents taught them to. Lucky X—you don't have rules at all! All you have to do is be yourself.

"P.S. We're not saying it'll be easy."

X liked being itself. But X cried a lot that night. So X's father held X tight, and cried a little, too. X's mother cheered them up with an Xciting story about an enchanted prince called Sleeping Handsome, who woke up when Princess Charming kissed him.

The next morning, they all felt much better, and little X went back to school with a brave smile and a clean pair of red and white checked overalls.

There was a seven-letter-word spelling bee in class that day. And a seven-lap boys' relay race in the gym. And a seven-layer-cake baking contest in the girls' kitchen corner.

X won the spelling bee. X also won the relay race.

And X almost won the baking contest, Xcept it forgot to light the oven. (Remember, nobody's perfect.)

One of the Other Children noticed something else, too. He said: "X doesn't care about winning. X just thinks it's fun playing boys' stuff *and* girls' stuff."

"Come to think of it," said another one of the Other Children, "X is having twice as much fun as we are!"

After school that day, the girl who beat X in the baking contest gave X a big slice of her winning cake.

And the boy X beat in the relay race asked X to race him home.

From then on, some really funny things began to happen.

Susie, who sat next to X, refused to wear pink dresses to school any more. She wanted red and white checked overalls—just like X's.

Overalls, she told her parents, were better for climbing monkey bars.

Then Jim, the class football nut, started wheeling his little sister's doll carriage around the football field.

He'd put on his entire football uniform, except for the helmet.

Then he'd put the helmet *in* the carriage, lovingly tucked under an old set of shoulder pads.

Then he'd jog around the field, pushing the carriage and singing "Rockabye Baby" to his helmet.

He said X did the same thing, so it must be okay. After all, X was now the team's star quarterback.

Susie's parents were horrified by her behavior, and Jim's parents were worried sick about his.

But the worst came when the twins, Joe and Peggy, decided to share everything with each other.

Peggy used Joe's hockey skates, and his microscope, and took half his newspaper route.

Joe used Peggy's needlepoint kit, and her cookbooks, and took two of her three baby-sitting jobs.

Peggy ran the lawn mower, and Joe ran the vacuum cleaner.

Their parents weren't one bit pleased with Peggy's science experiments, or with Joe's terrific needlepoint pillows.

They didn't care that Peggy mowed the lawn better, and that Joe vacuumed the carpet better.

In fact, they were furious. It's all that little X's fault, they agreed. X doesn't know what it is, or what it's supposed to be! So X wants to mix everybody *else* up, too!

Peggy and Joe were forbidden to play with X any more. So was Susie, and then Jim, and then *all* the Other Children.

But it was too late: the Other Children stayed mixed-up and happy and free, and refused to go back to the way they'd been before X.

Finally, the parents held an emergency meeting to discuss "The X Problem."

They sent a report to the principal stating that X was a "bad influence," and demanding immediate action.

The Joneses, they said, should be *forced* to tell whether X was a boy or a girl. And X should be *forced* to behave like whichever it was.

If the Joneses refused to tell, the parents said, then X must take an Xamination. An Impartial Team of Xperts would Xtract the secret. Then X would start obeying all the old rules. Or else.

And if X turned out to be some kind of mixed-up misfit, then X must be Xpelled from school. Immediately! So that no little Xes would ever come to school again.

The principal was very upset. X, a bad influence? A mixed-up misfit? But X was an Xcellent student! X set a fine Xample! X was Xtraordinary!

X was president of the student council. X had won first prize in the art show, honorable mention in the science fair, and six events on field day, including the potato race.

Nevertheless, insisted the parents, X is a Problem Child. X is the Biggest Problem Child we have ever seen!

So the principal reluctantly notified X's parents and the Joneses reported this to the Project X scientists, who referred them to page 85769 of the *Instruction Manual.* "Sooner or later," it said, "X will have to be Xamined by an Impartial Team of Xperts.

"This may be the only way any of us will know for sure whether X is mixed up—or everyone else is."

At Xactly 9 o'clock the next day, X reported to the school health office. The principal, along with a committee from the Parents' Association, X's teacher, X's classmates, and Ms. and Mr. Jones, waited in the hall outside.

Inside, the Xperts had set up their famous testing machine: the Superpsychiamedicosocioculturometer.

Nobody knew Xactly how the machine worked, but everybody knew that this examination would reveal Xactly what everyone wanted to know about X, but were afraid to ask.

It was terribly quiet in the hall. Almost spooky. They could hear very strange noises from the room.

There were buzzes.

And a beep or two.

And several bells.

An occasional light flashed under the door. Was it an X ray?

Through it all, you could hear the Xperts' voices, asking questions, and X's voice, answering answers.

I wouldn't like to be in X's overalls right now, the children thought.

At last, the door opened. Everyone crowded around to hear the results. X didn't look any different; in fact, X was smiling. But the Impartial Team of Xperts looked terrible. They looked as if they were crying!

"What happened?" everyone began shouting.

"*Sssh,*" ssshed the principal. "The Xperts are trying to speak."

Wiping his eyes and clearing his throat, one Xpert began: "In our opinion," he whispered—you could tell he must be very upset—"in our opinion, young X here—"

"Yes? Yes?" shouted a parent.

"Young X," said the other Xpert, frowning, "is just about the *least* mixed-up child we've ever Xamined!" Behind the closed door, the Superpsychiamedicossocioculturometer made a noise like a contented hum.

"Yay for X!" yelled one of the children. And then the others began yelling, too. Clapping and cheering and jumping up and down.

"SSSH!" SSShed the principal, but nobody did.   130

The Parents' Committee was angry and bewildered. How *could* X have passed the whole Xamination?

Didn't X have an *identity* problem? Wasn't X mixed up at *all*? Wasn't X *any* kind of a misfit?

How could it *not* be, when it didn't even *know* what it was?

"Don't you see?" asked the Xperts. "X isn't one bit mixed up! As for being a misfit—ridiculous! X knows perfectly well what it is! Don't you, X?" The Xperts winked. X winked back.

"But what *is* X?" shrieked Peggy and Joe's parents. "*We* still want   135 to know what it is!"

"Ah, yes," said the Xperts, winking again. "Well, don't worry. You'll all know one of these days. And you won't need us to tell you."

"What? What do they mean?" Jim's parents grumbled suspiciously.

Susie and Peggy and Joe all answered at once. "They mean that by the time it matters which sex X is, it won't be a secret any more!"

With that, the Xperts reached out to hug Ms. and Mr. Jones. "If we ever have an X of our own," they whispered, "we sure hope you'll lend us your instruction manual."

Needless to say, the Joneses were very happy. The Project Baby   140 X scientists were rather pleased, too. So were Susie, Jim, Peggy, Joe, and all the Other Children. Even the parents promised not to make any trouble.

Later that day, all X's friends put on their red and white checked overalls and went over to see X.

They found X in the backyard, playing with a very tiny baby that none of them had ever seen before.

The baby was wearing very tiny red and white checked overalls.

"How do you like our new baby?" X asked the Other Children proudly.

"It's got cute dimples," said Jim. "It's got husky biceps, too," said Susie. [145]

"What kind of baby is it?" asked Joe and Peggy.

X frowned at them. "Can't you tell?" Then X broke into a big, mischievous grin. *"It's a Y!"*

RESPONDING IN DISCUSSION OR WRITING

1. What does the reading tell you about Gould's attitude toward gender stereotyping? What are its dangers? Are there any advantages? What are your own views on distinguishing the way we treat little boys and little girls?

2. What instructions would you want to include in Gould's *Official Instruction Manual* for raising X? Why do you see these instructions as important?

3. Who seems to be more disturbed by X's genderless state: the adults who come into contact with the child or the child's classmates? What explanation can you give for your reply? What point do you think Gould wanted to make?

4. *Considerations of Style.* Gould writes many paragraphs that have only one or two sentences. What effect does that have on the reader? Why do you think Gould chose to write in that way?

5. At various points in the story, Gould lets us know what she sees as features of gender stereotyping. Make two lists, one of the features of the male stereotyping and the other of the female stereotyping she mentions. What are your reactions to those stereotypes? Have you ever seen them in operation?

6. What toys would you buy for a little girl, and what toys would you buy for a little boy? Why would you choose those particular toys?

WRITING ASSIGNMENTS

1. Put yourself into X's shoes and write an account describing some of your childhood experiences from your (X's) point of view, using *I* to describe your (X's) childhood experiences. Keep the same chronological order that Gould uses. Or pretend that you are a classmate of X's and write an account of a few selected incidents that show how you react to X.

2. Imagine parents who are so delighted to have a son or daughter (choose either one) that they do whatever they can to emphasize that this is their "little boy" or "little girl." Write an essay describing the kinds of things they would do and how you feel about such treatment. In your essay, discuss and evaluate the effects (positive, negative, neutral) that gender stereotyping could have on a young child.

❖

HIS POLITENESS IS HER POWERLESSNESS

DEBORAH TANNEN

Deborah Tannen, born in 1945, is Professor of Linguistics at Georgetown University and has held a Distinguished Lecturer post at Princeton University. She is the author of three popular books that examine people's conversational interactions: That's Not What I Meant! How Conversational Style Makes or Breaks Your Relationship with Others *(1986),* Talking from 9 to 5 *(1994), and the book from which this excerpt is taken,* You Just Don't Understand *(1990), as well as many scholarly books and articles. Her popular books are based on the data she gathers for her scholarly research, such as appears in* Gender and Discourse *(1994).*

THERE ARE MANY KINDS of evidence that women and men are judged differently even if they talk the same way. This tendency makes mischief in discussions of women, men, and power. If a linguistic strategy is used by a woman, it is seen as powerless; if it is done by a man, it is seen as powerful. Often, the labeling of "women's language" as "powerless language" reflects the view of women's behavior through the lens of men's.

Because they are not struggling to be one-up, women often find themselves framed as one-down. Any situation is ripe for misinterpretation, because status and connections are displayed by the same moves. This ambiguity accounts for much misinterpretation, by experts as well as nonexperts, by which women's ways of talking, uttered in a spirit of rapport, are branded powerless. Nowhere is this inherent ambiguity clearer than in a brief comment in a newspaper article in which a couple, both psychologists, were jointly interviewed. The journalist asked them the meaning of "being very polite." The two experts responded simultaneously, giving different answers. The man said, "Subservience." The woman said, "Sensitivity." Both experts were right, but each was describing the view of a different gender.

Experts and nonexperts alike tend to see anything women do as evidence of powerlessness. The same newspaper article quotes another psychologist as saying, "A man might ask a woman, 'Will you please go to the store?' where a woman might say, 'Gee, I really need a few things from the store, but I'm so tired.' " The woman's style is called "covert," a term suggesting negative qualities like being "sneaky" and "underhanded." The reason offered for this is power: The woman doesn't feel she has a right to ask directly.

Granted, women have lower status than men in our society. But this is not necessarily why they prefer not to make outright demands. The explanation for a woman's indirectness could just as well be her seeking connection. If you get your way as a result of having demanded it, the payoff is satisfying in terms of status: You're one-up because others are doing as you told them. But if you get your way because others happened to want the same thing, or because they offered freely, the payoff is in rapport. You're neither one-up nor one-down but happily connected to others whose wants are the same as yours. Furthermore, if indirectness is understood by both parties, then there is nothing covert about it: That a request is being made is clear. Calling an indirect communication covert reflects the view of someone for whom the direct style seems "natural" and "logical"—a view more common among men.

Indirectness itself does not reflect powerlessness. It is easy to think of situations where indirectness is the prerogative of those in power. For example, a wealthy couple who know that their servants will do their bidding need not give direct orders, but can simply state wishes: The woman of the house says, "It's chilly in here," and the servant sets about raising the temperature. The man of the house says, "It's dinner time," and the servant sees about having dinner served. Perhaps the ultimate indirectness is getting someone to do something without saying anything at all: The hostess rings a bell and the maid brings the next course; or a parent enters the room where children are misbehaving and stands with hands on hips, and the children immediately stop what they're doing.

Entire cultures operate on elaborate systems of indirectness. For example, I discovered in a small research project that most Greeks assumed that a wife who asked, "Would you like to go to the party?" was hinting that she wanted to go. They felt that she wouldn't bring it up if she didn't want to go. Furthermore, they felt, she would not state her preference outright because that would sound like a demand. Indirectness was the appropriate means for communicating her preference.

Japanese culture has developed indirectness to a fine art. For example, a Japanese anthropologist, Harumi Befu, explains the delicate exchange of indirectness required by a simple invitation to lunch. When his friend extended the invitation, Befu first had to determine whether it was meant literally or just *pro forma*, much as an American might say, "We'll have to have you over for dinner some time" but would not expect you to turn up at the door. Having decided the invitation was meant literally and having accepted, Befu was then asked what he would like to eat. Following custom, he said anything would do, but his friend, also following custom, pressed him to specify. Host and guest repeated this exchange an appropriate number of times, until Befu deemed it polite to answer the question—politely—by saying that tea over rice would be fine. When he arrived for lunch, he was indeed served tea over rice—as the last course of a sumptuous meal. Befu was not surprised by the feast, because he knew that protocol required it. Had he been given what he had asked for, he would have been insulted. But protocol also required that he make a great show of being surprised.

This account of mutual indirectness in a lunch invitation may strike Americans as excessive. But far more cultures in the world use elaborate systems of indirectness than value directness. Only modern Western societies place a priority on direct communication, and even for us it is more a value than a practice.

Evidence from other cultures also makes it clear that indirectness does not in itself reflect low status. Rather, our assumptions about the status of women compel us to interpret anything they do as reflecting low status. Anthropologist Elinor Keenan, for example, found that in a Malagasy-speaking village on the island of Madagascar, it is women who are direct and men who are indirect. And the villagers see the men's indirect way of speaking, using metaphors and proverbs, as the better way. For them, indirectness, like the men who use it, has high status. They regard women's direct style as clumsy and crude, debasing the beautiful subtlety of men's language. Whether women or men are direct or indirect differs; what remains constant is that the women's style is negatively evaluated—seen as lower in status than the men's.

RESPONDING IN DISCUSSION OR WRITING

1. *Considerations of Style.*   Tannen frequently juxtaposes sentences that present two sides of a picture. One example follows: "If a linguistic strategy is used by a woman, it is seen as powerless; if it is done by a man, it is seen as powerful." Find other examples, and evaluate what effect they have on the reader.

2. Tannen points out that "Japanese culture has developed indirectness to a fine art." How does she illustrate this? How could you complete the following statement: "American culture has developed_____to a fine art"? What examples can you use to support your statement?

3. What evidence can you provide from your own experience for Tannen's statement that "there are many kinds of evidence that women and men are judged differently even if they talk the same way"?

4. Compare your classmates' notes from reading Tannen's piece, or their annotations of the text, and respond to the following questions: What effect do you think Tannen is hoping to have on (a) her male readers and (b) her female readers? Would men and women be likely to underline and comment on different passages in this selection?

5. In elevators, cafeterias, and crowded places and on public transportation, pay attention to conversations going on around you and listen for instances of what Tannen calls "covert" conversational style (paragraph 3). Make notes on what is especially indirect about what you hear.

6. What conversation patterns have you noticed that are different for men and women? Consider, for example, situations like asking for directions, help, or information, interrupting, making a complaint in a restaurant, telling jokes, and making suggestions. What patterns might men and women typically use in these situations?

WRITING ASSIGNMENTS

1. Write an essay about some specific incidents that occurred when people you know have acted and spoken in a way you consider to be "typically male" or "typically female." Describe those incidents in detail, then reflect on them and analyze what was "typical" about the people's behavior. Draw conclusions about the effects that such stereotyping might have on how gender roles are perceived.

2. Tannen offers as an explanation for women's indirectness the fact that women may be "seeking connection." What do you think she means by this in this reading selection? Write an essay in which you discuss the thesis that Tannen proposes, agree or disagree with it, and provide evidence from your own knowledge and experience to support your opinion.

IRON BONDING

ALAN BUCZYNSKI

Alan Buczynski has a degree in English and has worked as an ironworker in the Detroit area for more than ten years. This article appeared in the "About Men" column in The New York Times Magazine *on July 19, 1992. The title connects Buczynski's theme to Robert Bly's book* Iron John, *which uses a parable to discuss the male role at a time when feminist causes are in the news.*

"I JUST DON'T GET IT." We were up on the iron, about 120 feet, waiting for the gang below to swing up another beam. Sweat from under Ron's hard hat dripped on the beam we were sitting on and evaporated immediately, like water thrown on a sauna stove. We were talking about the "men's movement" and "wildman weekends."

"I mean," he continued, "if they want to get dirty and sweat and cuss and pound on things, why don't they just get *real* jobs and get paid for it?" Below, the crane growled, the next piece lifting skyward.

I replied: "Nah, Ron, that isn't the point. They don't want to sweat every day, just sometimes."

He said: "Man, if you only sweat when you want to, I don't call that real sweatin'."

Although my degree is in English, I am an ironworker by trade; my girlfriend, Patti, is a graduate student in English literature. Like a tennis ball volleyed by two players with distinctly different styles, I am bounced between blue-collar maulers and precise academicians. My conversations range from fishing to Foucault, derricks to deconstruction. There is very little overlap, but when it does occur it is generally the academics who are curious about the working life.

Patti and I were at a dinner party. The question of communication between men had arisen. Becky, the host, is a persistent interrogator: "What do you and Ron talk about?"

I said, "Well, we talk about work, drinking, ah, women."

Becky asked, "Do you guys ever say, 'I love you' to each other?" This smelled mightily of Robert Bly and the men's movement.

I replied: "Certainly. All the time."

I am still dissatisfied with this answer. Not because it was a lie, but because it was perceived as one.

The notion prevails that men's emotional communication skills are less advanced than that of chimpanzees, that we can no more communicate with one another than can earthworms.

Ironworkers as a group may well validate this theory. We are not a very articulate bunch. Most of us have only a basic education. Construction sites are extremely noisy, and much of our communication takes place via hand signals. There is little premium placed on words that don't stem from our own jargon. Conversations can be blunt.

Bly's approach, of adapting a fable for instruction, may instinctively mimic the way men communicate. Ironworkers are otherwise very direct, yet when emotional issues arise we speak to one another in allegory and parable. One of my co-workers, Cliff, is a good storyteller, with an understated delivery: "The old man got home one night, drunk, real messed up and got to roughhousing with the cat. Old Smoke, well she laid into him, scratched him good. Out comes the shotgun. The old man loads up, chases Smoke into the front yard and blam! Off goes the gun. My Mom and my sisters and me we're all screamin'. Smoke comes walkin' in the side door. Seems the old man blew away the wrong cat, the neighbor's Siamese. Red lights were flashin' against the house, fur was splattered all over the lawn, the cops cuffed my old man and he's hollerin' and man, I'll tell you, I was cryin'."

Now, we didn't all get up from our beers and go over and hug him. This was a story, not therapy. Cliff is amiable, but tough, more inclined to solving any perceived injustices with his fists than verbal banter, but I don't need to see him cry to know that he can. He has before, and he can tell a story about it without shame, without any disclaimers about being "just a kid," and that's enough for me.

Ron and I have worked together for nine years and are as close as 29 is to 30. We have worked through heat and cold and seen each other injured in the stupidest of accidents. One February we were working inside a plant, erecting steel with a little crane; it was near the end of the day, and I was tired. I hooked onto a piece and, while still holding the load cable, signaled the operator "up." My thumb was promptly sucked into the sheave of the crane. I screamed, and the operator came down on the load, releasing my thumb. It hurt. A lot. Water started leaking from my eyes. The gang gathered around while Ron tugged gently at my work glove, everyone curious whether my thumb would come off with the glove or stay on my hand. [15]

"O.K., man, relax, just relax," Ron said. "See if you can move it." Ron held my hand. The thumb had a neat crease right down the center, lengthwise. All the capillaries on one side had burst and were turning remarkable colors. My new thumbnail was on back order and would arrive in about five months. I wiggled the thumb, an eighth of an inch, a quarter, a half.

"You're O.K., man, it's still yours and it ain't broke. Let's go back to work."

Afterwards, in the bar, while I wrapped my hand around a cold beer to keep the swelling and pain down, Ron hoisted his bottle in a toast: "That," he said, "was the best scream I ever heard, real authentic, like you were in actual pain, like you were really *scared*."

If this wasn't exactly Wind in His Hair howling eternal friendship for Dances With Wolves, I still understood what Ron was saying. It's more like a 7-year-old boy putting a frog down the back of a little girl's dress because he has a crush on her. It's a backward way of showing affection, of saying "I love you," but it's the only way we know. We should have outgrown it, and hordes of men are now paying thousands of dollars to sweat and stink and pound and grieve together to try and do just that. Maybe it works, maybe it doesn't. But no matter how cryptic, how Byzantine, how weird and weary the way it travels, the message still manages to get through.

RESPONDING IN DISCUSSION OR WRITING

1. How do you respond to the idea of "wildman weekends," in which men get together to do what they consider male activities?

2. When the author says that the guys say "I love you" to each other "all the time" (paragraph 9), what does he mean and how do you interpret and respond to his statement?

3. How does Cliff's story illustrate the idea that men discuss emotional issues in "allegory and parable"?

4. What stories can you tell of the ways in which men bond with each other in friendship?

5. In what ways are the settings in the article—the construction site, a dinner party, and a bar—representative of the worlds the author is writing about?

6. *Considerations of Style.* What stories does Buczynski tell to illustrate his thesis? How effective are the stories in supporting his point?

WRITING ASSIGNMENTS

1. Buczynski gives an example of a "backward way of showing affection." Do you think many people use this method of showing affection? In what ways do they show affection? Is the method used only by men? What are the effects on others of showing affection directly or in indirect, even backward, ways? Reflect on the issues involved in expressing emotions.

2. *The New York Times Magazine* alternates the "About Men" feature with one titled "Hers." Write a response to Buczynski's article for the "Hers" feature.

❖

BIG BOYS DON'T CRY: RETUNING THE MACHO MESSAGE

BERNICE KANNER

Bernice Kanner writes frequently for New York *magazine. This article, which examines how men are presented in advertising, appeared there on May 21, 1990.*

SENSITIVE MUSCLE MEN CRADLING newborns were as much an icon of 1989 advertising as the inept, bumbling male. But although men will continue to be presented in contradictory ways in the nineties, one thing is certain: "Guy" stuff is on its way back. The dud is becoming the dude again.

Yes, the sexes have become more similar. Sensitive, vulnerable men are "acceptable," and everyone agrees that traditional male attributes—physical strength, aggressiveness, and earning power —aren't as important as they once were. Still, men aren't willing to sacrifice their authoritarian style to become domesticated wimps. "Macho" may be gone (or, more likely, repressed), but "masculine" remains synonymous with *strong,* and men by and large still want products that are "tough," even to the point of pain—after-shave stings *because* men like that.

"The kinder, gentler image of men is losing momentum," says Ted Bell, president of Leo Burnett U.S.A. "Some men have rejected it, and so have women who want men to be men, though admittedly more sensitive and caring. A cigar and martini may be the new symbols to reach those who are starting to reject white wine and Perrier. I doubt you'll ever see the Marlboro man nuzzling a baby."

Yet symbols of domestication abound. A father nurses a sick child in a Tylenol commercial; in a commercial for Ivory soap, another rushes home to play with his infant daughter. Two men fret about dishwasher spots for Cascade. And Marine Midland's "Working things out together" campaign shows dads admitting insecurity about handling life's responsibilities—in one case, by shooting baskets at 3 A.M.

But for these pitches to work, the products must lend themselves to emotional license. "Life passages are almost always associated with banks," says John Neiman, vice-chairman of DMB&B, Marine Midland's agency. "Five years ago, you'd have seen a bank granting a loan so a man could buy a more powerful yacht." Budweiser's 1988 spot in which an Olympic winner cried while listening to the national anthem "would have been considered wimpy ten years ago," says Neiman.

Neiman blames the population's growing conservatism—a corollary of tougher economic times—for prompting the swing back somewhere between the sensitive eighties man and the unliberated macho man of the seventies. But he also feels that "while five years ago it was interesting to romanticize and lionize a man buying a head of lettuce, now it's a commonplace fact of life and no longer worthy of a commercial."

Others say clients resist showing men cooking, cleaning, and caring for children because they see little evidence of such activity in the real world. "The image of men has changed on TV but not in real life," says Jim Patterson, chairman of J. Walter Thompson North America. While researching a book, Patterson discovered that "men are shockingly recidivistic. They still don't buy women as equals, they're not interested in changing who they are, and they resent the prodding more than they did five years ago, when the women's movement was in bloom." Though men are doing more domestic chores, their style is different from women's. Thus, two guys pushing their children in strollers turns into a race to the 7-Eleven. Competitiveness makes the concept of child care more palatable to men.

The nurturing-ad genre turned off men "who have assumed these roles somewhat reluctantly or who don't want to see it as their entire accomplishment or interest. And it turned off women who couldn't get their husbands to live up to that perfect image," says Dick Karp, executive vice-president creative services at Grey

Advertising. Similarly, he says, though women like ads that poke fun at inept men, men have become too sophisticated as shoppers for advertisers to risk alienating them.

"Roles *are* changing, but we found it's important not to rob men of their masculinity," says Barbara Durham, an associate director of consumer resources at FCB/Chicago. Increasingly, ads will show guys doing guy things, or families together. Teamwork—men, women, and even the kids doing the chores—is the new standard, says Grey's Karp. "Pop is now a team player, not a supervisor, not the commanding officer, and, God knows, not a bumbling klutz. He's still allowed skepticism, but not ineptitude."

A MAN'S PLACE: *Cooking for Creamette.*
Courtesy Borden, Inc.

In a Grey spot for Creamette pasta, a man prepares dinner while his family looks on. "In the old days, a man's famous chili was the only thing he could—or would—cook," says Karp.

In the seventies, men were shown evaluating or enjoying women's efforts; in the eighties, they were "employees" who ran the vacuum cleaner as directed by women. Now "they know how to run the washer and use the oven, but not when it needs to be done," says Susan Small-Weil, director of strategic planning at Warwick Baker-Fiore. "Women are still directing, but now they're more or less equal partners. In the Cascade series, for instance, she asks if he's lighted the candles, started the music, and set the table. [A few years ago, he wouldn't have known how to set the table.] And yet *she's* the one still devastated by dishwasher spots. The way the house looks is still her responsibility."

An upcoming Wells, Rich, Greene campaign talks about "guys" and "girls," illustrating the former with a football and the latter with a ballet scene. "In the end, girls are pink and guys are tough," says executive vice-president Chris Hansen. "We thought about role-reversing but decided that showing a female plumber would cram the eighties down men's throats."

In the provocative Liz Claiborne for Men campaign, a man muses about looking in the mirror and seeing his father's face; in another ad, a man frets that a woman in a bar may be laughing at him. "It's too soon to say whether it's working," admits Robert Reitzfeld, creative director of Altschiller Reitzfeld Davis/Tracy-Locke, the agency responsible for the campaign.

DMB&B's Neiman warns that nothing suggesting "two-dimensional stereotypes" will succeed. He believes marketers will use neutral ads that appeal to different sides of men through different media. Certainly there will be plenty of magazines to reach the new men: Murdoch Magazine's *Men's Life,* due out in September, Norris Publishing's *Men*—for, among others, "untrendy suburbanites"—and a revamped *Details,* which is set to join *Men's Health, Esquire,* and *GQ* in declaring that it's okay to be a guy again.

Chris Kimball, publisher of *Men,* claims that after the complications and discomfort caused by the women's movement, men are re-emerging as "a homogeneous cultural unit desperate to be men again, doing the guy things they had put on hold—cars and sports and a drink with the boys. But while they'd still like to be kings, they've accepted and made peace with women's demands to be peers and equals." (Women apparently disagree. This spring, the Roper Organization found that more and more women feel that men are self-centered sex hounds who still don't help enough with household chores.) 15

Several men's organizations contend that the "men's liberation movement" is a consequence of their being pushed too far and put down too often. Certainly commercials persistently depict them as "evil incarnate or redneck, beer-swilling pigs," says Kenneth Pangborn, president of Men International, a national men's-rights organization. "While ads do portray men positively as authority figures—doctors, pharmacists, and repairmen—they just as often portray them as sleazy, disingenuous, or boobs."

In a commercial for Robitussin, Mom drags herself out of her sickbed to watch her hapless fellow wreak havoc while trying to run the house. The husband in a spot for Mrs. Smith's wonders whether he'll "ever be worthy" of the wife who has baked him a pie. In a Hallmark Cards spot, a woman who is despondent about a recent breakup receives a card from a friend: "Men are only good for one thing . . . and how important is parallel parking anyway?"

RESPONDING IN DISCUSSION OR WRITING

1. What responses do you have to the article's title? Does it make you want to read the whole article? What does the subtitle add?

2. What evidence does Kanner provide for saying that "'Guy' stuff is on its way back"? Do you find her evidence convincing? Were you aware that "'Guy' stuff" had ever disappeared?

3. Kanner makes a sweeping statement that "traditional male attributes . . . aren't as important as they once were." Do you agree with her? Why or why not?

4. Kanner makes a distinction between "macho" and "masculine." What are the differences? Make lists of actions that illustrate each type of behavior.

5. In paragraph 7, the implication is that men are more competitive than women. How do you respond to that assumption?

6. *Considerations of Style.* Kanner uses many specific examples to make her point. Which examples do you find particularly effective? What makes them stand out?

WRITING ASSIGNMENTS

1. Kanner points out that Jim Patterson has discovered that "the image of men has changed on TV but not in real life" (paragraph 7). Write about how you see men presented on TV nowadays and how that portrayal matches with the behavior of the men you know.

2. *For Further Research.* Find an advertisement in a newspaper or magazine that features either a man or a woman (or several men or women) as the main focus. Describe what you see in the ad and analyze what world and values are presented. What ideas is the ad selling, other than the product it is advertising? What does the ad

suggest to the consumer? Attach the advertisement to your piece of writing.

❖

WHAT ARE YOU?

ROSEMARY MAHONEY

Rosemary Mahoney, born in Boston in 1961, has won a Henfield/ Transatlantic Review *Award for creative writing. She is the author of* Whoredom in Kimmage: Irish Women Coming of Age *(1993), a result of ten months of interviews and experiences in Ireland. This article was published in the* New York Times *on March 17, 1993. It begins with a reference to the controversy surrounding the St. Patrick's Day parade in New York City in 1993: homosexuals wanted the right to march in this parade celebrating Irish pride, but were denied.*

BALTIMORE—TRY FOR A moment to forget the particulars of the dispute over the St. Patrick's Day parade and consider this: We would all like the right to march down Fifth Avenue and say who we are. Yet who are we but by our relationship to others? As often as not we define who we are by defining who we aren't.

The only thing I know about the Ancient Order of Hibernians is that they are not gay (they say) and do not want to be associated with those who are. But certainly they are more than this. The order was established in 1836 as a way of answering nativistic hatreds against the growing numbers of Irish in New York. (Nativism in this context is a misnomer—the people guilty of it were never truly native.) We know what the Hibernians are against. What are they for?

One midnight last year when I was living in Dublin, I was walking home from a party and met a young man. He crossed the street toward me, walking stiffly, with the mincing steps of a baby, as though his shoes—big black army boots—were too tight.

He was drunk, but not so drunk that he couldn't recognize my apprehension at his approach. He stopped before me, just beneath a streetlight, and with a great show of gentle courtesy raised his big hands in the gesture of surrender—a sign to me that he was harmless and that I should not be afraid. He leaned forward, pushed his thick-lensed eyeglasses higher on his nose, blinked at me for a minute, and with the fussy enunciation peculiar to the very drunk he said, "What are you?"

I studied his blinking face, unsure what exactly it was he wanted to know. Sensing my puzzlement he said, "I mean to ask, what sex are you? Girl or man." 5

I was certain I had never before been asked such a question and not certain that I shouldn't be insulted by it. I invited the man to tell me which sex I looked like to him. He stepped closer and peered at me, mouth open in intense concentration. He had a thicket of long black hair, wore an army jacket, and in the soft glow of the streetlight I could make out three large silver rings on his fingers, two depicting the figure of the Grim Reaper and one a skull and crossbones. The rings looked heavy and ugly and menacing, like knots of twisted chrome.

"Well, you look like a girl to me," said the man.

"Good," I said. "I am."

The man laughed—a high and surprisingly girlish laugh—and apologetically he said, "I only wanted to be sure I had you situated correctly." His voice was soft and pleasant and he had the confused demeanor of a stray dog, a blend of timidity and fierceness, diffidence and eagerness. Politely he asked how I intended to occupy myself the next day. I told him I planned to attend the Latin Mass at the Pro-Cathedral and afterward to meet a friend.

"Is it my turn now to ask you a question?" I said. 10

"Shoot," he said, rubbing his hands together, clearly delighted at having struck up this conversation in the middle of the night. I asked him about his rings. He responded by buffing them lovingly on his shirtfront, then held his hands out, admiring the rings in the glow of the streetlight, frowning with thoughtful interest. "These rings mean death," he said finally. "Are you afraid of death, miss?"

I told him I was not afraid of death.

"And you're dead right, too," he said eagerly, "for there is nothing to be afraid of. We're all going to die. Not even the rich escape that fate."

The man held up one hand for me. "The skull and crossbones on this ring symbolize the German SS," he said. I asked him why he wore a ring like that. He answered that he admired what he saw as their willingness to die. He didn't agree with the Nazi policy of killing the Jews, but death he was interested in, and as a matter of fact, while he didn't like what was done to the Jews, he might as well say he hated the Jews anyway. "I was in Israel once," he said, "and I knew some firsthand Jews. They are arrogant. They're always complaining about their six million. What about our four million?"

The four million he had in mind were, I assumed, the Irish victims of famine, emigration and hopeless battle. As if to clarify he said, "It doesn't matter how they kill you, but they kill you. Because of who you are. The British did it to us."

"Does that make the extermination of Jews all right?" I said.

"No, but it's better to forget and be peaceful and know yourself than be dragging up old fights all the time and be adopting the policies of your oppressor."

I told the man I thought it was better to remember our capacity for destruction and be vigilant than to fall into torpor. The conversation had become a heated argument, and it was clear that he felt he was losing ground. He crossed his long arms defensively, and sounding nearly tearful he stuttered, "I don't give a damn about history or Jews. You're only an American anyway. Americans don't know what they're talking about. Foreigners never do."

Though it would have been immediately obvious to any half-sensate Dubliner that my accent was American, I said, "What makes you think I'm American?" My words sounded angular and brutish compared to his gentle, singing ones.

"The way you sound, of course!" he cried.

I told the man that the way I sound had little to do with who I was, that it was simply an accident of history that I had been born in America and talk the way I do, that if things had been slightly different in Ireland, my family might never have left. I told the man the truth, that I had always felt more Irish than American.

"But you're not!" he said.

"I am," I said.

"Prove it," he said.

I told him the Irish Government had given me a passport.

"Rot!" was his response. We argued this way for several minutes until finally he seemed to give in. Softly he said, "I like you, miss.

You're mean and you're not afraid of me. A lot of girls are afraid of me. They don't like my rings and my clothes, so they don't like me. They think they know who I am and what I'm about."

"Precisely the way you think you know something about me because of my accent," I said.

The man smiled, and then he grew serious again. He told me a little about himself; he liked music and movies and cars. "I can talk to you," he said. "Know where I've been tonight? I've been in a homosexual bar. I think there are a lot of homosexuals in the world, so I'm curious. When I was in there tonight an old man came in and started hollering at us. He called us a lot of rude names. He was angry about us being there, about who we were. I felt bad about that.

"I don't really know what I am myself, to tell you the truth. I haven't had a girlfriend in years. I can hardly talk to girls. I have some kind of block. That's why I asked you what you were before—girl or boy. I meant what are you in your head. Because to me the important thing is what you are in your head."

I told him that in my head I was a woman, an Irish one.   30

"O.K.," he said, grinning. "O.K. I believe you. But you still have that accent."

I imitated a Boston accent for him, which he thought was tremendously funny. I imitated a Baltimore accent, and that he found even funnier. I said, "Open the door, hon'," in the sliding way a Baltimorean would, and he laughed uproariously, rocking in his army boots, and when he had recovered enough to speak he shook his head and said, "People are really different. Jesus, you have to love them."

RESPONDING IN DISCUSSION OR WRITING

1. How do you react to the young man's comment that "the important thing is what you are in your head"? How would you define yourself in your head?

2. How do you feel about the young man Mahoney talks to, particularly about his views on the Jews and the Irish? If you had been talking to the young man, would your conversation have continued in the same way as Mahoney's? Why or why not?

3. Mahoney begins with a comment about a St. Patrick's Day parade at which the organizers wanted to ban gay marchers. What

can you learn from the rest of the article about her views on that topic?

4. What connections are there between Mahoney's question at the end of paragraph 2: "What are they [the Hibernians] for?" and the young man's final comment: "People are really different. Jesus, you have to love them"?

5. The title of this article is "What Are You?" and not the more usual "Who Are You?" What issues of identity does this article address?

WRITING ASSIGNMENTS

1. From Mahoney we get details about the young man's clothes, hair, and rings, his "thick-lensed eyeglasses," his "girlish laugh," and his "gentle, singing" tone of voice. Write about an incident that is connected to the way people define who they are (or aren't). Include your own vivid details so that your readers can picture all the details of the people and place.

2. The young man Mahoney meets complains that people look at his clothes and think they know who he is and what kind of person he is. Discuss in an essay whether you think that judging someone from the way he or she dresses is a common approach to evaluating identity. If it is, what benefits or problems can result? If it is not a common approach, what criteria do you think people use to judge others? Try to use examples, and tell stories to illustrate your ideas.

❖

GEORGE SAND

CAROLYN G. HEILBRUN

Carolyn G. Heilbrun, born in 1926, was a professor of English at Columbia University in New York City until she retired in 1992, protesting that Columbia did not support feminist studies and feminist scholars.

She is the author of many works of criticism and has published mystery novels under the pseudonym Amanda Cross. This is an excerpt from her book Writing a Woman's Life, *published in 1988.*

> Women will starve in silence until new stories are created
> which confer on them the power of naming themselves.
>
> —*Sandra Gilbert and Susan Gubar*

THIS IS THE TRUE story of a woman who was born exactly a century before Freud published *The Psychopathology of Everyday Life.*

At the age of four, living on a large estate with horses and space for vigorous activity, she dressed as a boy in order to be able to play more freely. As she grew up, she dressed as a boy for riding and played the male roles opposite conventionally pretty girls in village productions. She found cross-dressing fun, sometimes going to the village near her estate dressed as a young man with her brother who would dress as a girl.

She was married at eighteen to a man of whom Henry James was to observe that he thought he had married an ordinary woman, and found on his hands a (spiritual) sister of Goethe. A year later her first child was born, six years later her second, who was probably not her husband's. By then she had already taken her first lover, years after her husband had taken many mistresses, including her own maid, and behaved brutally toward her. She left her husband eight years after the marriage began and went to live with a lover and collaborator in the nation's capital. Gaining from her husband a separation and an allowance (from her own money), she published two novels and several novelettes under a male pseudonym. Here is her description of how she dressed when she first came to the city:

> Above all, I hungered for the theater. I had no illusions that a poor woman could indulge such longings. [They] used to say, "You can't be a woman [here] on under twenty-five thousand." And this paradox, that a woman was not really a woman unless she was smartly dressed, was unbearably hampering to the poor woman artist.
>
> Yet I saw that my young male friends—my childhood companions— were living on as little as I, and knew about everything that could possibly interest young people. The literary and political events, the excitements of the theaters and picture salons, of the clubs and of the

streets—they saw it all, they were there. I had legs as strong as theirs, and good feet which had learned to walk sturdily in their great clogs upon the rutted roads of [the country]. Yet on the pavement I was like a boat on ice. My delicate shoes cracked open in two days, my pattens sent me spilling, and I always forgot to lift my dress. I was muddy, tired and runny-nosed, and I watched my shoes and my clothes—not to forget my little velvet hats, which the drainpipes watered—go to rack and ruin with alarming rapidity.

Distressed, she consulted her mother, who said: "When I was young and your father was hard up, he hit on the idea of dressing me as a boy. My sister did the same, and we went everywhere with our husbands: to the theater—oh, anywhere we wanted. And it halved our bills." Here, of course, was the perfect solution. "Having been dressed as a boy in my childhood, and having hunted in knee breeches and shirt, such dress was hardly new to me, and I was not shocked to put it on again." She became famous and had many lovers, including one woman, but she loved one man at a time, and these men were usually younger than she and were not married or the lovers of other women. She liked women, and encouraged younger women all her life. She was the lover and friend of some of the outstanding creative men of her day. She ran a comfortable, hospitable home, eventually delighted in her grandchildren, her garden, conversation, and the possibility of social revolution. Her name, of course, was George Sand.[1]

To describe her further to you I shall borrow the words of the late Ellen Moers, who in turn calls upon descriptions by Sand's contemporaries to compose this portrait: "She has a brilliant, well-stocked mind and a warm heart; she has courage, energy, vitality, generosity, responsibility, good humor, and charm; she has aristocratic distinction combined with bohemian informality; she is a wise, passionate, down-to-earth human being, and disappointingly sane." Moers continues:

She was a woman who was a great man: that is what her admirers most wanted to say about George Sand. But words of gender being what they are, suggestions of abnormality and monstrosity cling to their portraits of Sand, all unintentionally and quite the reverse of what her admirers had in mind. Elizabeth Barrett Browning began a sonnet to Sand with the line "Thou large-brained woman and large-hearted man" and what she intended as a tribute to wholeness came out sounding grotesque. Similarly Balzac: "She is boyish, an artist, she is great-hearted, generous, devout, and chaste; she has the main characteristics of a man; ergo, she is not a woman." Similarly Turgenev: "What a brave man she was, and what a good woman." . . . Reading George Sand is to encounter a great man who was all woman.[2]

And, indeed, if we read her life in any available form, we come again and again to this description of her as both man and woman. She enacted, through lovers and friends, all relationships from mother to master (Flaubert called her "dear master"). She had the power both to give and to receive, to nurture and to be nurtured. Yet all who knew and admired her found themselves without language to describe or address her, without a story, other than her own unique one, in which to encompass her. Although she played every role, including conventionally female ones, although she wrote, in her letters, stereotypically romantic phrases, she did not herself become the victim of these roles or phrases. In one of her novels, the heroine lives dressed as a man, though married and spending intervals in women's clothes; she dies as a man with the word *liberté* on her lips, having said, "I have always felt more than a woman," meaning, of course, more than woman as she is defined.

"Oh you, of the third sex," Flaubert hailed her, and those words that would today sound sneering or disturbing were wholly complimentary then. Flaubert, the ultimate master of words, found it impossible to discover any other way to describe the greatest friend of his life. Henry James, a lifelong admirer of her work, tried many times to describe Sand, and this artist of language and narrative faltered again and again in the attempt. George Sand's, he wrote, was "a method that may be summed up in a fairly simple, if comprehensive statement: it consisted in her dealing with life exactly as if she had been a man—exactly not being too much to say." After her death, James would remark to Flaubert that "the moral of George Sand's tale, the beauty of what she does for us, is not the extension she gives to the feminine nature, but the richness that she adds to the masculine." Flaubert wrote sadly to Turgenev of how at Sand's funeral he had wept "on seeing the coffin pass by." To a woman whose friendship he had shared with Sand, he wrote: "One had to know her as I knew her to realize how much of the feminine there was in that great man, the immensity of tenderness there was in that genius. She will remain one of the radiant splendors of France, unequaled in her glory."[3]

If we compare this story with the now famous account of the probable life of Shakespeare's imagined sister in Virginia Woolf's *A Room of One's Own,* we are moved to explain the miracle that was George Sand's life with the failure of Judith Shakespeare and of so many anonymous women poets. It is easy enough to point to Paris and to French mores for an explanation, but this is not what matters. What matters is that lives do not serve as models; only stories do that. And it is a hard thing to make up stories to live by. We can only retell and live by the stories we have read or heard. We live our lives through texts. They may be read, or chanted, or experienced electronically, or come to us, like the murmurings of our mothers, telling us what conventions demand. Whatever their form or medium, these stories have formed us all; they are what we must use to make new fictions, new narratives.

George Eliot, who did in her life what she could never portray in the lives of her heroines, allowed a minor character in *Daniel Deronda* to protest women's storylessness: "You can never imagine," Daniel's mother tells him, "what it is to have a man's force of genius in you, and yet to suffer the slavery of being a girl. To have a pattern cut out . . . a woman's heart must be of such a size and no larger, else it must be pressed small, like Chinese feet; her happiness is to be made as cakes are, by a fixed receipt."

No careful study of nineteenth-century literature can overlook Sand's tremendous effect on the writers of her time. Hers is the work that explains the Brontës, whose passionate novels lay outside the English tradition, and that goes far to explain the work of Dostoyevski, Whitman, Hawthorne, Matthew Arnold, George Eliot, and many others, to mention only writers who did not meet her but were influenced by her work. Yet few courses in Victorian literature, Russian literature, or American literature even mention George Sand. She and her tremendous influence have disappeared from the canons of French and American literature classes with scarcely a trace. Had she not been a woman, such a disappearance would be inconceivable. But, what is most important, the story of her life has not become an available narrative for women to use in making fictions of their lives. The liberating effect of her novels is greater upon male writers than upon women in England and the United States. The narrative she lived is not yet textually embodied. How may new narratives for women enter texts and then other texts and eventually women's lives?

Notes

1. These passages are drawn from Ellen Moers, "Introduction" to *George Sand: In Her Own Words,* ed. Joseph Barry (Garden City, N.Y.: Anchor, 1979), and from George Sand, *My Life,* trans. Dan Hofstadter (New York: Harper Colophon, 1979).

2. Moers, xv.

3. Barry, ed. *George Sand,* 384.

RESPONDING IN DISCUSSION OR WRITING

1. Discuss what Heilbrun means when she says, "We can only retell and live by the stories we have read or heard. We live our lives through texts." What texts does she mean? How can you apply what she says here to your own life?

2. *Considerations of Style.*   Heilbrun does not reveal the name of her subject until the end of her fourth paragraph; up until that point we read only about "she." Why do you think Heilbrun chose to do that, and what effect does it have on the reader?

3. What do you think is Heilbrun's point in mentioning Freud in the very first paragraph? What does Freud and his book have to do with George Sand?

4. What is Heilbrun's purpose in mentioning other nineteenth-century writers such as George Eliot, the Brontës, Whitman, and Hawthorne? Why does she use so many names?

5. Do you think you would have liked George Sand as a person? Why or why not?

6. How do you think your own life would have been different if you had been born the opposite sex or if you had learned to live and dress comfortably as the opposite sex?

WRITING ASSIGNMENTS

1. If you performed in a drama in which you had to play someone of the opposite sex, consider how you would behave, walk, and talk and what gestures you would adopt. Write an essay describing what changes you would make from your usual behavior and give

examples of specific behavior you would adopt. How much of you as you know yourself would remain?

2. *For Further Research.* Do library research to discover more about George Sand's life, works, and reputation. Write an essay exploring in what ways "passing" as a man was a feature of her identity and to explain how she was perceived by her contemporaries. You could also see the film *Impromptu,* which tells the story of the relationship between Sand and the composers Liszt and Chopin, and comment on the way the film portrays her.

❖

GAY POLITICS, ETHNIC IDENTITY

STEVEN EPSTEIN

This is the introductory section of a long article by Steven Epstein, originally published in Volume 17 of Socialist Review *(1987) with the subtitle "The Limits of Social Constructionism." Epstein, born in 1943, is the author of many articles and book reviews on issues of gay culture, AIDS, and education. He wrote this article while he was a graduate student in sociology at Berkeley, University of California.*

> I seem to be surrounded at all times in all ways by who I am. . . . It goes with me wherever I go . . . and my life is gay and where I go I take my gay life with me. I don't consciously sit and think while I'm eating soup that I'm eating this "gayly," but, you know, it surrounds me.

> To me, being gay is like having a tan. When you are in a gay relationship, you're gay. When you're not in a gay relationship, you're not gay.

> As I sit at a concert or engage volubly in a conversation in the office or at home, or as I look up from my newspaper and glance at the people occupying the seats of the bus, my mind will suddenly jump from the words, the

thoughts", or the music around me, and with horrible
impact I will hear, pounding within myself, the fateful
words: *I am different.* I am different from these people, and
I must always be different from them. I do not belong to
them, nor they to me.

   There's nothing in me that is not in everybody else, and
nothing in everybody else that is not in me. We're trapped
in language, of course. But homosexual is not a noun. At
least not in my book.

WHAT DOES IT MEAN to be gay? Do lesbians and gay men constitute a "deviant subculture"? A "sexual minority"? A privileged "revolutionary subject"? Is homosexuality a "preference" (like a taste
for chocolate ice cream)? Or perhaps an "orientation" (a fixed
position relative to the points of a compass)? Or maybe it's a
"lifestyle," like being a "yuppie" or a surfer? Is being gay something that has some importance? Or is it a relatively inconsequential difference?

   The gay men and women quoted above are undoubtedly not a
representative sample, but the range of contradictory opinions
certainly testifies to the difficulties involved in answering these
questions.[1] And the types of disagreements observed in these
quotes are present not only between individuals, but also within
them. Most people who identify as gay or practice homosexuality
adopt some variety of relatively inconsistent positions regarding
their identity over the course of time, often depending on the
needs of the moment. These contradictions are paralleled by the
attitudes of homophobic opponents of the gay movement, which
are typically even less consistent; for example, one frequently
hears the belief that homosexuality is an "illness" combined with a
simultaneous concern that youngsters can be "seduced" into it.
The whole issue, it seems, is a terminological and conceptual
minefield. Yet given the startling newness of the idea of there
being such a thing as a "gay identity"—neither that term, nor "lesbian identity," nor "homosexual identity" appeared in writing by
or about gays and lesbians before the mid-1970s—the confusion is
hardly surprising.[2]

   This article does not address the question of what "causes"
homosexuality, or what "causes" heterosexuality. Instead, what I

seek to explore is how lesbians and gay men, on a day-to-day basis, interpret their sexual desires and practices so as to situate themselves in the world; how these self-understandings relate to social theories about homosexuals; and how both the theories and the self-understandings can shape—or block—different varieties of political activism by gays.[3] I take as given that power inheres in the ability to name, and that what we call ourselves has implications for political practice. An additional assumption is that lesbians and gay men in our society consciously seek, in a wide variety of ways, to *legitimate* their forms of sexual expression, by developing explanations, strategies, and defenses. These legitimations are articulated both on an individual level ("This is who I am, and this is why I am that way") and on a collective level ("This is what we are, and here is what we should do"). Legitimation strategies play a mediating function between self-understandings and political programs, and between groups and their individual members.

Existing theories of sexuality fail to address these concerns adequately. For some time now, sexual theory has been preoccupied with a debate between "essentialism" and "constructionism"—a debate which, despite its importance in reorienting our thinking about sexuality, may well have outlived its usefulness. "Essentialists" treat sexuality as a biological force and consider sexual identities to be cognitive realizations of genuine, underlying differences; "constructionists," on the other hand, stress that sexuality, and sexual identities, are social constructions, and belong to the world of culture and meaning, not biology. In the first case, there is considered to be some "essence" within homosexuals that makes them homosexual—some gay "core" of their being, or their psyche, or their genetic make-up. In the second case, "homosexual," "gay," and "lesbian" are just labels, created by cultures and applied to the self.

Both essentialist and constructionist views are ingrained in the folk understandings of homosexuality in our society—often in a highly contradictory fashion. In a recent letter to Ann Landers, "Worried in Montana" expresses concern that her fourteen-year-old son may be "seduced" into homosexuality (folk constructionism) by the boy's friend, who she has "no question" is gay, because of his "feminine mannerisms" (folk essentialism). Ann reassures the mother that the only way her son would turn out to be gay is if "the seeds of homosexuality were already present" (folk essential-ism). At the same time, she questions the mother's certainty about the sexual orientation of the friend, claiming that it is "presump-tuous" to label a fourteen-year-old as "gay" (folk construc-tionism).[4] But if such inconsistent views can at times exist side by side, it is equally true that at other times they clash violently. Homosexuals who are advised to "change" and become straight, for example, might have more than a passing investment in the claim that they've "always been that way"—that their gayness is a fundamental part of who they "really are."

This debate is not restricted to the field of sexuality; it parallels similar ones that have taken place in many other domains, includ-ing gender, race, and class. For example, while some feminists have proposed that qualities such as nurturance constitute a femi-nine "essence," others have insisted that any differences between men and women, beyond the strictly biological, are the products of culture and history: men and women have no essential "nature."[5] But while the issues may be generalizable, they have a special salience for contemporary gay politics, because of a pecu-liar historical irony. With regard to sexuality, the constructionist critique of essentialism has become the received wisdom in left academic circles. And yet, curiously, the historical ascendancy of the new constructionist orthodoxy has paralleled a growing incli-nation within the gay movement in the United States to under-stand itself and project an image of itself in ever more "essentialist" terms.

As many observers have noted, gays in the 1970s increasingly came to conceptualize themselves as a legitimate minority group, having a certain quasi-"ethnic" status, and deserving the same pro-tections against discrimination that are claimed by other groups in our society.[6] To be gay, then, became something like being Italian, or black, or Jewish. The "politics of identity" have crystal-lized around a notion of "gayness" as a real, and not arbitrary, dif-ference. So while constructionist theorists have been preaching the gospel that the hetero/homosexual distinction is a social fic-tion, gays and lesbians, in everyday life and in political action, have been busy hardening the categories. Theory, it seems, has not been informing practice. Perhaps the practitioners are mis-guided; or perhaps there is something about the strict construc-tionist perspective which neither adequately describes the experiences of gays and lesbians nor speaks to their need to understand and legitimate their places in the world.[7]

Notes

1. The four quotes, in order, are: (1) an unnamed lesbian, interviewed by Barbara Ponse in *Identities in the Lesbian World: The Social Construction of Self* (Westport, Conn.: Greenwood Press, 1978), p. 178; (2) a different lesbian interview subject, quoted in Ponse, p. 189; (3) Donald Webster Cory [pseud.], *The Homosexual in America* (New York: Castle Books, 1951), p. 9; (4) James Baldwin, interviewed by Richard Goldstein, "Go the Way Your Blood Beats: An Interview with James Baldwin," *Village Voice*, 26 June 1984, p. 14.

2. Vivienne C. Cass, "Homosexual Identity: A Concept in Need of Definition," *Journal of Homosexuality*, vol. 9, nos. 2/3 (Winter 1983/Spring 1984), p. 105.

3. This analysis does not systematically explore the self-understandings or politics of people who identify as bisexuals, though the category of "bisexual" itself is important to the discussion. . . .

   At times, I will discuss gay men separately from lesbians; at other points, the analysis will refer to both at the same time. While this may be confusing from an analytic standpoint, it seems unavoidable if one wants to avoid simplistic assumptions of parallelism between the experiences of gay men and women.

4. *Oakland Tribune*, 6 March 1987, p. F-7.

5. See Nancy Chodorow, "Feminism and Difference: Gender, Relation, and Difference in Psychoanalytic Perspective," *Socialist Review*, no. 46 (July-August 1979), pp. 51–69. For an analogous discussion in the domain of race, see Michael Omi and Howard Winant, *Racial Formation in the United States: From the 1960s to the 1980s* (New York: Routledge & Kegan Paul, 1986), p. 68 and passim. For class, see Ernesto Laclau and Chantal Mouffe, *Hegemony and Socialist Strategy: Towards a Radical Democratic Theory of Politics* (London: Verso, 1985); or Pierre Bourdieu, "The Social Space and the Genesis of Groups," *Theory and Society*, vol. 14, no. 6 (November 1985), pp. 723–744. Similar arguments have also taken place with regard to mental illness, alcoholism, and drug addiction.

6. See, in particular, Dennis Altman, *The Homosexualization of America* (Boston: Beacon Press, 1982).

7. I do not mean to suggest that constructionism is the *only* theoretical perspective on homosexuality proposed by left academics. Clearly, feminist theory has played a significant role in informing debates on sexual politics. However, feminism has often been guilty of "gender reductionism" by treating questions of sexual identity as epiphenoma of gender debates. To the extent that there is a coherent theoretical perspective on homosexuality *as* homosexuality, it is constructionism.

RESPONDING IN DISCUSSION OR WRITING

1. The essay begins with four quotations. What attitudes do the speakers express toward being gay? Which one do you feel you understand best and respond to most positively? Why?

2. Respond to the first sentence in the second quotation, ". . . being gay is like having a tan." What connections can you make between that quotation and the issue of the way people shape their identity?

3. How would you answer the questions Epstein pose in paragraph 1: "Is being gay something that has some importance? Or is it a relatively inconsequential difference?" What makes you give your particular answer?

4. What examples can you offer to support Epstein's contention that "power inheres in the ability to name"? What does that mean for lesbians and gay men? And for other groups of people? Think of connections here to the selections in the first unit of this book.

5. Epstein draws parallels in his article between ethnicity and sexuality. What connections do you see between the ways gays and lesbians and ethnic minorities are treated in society?

6. The debate between "essentialism" and "constructionism" in sexual theory reflects the old nature versus nurture debate that concerns all aspects of human behavior. What are the difficulties that might be caused for homosexuals by an emphasis on each theory?

WRITING ASSIGNMENTS

1. Consider in what ways being gay can become, as Epstein says happened in the 1970s, "something like being Italian, or black, or Jewish." Write an essay discussing whether you see connections between being gay and being a member of an ethnic minority, and give your reasons. If you do see connections, explain what they are and what they mean for the individuals involved.

2. *For Further Research.* Read the interview with James Baldwin from which the fourth opening quotation was taken. (See endnote 1 for the source.) To let a reader know what the original interview contained, summarize the issues discussed in the interview and then discuss in an essay how the interview does or does not offer a response to Epstein's question: "Is being gay something that has some importance?"

❖

THE NEW AMERICAN DREAMERS

RUTH SIDEL

Ruth Sidel is Professor of Sociology at Hunter College, City University of New York, and the author of many books that examine social class and the position of women, such as Women and Children Last *(1986) and* On Her Own: Growing Up in the Shadow of the American Dream *(1990), from which this excerpt from the first chapter is taken. Recognizing that the American vision had been "for the most part a male dream" but that over two decades there had been a change in women's perceptions of "their roles, their rights, and their responsibilities," Sidel conducted over 150 interviews in many parts of the country with young women, people who worked with the young women, and older women to find out about their dreams and expectations after more than twenty years of feminism. She found three groups: "Neotraditionalists" (those who plan to work or have careers but have a "strong commitment to their future roles within the family"), the "Outsiders" (those "who can barely see beyond tomorrow"), and the "New American Dreamers," who are the subject of the following piece. Sidel's most recent book is* Battling Bias: The Struggle for Identity and Community on College Campuses *(1994).*

> It's your life. You have to live it yourself . . . If you work
> hard enough, you will get there. You must be in control of
> your life, and then somehow it will all work out.
>
> *Angela Dawson*
> *high-school junior, Southern California*

SHE IS THE PROTOTYPE of today's young woman—confident, outgoing, knowledgeable, involved. She is active in her school, church, or community. She may have a wide circle of friends or simply a few close ones, but she is committed to them and to their friendship. She is sophisticated about the central issues facing young people today—planning for the future, intimacy, sex, drugs, and alcohol—and discusses them seriously, thoughtfully, and forthrightly. She wants to take control of her life and is trying to figure out how to get from where she is to where she wants to go. Above all, she is convinced that if she plans carefully, works hard, and makes the right decisions, she will be a success in her chosen field; have the material goods she desires; in time, marry if she wishes; and, in all probability, have children. She plans, as the expression goes, to "have it all."

She lives in and around the major cities of the United States, in the towns of New England, in the smaller cities of the South and Midwest, and along the West Coast. She comes from an upper-middle-class family, from the middle class, from the working class, and even sometimes from the poor. What is clear is that she has heard the message that women today should be the heroines of their own lives. She looks toward the future, seeing herself as the central character, planning her career, her apartment, her own success story. These young women do not see themselves as playing supporting roles in someone else's life script; it is their own journeys they are planning. They see their lives in terms of *their* aspirations, *their* hopes, *their* dreams.

Beth Conant is a sixteen-year-old high-school junior who lives with her mother and stepfather in an affluent New England college town. She has five brothers, four older and one several years younger. Her mother is a librarian, and her stepfather is a stockbroker. A junior at a top-notch public high school, she hopes to study drama in college, possibly at Yale, "like Meryl Streep." She would like to live and act in England for a time, possibly doing Shakespeare. She hopes to be living in New York by the age of twenty-five, in her own apartment or condo, starting on her acting career while working at another job by which she supports herself. She wants to have "a great life," be "really independent," and have "everything that's mine—crazy furniture, everything my own style."

By the time she's thirty ("that's so boring"), she feels, she will need to be sensible, because soon she will be "tied down." She hopes that by then her career will be "starting to go forth" and that she will be getting good roles. By thirty-five she'll have a child ("probably be married beforehand"), be working in New York and have a house in the country. How will she manage all this? Her husband will share responsibilities. She's not going to be a "supermom." They'll both do child care. He won't do it as a favor; it will be their joint responsibility. Moreover, if she doesn't have the

time to give to a child, she won't have one. If necessary, she'll
work for a while, then have children, and after that "make one
movie a year."

Amy Morrison is a petite, black, fifteen-year-old high-school
sophomore who lives in Ohio. Her mother works part-time, and
her father works for a local art museum. She plans to go to medical school and hopes to become a surgeon. She doesn't want to
marry until she has a good, secure job but indicates that she
might be living with someone. She's not sure about having children but says emphatically that she wants to be successful, to
make money, to have cars. In fact, originally she wanted to
become a doctor "primarily for the money," but now she claims
other factors are drawing her to medicine.

Jacqueline Gonzalez is a quiet, self-possessed, nineteen-year-old
Mexican-American woman who is a sophomore at a community
college in southern California. She describes her father as a "self-
employed contractor" and her mother as a "housewife."
Jacqueline, the second-youngest of six children, is the first in her
family to go to college. Among her four brothers and one sister,
only her sister has finished high school. Jacqueline's goal is to go
to law school and then to go into private practice. While she sees
herself as eventually married with "one or two children," work,
professional achievement, and an upper-middle-class life-style are
central to her plans for her future.

If in the past, and to a considerable extent still today, women
have hoped to find their identity through marriage, have sought
to find "validation of . . . [their] uniqueness and importance by
being singled out among all other women by a man,"[1] the New
American Dreamers are setting out on a very different quest for
self-realization. They are, in their plans for the future, separating
identity from intimacy, saying that they must first figure out who
they are and that then and only then will they form a partnership
with a man. Among the young women I interviewed, the New
American Dreamers stand apart in their intention to make their
own way in the world and determine their own destiny prior to
forming a significant and lasting intimate relationship.

Young women today do not need to come from upper-middle-
class homes such as Beth's or middle-class homes such as Amy's or
working-class homes such as Jacqueline's to dream of "the good
life." Even young women with several strikes against them see

material success as a key prize at the end of the rainbow. Some seem to feel that success is out there for the taking. Generally, the most prestigious, best-paying careers are mentioned; few women of any class mention traditional women's professions such as teaching or nursing. A sixteen-year-old unmarried Arizona mother of a four-and-a-half-month-old baby looks forward to a "professional career either in a bank or with a computer company," a "house that belongs to me," a "nice car," and the ability to buy her son "good clothes." She sees herself in the future as dating but not married. "There is not so much stress on marriage these days," she says.

Yet another young woman, a seventeen-year-old black unmarried mother of an infant, hopes to be a "professional model," have "lots of cash," be "rich," maybe have another child. When asked if a man will be part of the picture, she responds, "I don't know."

An eighteen-year-old Hispanic unmarried mother hopes to "be   10
my own boss" in a large company, have a "beautiful home," send her daughter to "the best schools." She wants, in her words, to "do it, make it, have money."

These young women are bright, thoughtful, personable. And they are quintessentially American: they believe that with enough hard work they will "make it" in American society. No matter what class they come from, their fantasies are of upward mobility, a comfortable life filled with personal choice and material possessions. The upper-middle-class women fantasize a life even more upper-middle-class; middle-class and working-class women look toward a life of high status in which they have virtually everything they want; and some young women who come from families with significant financial deprivation and numerous other problems dream of a life straight out of "Dallas," "Dynasty," or "L.A. Law." According to one young woman, some of her friends are so determined to be successful that they are "fearful that there will be a nuclear war and that they will die before they have a chance to live their lives. If there is a nuclear war," she explained, "they won't live long enough to be successful."

Young women are our latest true believers. They have bought into the image of a bright future. Many of them see themselves as professional women, dressed in handsome clothes, carrying a briefcase to work, and coming home to a comfortable house or condo, possibly to a loving, caring husband and a couple of well-behaved children. How widespread is the dream? How realistic is it? What is the function of this latest American dream? What about those young women who cling to a more traditional dream? What about those who feel their dreams must be deferred? What about those with no dream at all? And what about those who "share the fantasy," as the Chanel No. 5 perfume advertisement used to say, but have little or no chance of achieving it?

Perhaps the most poignant example of the impossible dream is Simone Baker, a dynamic, bright, eighteen-year-old black woman from Louisiana. Simone's mother is a seamstress who has been off and on welfare over the years, and her father is a drug addict. Simone herself has been addicted to drugs of one kind or another since she was five. She has been in and out of drug-abuse facilities, and although she attended school for many years and was passed from grade to grade, she can barely read and write. When I met her in a drug rehabilitation center, she was struggling to become drug free so that she could join the Job Corps, finish high school, and obtain some vocational training. Her dream of the future is so extraordinary, given her background, that she seems to epitomize the Horatio Alger myth of another era. When asked what she would like her life to be like in the future, Simone replies instantly, her eyes shining: "I want to be a model. I want to have a Jacuzzi. I want to have a *big*, BIG house and a BIG family—three girls and two boys."

"And what about the man?" I ask her.

"He'll be a lawyer. He'll be responsible, hardworking, and sensitive to my feelings. Everything will be fifty-fifty. And he'll take the little boys out to play football and I'll have the girls inside cooking. That would be a dream come true!"

Simone's dream is an incredible mixture of the old and the new—a Dick-and-Jane reader updated. And she's even mouthing the supreme hope of so many women in this age of the therapeutic solution to personal problems—that she'll find a man who is "sensitive" to her "feelings." She has lived a life far from the traditional middle class and yet has the quintessential image of the good life as it has been formulated in the last quarter of the twentieth century. But for Simone, it is virtually an impossible dream. One wishes that that were not so; listening to her, watching her excitement and hope at the mere thought of such a life, one gets caught up and wants desperately for it all to happen. The image is clear: the white house in the suburbs with the brass knocker on the front door, the leaves on the lawn in the fall, the boys playing football with this incredibly wonderful husband/father, and Simone sometimes the successful model, other times at home, cooking with her daughters. But we know how very unlikely it is that this particular dream will come true. And yet, maybe . . .

How have young women come to take on the American Dream as their own? That this is a relatively new dream for women is clear. Until recent years women, for the most part, did not perceive themselves as separate, independent entities with their own needs and agendas. Women fit themselves into other people's lives, molded their needs to fit the needs of others. For the full-time homemaker the day began early enough to enable husband and children to get to work and school on time. Chores had to be done between breakfast and lunch or between lunch and the end of school. Dinnertime was when the man of the house returned from work. When a woman worked outside of the home, her work hours were often those that fit into the schedules of other family members. Her needs were determined by the needs of others, as often her identity rested on her affiliation with them.

What some women seem to be saying now is that they will form their own identities, develop their own styles, and meet their own needs. They will be the central characters in their stories. They will work at jobs men work at, earn the money men earn; but many of them also plan at the same time to play all the roles women have traditionally played.

What has become clear in talking with young women throughout the country is that many of them are planning for their future in terms of their "public" roles as well as their "domestic" roles, that they are "laying claim to significant and satisfying work . . . as a normal part of their lives and laying claim also to the authority, prestige, power, and salary that . . . [that] work commands."[2] Historically, women have been confined primarily to the "domestic" sphere of life, particularly to child rearing and homemaking, and men, for the most part, have participated in the "public" sphere—that is, in social, economic, and political institutions and forms of association in the broader social structure. This dichotomy between "public" and "domestic" has led to "an asymmetry in the cultural evaluation of male and female that appears to be universal."[3] Margaret Mead noted this asymmetry when she observed that "whatever the arrangements in regard to descent or ownership of property, and even if these formal outward arrangements are reflected in the temperamental relations between the sexes, the prestige values always attach to the activities of men."[4]

In New Guinea, women grow sweet potatoes and men grow yams; yams are the prestige food. In societies where women grow rice, the staple food, and men hunt for meat, meat is the most valued food.[5] Traditionally, the more exclusively male the activity, the more cultural value is attached to it. Because male activities have been valued over female activities and women have become "absorbed primarily in domestic activities because of their role as mothers,"[6] women's work of caring has traditionally been devalued. However, as political scientist Joan Tronto has pointed out, it is not simply the dichotomy between the public and the private that results in the devaluation of the female but the immense difference in power between the two spheres.[7] So long as men have a monopoly on the public sphere and it in turn wields great power within society, women, identified with the private sphere, which is seen as relatively powerless, will be devalued.

Since the emergence of the women's movement in the 1960s, women in the U.S. as well as in many other parts of the world have been questioning the traditional asymmetry between men and women, seeking to understand its roots, its causes, and its consequences, and attempting to modify the male monopoly of power. Many strategies have developed toward this end: laws have been passed in an attempt to eliminate discrimination; groups have formed to elect more women to positions of power; those already in power have been urged to appoint more women to administrative roles; dominant, high-status, high-income professions have been pressured to admit more women to their hallowed ranks; and strategies to bring greater equity to male and female salaries have been developed.

Great stress has been placed on raising the consciousness of both women and men concerning this imbalance of power, but particular attention has been devoted to raising the consciousness of women. Discussion about the relative powerlessness of the non-wage-earning "housewife" has been widespread. Books and articles about the impoverishment of the divorced woman, the problems of the displaced homemaker, and the often desperate plight of the single, female head of household have been directed at women. During the 1970s and 1980s, the message suddenly became clear to many women: perhaps they are entitled to play roles formerly reserved for men; perhaps they would enjoy these challenges; perhaps they have something special to offer and can make a difference in the practice of medicine or law or in running the country. Moreover, it became clear that if women want power, prestige, and paychecks similar to those men receive, if they want to lessen the asymmetry between male and female, then perhaps they must enter those spheres traditionally reserved for men. If men grow yams, must women grow yams? If men hunt and women gather, must women purchase a bow and arrow? If men are in the public sphere while women are at home caring for children and doing the laundry, the consensus seems to say that women must enter the public sphere. If men are doctors and lawyers and earn great rewards while women are nurses and teachers and earn meager rewards, then women see what they obviously must do. If men have focused on doing while women have focused on caring, then clearly women must become doers.

It is not sufficient, however, to become a doer in a traditionally female occupation, for, as we know, these occupations are notoriously underpaid and underesteemed. Women must become *real* doers in the arena that counts: they must learn to play hardball, or, as Mary Lou Retton says in her breakfast-cereal advertisements, "eat what the big boys eat." For real power, status, money, and "success," it's law, medicine, and finance—also, possibly, acting, modeling, or working in the media, if one is very lucky.

An illustration of the current emphasis on male-dominated careers as the road to success for young women are the career goals of *Glamour* magazine's "Top Ten College Women '88." One woman hopes to become an astronaut; a second plans to work in the area of public policy, another to be a biologist, another to obtain a degree in business administration, yet another to obtain a degree in acting; and one young woman is currently working in journalism. One college senior is undecided between journalism and law, and the last three are planning to go to law school. These young women, according to *Glamour,* "possess the talents and ambition necessary to shape tomorrow's society." It is noteworthy that none of the women *Glamour* chose to honor are entering any traditionally female occupation or any "helping" profession—not even medicine. Don't nurses, teachers, and social workers "possess the talents and ambition necessary to shape tomorrow's society"? The word has gone out and continues to go out that the way to "make it" in American society and the way to "shape tomorrow's society" is the traditional male route.[8]

Once singled out, these young women play their part in spreading the ideology of the American Dream. Three of the ten honorees appeared on NBC's "Today" show. When asked about the significance of their being chosen, one woman replied without hesitation that if you work hard, you can do whatever you want to do. This statement was greeted by smiles and nods; she had clearly given the right message.

In addition to wanting to break out of the mold of a secondary worker receiving inferior wages and benefits and having little authority or opportunity for advancement, women have been motivated to make real money and to acquire valued skills and some semblance of security because of their relatively recent realization that women, even women with children, may well be forced to care for themselves or, at the very least, to participate in providing for the family unit. Women have come to realize that whether because of divorce (which leaves women on the average 73 percent poorer and men on the average 42 percent richer),[9] childbearing outside of marriage, the inability of many men to earn an adequate "family wage," or their remaining single— either through design or through circumstance—they must be prepared to support themselves and anyone else for whom they feel responsible.

But what of all that caring women used to do—for children, for elderly parents, for sick family members, for the home? What about Sunday dinner, baking chocolate-chip cookies with the kids eating up half the batter, serving Kool-Aid in the backyard on a hot summer day? What about sitting with a child with a painful ear infection until the antibiotic takes effect, going with a four-year-old to nursery school the first week until the child feels comfortable letting you leave, being available when there's an accident at school and your second grader must be rushed to the emergency room? Who's going to do the caring? Who is going to do the caring in a society in which few institutions have been developed to take up the slack, a society in which men have been far more reluctant to become carers than women have been to become doers. Members of the subordinate group may gain significantly in status, in self-image, and in material rewards when they take on the activities and characteristics of the dominant group, but there is little incentive for members of the dominant group to do the reverse.

Above all, how do young women today deal with these questions? How do they feel about doing and caring, about power, prestige, and parenting? What messages is society giving them about the roles they should play, and how are they sorting out these messages?

A key message the New American Dreamers are both receiving and sending is one of optimism—the sense that they can do whatever they want with their lives. Many Americans, of course—not just young people or young women—have a fundamentally optimistic attitude toward the future. Historically, Americans have believed that progress is likely, even inevitable, and that they have the ability to control their own destinies. A poll taken early in 1988 indicates that while the American public was concerned about the nation's future and indeed more pessimistic about "the way things [were] going in the United States" than they had been at any other time since the Carter presidency in the late 1970s, they nonetheless believed that they could "plan and regulate their own lives, even while the national economy and popular culture appear[ed] to be spinning out of control."[10] As one would expect, those with higher incomes and more education are more optimistic than those with less; Republicans are more optimistic than Democrats or Independents; and, significantly, men are more hopeful than women.[11] In looking toward the future, young men clearly dream of "the good life," of upward mobility and their share of material possessions. While young women historically have had far less control over their lives than men, for the past twenty-five years they have been urged to take greater control, both in the workplace and in their private lives, and they have clearly taken the message very much to heart.

Angela Dawson, a sixteen-year-old high-school junior from southern California, sums up the views of the New American Dreamers: "It's your life. You have to live it yourself. You must decide what you want in high school, plan your college education, and from there you can basically get what you want. If you work hard enough, you will get there. You must be in control of your life, and then somehow it will all work out."

Notes

1. Rachel M. Brownstein, *Becoming a Heroine: Reading About Women in Novels* (New York: Penguin, 1984), p. xv.

2. Nadya Aisenberg and Mona Harrington, *Women of Academe: Outsiders in the Sacred Grove* (Amherst, Mass.: University of Massachusetts Press, 1988), p. 3.

3. Michelle Zimbalist Rosaldo, "Women, Culture, and Society: An Overview," in *Women, Culture, and Society,* Michelle Zimbalist Rosaldo and Louise Lamphere, eds. (Stanford, Calif.: Stanford University Press, 1974), p. 19.

4. Ibid.

5. Ibid.

6. Ibid., p. 24.

7. Joan C. Tronto, "Women and Caring: What Can Feminists Learn About Morality from Caring?" in *Body, Gender and Knowledge,* Alison Jagger and Susan Brodo, eds. (New Brunswick, N.J.: Rutgers University Press, in press). See also Linda Imray and Audrey Middleton, "Public and Private: Marking the Boundaries," in *The Public and the Private,* Eva Gamarnikow et al., eds. (London: Heinemann, 1983), pp. 12–27.

8. *Glamour* (August 1988), pp. 208–9.

9. Terry Arendell, *Mothers and Divorce: Legal, Economic, and Social Dilemmas* (Los Angeles: University of California Press, 1986), p. 2.

10. Steven V. Roberts, "Poll Finds Less Optimism in U.S. on Future, a First Under Reagan," *The New York Times,* February 21, 1988.

11. Ibid.

RESPONDING IN DISCUSSION OR WRITING

1. Sidel begins the first chapter of her book with a quotation. How do you respond to that quotation? Do you agree with the idea expressed in it or not?

2. *Considerations of Style.*   In paragraph 12, Sidel asks seven questions, one after the other. What is the effect of those questions? Why do you think Sidel asks so many all at the same time? Look at other places where Sidel uses questions, and discuss their effect.

3. *Considerations of Style.*   Why do you think Sidel begins her first chapter by discussing an unidentified "she"? What is the effect of using a pronoun at the beginning with no noun that it refers back to?

4. Sidel uses material and quotations from interviews to support her points. What supporting evidence does she provide for the following statements?

These young women do not see themselves as playing supporting roles in someone else's life script; it is their own journeys they are planning. (paragraph 2)

A key message the New American Dreamers are both receiving and sending is one of optimism—the sense that they can do whatever they want with their lives. (paragraph 29)

How convincing is that evidence for you, the reader?

5. How accurate do you think Sidel's "prototype of today's young woman" is? Do you think she is speaking for all young women, or does she seem to you to focus her analysis on women of a certain economic status?

6. To what extent do you think both women and men experience a dichotomy between "public" and "domestic" roles?

WRITING ASSIGNMENTS

1. How do Sidel's findings compare with what you know from your family, friends, and acquaintances about how they view their opportunities and hopes for the future? Write an essay in which you discuss this question, and illustrate your ideas with reference to specific people and their experiences and views.

2. Sidel contends that "traditionally, the more exclusively male the activity, the more cultural value is attached to it" (paragraph 20). Write an essay in which you discuss that proposition, and argue for or against it. Your reader will need to know what examples Sidel uses to provide evidence of her opinion; in addition, let your reader know about examples from your own culture that support or refute her idea.

WOMAN ENOUGH

ERICA JONG

*Erica Jong, born in 1942, is the author of many books of poetry and of
novels, including* Fear of Flying *(1973) and* Fanny *(1980). She frequently writes articles about writers and writing. This poem appears in the
collection* Becoming Light *(1991).*

Because my grandmother's hours
were apple cakes baking,
& dust motes gathering,
& linens yellowing
& seams and hems   5
inevitably unraveling—
I almost never keep house—
though really I *like* houses
& wish I had a clean one.

Because my mother's minutes   10
were sucked into the roar
of the vacuum cleaner,
because she waltzed with the washer-dryer
& tore her hair waiting for repairmen—
I send out my laundry,   15
& live in a dusty house,
though really I *like* clean houses
as well as anyone.

I am woman enough   20
to love the kneading of bread
as much as the feel
of typewriter keys
under my fingers—
springy, springy.

& the smell of clean laundry 25
& simmering soup
are almost as dear to me
as the smell of paper and ink.

I wish there were not a choice;
I wish I could be two women. 30
I wish the days could be longer.
But they are short.
So I write while
the dust piles up.

I sit at my typewriter 35
remembering my grandmother
& all my mothers,
& the minutes they lost
loving houses better than themselves—
& the man I love cleans up the kitchen 40
grumbling only a little
because he knows
that after all these centuries
it is easier for him
than for me. 45

RESPONDING IN DISCUSSION OR WRITING

1. How do the contents of the poem explain to you what Jong means by the title "Woman Enough"?

2. Jong focuses on her grandmother and her mother. Why do you think she does that, and what effect does it have on the reader? What connections can you make with other selections you have read in this book?

3. *Considerations of Style.*   In the first stanza, three lines begin with "&." Does that repetition seem to you to be unfortunate, or does it serve a purpose? In what ways can the repetition be seen as contributing to the meaning?

4. Jong makes use of specific details to achieve an effect. How many specific details does she provide about a woman's activities, and what do they add to your understanding?

5. Not all poems contain a message about a social issue. Does this poem? If so, what is the social issue, and how would you rank its importance?

WRITING ASSIGNMENTS

1. Jong says: "I wish I could be two women." What does she mean by that? Do you ever wish you could be two people? Why? What details can you give about the two lives that will let readers see why these two people are important? Write an essay in which you discuss Jong's statement and its relevance to the lives of others.

2. Even though housework is not a common topic for poetry, Jong raises the issue of who does household chores and how meticulous one is about how clean the house is. Joan Rivers, the comedian, has said: "I hate housework! You make the beds, you do the dishes—and six months later you have to start all over again." In an essay, discuss why housework can be an issue in a poem. What makes it an issue that is worthy of poetic treatment? Is it more important for men or women? Why? Why does Jong say at the end of her poem "it is easier for him/than for me"?

Making Connections: Gender and Sexual Orientation

1. Refer to two child-rearing manuals, such as ones by Dr. Benjamin Spock or T. Berry Brazelton, and analyze in an essay what they say to parents about gender roles as they rear their children. Give examples of the opinions they express on gender roles and the advice they derive from what they have observed. Does one of the authors appear to give more useful advice than the other? If so, which one, and why do you think that?

2. Use a tape recorder to tape a conversation between a man and a woman (you'll need their permission first). Tape a few conversations until you find one that provides interesting material. Write an essay describing in detail what was said and how representative it was of the different sexes. If someone just saw a transcript, would it be clear which speaker was a man and which one a woman? Explain your opinion.

3. The articles by Buczynski and Kanner discuss masculinity and men's roles in society. Do you think that men should take more of an active role in family life? How do policies of companies make that difficult? What changes would need to be made in the working world for significant changes to occur in male participation in family life?

4. Do research in the library or through interviews to explore the traditional roles of men and women in at least three different cultures. Discuss the roles of both sexes in the home and the workplace and the roles they play in social and religious life.

5. In the first unit, the section from the book by Mary C. Waters discusses how people try to pass as a member of a different ethnic group in order to escape discrimination. Other types of "passing" occur, however. See one of the following motion pictures: *Tootsie, Yentl, Orlando, M. Butterfly, Mrs. Doubtfire,* or *The Crying Game,* and write an essay describing how it handles the theme of passing as someone of the opposite sex. What

does it present as the motives for the attempt to pass, and what are the results? What problems does passing cause for the protagonists? What is learned by the characters involved?

6. Find reviews of two films about attempts to pass as a member of the opposite sex, *Some Like It Hot* (1959) and *Victor/Victoria* (1982), and write an essay in which you compare and contrast reactions to these two films produced twenty-three years apart and comment on what the reactions reveal.

7. Collect advertisements from magazines or describe popular Hollywood movies, TV soap operas, comics, or magazines, and analyze the ways in which men and women are portrayed in terms of who appears to be in charge and what kinds of roles they fill. Are idealized forms presented? What seems to make up "masculinity" and "femininity"? How would you define the features of the terms "masculinity" and "femininity" as they are presented in the material you examine?

8. Writers sometimes adopt the name of someone of the opposite sex. Discuss two writers who have done this (for example, George Sand, George Eliot, Isak Dinesen, or Currer Bell). Compare and contrast their circumstances and why it was important for them to adopt a pseudonym.

9. Rosemary Mahoney's essay asks the question "What Are You?" Write an essay in which you tell a reader about what Mahoney means by the question and how she develops her point, and then discuss how the readings in this unit have added to your understanding of the ramifications of that question.

10. Heilbrun says, "We can only retell and live by the stories we have read or heard. We live our lives through texts" (paragraph 8). Consider the selections by Gould and Sidel, and write an essay about how that idea can be illuminated by the stories they tell.

Ethnic Affiliation
and Class

It is a great shock at the age of five or six to find that in a world of Gary Coopers you are the Indian.

—JAMES BALDWIN, *speech at the Cambridge Union, England, 1965*

I have a dream that my four little children will one day live in a nation where they will not be judged by the color of their skin but by the content of their character.

—MARTIN LUTHER KING, JR. *speech at civil rights demonstration, Washington, D.C., 1963*

Ethnic Affiliation and Class

❖

Oɴʟʏ ᴛʜᴇ Nᴀᴛɪᴠᴇ Aᴍᴇʀɪᴄᴀɴs have lived on the North American continent since the time of its "discovery" by the rest of the world. All other residents came from elsewhere. So it is that most people claim affiliation to one or other of the ethnic groups that make up the culture: Italian American, African American, Chinese American, and so on. Yet the concept of what it is to be *ethnic* is a slippery one. Does ethnicity conflict with nationality? Is a person's primary affiliation with a nation or with an ethnic group? Who is usually called ethnic? Who can claim to be ethnic?

"Are we ethnic?"

Drawing by Wm. Hamilton; ©1972 The New Yorker Magazine, Inc.

As the cartoon suggests, the word *ethnic* is frequently applied only to minorities or working men and women of low socioeconomic status. The concept of ethnicity thus becomes linked to class. Ethnic affiliation is something common to everyone, however, and this is being recognized more and more. People routinely identify themselves as Irish American, Japanese American, French Canadian, Mexican American, and so forth. When Americans or Canadians are asked where they are from, they are as likely to say Taiwan or France as Kansas or Saskatchewan. Ethnicity adds a dimension to one's affiliation to a nation and is not necessarily linked to one's amount of money or status.

Our feeling of attachment to a particular ethnic group often forms a large part of our identity. Feelings of community and familiarity with others give us a sense of belonging. We have a group out there that is "like us," that has experienced what we have experienced, that knows and likes the same food or holiday traditions as we do. While physical characteristics (skin color, voice, facial features) may sometimes help identify us to others as belonging to a specific race and having a particular ethnic affiliation, our family heritage, customs, religion, and beliefs also contribute to our own sense of belonging to an ethnic culture.

Our choice of affiliation aligns us with a cultural group. We feel included in that group. The other side of inclusion is exclusion, however, and it is ethnic affiliation almost more than any other association that is perceived as being responsible for either our inclusion in or exclusion from social and political institutions and functions. Indeed, much of the strife in the world begins with intolerance toward those who are different from ourselves. Wars are fought over ethnic background and territorial rights. Social problems occur because of a lack of tolerance for those who are poorer than we are or who have a different ethnic affiliation or a different skin color. Affiliation to an ethnic group can be a source of social stratification, stereotyping, deprivation, prejudice, and oppression, as many have described in their writings. It is also a source of enormous pride and untold achievement, the foundation of the diversity celebrated as the mark of freedom in North America.

The readings in this unit explore ethnic affiliation and class from many different experiences and points of view. What role does ethnic affiliation play in shaping the identity of someone from parents of different background, different race, different color? Articles by Lisa Jones and Dexter Jeffries explore that question. How do the privileged and powerful view their ethnic heritage? Lang Phipps satirically describes the world of WASP (White Anglo-Saxon Protestant) privilege.

What role does ethnic affiliation play for those who have historically been seen as underprivileged minorities, fighting for survival and recognition? David J. Gordon explores his Jewish identity by reminiscing about his rabbi father; Lawrence Otis Graham reports his observations of racial discrimination when he switches temporarily from being a highly paid lawyer to working as a busboy at a country club. The feminist perspective on being both an ethnic minority and a woman is presented in essays by Gloria Anzaldúa and Anna Lisa Raya. A story by Lucy Honig shows a Guatemalan woman's awareness of her ethnic affiliation and poverty even as she is presented with an award by the Mayor of New York City. The unit ends with Aurora Levins Morales' autobiographical poem, a celebration of the writer's survival.

STARTING POINTS [FOR JOURNAL OR FREEWRITING]

As you begin to reflect on the role that race and class play in the formation of identity, respond in writing to the following questions.

1. What seem to you to be the distinguishing characteristics of the ethnic group to which you have the closest affiliation? How important is it to you to feel that you are a member of an ethnic group? Have you ever been a victim of ethnic stereotyping or prejudice? Recall exactly what happened.

2. What are the positive and negative connotations of the word *ethnic*?

3. What problems or privileges are the children of multiracial marriages likely to face? Or adopted children of a race different from their adoptive parents?

4. Which events in history have been characterized by conflict among people of different ethnic backgrounds? Which one of these events do you know the most about?

MAMA'S WHITE

LISA JONES

Lisa Jones was born in 1961, the daughter of poet/playwright Imamu Amiri Baraka (who was born LeRoi Jones) and Hettie Jones. She is the author of many articles and several books, notably Bulletproof Diva: Tales of Race, Sex, and Hair *(1994), in which a modified version of this article appeared. This article was originally published in* The Village Voice *on May 18, 1993. Lisa Jones writes a regular column for* The Village Voice *titled "Skin Trade," on the politics of fashion for African American women. She has also cowritten companion books to two Spike Lee films:* Do the Right Thing *and* Mo' Better Blues.

JUST ANOTHER RAINBOW BABY on the IRT, that's me, handing out flyers modeled after Adrian Piper's seminal art piece, "My Calling (Card) #1" (1986):

Dear Fellow Straphanger:

My mother is white. And I, as you may or may not have figured out, am black. This is how I choose to define myself and this is how America chooses to define me. I have no regrets about my racial classification other than to lament, off and on, that classifications exist period.

Actually, the mystery of my background is really not much of a mystery at all, despite those taboo-love-child stories you read in *People* or *Jet*. If you boned up on your world history, you'd know that unions between people of different racial classifications, such as my (white) mother and my (black) father, are not a recent phenomenon. Entire countries in South America are peopled by the offspring of such relationships. Even our own country is more of a creole outpost than we are ready to acknowledge.

Are you still staring? Let me guess. My white mother presents a different set of enigmas to you based on your own racial classification. Those of you who are black might find "evidence" of my white parent reason to question my racial allegiance. For those of you who are white, evidence of my white lineage might move you to voice deep-seated feelings of racial superiority. You might wonder why I would choose to identify as "fully" black when I have the "saving grace" of a white parent. I have no time for this sort of provinciality either. I realize both sets of responses display an ignorance of our shared cultural and racial history as Americans.

I'm sorry you're still staring. If you care to, I'll gladly engage 5 you in a lengthy conversation about this subject at another time. But right now I'm having just another "attitudinous"-black-girl day on the IRT, and if you keep staring, I'll just stare right back. I regret any discomfort my presence is causing you. Just as I'm sure you regret the discomfort your ignorance is causing me.

Yours (More Truly Than You Think),
L.J.

This is the story of Emily Sohmer Tai and Hettie Jones, two women who don't know each other and whose only connection is the melanin count of their skin.

Recently, Emily Sohmer Tai, who describes herself as the "white female half of an interracial marriage," wrote a letter to *The Village Voice*. The letter is worth returning to as an example of the closeted superiority trip I mentioned. And what I mean by superiority trip is the type of thinking that assigns whiteness highest value (and upholds white people as the only viable arbiters of experience), though this thinking may at times be draped in the gauze of liberalism.

I had written a sentimental tribute to my 65-year-old Aunt Cora for a series the paper ran for black history month. In one section I recount my aunt's visit to Minneapolis, where I was living at the time, her brushes with racism there, and her reaction to the large number of white female–black male couples that coexist there alongside this racism. I sized up these couples as "Debbies curled up with Sam"—to allude to the lady-stud legend that burdens them and, at the same time, to pry it apart. I was sure to note, in the same breath, that if one Debbie hadn't curled up with one Sam, I wouldn't be around. Clearly I was saying that these duos tangle up my emotions; I look at them as a child of an interracial marriage, but also as a black woman who has witnessed the market value put on white femininity.

Tai seems to have got stuck on one word, "Debbie," and looked   10
no further. Her letter responds to my entire article as if it were
merely a personal attack on her and other white women in interracial relationships. Tai never once mentions my aunt. In effect,
she completely erases Cora's story. What I got from this is that
there is nothing I could say about my aunt, her amazing life, and
our feelings as black women about interracial relationships—
some shared, some not—that could be as important as Tai's outrage as a white woman measuring herself against a stereotype.
Nothing, simply, was as worthy of readers' consideration as Tai's
story, Tai's version of history.

There's a shrillness to Tai's letter, and it seems to come from
the fact that I don't accept her view of what interracial identity
means. To her, it's a haven from racialized society; to me, it's not.
Tai rather smugly assumes that this safe house is indeed something I have a political or aesthetic interest in embracing. I've
been called "nigger bitch" more than once in my life, and I wonder if Tai would advise that I handle it by shouting back.
"Actually, guys, my mom's white, so call me half-white bitch, or
how about mongrel bitch, since it's better rhythmically?"

Left unsaid, but lurking in the margins of Tai's letter, is this
amazement that I, as a woman, would claim *black* over *interracial* or
white. The implication being that choosing black was somehow a
settlement, a compromise following a personal identity crisis
(another assumption whites often make), and not a much larger
cultural-historical calling or even just sheer love, romance, and
respect for blackness (in all its permutations), for better or for
worse, amen. Would Tai's mouth hang open if I told her my
story? That, among others, it was my (white) mother who raised
me to think politically about being a black woman.

Could Tai picture this complexity as well?—That I'm a black
writer whose work is dedicated to exploring the hybridity of
African American culture and of American culture in general.
That I don't deny my white forebears, but I call myself African
American, which means, to me, a person of African and Native
American, Latin, or European descent. That I feel comfortable
and historically grounded in this identity. That I find family there,
whereas no white people have embraced me with their culture,
have said to me, take this gift, it's yours and we are yours, no problem. And that, by claiming African American and black, I also

inherit a right to ask questions about what this identity means. And that, chances are, this identity will never be static, which is fine by me.

Tai's reaction to this "racial persona" of mine is nothing I haven't come across before. White women in particular have trouble seeing my black identity as anything other than a rebuff of my mother. Deep down I wonder if what they have difficulty picturing is this: not that I could reject, in their minds, my own mother, but that I have no desire to be *them*.

Friends of mine who are also rainbow babies have had similar run-ins, and sometimes we sit around and compare notes. We're not disinterested in our white "heritage," even though most of us don't know our white relatives (apart from the parent who raised us), or we were given up for adoption by a white biological parent and have never had white family. In my own case, my mother's parents, first-generation American Jews, disowned her for marrying black. When she announced she was pregnant, they begged her to have an abortion. On hearing that in her third year of marriage my mother was pregnant with a second child, they again begged her to abort.

We of the rainbow persuasion joke about whites' inability to imagine why we would want to see ourselves as people of color and as African Americans; how connected this makes us feel. What could they possibly think is "in it" for us to be white people? Would it extend refuge or protection, provide moral directive? If it helped us get better jobs and higher salaries, would it offer spiritual community? Would it bring us family?

Forget everything that the Emily Sohmer Tai example tells you about race, and meet Hettie Jones, author, poet, teacher, and my mother. Her memoir, *How I Became Hettie Jones*, revisits her life as a woman among the Beats as the starched-collar 1950s gave way to the guns-and-roses 1960s. It also tells of her marriage to my father, writer Amiri Baraka, and her own coming of age as a writer. If you want to know more, the book is in paperback. I will share this: The most dreadfully cute fact about my mother is that she has taken to checking "Other" on her census form. In the line slotted for explanation she writes, in her flowery longhand, "Semitic American mother of black children."

My mother is my mother, and I'm very protective of her and of our relationship. I find myself in this amusing little bind at times, which reminds me over and over that what I am, I guess, for lack of a more sexy and historically complex word, is a humanist. This is the bind of explaining that my mother is white, though I am black, then getting pissed when people reduce dear Mom to the calling card of "your white mother." Negotiating all this continues to be one of the challenges of my intellectual life. I'll crib from Greg Tate on this one: "The world isn't black and white, it just feels that way sometimes."

I owe Mom a couple of solids. One for being strong enough in her own self to let me be who I was gonna be. Being the sister/girlfriend/black woman individual that I take so much pride in being actually brings me closer to my (white) mom. This identity gives me a stronger sense of history and self, and I can come to my mother as what the New Age folks might call a "fully realized person." If I called myself "interracial" (in my mind, and I do know others see this differently), I would need her presence, her "whiteness," to somehow validate my "half-whiteness."

Another solid. Mom's a bohemian from way back. The journey 20 she's made as a woman, as an artist, making herself up in America, has been useful to me as a black woman living outside of society's usual paradigms of femininity. Mom knew that we—my sister and I—needed black female relatives and role models, and she made sure these ties were in place. She never tried to substitute for these; what she gave instead was her own DNA, her own boho Mama in the black stockings self, and she trusted that this would be enough.

Solid number three. My mother, more than anyone I know, has taught me difference as pleasure. Not as something feared or exotic, but difference as one of the rich facts of one's life, a truism that gives you more data, more power, and more flavor. These are the sort of things you needed to get by: a black South Carolinian grandfather who did the Moon Walk before Michael Jackson (though he called it the Camel Walk), a mother who speaks Yiddish and jazz, a Caribbean boyfriend to make you rice and peas, and a sister who's a Latin American art scholar so you won't lapse into thinking you're God's gift to all knowledge as an American Negro.

Today my mother is in town from Wyoming, where she's teaching for a stint. We hug, I cook her tofu and collard greens, we swap clothes, watch TV evangelism for a goof. We talk about race as the world places it on us. We argue sometimes, but we don't stumble on it. When our generational differences make themselves felt in how we see the world and race, it doesn't butt against our love, our trust.

I've got my pad and pen out and she's laughing at my official-ness. So, Mom, not *how*, but *why* did you become Hettie Jones?

"After the breakup of my marriage," she explains, "people asked me why I didn't change my name, why I didn't, quote, 'go back to the Jews.' There was no going back to something that denied you."

And why was it important to you that we be black and not "biracial"?   25

"I was not about to delude you guys into thinking you could be anything different in this country. And, frankly, I didn't think that being anything other than black would be any more desirable."

Mom, what you say in the book about black people's anger in the '60s being necessary to America, how did you come to this?

"Some people think that I'm dishonest and that I'm a martyr for saying that, but there's a certain time in your life if you're a white person and you have black children that you have to see that the world is ready to take them on. I love my children and I just sensed that the world had to go through this period in order for it to be a better place for them."

Motherhood has always been more than a domestic chore or emotional bond for my mother. It's a political vocation—one she's taken seriously enough to go up against the world for. And she's always been ready to testify about how her children and blackness have broadened her own life. In the music—the jazz, blues, language—she found her own.

Mom's headed back to Wyoming. The cab driver offers to put   30
her backpack in the trunk. "May I take your parachute?" he asks. People of all ages and backgrounds say fetching things like this to my mother. She's led, as she wrote once, a "charmed life in the middle of other people's wars," and it comes through in her smile. When Mom sends the mojo his way, the cab driver lights up like New Year's Eve on Forty-Deuce. I'm reminded, right then,

that there is no place that I'm ever gonna go (by way of geography or ideology) where I can't bring my mother, and where I can't bring myself, which she has in large part made possible. And, as Adrian Piper would have me ask, what are all you—black and white—gonna do about that?

RESPONDING IN DISCUSSION OR WRITING

1. Lisa Jones begins her article with a flyer designed to be handed out to passengers on a New York City subway train. If you were a passenger, how would you react to having this flyer put into your hand? What do you think is the purpose of the flyer, and what is Jones's purpose in beginning her essay with this?

2. What is Jones's purpose in devoting a large part of the article to Emily Sohmer Tai and Hettie Jones? What do they represent for her? Why does she want her readers to know about these two women? How does describing them serve Jones's purpose as a writer?

3. Jones takes a stand against Tai in that she does not accept "her view of what interracial identity means." How do the two women differ on this issue?

4. *Considerations of Style.*   How would you describe the tone of this article? Make a list of the adjectives you would use to describe the article to somebody who hadn't read it. Find a sentence in the article that will support each adjective you choose.

5. Jones tells her readers how her white mother raised her "to think politically about being a black woman" (paragraph 12). What do you think that raising process involves?

6. Twice in her article, Jones refers to a "calling card" (paragraphs 1 and 18). What effect does this image of the calling card have? Is the image effective?

WRITING ASSIGNMENTS

1. Jones devotes a large part of her essay to explaining reasons why she chooses the definition "black" over "white," positive reasons, not a "settlement" or a "compromise." In an essay, describe what reasons she gives and discuss how you stand in relation to the position she takes. What would you do in her place? Why?

2. *Considerations of Style.* Jones divides her article into three parts: the flyer, the incident with Tai, and a description of her mother. How are these parts connected? Do they build on each other, or do they each move to a new point? Which part do you think makes the strongest statement, and which one do you think fulfills Jones's purpose most effectively?

WHO I AM

DEXTER JEFFRIES

Dexter Jeffries, born in 1953 in Queens, New York, has taught English at Borough of Manhattan Community College for eight years. Before that he drove a taxi for many years. He is a writer and filmmaker as well as a teacher and has just completed a documentary film about jazz and its influence on poetry and film in the 1930s and 1940s. The following article appeared in Present Tense *in August 1988.*

IT IS A COMMON practice to look back at one's life and search for some thread, some theme that has run through it. For me, fortunately or unfortunately, color is the cord that ties up most of my life's successes, failures and contradictions. When Thoreau stumbled upon the gravestone of a slave, he ruminated on the words "a man of color" and remarked to himself, "As though he were discolored." That is how America has always made me feel: discolored. American ambivalence about color has followed me wherever I have traveled. That ambivalence—and my attempts to cope with it—have formed a major part of my life. Yet I feel that I am a richer person for this struggle, a better teacher, writer and friend because of it.

I grew up in the 1950s in a neighborhood with an idyllic name, Springfield Gardens, a small neighborhood in the southeastern section of the borough of Queens in New York City. It is provincial now, and it was provincial 30 years ago. At that time, it was considered a suburban haven for second-generation immigrants from the tenements of Manhattan. The population was a mixture of Italians and Irish, most of whom were blue-collar workers. My father was a lithographer and my mother worked as an executive secretary in a law firm. My parents did not exactly view Springfield Gardens as a sanctuary; it was their second choice. They were learning to settle for second choice with the inevitable consequences: anger, frustration, despair.

My parents, who were married in 1936 and remained so until my father's death in 1977, always had difficulty in finding suitable housing. They were an interracial couple, a real anomaly for their times. My father was a black from Virginia, and my mother was the daughter of Russian Jews from Odessa. They suffered. America was a nation of apartheid in the 1930s. Separate facilities in all areas of society were common. Practically everything worked to keep them apart. When they lived in Washington, D.C., for instance, whenever they attended the movies, my father would have to sit in the balcony, which was for "Colored Only," while my mother sat down in the orchestra. They endured.

I have often wondered about the source of their courage and strength. Many of my peers, black and white, have suggested that even now, in the 1980s, they would not venture into an interracial relationship because of the inevitable psychological hardships, particularly raising the children of such a union. They are frightened. So were my parents, but something told them, back in the 1930s, that Jim Crow would not remain a permanent facet of American life. They believed that the world could be built anew. My parents were Communists; they had an ideology, a political agenda, a gospel that inspired them with the conviction required for an epic journey.

By 1953 they had become accustomed to following a certain pattern whenever there was a search for housing. My mother would venture forth alone and hope to find something within their means. She would make no mention of my father's being black, relying on her intuition as to whether a landlord or real estate agent harbored prejudice against an interracial couple. My father remained behind rather than be humiliated. He was humiliated anyway. He said to me in later years, "What kind of man allows his wife to look for an apartment or house?" I said nothing.

My parents did what they could to resist the general climate of racism and even hoped to share in the popular American dream of moving into Levittown, on Long Island. My father was a veteran of the United States Army Air Corps and had fought in the Pacific in World War II. (When I asked him what it was like fighting the Japanese, he would always say, "The Japs weren't the problem. We were busy fighting with the white guys in our outfit.") And as a G.I., he was eligible for a number of benefits, one of them being a low-interest mortgage on a house with no down payment in places such as Levittown. I remember that my mother took the Long Island Rail Road to this new suburban experiment, that she filled out the necessary papers and that everything looked promising—until my father showed up for the final signing of the contract. At that point, they were informed that Levittown—built with a good deal of Federal money—had restrictive covenants and was to be a segregated community.

My parents despaired nightly at the dinner table. Exposed to these harsh realities early, my sister, Elizabeth, my brother, Gregory, and I quickly became aware of our place in society. We were not wanted. We were not desirable. The problem was compounded by our not being dark enough to be taken as Negro nor light enough to be accepted as white. To this day, people are still confused by my appearance. Students at the college where I teach have asked about my identity. Am I black? White? Am I Hispanic? Because of the recent influx of new immigrants, the guesses are sometimes more exotic. Am I Egyptian? Am I Iranian? No one ever enunciates what I would really like to hear: human, *homo erectus,* a member of the species, just like you.

As an adult, I am politely asked questions. As youngsters, my sister, brother and I were usually expected to behave in a manner consistent with how we were perceived. If people thought we were white, we were expected to act "white." If neighbors suggested that we were black, we were expected to act "black." We all made feeble attempts at dealing with a society that thrives on racial and ethnic identification. My sister suffered the most because she was the oldest and therefore born a bit too soon as far as American history was concerned.

To the historian, history is a chain of events that only make sense when they are placed in a particular order, in line with a certain theme that is interwoven throughout an arbitrary number of years. History is more than this. History is alive, and it affects the people who live through it. Events are connected when they are examined from the perspective of the individual. The eradication of racism in America is an ongoing process that stems from the early days of the abolitionist movement in the 19th century.

I was born eight years after my sister, and there were some events that occurred that perceptibly changed the general social climate of race relations in the United States and the course of our lives. In 1947, Jackie Robinson joined the Brooklyn Dodgers and sports would never be the same. In 1948, the Armed Forces of the United States were integrated, and millions of volunteers and draftees were exposed to the idea of blacks and whites working together. Finally, in 1954, *Brown v. Topeka* was a phrase on the lips of many people who lived thousands of miles from Kansas. These events made a difference.

My sister grew up while these events were in the making. By the time I was born, their reverberations could be felt throughout the nation. But she was to suffer more racial discrimination and hatred than I. And as a consequence, she was hostile and bitter and had a potential for self-destruction. By the time my sister reached her adolescence, she had been so traumatized by growing up in a world of hate, fear and misunderstanding that my mother decided that therapy and a less hostile environment were the only answer. As a child, I vaguely remember my sister going away and my not knowing where she was. My parents never told me, but I figured it out in later years.

I have followed my sister's career as an itinerant artist, student and writer. She knew what it would mean to stay in a country that preached equality but rarely applied it. So, following the path of Richard Wright and James Baldwin, Elizabeth became an expatriate, living for years in Europe and Mexico. To me, at the age of 10, my sister seemed heroic as she left New York in the early 1960s with a pack on her back, a Ginsbergian figure fleeing a contaminated world. I now realize that Elizabeth had problems other than race; yet I also know that these continuing problems have been exacerbated by the anguish of being "colored" and "not colored" at the same time.

My brother was not born at the right time in history either. He felt the full brunt of discrimination as he was not permitted ever to become a part of the youthful male community of Springfield

Gardens. Whether it was Little League, Davy Crockett and the Alamo, Boy Scouts or after-school activities, he was always aware that something was wrong. Some children are too fat, too skinny, too short or too tall. You can also be too dark. One of the confounding problems of this situation is the realization that the bearer of this problem can do nothing about it. When I look at my brother, I see that not fitting into a peer group at an important age can leave one desolate. Gregory's reaction was not as drastic as my sister's, but it was certainly negative. My brother was a James Dean–like figure. Had he been thought of as white, he might have been seen as having normal growing pains—mistakes, corrections and adjustment. However, Springfield Gardens was not quite prepared then for a black rebel, and instead, my brother developed into a maladjusted young man: "Juvenile delinquent" was the sociological label of the 1950s. He entered a world of petty crime that he has never really been able to escape. In the 1960s, my brother was to become one of the first casualties of the drug revolution. Since that time, he has followed a heartbreaking trail from one institution to another: drug rehabilitation programs and prison.

Things had begun to change by the middle and late 1950s. Certain progressive ideals and notions had started to take hold. There were small and evolving changes, but they assuaged the rage and mistrust between whites and blacks just enough so that I did not have to suffer all of the racial indignities that my brother and sister were forced to brave. It might have been the elementary school teacher who acknowledged Negro History Week in the class and spoke about Paul Robeson, Negro soldiers in the Civil War and Dr. Ralph Bunche. Or it could have been a young white boy who uttered words evocative of a heroic Huck Finn, "Ah, let the colored guy play. They're pretty good sometimes." These were events that would never enter a history text, but they changed my present and future.

However, for the most part, I was a bit befuddled as a youngster, since my parents had never prepared me for—nor could they foresee—the problems I would meet. I loved them, of course, and I did not see them as black or white. They were my mother and father. The issue of race did arise, but it was always in a positive historical and social vein. My father would become rhapsodic as he spoke about his heroes, Paul Robeson, Duke

Ellington, Alexandre Dumas, Pushkin and Charlie Parker. My mother was also well versed in Afro-American history. Elizabeth, Gregory and I now know that the education we received from our parents about Negro history was more comprehensive than any book written or documentary produced by the late 1960s, when black awareness became a facet of American culture.

I remember loving school and very earnestly digesting everything that was dished out. One day, a neighbor asked me what I was. In kindergarten I had just learned about the Pilgrims (I loved making those hats), and I replied quickly, with all the confidence and innocence of that age, "I'm an Englishman." That was the last time I ever answered that question so quickly and unwittingly. With just as much confidence and a trace of contempt, this blond Irishwoman said, "Ah, no. You're a little Puerto Rican or maybe colored." It was on that day that the "veil," as W.E.B. Du Bois labeled it, was cast over me. I have never forgotten it. Du Bois also wrote: "The problem of the twentieth century is the problem of the color line." It is. Howard Beach. South Ozone Park. Canarsie. Michael Stewart.

As I grew older, I developed a dualistic view of the world. I viewed things literally in black and white. People were quick to label me, and I spent a great deal of time and energy attempting to live out their visions. This manner of existence would make life bearable for two or three months, but the inevitable would always occur: a joke about niggers or a frenetic speech about the cheapness of Jews in which the speaker demonstrated that, in the American black ghetto, the Jew was supposedly the cause of all the misery. These insults caused a physical reaction. I would feel faint for a few moments as I realized that the person whom I had befriended had betrayed me. The friends with whom I had eaten hamburgers, played ball and shared the intimate moments of growing up had torn me asunder. With clenched fists, I wept.

Because I had my secret and extraordinary vantage point— black and Jewish—one that allowed me access to the inner recesses of whites and blacks, there was a part of me that felt the jokes I heard were actually on the people who told them. They had taken me into their confidence and believed that I was just like them, black or white. And perhaps I was the one who was the betrayer of trust and faith, for I listened and never said a word. I listened to whites assault blacks and remained silent. Blacks heaped invective upon whites, usually selecting Jews as the specific enemy, and I listened and nodded my head. During the 1960s, I had a front-row seat on one of the most momentous social struggles in America, but the price of the ticket left me reeling. Every derogatory remark about blacks left me weaker. Every anti-Semitic remark left me sadder.

But wearing a mask, being a spy in the enemy's camp, also made me intensely paranoid. I was constantly worried that my fraudulent behavior would be discovered, yet I managed to hide it from my family. I did a lot of thinking. I was invariably in a quandary about what to do if someone wished to visit me at home. This almost always involved the logistical shifting of one parent or both out of the house or an awkward last-minute cancellation of an appointment. And I was wary and cunning. No matter what group I was currently holding favor with, I had to keep myself under control constantly in order not to blurt out, "Jews don't own the banks. That's a myth." Or "How can you say a black person is lazier than a white? What do you base that on?"

Repressing these responses and the pain that went along with them ate away at my soul. How long can a man, a young man at that, live a lie? These people hate a part of me, I would think, and if they really knew . . . I sometimes toyed with that idea. Tell them. Don't hide. Just tell them the truth and see what they say. I am ashamed to say that impotence and paralysis prevented me from taking such action for most of my life. It is difficult to discard love and affection even if it is tainted, to surrender friendship and its bonds for principles when you are confused about the principles yourselves.

I searched for simplistic solutions. I tried to be "white" for six months. I ended up hating all white people. I tried being "black" for a similar span of time and ended up hating blacks just as much as whites. To be a Jew had a specific meaning to me, something different from just being white. There were a lot of rules that had to be obeyed and followed. Anyone can be white. I tried to be Jewish and failed at that also. When I was in my late teens, the remedy became clear. Be nothing. Identify with no one and no group. When I was asked about my racial background, I informed people that I was nothing: "Nothing. I'm just nothing."

People reacted in their own peculiar way to me. They were silent.
I brooded.

During high school, I became a secretive and withdrawn person
in dealing with this issue. I made few friends and avoided the
topic of race. I felt that I possessed something of a strange and
forbidding nature. I fantasized about meeting people who were
like myself, racially mixed or others who were not concerned with
racial identity. I spent countless hours imagining how things
should be. In conjunction with these feelings of anxiety and
apprehension, there was an incredible desire to talk to someone
and tell that person about my inner turmoil. By the 10th grade, I
had decided to search for this particular someone actively.

In the fall of 1968, I met an English teacher, Paul Golden. He
was a young teacher and displayed a particular sensitivity when we
read novels, plays or poems. I wondered if he would be just as perceptive if I were to disclose my numerous and troublesome
thoughts. I made a decision that somehow I had to approach him.
I was completely bewildered as to how to speak to an adult, a
teacher. I was terrified of all the possible negative reactions. He
could have summarily brushed me aside. He could have politely
informed me that I had made a mistake in approaching him and
that as a teacher it was not within his province to act as a counselor. I was scared.

Near the end of the semester he assigned a composition entitled "The American Dream." I wrote with all the conviction that I
possessed about my American dream, a place where a person like
me could live with dignity and pride, a place where I would not
have to live an underground existence. I was tired of being an
invisible man. I prayed. I prayed that he would receive my message. I hoped that when he graded the essays he would hear my
plea for understanding and compassion. I did not believe in God,
but I still prayed. My parents' political beliefs were strong ones,
and they always felt that if there was to be a solution to the problem of race in America, it would be political, social and economic,
not religious. I still prayed. My God was neither the Christian God
nor the Jewish God. He came to the aid of everybody and anybody
who was persecuted by a harsh world afflicted with injustice. He
was a witness with a vivid memory. My God would always remember the look on the small Jewish boy's face as he was herded out
of the Warsaw ghetto by an arrogant Nazi infantryman. He saw

the Negro battered by Bull Connor's deputies with clubs, then set upon by German shepherds. And he saw me, not every day, but on special days when the brutality that I was subjected to bordered on the absurd, harassed by militant blacks in the morning because I was too light-skinned to be accepted by them and then hit with a slingshot by some white ruffians for being a "nigger" in the afternoon. He listened.

Paul Golden heard my story and empathized with me. He did not turn away, and we ended up becoming friends. We spent many an afternoon walking around the athletic field behind Springfield Gardens High School talking about blacks, Jews and what I was supposed to be. I felt better just because I had finally found an outlet for my feelings of rage and fear. He hinted at a resolution that I was a bit too immature or too inexperienced to take up at the time, but it did provide some direction: I would somehow just have to be me.

By college, where social relationships have the potential to play such a major role in one's life, I realized that a human being could survive this sort of misery for only a limited time. A crisis brought on a final scream for help. I was dating a Greek girl at Queens College. She had met my family on numerous occasions, but I noticed that this exchange was not reciprocal. One night, just out of curiosity, I asked her why she had never invited me to her house. She avoided the question. I should have known. I pushed hard for an answer. She burst into tears. After she cried for a while, we hugged and then she said, "Dexter, my mom said it's all right to bring anyone home, anyone. Jewish, Italian, Irish, anyone. She said I can bring any boy home as long as he's not colored."

This event forced me into therapy. I had intentionally avoided this one possibility of help. Therapy was a strange and mysterious process that my father had attacked for years. He ridiculed my mother for going and mocked my brother and sister for their weekly visits. I felt a certain allegiance to my father, and I automatically surrendered any degree of autonomy I could have in his presence. I was loyal to him at all costs, right or wrong. Consequently, I had joined him and attacked my brother for being "crazy." When I finally went to the therapist at Queens

College, I was possessed by a certain fear and loathing. I was ashamed and embarrassed. I made a pledge never to allow my father to know that I was in therapy. He went to his grave without that knowledge. Whenever he, or anyone else for that matter, asked why I was never available Friday afternoons, I lied and said that I was working in the library.

Lying: That's how I spent my first six months in therapy. It was a waste of valuable time and energy, but I imagined it was the normal course of affairs, particularly for someone who had already lived a lie. I walked into the office. The therapist, a middle-aged woman, asked me what I would like to accomplish, talk about or discuss. I said, with dispatch and confidence in my voice, "I have this problem, something to do with identity. I'm sure you've handled many cases like it." (I had prepared a speech.) "It is a little unusual, but I'm sure if you take some time and do some research, you'll find the answer. You see, I have a black father and a white mother and have had a difficult time finding myself, who I am, what I am. Can you help me with this? How long do you think it will take? A few weeks? A month? What do you think?"

Dr. Hannah Sallinger smiled at me, leaned back in her chair, and said, "Well, it's good that you know what you want to talk about, but do you really think that I should do all the work, read the books, go to the library, research articles? What will you do? Don't you think we could solve your problem a little more quickly if we worked together, like a team, same goals?" Yes, I was to find out that we would work together, a lot of work, many discoveries, exploring, crying, reflecting and mourning. It's a long story with so many different facets and anecdotes, but there is one incident that stands out not just as a paradigm of the workings of therapy but also as a representation of my conflicted views of the world.

Some time in the first year, I became angry at Dr. Sallinger, perhaps because the psychological excavations that we were conducting together were finding too much grist, too much evidence of the sad life I had led. I developed a new strategy and attacked her. My overall plan was to prove that she was a racist and that all the therapy was distorted just on the basis of her being white. It was the early 1970s, and black militancy was still popular on American colleges. Black militants had dominated certain college campuses with their rhetoric, which always seemed to revolve around forcing white people, most of whom were completely innocent of the many petty intrigues that were being foisted upon them, to bear the burden and subsequent guilt for every act of racial injustice committed in American history since the landing of the first 19 African slaves at Jamestown, Virginia, in 1619. I too was a victim of this distorted ideology. It possessed a certain delicious appeal when the alternative was hard work, honesty and a constant struggle to uphold one's integrity under trying conditions. If I could uncover or detect some evidence of racism on the part of an authority figure, Dr. Sallinger, this would discredit and invalidate all of this person's work, findings and profound insights into my life.

I started to do a little research myself. From the listing in the back of the college catalog, I found out that Dr. Sallinger had completed her degree at the University of Maryland in the 1950s. The University of Maryland was segregated at the time. There was my evidence. This is what I had been waiting for, the triumph of client over therapist. It wasn't much, but a desperate person does not require that much concrete evidence to convict someone whom he has already found guilty in his heart. I walked into her office the following Friday, swaggering, plopped myself down in the chair, folded my arms across my chest and smiled. She was aware that something was up, but she allowed me to see my fantasy through to its conclusion.

I commenced a barrage: "Dr. Sallinger, you never talk about your college days too much. How was it? Did you meet a lot of black people then?" She shook her head and said, "I get the feeling you found out that I attended the University of Maryland, and yes, you're right. It was segregated while I was there. Segregation always made me feel uncomfortable. I doubt if this is a satisfactory answer, but what special meaning does all of this information have for you?"

I quickly explained that her having gone to a segregated college demonstrated a certain racist sensibility and insensitivity on the part of her family and herself and that it was obvious that she would have a difficult time really understanding a black person's point of view. I should have worded it differently and said a half-black person's point of view, but I was so mixed up at the time I was never quite sure how much I was of anything. Finally, I informed her that her having had absolutely no contact with black people would prevent her from comprehending any of my problems. At this point, and it was probably the only time she lost her objectivity, she leaned forward, gave me a stern look and said, "I want you to know that my father spent his entire academic career at Howard University, teaching black students at an all-black school. Does that pass your test? Now, are you going to keep on wasting this hour or are we going to do some serious work today?"

From that day, I kept on the main track with only some minor digressions. She helped me understand who I was, from a human point of view. And when it comes down to it, race is not human; it's an artificial categorization employed to justify what is inherently human: weakness, fear, diffidence and timidity. By focusing on the human side—my family, my relationships with my father, mother, brother and sister—I was able to make some substantial progress in consolidating a genuine identity.

In addition, there were other cures that worked in conjunction with therapy and helped bring about my emancipation: friends, my fellow soldiers when I was in the Army, lovers, radical politics, jazz and literature. It was in the last years of high school and then during college that I discovered books. It was on pages with words composed by Camus, Wright, Woolf, Kesey, Kafka, Ellison and Dostoyevski that a voice sounded like my voice. I embraced fictional characters as I watched them confront a world similar to mine, no matter if they were white, black, insane, women or Russian. Books made me feel whole and instilled in me a feeling that I was part of something much larger and more important than Queens, than being white, black or even American. No matter what shape or form the writer's pronouncement took, the message was always the same: Do not allow the external world to denigrate you. Create your own identity. I heard it in Joyce, Thoreau and Du Bois. Literature always affirmed what was best in men and women, and with that affirmation I was able, for the first time, to withstand the onslaught threatened by the world.

It was in the army that I began to take stands. By that time I had been through college, had received my degree in English and had had therapy. My first night in the barracks I talked to young men from California, Texas and Maine. There were Indians, Mexican-Americans, Samoans, farm boys and city toughs. Some were racist, some not. Some were anti-Semitic, some not. However, by that time I refused to tolerate anyone who harbored any prejudice.

When someone said the word "nigger" I would tell that person to "get the hell out of here," and if a soldier started to inform me that "Jews shouldn't tell white people what to do," I would say, "Well, you're talking to one now and he's telling you what to do."

I began to write. I kept journals and wrote short stories. I reread my favorite books again and again. I was so moved by the ideas and feelings in these books that I sought opportunities to thank their authors for what they had done, for liberating me, for showing me another way to live, hope, think and feel. When I was teaching at Queens College, I went to hear Ralph Ellison read from his work. The English department managed the affair, and I was happy knowing that I would actually meet one of my heroes. After the reading, I waited on line anticipating the handshake and the few brief words. The chairman and the upper ranks of the department stood by Ellison's side while teachers filed by. I was excited, much like the boy with a Pilgrim hat at Thanksgiving time. It was finally my turn. I shook his hand and said, "I want you to know that *Invisible Man,* especially the part about 'I yam what I am,' really changed my life for the better." The chairman looked at me as though I had embarrassed him, and the others shook their heads and smiled. I felt foolish for being who I was. But as I walked away, Ellison touched my shoulder lightly and said, "That's the greatest compliment an author can ever receive."

I have frequently thought about what Ellison said to me that evening and other evenings while I was reading his novel and his essays. He not only gave me strength to see and accept myself as a whole human being with inalienable rights to just as much self-worth and integrity as anyone else; Ellison, along with other writers, prepared me for America's continual problem of racial strife.

These times are difficult for the country and particularly for New York City, my home. It seems as if the Kerner Commission's prediction of a racially divided society has arrived. I have heard and witnessed much hate in the last four years. People—whites and blacks—seem always to be on the edge of reacting violently. Which side should I take, white or black?

No American should be coerced into taking either side because both are inherently racist. Those who force us to take sides make things extremely difficult for people like me—black, Jewish and American—people caught in the middle of their ambivalence, their lost dreams and aspirations.

RESPONDING IN DISCUSSION OR WRITING

1. Jeffries says that as he searches for a theme that has run through his life, "color is the cord that ties up most of my life's successes, failures and contradictions." How important is your color to your life, ambition, relationships, achievements, opportunities, self-worth, and prospects?

2. What do you think Jeffries means when he says that his sister and brother were "not born at the right time in history"? Do you feel you were born at the right time in history? Why or why not? What could be seen as a "right time" for people in the ethnic group with which you most closely identify?

3. In paragraph 14, Jeffries mentions events and words spoken to him that changed his "present and future." Why were those events and words momentous? Do you think they would make a difference to a child growing up in the 1990s? Why or why not?

4. In paragraphs 18–22, Jeffries discusses how he kept silent when he heard racial insults and how he constantly tried to control himself. What are the advantages and disadvantages of silence and control in such situations? How do you respond to the author's account of his silence and control?

5. In paragraph 19, Jeffries describes "wearing a mask" as he hid his race from others. In what other ways do people wear masks to conceal aspects of their identity? What other things do people try to hide and why?

6. In paragraph 26, Jeffries tells a powerful anecdote about the issue of dating. What attitudes to dating people of other ethnic groups prevail in households with which you are familiar? Do the attitudes cause problems?

WRITING ASSIGNMENTS

1. Jeffries begins in paragraph 2 with an autobiographical account of his life. He does not tell us every detail; rather he selects events, focusing on those that deal with perceptions of race and color. Write your own autobiography of race, color, class, or ethnicity. Select your own focus, one that will help you highlight events relevant to your choice.

2. Jeffries quotes W.E.B. Du Bois, who said, "The problem of the twentieth century is the problem of the color line" (paragraph

16). Consider that statement as applicable to the North American continent and to other places in the world you have lived in or have learned about. Write an essay in which you explore the claim made by Du Bois, draw conclusions about whether or not you agree with him, and explain why.

❖

CONFESSIONS OF A YOUNG WASP

LANG PHIPPS

Lang Phipps is a self-confessed WASP. This article appeared in New York *magazine on September 2, 1991. In it Phipps dissects the WASP mentality and lifestyle.*

ALMOST EVERY SUMMER WEEKEND, as I have since I was a small boy, I go out East to Southampton, Long Island. There, in a locale my father knew in the early thirties when the Montauk Highway was still a dirt road, I enter a world of private beach and tennis clubs, of properties and houses that have been "in the family" for three quarters of a century.

Typically, I will spend the afternoon on one of the world's most beautiful beaches, usually with old friends, often on a stretch of beach that is marked off with a sign reading MEMBERS ONLY— that is the subtext of the weekend, MEMBERS ONLY. In preternaturally attractive settings, preternaturally attractive people enact social rituals that flaunt their elitism in a resort of stratospheric privilege and exclusivity.

The place has a lyrical beauty in summertime—it seemed like paradise to me as a child. Biking down sunny lanes through the swirl of honeysuckle and privet in bloom, I easily recover the sense of a near-perfect place. And all of us who grew up there feel proprietary about it, that we are a part of it, that it is *our* sanctuary. It is almost painful to pull away from there on Sunday afternoon and return to the city.

Sticky-hot and choked with the reek of urine, I emerge from the subway in Brooklyn experiencing something like cognitive dissonance as I take in the full reality of Fourth Avenue and Atlantic. It disturbs me to think these two places—Brooklyn, where I now live, and Southampton—can exist simultaneously on the same island.

The first thing I notice when walking down Fourth Avenue is that very few people look like me: There aren't many blond heads. The Northern European type that dominated the society I found myself in all weekend is all but gone, and the unnatural but comfortable experience of facing döppelgangers at every turn is now replaced by the discomfort of being different, of suddenly being what's "wrong with the picture." This feeling has taken some getting used to since I moved to Brooklyn: After all, I'm a New York Wasp, and my upbringing has always reassured me that I am "in" and the rest of the world "out." All weekend, my appearance and background have been my armor. But as I walk down Fourth Avenue, I'm aware these strengths are suddenly my vulnerability. I feel a sudden fear for the people I've grown up with who still hold on to the fiction of tribal superiority that confuses style with substance, unaware that the dust of their crumbling bastion is already obscuring their vision.

I was born and grew up in a strictly bounded section of Manhattan that began at 59th Street and ended at 96th Street. This northern limit was the deadline, and any knowledge of what lay north of it came through the window of the Campus Coach bus that took me and my schoolmates to and from Randall's Island, where we played afternoon sports.

On my father's side of the family, my forebears are New Englanders, old New Yorkers, Virginians, and a lot of English. His mother was one of the Langhorne sisters, five Virginia beauties of vivid romance. Irene married the artist Charles Dana Gibson and was the original "Gibson Girl." Nancy married Waldorf Astor and became the first woman member of Parliament. Her country house, Cliveden, where my father spent much time with his cousins as a boy, was a controversial cynosure of culture and politics before the Second World War. My mother is from an old southern family that has the obligatory Confederate general in it somewhere, rattling an illustrious saber.

My schooling went along classic English guidelines: all-boy private grade school, Buckley; all-boy private boarding school, Brooks; and then on to college at Duke. The gist of my training for college consisted of a thorough knowledge of Greek mythology and European history, the ability to translate Latin, and the art of proper essay writing. As a child, I was sent to dancing school at the Colony Club and began there the chaperoned social life that culminated in the Gold and Silver Ball when I reached my teens.

From birth through early childhood, I was raised by a professional English nanny in the days when Wasp mothers had as little to do with hands-on child raising as possible. My nanny would wheel me in a pram through the mall in Central Park to the sailboat pond, where she met the other nannies and their charges. I grew up with these boys and girls. I learned to swim at the Southampton Bathing Corporation and to play tennis at the Meadow Club. Camp was a place run by a sports teacher from Buckley, and I knew most everybody there. Everywhere I went, I knew everyone from childhood and the recognition was precisely tribal.

The constrictions of the tribe, the clan, the club of the New York Wasp to this day include maintaining the appearance of propriety at all times—the right job, an almost military adherence to grooming and dress based on turning yourself out as your nanny did—the result being men and women in their forties who haven't changed their hairstyle *ever,* the men parted on the left and combed dead across with a wet comb, the women pulling their lank, shoulder-length hair tight off their face with a barrette: They look like nothing more than very old children.

The great emphasis is on the idea of tradition, the tidal repetitions of inherited form and their patterns of sameness. The tribe *is* the world and has no need to change or assimilate; others will try to assimilate into the tribe, it is assumed. Naturally xenophobic and insulated, the Wasp has the moated psychology of an islander. The island is, in fact, a classic Wasp motif. So natural is their islophilia, I wonder if it isn't something of an atavistic call to England, the Wasp's ancestral island.

In my life I have known three types of Wasp, whom I will call Old, Vestigial, and New. The difference between these generations has everything to do with how meaningfully their traditions and values have connected with the country at large, and their personal weight in the marketplace and affairs of state.

The men and women of my great-grandparents' generation were the mold, the Ur-Wasps. They lived in an America, still small, where there was a plutocratic ruling class of mostly English stock. Beginning in the mid-nineteenth century, capitalist dynasties like Morgan, Whitney, Vanderbilt, Mellon, and Harriman, whose fortunes were founded on the industrialization of America, replaced the older agrarian or merchant families with roots in the eighteenth century.

Suddenly a new strain of Wasp emerged whose power was based in industry and banking, leaving behind forever the Adamses and their ilk, whose power reposed more in ideas than in commerce. The Ur-Wasps, whether or not you agreed with their capitalist tactics, had, to say the least, a robust and substantial vision of who they were and what they were about. And because of the wealth they accumulated and the privilege they assumed, they opened a psychic space in American history that, despite the weakening of the Wasps, endures to this day and still makes them a subject of cultural preoccupation.

The offspring of the Ur-Wasps, first in line of inheritance, were the Old Wasps. Old Wasps like W. Averell Harriman, John Hay Whitney, and Paul Mellon had a sense of sovereign power, a long-term and tangible connection with the physical country and its development. Their fathers had made great piles of money here, and in gratitude, they refunded their good fortune by leading lives of generous service. In their houses, clothes, and sporting lives, they had the grand style of European dukes.

In a long career that began at the family's railroad concern, Averell Harriman moved into public life in the thirties as an officer with the National Recovery Administration, then was named ambassador to Russia and the Court of St. James's. He served as secretary of commerce in the late forties and in 1948 was appointed U.S. representative abroad for the Marshall Plan. The last stroke of this distinguished career was Harriman's vital role at the Paris Peace Talks in 1968–1969.

John Hay "Jock" Whitney had another protean career, in which he managed to combine publishing, horse-racing, diplomacy, and philanthropy. He owned and ran the New York *Herald Tribune*, owned and raced a world-class stable, served as the ambassador to the Court of St. James's, and served on many corporate boards.

The second generation of inheritors I call Vestigial Wasps. These people, my father's contemporaries, have survived the mid- and late-twentieth century, whose seismic events changed America irrevocably. Decade after decade, their America has become more unrecognizable, and they've begun to sense that Wasp traditions and values are being swept off to the side of the turbid current of national life. Accustomed to sailing surely in the swiftest waters of this force of history, the Vestigial Wasps find themselves suddenly in a brackish tributary. Their ethos has only a personal resonance now, and, like the British royal family, they must resort to ceremony and "style" to keep alive traditions that once buttressed empire.

The gentleman's club like the Brook or the Racquet is a refuge of tribal sanctity for the male Vestigial Wasp. A visit to the bar or steam room, seeing the portraits of venerable members or the very stolidity of the building, is a balm to him.

George Bush is of the right generation and background for Vestigial Wasphood. He is Greenwich, Andover, Yale, Skull and Bones, and so on. But Bush has tried to adapt to the wider world. He uprooted from the Northeast and made his mark in politically tough, all-American Texas. He bombs around the Maine coast in a gas-guzzling powerboat instead of a genteel ketch, and claims he likes pork rinds and country music as much as any truck driver. He practices divisive, hardball, ungentlemanly politics at home and seems to revel in war. But how much of this is genuine and how much the contrivance of handlers is impossible to say. Is Bush's syntax so strangled and baffling because he's afraid his natural patrician speech will chill the electorate?

In better times, Vestigial Wasps gave coming-out parties for their eighteen-year-old daughters. Often the high point of the summer's social calendar, the coming-out party was a lavish deal "created" by the decorator of the moment. Tens of thousands were spent on getting it right: a tidal wave of flowers, catered food that was often hot when you got to it, at least two fevered bars, the society orchestra, and, of course, clouds of pink and white balloons that, blissfully buoyant, bobbed in the breeze.

For Vestigial Wasp women, the charity committee is a career obligation. The Ladies Who Lunch do so at Upper East Side restaurants like Mortimer's or Le Bilboquet, but they talk like captains of industry about selling the annual events that raise funds for the Central Park Conservancy or Sloan-Kettering or the Southampton Hospital. It is a ceremony that will always be enacted by Wasp Women, whether the dewiest newlywed or the crustiest dowager.

One bit of Vestigial Wasp style that seems nontransferable, though, is the way of speaking.

If you were to sit quietly for a while, some late afternoon in the library of the Racquet, Harvard, or Brook Club, you would hear, over the unmistakably Waspy creak of an old leather armchair in which a big-boned body is moving, the sonorous drone of the Vestigial Wasp. It has been called "Wasp lockjaw," although that doesn't really describe it very well.

Familiar but rarefied, this accent has simply disappeared in the transit from my father's generation to mine. I know no one my age who speaks like this, and anyone who attempted to do so I would assume to be a fraud. Most of America thinks Thurston Howell III of TV's *Gilligan's Island* has the accent, but the real thing is closer to George Plimpton, who recently lent his voice, to great effect, to Ken Burns's award-winning series *The Civil War.* The accent prevailed in a pre-television America, before the onset of mass culture. It remained unchallenged until my generation, which, despite its privilege, is no more immune to the effects of an invasive culture than any other part of American society.

It is an accent that belongs to the past, to things "lawn gawn." It's simply "obsuhd" to hear a Vestigial Wasp talking about modernisms like Nintendo or rap music. Imagine Nelson Doubleday intoning "Grandmaster Flash and the Furious 5." He'd make it sound like a hot jazz combo that played his older sister's coming-out party back in 1925.

The accent is actually rather beautiful and pleasant. I think part of its beauty is its fragility, which is like the tenuousness of a white rhino or a California condor, poised at extinction.

It can be devastating when used in a haughty or arrogant manner. Years ago, my father overheard this exchange in a club. A

man who was listening to another tell a rather long-winded story
suddenly stopped a passing waiter and said, "Would you mind listening to the rest of this man's story; I have somewhere to go,"
and got up to leave.

Like too much of the world of Vestigial Wasps, their accent
belongs to another time, further pushing them into the margin
of the present day, making them more and more a historical
curiosity.

The children of the Vestigial Wasps are the New Wasps, my generation. In Whit Stillman's film *Metropolitan,* the type is pretty
much put under a slide for the world to see. The characters in the
film are all people I have known and probably been myself.

The New Wasps are vain and silly people, terminally blinkered
and naïve. They have the unmistakable lifelessness of people who
even at apparently spontaneous moments are stiltedly self-
conscious. They define that meaning of the word *fey* that is
"weak." They wouldn't know a feeling if it fell on them and live
carefully scripted and bounded lives designed to keep messy emotions at a safe remove.

They pride themselves on a limited view of life, arrogantly calling their fear of things unfamiliar "discretion." They drink too
much and lack passion. When encountered one-on-one,
marooned without the blanket identity of the tribe, they suffer
from a complete loss of personal force.

By "vanity" I mean the time I was fourteen and a boy my age
approached me at the beach club and, pointing out that we had
on the very same shirt, asked was I going home to change it or
should he.

By silliness I mean, for example, the New Wasp male's sense of
humor, which is still giddy and scatological in men 35 years old,
and the obsession with having "fun"—light, unchallenging, usually liquor-assisted activity that fills a disproportionate part of the
New Wasp's life. It is as though meaningful work were not fun and
had to be compensated for, as if life consisted of the school
vacations when one was ten and it was okay to do nothing but
have fun.

New Wasp women have the cosmetic side of their sexuality
down—they know how to catch a man's eye, but they don't know
what to do once they have him. They are at once naïve and filled
with a hard-edged sexual acquisitiveness.

The naïveté doesn't come any purer than the moment a 30-year-old New Wasp woman asked me *in complete mystification* at a dinner party what this word *clitoris* was that she'd just overheard at the table. She'd never bothered to ask Mom about that one, and evidently Mom hadn't bothered to tell.

A general immaturity about sex and the odd combination of childish apprehension and obsession with it make the New Wasps as lousy in bed as upper-class Brits, who suffer the same symptoms.

An example of their pathetic misuse of "discretion" is a New Wasp male's categorical refusal to buy something he needed because the store was on the West Side. "I don't go to the West Side," he said, as if announcing he never drank Beaujolais Nouveau. What he meant was "I'm uncomfortable unless everyone looks and talks like me."

This xenophobia readily twists into anti-Semitism, which is alive and unwell in Wasp culture. The Upper East Side nightclub called the Living Room—now closed—drew people from everywhere but was tagged "the Levine Room" by some clan members who wouldn't set foot in the place for the same reason they eschew the Upper West Side.

New Wasps love to drink. Liquor helps them keep feelings buried and supplies giddy fuel for fun time. They favor sweet rum drinks, like novice drinkers or college kids at Trader Vic's. 40

New Wasps favor places like the bars at private clubs where drinks can be signed for (in someone else's name, it's hoped: Wasps are cheap, cheap, cheap), parties where the liquor is free and plentiful, and certain meeting places they can take over en masse, like Mortimer's and Shelby.

New Wasp status symbols are not heavy handed like Rolexes or BMWs but things we grew up with—like the perfectly rendered black tie. The trophy woman, the "babe," is how New Wasp men conduct their one-upmanship. The hotter the babe, breast implants, nose job notwithstanding, the better the impact upon entrance to a party or club. Any evidence you're getting laid a lot earns high points and envy.

In many ways, New Wasp men are like little boys when it comes to women, who are seen as both threat and quarry, never as equal. For a New Wasp male to be perceived as a lady-killer is vital to his sense of masculinity and power. I can't help wondering (*pace* Sigmund) if all this frantic skirt chasing isn't a maneuver to engage Mother in some way.

For New Wasp women, status is celebrated in expensive objects like Chanel bags or Cartier baubles or bibelots from A La Vieille Russie. And more and more lately, they go in for surgery to help them fill out their Fendis, making them better trophies and more appetizing to the much older, often married, men of power and wealth who are *their* trophies.

Although inept in practice, they focus much energy on sex to achieve certain ends. I jotted this in a notebook not long ago about young New Wasp women I have known:

"What's sickening about these young women is the lack of innocence—were they ever innocent? Brought up materialistically, the cosmetically desirable object, the status prize, and they are never satisfied, because they always find they don't want what they have. Shiny new, new things carry meaning about who they are in the world.

"Bred to be always clean and comely, perfectly groomed, they want a look that is idealized and new, like a diamond cut into symmetrical facets that never ages. They are very like their jewels, cold and artificially refined: Précieux Stones."

More than their fathers, who might still have substantial jobs at the family firm or a diplomatic post, the New Wasps are entirely about style. In three generations, the connection with a system of human values that derives from a knowledge of why you are what you are has been lost in the frenzy to get into clubs, stay on the "A" list, wear the right clothes, do the charity balls, weekend at Newport, Southampton, and Greenwich, and marry not so much the right background anymore as the right look. The high-Wasp fraternity may have been socially aggressive in the past, but that aggressiveness was fueled by great vitality that led to the founding of railroads, banks, and such. I imagine the salon of Mrs. Astor's 400 contained not only some great pictures but also some pretty heavyweight conversation.

With an identity no deeper than the layers of oil paint in the ancestral portrait, the New Wasp is a parody of himself. This fact has not been lost on Seventh Avenue, which has been making an Old Wasp fortune knocking off a look that is already once removed from the original. Stung (pardon the pun) by the irony, certain hard-core Wasps swear they wouldn't be caught dead in Ralph Lauren.

And yet, peeking into the enclave, I have begun to notice some-   50
thing very interesting and telling: An outsider of any background, ethnicity, or sexual orientation will be welcomed inside, *only so long as* he or she has perfectly nailed down the Wasp look. The studious and hardworking epigone who has mastered the style, burnished the Old Guard glamour to a shining ideal, will not only be accepted but fêted, gushed over, adored, talked about, and, in some cases, proposed to.

The rub is simply that Wasp image has become Wasp identity, and anyone who cultivates the image lovingly enough validates it. Their idolatry says, "Being a Wasp is still desirable, is still impor-tant." To a group that must intuitively sense its dwindling clout in the world, this is food for the soul. It is a case of safety in numbers now, and new believers add more voices to the chorus of denial of the fact that, like the British empire, the sun has set on Old Wasp hegemony.

The fantastic success of Ralph Lauren, who represents to the clan the bellwether agent of the appropriation of Wasp style, could have happened only now, in the era of the New Wasp.

The key to Lauren's multi-million-dollar business is the market-ing and the advertisements that so brilliantly capture the "look." I would be hard-pressed to find any photo from my boarding-school or summer days that, placed side by side with a Polo ad, would show its artifice. If anything is wrong, it is the newness of the clothes and accessories; no matter how good our clothes, Lacoste shirts or Gucci loafers attained classic status only after a couple of summers' abuse when they were thoroughly worn-in and comfortable. With Polo, J. Crew, the Gap, and such, there is a worldwide glut of clothing that pays homage to the Wasp image. I am fascinated that this is happening in a time when Wasps are fading like a summer tan in October.

Could the attraction be the homogeneity of breeding, the illu-sion of purity and order that projects from these tribal pictures of a people of stereotyped good looks: tall, sturdily built, with healthy skin and hair and teeth and idealized coloring—blond or highlit-brown hair and blue eyes? In a universe where we are told chaos is the only law, is it a comfort to see the order these people seem to bring to living, to their immaculate houses, the jewellike precision of their gardens, their "model" children, and their clubs, a utopian society not so much in its harmony as its lack of dissonance?

In some of these clubs, the effect, of course, is monotony. Two of the most coveted clubs in Southampton—the Bathing Corp. and the Meadow Club—are traditionally Old Guard bastions. Neither is officially restricted, but the two societies couldn't feel more different. In the interest of bending a little to the prevailing wind, one—the beach club—has loosened up a policy that had let in only "legacy" types or those with an acceptable lineage and social profile: aquiline, yes; Levantine, only a tiny few of the most assimilated. The sense here is artificial, as in artifice, as in art. Spending a lot of time here, one feels like the real world has vanished.

Down the lane, the Meadow Club is another place entirely. I have thought often about its relative progressiveness in admitting a few Jewish people and dynamic, controverial businesspeople. I have thought about it in particular because my father is its president. A few summers ago, I wrote down these thoughts on the two clubs:

"Against the Meadow, which has an appearance of Old World propriety but whose membership puts it near the hot center of a new world of successful men and women on all sides of the genera 'ladies and gentlemen,' the beach club is blandly uniform. It has none of the scary New York edge that is felt when people sharing only ambition and talent cross-pollinate in one marketplace or another.

"Whether the Meadow Club is a marketplace or not, I'm sure scuttlebutt on current deals is often volleyed back and forth on the courts or even the clubhouse porch. Compelling is the sense there of bare, ugly, miscegenating lust for power all dressed out in white, behind a façade of . . . green-and-white awnings that wave down on perfect grass courts laid out in reassuringly unvarying rows.

"Not remotely a 'sunny place for shady people' but a more real world than the beach club, which is so pure it seems endangered."

And yet a childhood of programming in tribal life, with its strict conventions of style, its protocol, left me momentarily unprepared when I entered the Meadow Club two summers ago and came face to face with the Hollywood actor James Woods. "What's *he* doing here?" I thought reflexively, aghast, feeling like sanctuary had been penetrated by an interloper.

In an instant, I remembered that one of the club members is tight with Oliver Stone, the film director and Woods's friend. Woods was obviously a guest of this member, staying the weekend at the club. A pretty cool thing actually, but for just a moment I was thrown: The contrast had been *too* much.

Should one continue to hide behind the façade of style and "insulate, insulate," one could end up like Sherman McCoy, Tom Wolfe's paragon of New Waspitude in *The Bonfire of the Vanities.* Sherman wouldn't dream of taking the subway down to Wall Street, as his father always did; Sherman rode in a liveried car, windows shut tight on a chaotic, Third World New York. He played life in strict accordance to the script: the fictional equivalents of the Racquet Club, the Park Avenue duplex, Chapin for the child, the Bathing Corp.

But he was not quite prudent enough. He fell for a lusty married woman of questionable background who released his strangled sexual energies, and soon found he'd unlidded Pandora's box. For her, he did proscribed things that blew away the chalk-line boundaries.

There are easier ways for the New York Wasp to join the world outside the enclave, to become alloyed by exposure to a more flexible and robust metal. Losing your family money is one way, though scarcely easier than Sherman's. It is embittering, and many people in this situation will do anything to carry on the game. They will borrow, freeload, steal, even get a job (horrors!) to keep up appearances. Or, if their prayers are answered, they may marry back in.

But the best reason to leave it all behind and assimilate is that assimilation is more attractive. The traditional Wasp reading of "attractive" has to do with patterns that don't clash, rigidly polite children, and soigné surfaces. I mean "attractive" in the sense that assimilating the wider world makes life, certainly life in this city, easier and *safer;* it is empowering.

Presuming myself to be a creative type and a maverick, I have always felt a little out of step with the tribe. Moving away has been natural, although never easy. I left Manhattan for Brooklyn—an almost unthinkable notion for a member of a group that won't even go to the West Side—four years ago and had awful doubts about what I'd given up. Had I finally passed the point of no return? (I settled well beyond the confines of Brooklyn Heights and its old-Wasp history.) I have pursued things members of the tribe aren't meant to. For instance, since earliest childhood I have been fascinated by the drums. It probably all started the first time I witnessed a parade on Fifth Avenue, my tiny heart pounding along with the great mythic voice of the bass drum. Over the years in dozens of bands, I've played every conceivable style, including the polka when I lived for a time in Montana. Recently, I have played in a Latin rock band in which I was the lone *blanco*. I am a reggae specialist who went by the name "Drummie."

After a year, I realized I was very comfortable in Brooklyn; it made sense to me. I live in a civilized amount of space for a sane rent, and the neighborhood, at the margin of Park Slope, is human in scale and cozy. With its gas lamps and well-tended little garden plots, it is a place my English antecedents would far prefer to Manhattan. The fact that my street is racially mixed and I feel at home here has been a source of pride and security to me.

Once one gets over the obsession with style, I have found qualities of substance may emerge. I realize that no matter where I live or what I wear, I will always value politeness, order, books and learning, tradition and family pride, and hard work: Here is the real legacy of my background.

I still go to a couple of black-tie parties every year and still find Southampton irresistible. But I don't confuse these things with those true values that can still be called "Wasp" values.

I recently overheard someone at the beach use the phrase "the browning of America." As they read more and more about new demographics in the newspapers, the tribe may feel a fear of becoming part of a minority of European whites in New York City. They are still wealthy, though few on the scale of the new, non-Wasp billionaires, and have political influence, but it seems to me their real capital is the notion of natural sovereignty. This idea's collective power can obtain only as long as the clan stays together, for a Wasp diaspora will mean the loss of identity to those who look to the group, to the style ethos, for identity. A Wasp diaspora will surely mean the final dispersal of Empire.

And what will happen when the world loses its taste for Wasp style, moves on to the comfort of the next selected fiction? Chagrined to realize they needed Ralph Lauren all along, the New Wasps will have to dig down deep and relocate their very selves to find the stuff to survive on. If they can think of themselves as avatars of the Ur-Wasp, exploit and develop their inner resources the way their great-grandfathers capitalized on iron and oil and livestock and gold, they may come into their own.

But without pluck, imagination, and drive, they will end up like the children of the "ruling" classes in England who have nothing in the world anymore but the grandiose alcoholic lie that they are better than everyone else, when in fact they are just barren, prating ghosts: a horrible fate. Complacency will topple any top dog. It's not too late for the Wasp to start looking over his shoulder, back to his forebears for inspiration, and at the new world rising that would bury him.

RESPONDING IN DISCUSSION OR WRITING

1. What are your reactions to this article and to the values the author discusses? Do you feel close to or remote from the issues he describes?

2. At one point, Phipps says that "assimilation is more attractive." Do you think that applies to all ethnic groups? Is it better for them to "join the world outside the enclave"? Why or why not?

3. *Considerations of Style.* This essay was published in the popular weekly magazine *New York*. What features can you point to that show how Phipps's audience is a general audience, not a specialized academic audience? In other words, what indications are there in the writing that this article appeared in a popular magazine and not in an academic sociological journal? Whom do you think Phipps envisions as his readers?

4. In paragraph 6, Phipps begins a chronological autobiographical account. What is the effect of his inserting it at this point—just after he has introduced the idea of the contrast between Southampton and Brooklyn?

5. In paragraph 49, Phipps remarks on the identity of the type he calls the "New Wasp": "With an identity no deeper than the layers of oil paint in the ancestral portrait, the New Wasp is a parody of himself." What is Phipps conveying here about the concept of

identity? What leads him to see a parody? Can you think of other groups that you might call parodies of themselves?

6. *For Further Research.* Look for advertisements in magazines that appear to cater to the "New Wasp" mentality. Label each one that you find, identifying the features that make you see this as characteristic of the New Wasps.

WRITING ASSIGNMENTS

1. Phipps classifies Wasps into three types, Old, Vestigial, and New, and describes each fully, with examples and stories. Write an article as a counterpart to Phipps's article, e.g., "Confessions of a Twenty-Something Chinese American," "Confessions of a Middle-Aged Mexican," "Confessions of a Not-So-Rich WASP," "Confessions of a Young Socialist," "Confessions of a Fading Baseball Star," in which you classify your own ethnic group or any social, political, or athletic group that you know well into its constituent parts and use that classification to make criticisms of some aspects of the group.

2. Phipps uses the adjective "tribal" a few times. In an essay, discuss how justified you think he is in using this adjective applied to an ethnic group in the contemporary North American continent. Discuss any tribal features you see displayed by ethnic groups.

❖

WRESTLING WITH THE ANGEL: A MEMOIR

DAVID J. GORDON

David J. Gordon, born in 1929, grew up in St. Louis before going to Harvard and then Yale. Since 1960 he has been a professor of English at Hunter College, City University of New York, and at the CUNY Graduate Center. He is the author of books on D. H. Lawrence and Bernard Shaw and on the relationship between literary art and the unconscious. His most recent book is Iris Murdoch's Fables of Unselfing *(1995). The following memoir was read at a conference on biography and auto-*

biography in Spring 1993 at the CUNY Graduate Center. It has not been published until now.

WITH A BIBLICAL FLOURISH, Julius and Mildred Gordon named their long awaited first-born David Jacob. But a few years later, as Hitler's fulminations aroused anti-Semites and frightened Jews as far away as St. Louis, Missouri, they officially changed Jacob to James. They did not know that the two names were connected; James merely had a softer sound, and for a boy growing up in a gentile society, surely the name of David would serve as a sufficient assertion of Jewish identity. And so, when in the fullness of time I graduated from Harvard College and received a diploma printed in Latin—David James becoming Davidem Jacobum—my mother looked proudly at the document, then suddenly gasped, "How did they find out?"

This story epitomizes for me the unease felt by my parents as rapidly assimilating American Jews during the Depression and War years, the age of Roosevelt and Hitler in which I grew up. Almost every question raised at the family dinner table was discussed in terms of its Jewish relevance. So much so that, as my sisters and I got older and sassier, we liked to ask about some quite extraneous issue, like a trade of baseball players or a change in one of our lessons, "Is it good for the Jews?"

My father spent the first fourteen years of his life in a Polish shtetl, speaking Yiddish and studying Hebrew. His own father had briefly tried out the New World but found that it turned Jews into goyim. Then he and a brother came on their own, joining cousins (and eventually their reluctant parents) in Cleveland. He learned English well enough in a few strenuous years of schooling to be admitted simultaneously to the University of Cincinnati and the rabbinical seminary across the street from it. The seminary was a citadel of Reform Judaism, and attending constituted an act of rebellion against his strictly orthodox parents; even his favorite brother maintained his orthodoxy, and seemed very old-world to us. My father was becoming a *rabbi*, to be sure, but that aggravated the problem: he would be *teaching* non-orthodox ways, not merely *adopting* them.

His appointment in 1929 to a new and growing congregation of mostly American-born German Jews was notable. In St. Louis,

Julius Gordon was the first Reform rabbi of Eastern European origin. He overcame a prejudice by his ability and by his evident
interest in preaching a modern, liberal Judaism. The prejudice,
however, lingered. Throughout my childhood I heard Eastern
European Jews referred to as "the other element" or "you know,
those *Jewish* Jews." He paid a price for rebelling against the world
of his fathers with a nagging sense of guilt that led him to devote
many hours in the midst of a busy life as the rabbi of large, active
congregation to writing a doctoral dissertation on 18th-century
Jewish mysticism for the College that had already ordained him.
Yet it was his struggle to become more completely American that I
remember best. Although his sermons were admired for their elo-
quence, he spoke with an accent that always troubled him. He was
fascinated by the novelties of his adopted language and culture,
delighting in colorful slang and in jokes that mocked the immigrant's awkwardness in learning English—the one, for example,
about the young husband who is trying to tell the doctor that his
wife is infertile and can only come up with the words unbearable,
inconceivable and impregnable; or the one about the greenhorn
who happens to read on a theater door, "*Macbeth* pronounced
marvelous," and in despair shoots himself. He listened passionately to broadcasts of the St. Louis Cardinal baseball games. Once
he missed a train in order to hear out a tenth inning on an
automobile radio; I think it was Johnny Mize who singled home
the winning run and amply compensated him for the inconve-
nience—though doubtless my mother, who chauffeured him and
took no joy in baseball, felt otherwise.

   Along with his growing children, my father was fascinated by
words. One of my tenderest memories is of drinking cocoa in the
kitchen before bedtime and looking together at a pamphlet that
came to the house each week called *Word Study*. We fondled the
newly learned etymologies like merchants fingering a shipment of
gems. But his taste had been formed on wisdom literature and
what he appreciated most in the poems and novels that his children were beginning to devour was the sententious passage, something that could find its way into a Friday evening sermon, and
especially something that clarified his sense of what it meant to be
a Jew in modern America.

   Judaism was to my parents a binding condition. When we told
them that we sang Christmas carols at public school, they asked us

please just to *hum* the unJewish words "Christ" and "Saviour." My mother was still thanking God a decade and more after the event that Leopold and Loeb had murdered a *Jewish* boy and therefore offered less incitement to anti-Semites. But the anti-Semites were indeed out there, even if our experience in St. Louis could not be compared to what was happening in Europe. It was commonplace to hear slurs against Jews on streets, on buses, at school, and even on the radio and in the newspapers, quoted from religious leaders or from politicians, one of whom referred casually to "the Jews, the niggers, and the real Americans." I remember especially a 7th-grade manual training teacher known as Pop Prebble. Prebble had us clear our benches early so he could impart his little lessons. "What is a kike?" he asked one day in, it must have been, 1942. Noting with satisfaction our awkward silence, he supplied the answer: "A Jew that not even Jews like." Another time, turning to me, whom he knew to be a rabbi's son, he asked, "How would *your* father explain the creation of the world?" I muttered something about gases and explosions, which irritated him since he had prepared an attack on the stupidity of the rabbi.

Many members of our temple were eager to minimize their Jewish identity. At the Christmas season they wanted their Rabbi's permission to display trees, which they called Hanukkah bushes, so as to spare their children an unhealthy envy of their gentile neighbors. Some belonged to the anti-Zionist American Council for Judaism based in Chicago. My father reported one day that a temple bigwig challenged the Zionist bias of his last sermon; my father replied testily, "75% of the members are Zionists!"; "I doubt your figures," came the challenge. "So do I," cried my father, his voice rising in anger to a still wilder figure, "—it's 90%!"

In 1940 the coming war with Nazi Germany compelled my parents to support Roosevelt not just as liberals but specifically as Jews. As the campaign for his third term heated up, school bullies challenged me to explain why I was "voting" for Roosevelt, whose name was indeed sacred in our household. The only answer I knew how to give them was that he was "good to the Jews"—after which they took my trousers off and threw them into a tree.

The theme of my father's life was the conflict between his American and Jewish loyalties, still symbolized for me in the alternating inscriptions of presidents and patriarchs around the ceiling of the YMHA Auditorium in New York City. How to be both a good Jew and a good American—that was the question in those days when assimilation rather than diversity defined the spirit of the age. Looking through my father's surviving sermons (lightly edited, with a concern for idiom, in my mother's neat script), I found this quintessential paragraph, facile in its rhetoric and innocent of irony yet touching in its declaration of "my entire story":

> I do not mind going back, but I do not wish to go backwards. This tells my entire story. I do not mind going back to the sources of Jewish strength, to the fountains of Jewish inspiration, to the well of Jewish learning, to the richness and beauty of Jewish living. But I do not wish to be thrown backwards. I do not want to become a slave to ancient taboos, antiquated superstitions, and archaic customs. I want my Judaism to be vital and vibrant. I want my Judaism to be enlightened and progressive, perfectly attuned to the Zeitgeist. I want my Judaism to be in harmony with the spirit of America which is the spirit of freedom.

I am still moved by this unquestioned faith in America, now lost amid the corruptions of power, expressed then by immigrants so grateful to their adopted land.

A questionnaire not long ago asked respondents to make a distinction between a "religious" and a "cultural" Jew. My parents could not have wedged these categories apart, and I in my second-generational turn find it impossible to make the further distinction called for on the questionnaire between a "cultural Jew" and a "non-Jew." "Cultural Jew" implies more commitment than I feel and show, but "non-Jew" seems to imply an act of repudiation. My own sense of Jewish identity is expressed nicely by the joke in which the question, "Are you Jewish?" is followed by the answer, "On my parents' side."

My father's position in the world of St. Louis loomed large in my childish perception. My sixth grade teacher at public school defined the word "prominent" by using my father as an example, and the matrons at the temple would pinch my cheek and ask if I was going to grow up and be famous too. Being a rabbi's son was not an easy matter for me, and the very moral authority his position represented had something to do with it. Our schoolfriends were reluctant to play at our house, where the monitory presence of an intimidating spiritual leader might materialize at any time. They seemed to wonder how we could go about doing ordinary things. And although this didn't seem a problem to us, my father was in fact a man hard to get close to, even for his children. "What does your father do?" one of my sisters was asked by a playmate when they were about eight. "He's a rabbi." Pause. "What's that?" Summoning to mind the image of our parent memorizing his weekly sermon, my sister answered, "That's someone who walks up and down and talks to himself." In essence that was my picture too. He was remote, preoccupied, not so much cold as veiled. "Pondering a platitude" is how I put it in my rebellious adolescence. "A distant, passionate man" is how my other sister put it later. When I was fourteen and away at summer camp, he wrote a letter in response to one of mine that must have referred to some boyish unhappiness, a phrase from which has stuck in my mind: ". . . and when shall we, like the biblical Jacob, wrestle with the angel of our destiny." That was Rabbi Gordon's style exactly— sincerely, naturally, unaffectedly pompous. The same in a letter to a fourteen-year-old son as in a sermon.

I do not recall that my father ever touched me, either in anger or tenderness, although I've seen a photo of him holding his one and a half year old son on a beach, a cigarette held away. He was afraid to impose discipline, yet I feared *some* retributive wrath because I remember well a terrifying incident (singled out later by a psychoanalyst for special attention) when at a baseball game on a corner lot, I hit a ball that broke a window in an adjacent synagogue, and ran home as fast as my ten year old legs could carry me, bawling into the arms of our maid that the police were sure to come after me and lock me up.

My parents' division of labor was clearly a version of the common shtetl arrangement by which the husband studied and the wife dealt with the world. Although my father held a salaried job, he did not drive, did not deal with money and could not be trusted to buy his own clothes because he would passively take whatever the salesman had a mind to sell him. My mother, contrary to stereotype, never complained. Listening to her husband and children leaning into a conversation about sports or symptoms, she must have sometimes wondered how she ever became a member of this particular family. She hardly ever bought anything in those days for herself, and it was a surprise to us to discover, after my father's death, that she actually liked to buy and wear nice clothes.

Their diffidence about giving us a Jewish education grew out of their fear of our being handicapped in a gentile society. My father himself would love to have written *Peace of Mind: A Guide to Happy Living* by his friend Joshua Loth Liebman, one of the all-time best-sellers in American publishing history, and actually did write two similar but far less successful books. A year before my thirteenth birthday I had of course to take Hebrew lessons, but these were not continued. About the Bar Mitzvah ceremony itself, I remember only leaving the pulpit too early, whereupon I looked up and saw my father's long arm summoning me back. Standing beside me again, he imparted some solemn wisdom concerning the responsibilities of manhood, and raised his hands over my head in the ritual blessing.

All the memories of boyhood that are tinged with nostalgia for me are unrelated to religion—the nightwatchman tapping his stick on the street at bedtime, the milkman leading his horse-drawn cart down the cobblestone alley, the Saturday afternoon double-bills at the Varsity and Tivoli theaters, the striped awnings that kept the heavy summer heat from the brick apartment buildings, the standing radio (which would now be styled "art deco") in front of which we listened every weekday around 5:30 to Superman, the Lone Ranger and The Green Hornet, the after-dinner games of kick-the-can in the backyard that ended as the fireflies lit up around us in the thickening dusk, the screened porch on which my sisters and I read for many hours our first grownup books while large insects pounded lightly against it, the smell of autumn leaves burning in curbside piles, the touch football games in the corner lot, the endless pingpong games with my sisters in the musty basement, the rigging up of wires for Morse-code communications with our neighbor, the talks with the black handyman who could predict rain from the discomfort in his toes.

In the autumn of my senior year of high school, I was interviewed in downtown St. Louis by a group of lawyers who were Harvard College alumni. Although our discussion centered on the recently announced Marshall Plan, one of them took me aside afterward and, placing a hand on my shoulder, advised me earnestly not to let being Jewish ruin my life. It has not done so. In the academic circles and large cities in which most of my life has been spent, I have, unlike my father, seldom been forced into Jewish self-consciousness, except ironically, in recent years, as the newer claims of under-represented minorities have placed upon Jews the strange mantle of the establishment.

Wrestling with *his* angel for a blessing, my father thrashed out the conflict between being a Jew, as his father was, and being an American, as his children would be. My own dark angel is more obscure but is also an agent of the patriarchal law, and has involved me in no less struggle and anguish. My record in college and graduate school was a crazy sequence of dramatic failures and dramatic successes, of expulsions and prizes—the failures perhaps a sacrificial wound to make the successes possible. My early scholarly publications—painfully brought forth somewhere between a first divorce and another marriage that would also end in divorce—bore such titles as "The Son and the Father (in Hemingway's Fiction)," "Attitudes Toward Authority (in *Paradise Lost*)," "Parricide, Regicide and Deicide (in *Hamlet*)." When a group of us as young teachers asked each other with what literary character we most identified, I named Milton's Satan. My favorite self-image in those days was indeed of someone on the ropes but battling back bravely from a defensive and basically hopeless position.

I cannot summon that image anymore except as a memory and do not even know what image would replace it—not an embattled one at any rate. I no longer wrestle with an image of the man who has been dead now for more than thirty years, and no longer even wish, as I once did, that he could see me much less unhappy, more settled and assured. In the mild air of middle-age, he is but a pale form in the distance, no longer active enough either to interrogate me or to confer a blessing. It is a kind of loss, but perhaps the very absence of a *need* for a blessing *is* the blessing I long wrestled for and have, after many years, received.

RESPONDING IN DISCUSSION OR WRITING

1. Gordon describes a questionnaire (paragraph 11) that makes a distinction between "religious" and "cultural" affiliation to an ethnic group. How could such a distinction apply within the ethnic group with which you primarily identify? Do people in that group have both religious and cultural affiliations? Would you describe

yourself as having either religious or cultural affiliation to an ethnic group, or both, or neither?

2. What connections can you make between the passage quoted from Julius Gordon's sermon and the notion that ethnic affiliation is a matter of heritage *and* choice?

3. *Considerations of Style.* To introduce a memoir about his father, Gordon tells a story about his name. How effective is the use of a story as an introduction to this memoir? How do you react to the story? What is the connection between the story and the main point of the memoir?

4. *Considerations of Style.* Why do you think Gordon decides, in this piece about religion and culture, to give many details to describe boyhood memories that are "unrelated to religion" (paragraph 16)? What function does paragraph 16 serve, and how do you respond to it?

5. Why do you think Gordon wrote this memoir? What audience did he have in mind? Does the memoir have resonance only for Jews or are its ideas applicable to other ethnic groups?

6. How does Gordon's parents' division of labor compare to the division in the household in which you grew up? Who did which household jobs? Did the division of labor cause any friction?

WRITING ASSIGNMENTS

1. Do you think parents and schools should instill in children a knowledge of and attachment to their own culture, language, and religion? If so, how should they do that, and who should have primary responsibility for doing it? If not, why not? What other responsibilities take precedence? What makes these issues important in a multicultural society?

2. Gordon says that as he was growing up "assimilation rather than diversity defined the spirit of the age." In an essay, discuss the different types of behavior and values that are evident in a society that values assimilation and one that values diversity. Give your reader examples to help illustrate the types of behavior and values you include.

3. Write your own memoir, about either your mother or your father, exploring your relationship with that parent, your own

feelings of ethnic identity, and what facts and images you have to wrestle with.

INVISIBLE MAN

LAWRENCE OTIS GRAHAM

Lawrence Otis Graham, born in 1962 in New York City and known professionally as Larry Graham, is an African American lawyer and a prolific writer. He has written many books on applying to college and professional schools. His first book was published while he was a student and he published a book each year he was a student at Princeton and Harvard Law School. He also researches issues of color and ethnicity. He has, for example, lived in a Harlem rooming house in order to report on conditions there in an article called "Harlem on My Mind" (1993). A chapter in his recent collection of essays, Member of the Club *(1995), describes how when dining in ten top New York restaurants he was frequently given the worst table; was mistaken for a waiter, coat-check attendant, or bathroom attendant; and, when making a telephone call, was threatened by another customer with losing his job for tying up the phone. The following article was published in* New York *magazine on August 17, 1992. The title recalls Ralph Ellison's book* Invisible Man, *called "the classic representation of American black experience" by R.W.B. Lewis.*

I DRIVE UP THE winding lane past a long stone wall and beneath an archway of 60-foot maples. At one bend of the drive, a freshly clipped lawn and a trail of yellow daffodils slope gently up to the four-pillared portico of a white Georgian colonial. The building's six huge chimneys, the two wings with slate-gray shutters, and the white-brick façade loom over a luxuriant golf course. Before me stands the 100-year-old Greenwich Country Club—*the* country club—in the affluent, patrician, and very white town of Greenwich, Connecticut, where there are eight clubs for 59,000 people.

I'm a 30-year-old corporate lawyer at a midtown Manhattan firm, and I make $105,000 a year. I'm a graduate of Princeton University (1983) and Harvard Law School (1988), and I've written eleven nonfiction books. Although these might seem like good credentials, they're not the ones that brought me here. Quite frankly, I got into this country club the only way that a black man like me could—as a $7-an-hour busboy.

After seeing dozens of news stories about Dan Quayle, Billy Graham, Ross Perot, and others who either belonged to or frequented white country clubs, I decided to find out what things were really like at a club where I saw no black members.

I remember stepping up to the pool at a country club when I was 10 and setting off a chain reaction: Several irate parents dragged their children out of the water and fled. Back then, in 1972, I saw these clubs only as a place where families socialized. I grew up in an affluent white neighborhood in Westchester, and all my playmates and neighbors belonged somewhere. Across the street, my best friend introduced me to the Westchester Country Club before he left for Groton and Yale. My teenage tennis partner from Scarsdale introduced me to the Beach Point Club on weekends before he left for Harvard. The family next door belonged to the Scarsdale Golf Club. In my crowd, the question wasn't "Do you belong?" It was "Where?"

My grandparents owned a Memphis trucking firm, and as far back as I can remember, our family was well off and we had little trouble fitting in—even though I was the only black kid on the high-school tennis team, the only one in the orchestra, the only one in my Roman Catholic confirmation class.

Today, I'm back where I started—on a street of five- and six-bedroom colonials with expensive cars, and neighbors who all belong somewhere. As a young lawyer, I realize that these clubs are where business people network, where lawyers and investment bankers meet potential clients and arrange deals. How many clients and deals am I going to line up on the asphalt parking lot of my local public tennis courts?

I am not ashamed to admit that I one day want to be a partner and a part of this network. When I talk to my black lawyer or investment-banker friends or my wife, a brilliant black woman who has degrees from Harvard College, law school, and business school, I learn that our white counterparts are being accepted by dozens of these elite institutions. So why shouldn't we—especially when we have the same ambitions, social graces, credentials, and salaries?

My black Ivy League friends and I talk about black company vice-presidents who have to beg white subordinates to invite them out for golf or tennis. We talk about the club in Westchester that rejected black Scarsdale resident and millionaire magazine publisher Earl Graves, who sits on *Fortune* 500 boards, owns a Pepsi-distribution franchise, raised three bright Ivy League children, and holds prestigious honorary degrees. We talk about all the clubs that face a scandal and then run out to sign up one quiet, deferential black man who will remove the taint and deflect further scrutiny.

I wanted some answers. I knew I could never be treated as an equal at this Greenwich oasis—a place so insular that the word *Negro* is still used in conversation. But I figured I could get close enough to understand what these people were thinking and why country clubs were so set on excluding people like me.

March 28 to April 7, 1992

I invented a completely new résumé for myself. I erased Harvard,   10
Princeton, and my upper-middle-class suburban childhood from my life. So that I'd have to account for fewer years, I made myself seven years younger—an innocent 23. I used my real name and made myself a graduate of the same high school. Since it was ludicrous to pretend I was from "the streets," I decided to become a sophomore-year dropout from Tufts University, a midsize college in suburban Boston. My years at nearby Harvard had given me enough knowledge about the school to pull it off. I contacted some older friends who owned large companies and restaurants in the Boston and New York areas and asked them to serve as references. I was already on a leave of absence from my law firm to work on a book.

I pieced together a wardrobe with a polyester blazer, ironed blue slacks, black loafers, and a horrendous pink-black-and-silver tie, and I set up interviews at clubs. Over the telephone, five of the eight said that I sounded as if I would make a great waiter. But when I met them, the club managers told me I "would probably make a much better busboy."

"Busboy? Over the phone, you said you needed a waiter," I argued. "Yes, I know I said that, but you seem very alert, and I think you'd make an excellent busboy instead."

The maître d' at one of the clubs refused to accept my application. Only an hour earlier, she had enthusiastically urged me to come right over for an interview. Now, as two white kitchen workers looked on, she would only hold her hands tightly behind her back and shake her head emphatically.

April 8 to 11

After interviewing at five clubs and getting only two offers, I made my final selection in much the way I had decided on a college and a law school: I went for prestige. Not only was the Greenwich Country Club celebrating its hundredth anniversary but its roster boasted former president Gerald Ford (an honorary member), baseball star Tom Seaver, former Securities and Exchange Commission chairman and U.S. ambassador to the Netherlands John Shad, as well as former Timex spokesman John Cameron Swayze. Add to that a few dozen *Fortune* 500 executives, bankers, Wall Street lawyers, European entrepreneurs, a Presbyterian minister, and cartoonist Mort Walker, who does "Beetle Bailey." [The Greenwich Country Club did not respond to any questions from *New York* Magazine about the club and its members.]

For three days, I worked on my upper-arm muscles by walking around the house with a sterling-silver tray stacked high with heavy dictionaries. I allowed a mustache to grow in, then added a pair of arrestingly ugly Coke-bottle reading glasses.

April 12 (Sunday)

Today was my first day at work. My shift didn't start until 10:30 A.M., so I laid out my clothes at home: a white button-down shirt, freshly ironed cotton khaki pants, white socks, and white leather sneakers. I'd get my official club uniform in two days. Looking in my wallet, I removed my American Express gold card, my Harvard Club membership ID, and all of my business cards.

When I arrived at the club, I entered under the large portico, stepping through the heavy doors and onto the black-and-white checkerboard tiles of the entry hall.

A distracted receptionist pointed me toward Mr. Ryan's[1] office. I walked past glistening silver trophies and a guest book on a pedestal, to a windowless office with three desks. My new boss waved me in and abruptly hung up the phone.

"Good morning, Larry," he said with a sufficiently warm smile. The tight knot in his green tie made him look more fastidious than I had remembered from the interview.

"Hi, Mr. Ryan. How's it going?" 20

Glancing at his watch to check my punctuality, he shook my hand and handed me some papers. "Oh, and by the way, where'd you park?"

"In front, near the tennis courts."

Already shaking his head, he tossed his pencil onto the desk. "That's off limits to you. You should always park in the back, enter in the back, and leave from the back. No exceptions."

"I'll do the forms right now," I said. "And then I'll be an official busboy."

Mr. Ryan threw me an ominous nod. "And, Larry, let me stop 25 you now. We don't like that term *busboy*. We find it demeaning. We prefer to call you busmen."

Leading me down the center stairwell to the basement, he added, "And in the future, you will always use the back stairway by the back entrance." He continued to talk as we trotted through a maze of hallways. "I think I'll have you trail with Carlos or Hector—no, Carlos. Unless you speak Spanish?"

"No." I ran to keep up with Mr. Ryan.

"That's the dishwasher room, where Juan works. And over here is where you'll be working." I looked at the brass sign. MEN'S GRILL.

It was a dark room with a mahogany finish, and it looked like a library in a large Victorian home. Dark walls, dark wood-beamed ceilings. Deep-green wool carpeting. Along one side of the room stood a long, highly polished mahogany bar with liquor bottles, wineglasses, and a two-and-a-half-foot-high silver trophy. Fifteen heavy round wooden tables, each encircled with four to six broad wooden armchairs padded with green leather on the backs and seats, broke up the room. A big-screen TV was set into the wall along with two shelves of books.

"This is the Men's Grill," Mr. Ryan said. "Ladies are not allowed 30 except on Friday evenings."

Next was the brightly lit connecting kitchen. "Our kitchen serves hot and cold foods. You'll work six days a week here. The club is closed on Mondays. The kitchen serves the Men's Grill and

an adjoining room called the Mixed Grill. That's where the ladies
and kids can eat."

"And what about men? Can they eat in there, too?"

This elicited a laugh. "Of course they can. Time and place
restrictions apply only to women and kids."

He showed me the Mixed Grill, a well-lit, pastel-blue room with
glass French doors and white wood trim.

"Guys, say hello to Larry. He's a new busman at the club."   35
I waved.

"And this is Rick, Stephen, Drew, Buddy, and Lee." Five white
waiters dressed in white polo shirts with blue "1892" club insignias
nodded while busily slicing lemons.

"And this is Hector and Carlos, the other busmen." Hector,
Carlos, and I were the only nonwhites on the serving staff. They
greeted me in a mix of English and Spanish.

"Nice to meet all of you," I responded.

"Thank God," one of the taller waiters cried out. "Finally—   40
somebody who can speak English."

Mr. Ryan took me and Carlos through a hall lined with old
black-and-white portraits of former presidents of the club. "This is
our one hundredth year, so you're joining the club at an important time," Mr. Ryan added before walking off. "Carlos, I'm going
to leave Larry to trail with you—and no funny stuff."

Standing outside the ice room, Carlos and I talked about our
pasts. He was 25, originally from Colombia, and hadn't finished
school. I said I had dropped out, too.

As I stood there talking, Carlos suddenly gestured for me to
move out of the hallway. I looked behind me and noticed something staring down at us. "A video camera?"

"They're around," Carlos remarked quietly while scooping ice
into large white tubs. "Now watch me scoop ice."

After we carried the heavy tubs back to the grill, I saw another   45
video camera pointed down at us. I dropped my head.

"You gonna live in the Monkey House?" Carlos asked.

"What's that?"

We climbed the stairs to take our ten-minute lunch break
before work began. "Monkey House is where workers live here,"
Carlos said.

I followed him through a rather filthy utility room and into a
huge white kitchen. We got on line behind about twenty Hispanic

men and women—all dressed in varying uniforms. At the head of
the line were the white waiters I'd met earlier.

I was soon handed a hot plate with two red lumps of rice and   50
some kind of sausage-shaped meat. There were two string beans,
several pieces of zucchini, and a thin, broken slice of dried meat
loaf that looked as if it had been cooked, burned, frozen, and
then reheated.

I followed Carlos, plate in hand, out of the kitchen. To my surprise, we walked back into the dank and dingy utility room, which
turned out to be the workers' dining area.

The white waiters huddled together at one end of the tables,
while the Hispanic workers ate quietly at the other end. Before I
could decide which end to integrate, Carlos directed me to sit
with him on the Hispanic end.

I was soon back downstairs working in the grill. At my first few
tables, I tried to avoid making eye contact with members as I
removed dirty plates and wiped down tables and chairs. I was sure
I'd be recognized.

At around 1:15, four men who looked to be in their mid- to late
fifties sat down at a six-chair table while pulling off their cotton
Windbreakers and golf sweaters.

"It's these damned newspeople that cause all the problems,"   55
said Golfer No. 1, shoving his hand deep into a popcorn bowl.
"These Negroes wouldn't even be thinking about golf. They can't
afford to join a club, anyway."

Golfer No. 2 squirmed out of his navy-blue sweater and nodded
in agreement. "My big problem with this Clinton fellow is that he
apologized." As I stood watching from the corner of the bar, I
realized the men were talking about Governor Bill Clinton's
recent apology for playing at an all-white golf club in Little Rock,
Arkansas.

"Holt, I couldn't agree with you more," added Golfer No. 3, a
hefty man who was biting off the end of a cigar.

"You got any iced tea?" Golfer No. 1 asked as I put the silverware and menus around the table. Popcorn flew out of his mouth
as he attempted to speak and chew at the same time.

"Yes, we certainly do."

Golfer No. 3 removed a beat-up Rolex from his wrist. "It just   60
sets a bad precedent. Instead of apologizing, he should try to discredit them—undercut them somehow. What's to apologize for?"
I cleared my throat and backed away from the table.

Suddenly, Golfer No. 1 waved me back to his side. "Should we get four iced teas or just a pitcher and four glasses?"

"I'd be happy to bring whatever you'd like, sir."

Throughout the day, I carried "bus buckets" filled with dirty dishes from the grill to the dishwasher room. And each time I returned to the grill, I scanned the room for recognizable faces. After almost four hours of running back and forth, clearing dishes, wiping down tables, and thanking departing members who left spilled coffee, dirty napkins, and unwanted business cards in their wake, I helped out in the coed Mixed Grill.

"Oh, busboy," a voice called out as I made the rounds with two pots of coffee. "Here, busboy. Here, busboy," the woman called out. "Busboy, my coffee is cold. Give me a refill."

"Certainly, I would be happy to." I reached over for her cup.   65

The fiftyish woman pushed her hand through her strawblonde hair and turned to look me in the face. "Decaf, thank you."

"You are quite welcome."

Before I turned toward the kitchen, the woman leaned over to her companion. "My goodness. Did you hear that? That busboy has diction like an educated white person."

A curly-haired waiter walked up to me in the kitchen. "Larry, are you living in the Monkey House?"

"No, but why do they call it that?"   70

"Well, no offense against you, but it got that name since it's the house where the workers have lived at the club. And since the workers used to be Negroes—blacks—it was nicknamed the Monkey House. And the name just stuck—even though Negroes have been replaced by Hispanics."

April 13 (Monday)

I woke up and felt a pain shooting up my calves. As I turned to the clock, I realized I'd slept for eleven hours. I was thankful the club is closed on Mondays.

April 14 (Tuesday)

Rosa, the club seamstress, measured me for a uniform in the basement laundry room, while her barking gray poodle jumped up on my feet and pants. "Down, Margarita, down," Rosa cried with pins in her mouth and marking chalk in her hand. But Margarita ignored her and continued to bark and do tiny pirouettes until I left with all of my new country-club polo shirts and pants.

Today, I worked exclusively with the "veterans," including 65-year-old Sam, the Polish bartender in the Men's Grill. Hazel, an older waitress at the club, is quick, charming and smart—the kind of waitress who makes any restaurant a success. She has worked for the club nearly twenty years and has become quite territorial with certain older male members.

Members in the Mixed Grill talked about hotel queen and 75 Greenwich resident Leona Helmsley, who was on the clubhouse TV because of her upcoming prison term for tax evasion.

"I'd like to see them haul her off to jail," one irate woman said to the rest of her table. "She's nothing but a garish you-know-what."

"In every sense of the word," nodded her companion as she adjusted a pink headband in her blondish-white hair. "She makes the whole town look bad. The TV keeps showing those aerial shots of Greenwich and that dreadful house of hers."

A third woman shrugged her shoulders and looked into her bowl of salad. "Well, it is a beautiful piece of property."

"Yes, it is," said the first woman. "But why here? She should be in those other places like Beverly Hills or Scarsdale or Long Island, with the rest of them. What's she doing here?"

Woman No. 3 looked up. "Well, you know, he's not Jewish." 80

"Really?"

"So that explains it," said the first woman with an understanding expression on her tanned forehead. "Because, you know, the name didn't sound Jewish."

The second woman agreed: "I can usually tell."

April 15 (Wednesday)

Today, we introduced a new extended menu in the two grill rooms. We added shrimp quesadillas ($6) to the appetizer list—and neither the members nor Hazel could pronounce the name of the dish or fathom what it was. One man pounded on the table and demanded to know which country the dish had come from. He told Hazel how much he hated "changes like this. I like to know that some things are going to stay the same."

Another addition was the "New Dog in Town" ($3.50). It was 85 billed as knackwurst, but one woman of German descent sent the dish back: "This is not knackwurst—this is just a big hot dog."

As I wiped down the length of the men's bar, I noticed a tall stack of postcards with color photos of nude busty women waving hello from sunny faraway beaches. I saw they had been sent from vacationing members with fond regards to Sam or Hazel. Several had come from married couples. One glossy photo boasted a detailed frontal shot of a red-haired beauty who was naked except for a shoestring around her waist. On the back, the message said, DEAR SAM, PULL STRING IN AN EMERGENCY. LOVE ALWAYS, THE ATKINSON FAMILY.

April 16 (Thursday)

This afternoon, I realized I was doing okay. I was fairly comfortable with my few "serving" responsibilities and the rules that related to them:

- When a member is seated, bring out the silverware, cloth napkin, and a menu.
- Never take an order for food, but always bring water or iced tea if it is requested by a member or waiter.
- When a waiter takes a chili or salad order, bring out a basket of warm rolls and crackers, along with a scoop of butter.
- When getting iced tea, fill a tall glass with ice and serve it with a long spoon, a napkin on the bottom, and a lemon on the rim.
- When a member wants his alcoholic drink refilled, politely respond, "Certainly, I will have your waiter come right over."
- Remember that the member is always right.
- Never make offensive eye contact with a member or his guest.
- When serving a member fresh popcorn, serve to the left.
- When a member is finished with a dish or glass, clear it from the right.
- Never tell a member that the kitchen is out of something.

But there were also some "informal" rules that I discovered (but did not follow) while watching the more experienced waiters and kitchen staff in action:

- If you drop a hot roll on the floor in front of a member, apologize and throw it out. If you drop a hot roll on the floor in the kitchen, pick it up and put it back in the bread warmer.

- If you have cleared a table and are 75 percent sure that the member did not use the fork, put it back in the bin with the other clean forks.

- If, after pouring one glass of Coke and one of diet Coke, you get distracted and can't remember which is which, stick your finger in one of them to taste it.

- If a member asks for decaffeinated coffee and you have no time to make it, use regular and add water to cut the flavor.

- When members complain that the chili is too hot and spicy, instead of making a new batch, take the sting out by adding some chocolate syrup.

- If you're making a tuna on toasted wheat and you accidentally burn one side of the bread, don't throw it out. Instead, put the tuna on the burned side and lather on some extra mayo.

April 17 (Friday)

Today, I heard the word *nigger* four times. And it came from someone on the staff.

In the grill, several members were discussing Arthur Ashe, who   90
had recently announced that he had contracted AIDS through a blood transfusion.

"It's a shame that poor man has to be humiliated like this," one woman golfer remarked to a friend over pasta-and-vegetable salad. "He's been such a good example for his people."

"Well, quite frankly," added a woman in a white sun visor, "I always knew he was gay. There was something about him that just seemed too perfect."

"No, Anne, he's not gay. It came from a blood transfusion."

"Umm," said the woman. "I suppose that's a good reason to stay out of all those big city hospitals. All that bad blood moving around."

Later that afternoon, one of the waiters, who had worked in the   95
Mixed Grill for two years, told me that Tom Seaver and Gerald Ford were members. Of his brush with greatness, he added, "You know, Tom's real first name is George."

"That's something."

"And I've seen O. J. Simpson here, too."

"O. J. belongs here, too?" I asked.

"Oh, no, there aren't any black members here. No way. I actually don't even think there are any Jews here, either."

"Really? Why is that?" I asked.

"I don't know. I guess it's just that the members probably want to have a place where they can go and not have to think about Jews, blacks, and other minorities. It's not really hurting anyone. It's really a Wasp club. . . . But now that I think of it, there is a guy here who some people think is Jewish, but I can't really tell. Upstairs, there's a Jewish secretary too."

"And what about O. J.?"

"Oh, yeah, it was so funny to see him out there playing golf on the eighteenth hole." The waiter paused and pointed outside the window. "It never occurred to me before, but it seemed so odd to see a black man with a golf club here on this course."

April 18 (Saturday)

When I arrived, Stephen, one of the waiters, was hanging a poster and sign-up sheet for a soccer league whose main purpose was to "bridge the ethnic and language gap" between white and Hispanic workers at the country clubs in the Greenwich area. I congratulated Stephen on his idea.

Later, while I was wiping down a table, I heard a member snap his fingers in my direction. I turned to see a group of young men smoking cigars. They seemed to be my age or a couple of years younger. "Hey, do I know you?" the voice asked.

As I turned slowly toward the voice, I could hear my own heartbeat. I was sure it was someone I knew.

"No," I said, approaching the blond cigar smoker. He had on light-green khaki pants and a light-yellow V-neck cotton sweater adorned with a tiny green alligator. As I looked at the other men seated around the table, I noticed that all but one had alligators on their sweaters or shirts.

"I didn't think so. You must be new—what's your name?"

"My name is Larry. I just started a few days ago."

The cigar-smoking host grabbed me by the wrist while looking at his guests. "Well, Larry, welcome to the club. I'm Mr. Billings. And this is Mr. Dennis, a friend and new member."

"Hello, Mr. Dennis," I heard myself saying to a freckle-faced young man who puffed uncomfortably on his fat roll of tobacco.

The first cigar smoker gestured for me to bend over as if he were about to share some important confidence. "Now, Larry, here's what I want you to do. Go get us some of those peanuts and then give my guests and me a fresh ashtray. Can you manage that?"

April 19 (Sunday)

It was Easter Sunday, and the Easter-egg hunt began with dozens of small children scampering around the tulips and daffodils while well-dressed parents watched wistfully from the rear patio of the club. A giant Easter bunny gave out little baskets filled with jelly beans to parents and then hopped over to the bushes, where he hugged the children. As we peered out from the closed blinds in the grill, we saw women in mink, husbands in gray suits, children in Ralph Lauren and Laura Ashley. Hazel let out a sigh. "Aren't they beautiful?" she said. For just a moment, I found myself agreeing.

As I raced around taking out orders of coffee and baskets of hot rolls, I got a chance to see groups of families. Fathers seemed to be uniformly taller than six feet. Most of them were wearing blue blazers, white shirts, and incredibly out-of-style silk ties—the kind with little blue whales or little green ducks floating downward. They were bespectacled and conspicuously clean-shaven.

The "ladies," as the club prefers to call them, almost invariably had straight blonde hair. Whether or not they had brown roots and whether they were 25 or 48, ladies wore their hair blonde, straight, and off the face. No dangling earrings, five-carat diamonds, or designer handbags. Black velvet or pastel headbands were de rigueur.

There were also groups of high-school kids who wore torn jeans, sneakers or unlaced L. L. Bean shoes, and sweatshirts that said things like HOTCHKISS LACROSSE or ANDOVER CREW. At one table, two boys sat talking to two girls.

"No way, J.C.," one of the girls cried in disbelief while playing with the straw in her diet Coke.

The strawberry-blonde girl next to her flashed her unpainted nails in the air. "Way. She said that if she didn't get her grades up by this spring, they were going to take her out altogether."

"And where would they send her?" one of the guys asked.

The strawberry blonde's grin disappeared as she leaned in close. "Public school." 120

The group, in hysterics, shook the table. The guys stomped their feet.

"Oh, my God, J.C., oh, J.C., J.C.," the diet-Coke girl cried.

Sitting in a tableless corner of the room, beneath the TV, was a young, dark-skinned black woman dressed in a white uniform and a thick wool coat. On her lap was a baby with silky white-blond hair. The woman sat patiently, shifting the baby in her lap while glancing over to where the baby's family ate, two tables away.

I ran to the kitchen, brought back a glass of tea, and offered it to her. The woman looked up at me, shook her head, and then turned back to the gurgling infant.

April 21 (Tuesday)

While Hector and I stood inside a deep walk-in freezer, we 125 scooped balls of butter into separate butter dishes and talked about our plans. "Will you go finish school sometime?" he asked as I dug deep into a vat of frozen butter.

"Maybe. In a couple years, when I save more money, but I'm not sure."

I felt lousy about having to lie.

Just as we were all leaving for the day, Mr. Ryan came down to hand out the new policies for those who were going to live in the Monkey House. Since it had recently been renovated, the club was requiring all new residents to sign the form. The policy included a rule that forbade employees to have overnight guests. Rule 14 stated that the club management had the right to enter an employee's locked bedroom at any time, without permission and without giving notice.

As I was making rounds with my coffeepots, I overheard a raspy-voiced woman talking to a mother and daughter who were thumbing through a catalogue of infants' clothing.

"The problem with au pairs is that they're usually only in the 130 country for a year."

The mother and daughter nodded in agreement.

"But getting one that is a citizen has its own problems. For example, if you ever have to choose between a Negro and one of these Spanish people, always go for the Negro."

One of the women frowned, confused. "Really?"

"Yes," the raspy-voiced woman responded with cold logic. "Even though you can't trust either one, at least Negroes speak English and can follow your directions."

Before I could refill the final cup, the raspy-voiced woman 135 looked up at me and smiled. "Oh, thanks for the refill, Larry."

April 22 (Wednesday)

"This is our country, and don't you forget it. They came here and have to live by our rules!" Hazel pounded her fist into the palm of her pale white hand.

I had made the mistake of telling her I had learned a few Spanish phrases to help me communicate better with some of my co-workers. She wasn't impressed.

"I'll be damned if I'm going to learn or speak one word of Spanish. And I'd suggest you do the same," she said. She took a long drag on her cigarette while I loaded the empty shelves with clean glasses.

Today, the TV was tuned to testimony and closing arguments from the Rodney King police-beating trial in California.

"I am so sick of seeing that awful videotape," one woman said to 140 friends at her table. "It shouldn't be on TV."

At around two, Lois, the club's official secretary, asked me to help her send out a mailing to 600 members after my shift.

She took me up to her office on the main floor and introduced me to the two women who sat with her.

"Larry, this is Marge, whom you'll talk with in three months, because she's in charge of employee benefits."

I smiled at the brunette.

"And Larry, this is Sandy, whom you'll talk with after you 145 become a member at the club, because she's in charge of members' accounts."

Both Sandy and I looked up at Lois with shocked expressions.

Lois winked, and at the same moment, the three jovial women burst out laughing.

Lois sat me down at a table in the middle of the club's cavernous ballroom and had me stamp ANNUAL MEMBER GUEST on the bottom of small postcards and stuff them into envelopes.

As I sat in the empty ballroom, I looked around at the mirrors and the silver-and-crystal chandeliers that dripped from the high ceiling. I thought about all the beautiful weddings and debutante balls that must have taken place in that room. I could imagine members asking themselves, "Why would anybody who is not like us want to join a club where they're not wanted?"

I stuffed my last envelope, forgot to clock out, and drove back to the Merritt Parkway and into New York.   150

April 23 (Thursday)

"Wow, that's great," I said to Mr. Ryan as he posted a memo entitled "Employee Relations Policy Statement: Employee Golf Privileges."

After quickly reading the memo, I realized this "policy" was a crock. The memo opened optimistically: "The club provides golf privileges for staff. . . . Current employees will be allowed golf privileges as outlined below." Unfortunately, the only employees that the memo listed "below" were department heads, golf-management personnel, teaching assistants, the general manager, and "key staff that appear on the club's organizational chart."

At the end of the day, Mr. Ryan handed me my first paycheck. The backbreaking work finally seemed worthwhile. When I opened the envelope and saw what I'd earned—$174.04 for five days—I laughed out loud.

Back in the security of a bathroom stall, where I had periodically been taking notes since my arrival, I studied the check and thought about how many hours—and how hard—I'd worked for so little money. It was less than one tenth of what I'd make in the same time at my law firm. I went upstairs and asked Mr. Ryan about my paycheck.

"Well, we decided to give you $7 an hour," he said in a tone   155
overflowing with generosity. I had never actually been told my hourly rate. "But if the check looks especially big, that's because you got some extra pay in there for all of your terrific work on Good Friday. And by the way, Larry, don't tell the others what you're getting, because we're giving you a special deal and it's really nobody else's business."

I nodded and thanked him for his largess. I stuffed some more envelopes, emptied out my locker, and left.

The next morning, I was scheduled to work a double shift. Instead, I called and explained that I had a family emergency and would have to quit immediately. Mr. Ryan was very sympathetic and said I could return when things settled down. I told him, "No, thanks," but asked that he send my last paycheck to my home. I put my uniform and the key to my locker in a brown padded envelope, and I mailed it all to Mr. Ryan.

Somehow it took two months of phone calls for me to get my final paycheck ($123.74, after taxes and a $30 deduction).

I'm back at my law firm now, dressed in one of my dark-gray Paul Stuart suits, sitting in a handsome office 30 floors above midtown. It's a long way from the Monkey House, but we have a long way to go.

Notes

1. All names of club members and personnel have been changed.

RESPONDING IN DISCUSSION OR WRITING

1. How do you react to Graham's way of "find[ing] out what things were really like" at a club where he saw no black members?

2. Which parts of Graham's story made the biggest impact on you? Why? Do you think he was aiming for the effect he had on you?

3. What does Graham mean by his last sentence? What connections does it lead you to make to other parts of the article?

4. What kind of reaction do you imagine the article caused from the club's management and members?

5. How accurate a picture do you think you find here of racism in the present-day North American continent? What incidents provide evidence for your point of view?

WRITING ASSIGNMENTS

1. In an essay, consider the issue of the deception involved in creating this article. Do you think it matters that Graham had to lie in order to get this story? Do you see any ethical dilemma in how he got the material? Do Graham's ends (purposes) justify his means? Do the ends always justify the means?

2. Write a letter to *New York* magazine from the manager of the Greenwich Country Club, replying to the issues Graham raises.

3. Write an exploratory essay in which you discuss the corporate and personal issues of race that are prominent in this article. Consider issues such as the following: Why would race be more important to the country club in assigning jobs than qualifications or language ability? Why would an African American lawyer want to go undercover to work in a menial job in order to write a story like this, and why would a mainstream magazine want to publish it? What does the situation reveal about the society in which the events took place?

LINGUISTIC TERRORISM

GLORIA ANZALDÚA

Gloria Anzaldúa was born in 1942 and grew up in Texas, close to the border between Texas and Mexico. She is a Chicana, feminist, lesbian writer who has worked to improve conditions for migrant farm workers. She sees herself in many ways as on the border between cultures, and in her writing she relentlessly works to obliterate borders, mixing poetry and prose; history and fiction; and English, Spanish, their dialects, and American Indian languages. She has taught at several universities, including the University of Texas at Austin and San Francisco State University. This selection is from Borderlands/La Frontera: The New Mestiza *(1987), which is an exploration of multiple issues, including ethnicity, sexuality, and language.* Mestiza *means a woman with a mixed racial background.*

> *Deslenguadas. Somos los del español deficiente.* We are your linguistic nightmare, your linguistic aberration, your linguistic *mestisaje,* the subject of your *burla.* Because we speak with tongues of fire we are culturally crucified. Racially, culturally and linguistically *somos huérfanos*—we speak an orphan tongue.

CHICANAS WHO GREW UP speaking Chicano Spanish have internalized the belief that we speak poor Spanish. It is illegitimate, a bastard language. And because we internalize how our language has been used against us by the dominant culture, we use our language differences against each other.

Chicana feminists often skirt around each other with suspicion and hesitation. For the longest time I couldn't figure it out. Then it dawned on me. To be close to another Chicana is like looking into the mirror. We are afraid of what we'll see there. *Pena.* Shame. Low estimation of self. In childhood we are told that our language is wrong. Repeated attacks on our native tongue diminish our sense of self. The attacks continue throughout our lives.

Chicanas feel uncomfortable talking in Spanish to Latinas, afraid of their censure. Their language was not outlawed in their countries. They had a whole lifetime of being immersed in their native tongue; generations, centuries in which Spanish was a first language, taught in school, heard on radio and TV, and read in the newspaper.

If a person, Chicana or Latina, has a low estimation of my   5
native tongue, she also has a low estimation of me. Often with *mexicanas y latinas* we'll speak English as a neutral language. Even among Chicanas we tend to speak English at parties or conferences. Yet, at the same time, we're afraid the other will think we're *agringadas* because we don't speak Chicano Spanish. We oppress each other trying to out-Chicano each other, vying to be the "real" Chicanas, to speak like Chicanos. There is no one Chicano language just as there is no one Chicano experience. A monolingual Chicana whose first language is English or Spanish is just as much a Chicana as one who speaks several variants of Spanish. A Chicana from Michigan or Chicago or Detroit is just as much a Chicana as one from the Southwest. Chicano Spanish is as diverse linguistically as it is regionally.

By the end of this century, Spanish speakers will comprise the biggest minority group in the U.S., a country where students in high schools and colleges are encouraged to take French classes because French is considered more "cultured." But for a language to remain alive it must be used.[1] By the end of this century English, and not Spanish, will be the mother tongue of most Chicanos and Latinos.

So, if you want to really hurt me, talk badly about my language. Ethnic identity is twin skin to linguistic identity—I am my language. Until I can take pride in my language, I cannot take pride in myself. Until I can accept as legitimate Chicano Texas Spanish, Tex-Mex and all the other languages I speak, I cannot accept the legitimacy of myself. Until I am free to write bilingually and to switch codes without having always to translate, while I still have to speak English or Spanish when I would rather speak Spanglish, and as long as I have to accommodate the English speakers rather than having them accommodate me, my tongue will be illegitimate.

I will no longer be made to feel ashamed of existing. I will have my voice: Indian, Spanish, white. I will have my serpent's tongue —my woman's voice, my sexual voice, my poet's voice. I will overcome the tradition of silence.

> My fingers
> move sly against your palm
> Like women everywhere, we speak in code. . . .
> —*Melanie Kaye/Kantrowitz*[2]

"Vistas," corridos, y comida: My Native Tongue

In the 1960s, I read my first Chicano novel. It was *City of Night* by John Rechy, a gay Texan, son of a Scottish father and a Mexican mother. For days I walked around in stunned amazement that a Chicano could write and could get published. When I read *I Am Joaquín*[3] I was surprised to see a bilingual book by a Chicano in print. When I saw poetry written in Tex-Mex for the first time, a feeling of pure joy flashed through me. I felt like we really existed as a people. In 1971, when I started teaching High School English to Chicano students, I tried to supplement the required texts with works by Chicanos, only to be reprimanded and forbidden to do so by the principal. He claimed that I was supposed to teach "American" and English literature. At the risk of being fired, I swore my students to secrecy and slipped in Chicano short stories, poems, a play. In graduate school, while working toward a Ph.D., I had to "argue" with one advisor after the other, semester after semester, before I was allowed to make Chicano literature an area of focus.

Even before I read books by Chicanos or Mexicans, it was the Mexican movies I saw at the drive-in—the Thursday night special of $1.00 a carload—that gave me a sense of belonging. "*Vámonos a las vistas,"* my mother would call out and we'd all—grandmother, brothers, sister and cousins—squeeze into the car. We'd wolf down cheese and bologna white bread sandwiches while watching Pedro Infante in melodramatic tearjerkers like *Nosotros los pobres,* the first "real" Mexican movie (that was not an imitation of European movies). I remember seeing *Cuando los hijos se van* and surmising that all Mexican movies played up the love a mother has for her children and what ungrateful sons and daughters suffer when they are not devoted to their mothers. I remember the singing-type "westerns" of Jorge Negrete and Miquel Aceves Mejía. When watching Mexican movies, I felt a sense of homecoming as well as alienation. People who were to amount to something didn't go to Mexican movies, or *bailes* or tune their radios to *bolero, rancherita,* and *corrido* music.

The whole time I was growing up, there was *norteño* music sometimes called North Mexican border music, or Tex-Mex music, or Chicano music, or *cantina* (bar) music. I grew up listening to *conjuntos,* three- or four-piece bands made up of folk musicians playing guitar, *bajo sexto,* drums and button accordion, which Chicanos had borrowed from the German immigrants who had come to Central Texas and Mexico to farm and build breweries. In the Rio Grande Valley, Steve Jordan and Little Joe Hernández were popular, and Flaco Jiménez was the accordion king. The rhythms of Tex-Mex music are those of the polka, also adapted from the Germans, who in turn had borrowed the polka from the Czechs and Bohemians.

I remember the hot, sultry evenings when *corridos*—songs of love and death on the Texas-Mexican borderlands—reverberated out of cheap amplifiers from the local *cantinas* and wafted in through my bedroom window.

Corridos first became widely used along the South Texas/Mexican border during the early conflict between Chicanos and Anglos. The *corridos* are usually about Mexican heroes who do valiant deeds against the Anglo oppressors. Pancho Villa's song, *"La cucaracha,"* is the most famous one. *Corridos* of John F. Kennedy and his death are still very popular in the Valley. Older Chicanos remember Lydia Mendoza, one of the great border *corrido* singers who was called *la Gloria de Tejas.* Her *"El tango negro,"* sung during the Great Depression, made her a singer of the people. The everpresent *corridos* narrated one hundred years of border history, bringing news of events as well as entertaining. These folk musicians and folk songs are our chief cultural mythmakers, and they made our hard lives seem bearable.

I grew up feeling ambivalent about our music. Country-western and rock-and-roll had more status. In the 50s and 60s, for the slightly educated and *agringado* Chicanos, there existed a sense of shame at being caught listening to our music. Yet I couldn't stop my feet from thumping to the music, could not stop humming the words, nor hide from myself the exhilaration I felt when I heard it.

There are more subtle ways that we internalize identification, especially in the forms of images and emotions. For me food and certain smells are tied to my identity, to my homeland. Woodsmoke curling up to an immense blue sky; woodsmoke perfuming my grandmother's clothes, her skin. The stench of cow manure and the yellow patches on the ground; the crack of a .22 rifle and the reek of cordite. Homemade white cheese sizzling in a pan, melting inside a folded *tortilla*. My sister Hilda's hot, spicy *menudo, chile colorado* making it deep red, pieces of *panza* and hominy floating on top. My brother Carito barbequing *fajitas* in the backyard. Even now and 3,000 miles away, I can see my mother spicing the ground beef, pork and venison with *chile*. My mouth salivates at the thought of the hot steaming *tamales* I would be eating if I were home.

Notes

1. Irena Klepfisz, "Secular Jewish Identity: Yidishkayt in America," in *The Tribe of Dina,* Melanie Kaye/Kantrowitz and Irena Klepfisz, eds. (Montpelier, VT: Sinister Wisdom Books, 1986), 43.

2. Melanie Kaye/Kantrowitz, "Sign," in *We Speak In Code: Poems and Other Writings* (Pittsburgh, Pa: Motheroot Publications, Inc., 1980), 85.

3. Rodolfo Gonzales, *I Am Joaquín/Yo Soy Joaquín* (New York, N.Y.: Bantam Books, 1972). It was first published in 1967.

RESPONDING IN DISCUSSION OR WRITING

1. *Considerations of Style.* If you don't know what the Spanish phrases mean, what guesses can you make from the context in

which they appear? What effect do the Spanish phrases have on you as you read? What do you think Anzaldúa hopes and expects her readers will do as they read her work?

2. Whom do you think Anzaldúa is addressing with the "your" of the first paragraph? What makes you draw that conclusion?

3. How does Anzaldúa convey and justify the section title of "Linguistic Terrorism"?

4. Anzaldúa describes vividly the role that movies played in developing her sense of belonging to a culture. What other cultural experiences can also help develop a sense of belonging to a particular group or culture? Which cultural experiences have been particularly memorable for you in contributing to a sense of belonging?

5. Do you agree with Anzaldúa when she says that "folk musicians and folk songs" create cultural myths? What reasons do you have for your opinion? What experiences of your own have helped form your opinion?

6. Anzaldúa gives many examples of specific smells and specific types of food. What images occur to you about your own life as you consider her statements? In what ways could you, too, say that food and smells are tied to your identity?

WRITING ASSIGNMENTS

1. Experiment with writing an unusual text like Anzaldúa's. Cross some borders of your own choosing, and mix dialects or languages, poetry and prose, slang and formal language as you write to tell a reader about your own experiences with language, books, music, or food—or all of them.

2. *For Further Research.* Anzaldúa writes about language and its links to identity. Explore that issue with regard to some other languages or dialects and the cultural identities that relate to them. You might, for instance, do research on Black English, Russian, Chinese, or another Asian language as representative of the culture in which it is spoken.

3. When Anzaldúa says "Ethnic identity is twin skin to linguistic identity—I am my language," how do you react? Write an essay in which you support that statement or argue against it, using examples from your own experience and use of language and dialect.

IT'S HARD ENOUGH BEING ME

ANNA LISA RAYA

Anna Lisa Raya, born in 1973 in Los Angeles, is a member of the class of 1995 at Columbia University, New York, majoring in English. This article first appeared in Columbia's Latino Alumni Newsletter *(February 1994) and was then republished in* Columbia College Today *the same year. Raya first wrote this essay for a course in magazine and feature writing, where the assignment was to write about a personal experience.*

WHEN I ENTERED COLLEGE, I *discovered* I was Latina. Until then, I had never questioned who I was or where I was from: My father is a second-generation Mexican-American, born and raised in Los Angeles, and my mother was born in Puerto Rico and raised in Compton, Calif. My home is El Sereno, a predominantly Mexican neighborhood in L.A. Every close friend I have back home is Mexican. So I was always just Mexican. Though sometimes I was just Puerto Rican—like when we would visit Mamo (my grandma) or hang out with my Aunt Titi.

Upon arriving in New York as a first-year student, 3000 miles from home, I not only experienced extreme culture shock, but for the first time I had to define myself according to the broad term "Latina." Although culture shock and identity crisis are common for the newly minted collegian who goes away to school, my experience as a newly minted Latina was, and still is, even more complicating. In El Sereno, I felt like I was part of a majority, whereas at the College I am a minority.

I've discovered that many Latinos like myself have undergone similar experiences. We face discrimination for being a minority in this country while also facing criticism for being "whitewashed" or "sellouts" in the countries of our heritage. But as an ethnic group in college, we are forced to define ourselves according to some vague, generalized Latino experience. This requires us to know our history, our language, our music, and our religion. I can't even be a content "Puerto Mexican" because I have to be a politically-and-socially-aware-Latina-with-a-chip-on-my-shoulder-because-of-how-repressed-I-am-in-this-country.

I am none of the above. I am the quintessential imperfect Latina. I can't dance salsa to save my life, I learned about Montezuma and the Aztecs in sixth grade, and I haven't prayed to the *Virgen de Guadalupe* in years.

Apparently I don't even look Latina. I can't count how many   5 times people have just assumed that I'm white or asked me if I'm Asian. True, my friends back home call me *güera* ("whitey") because I have green eyes and pale skin, but that was as bad as it got. I never thought I would wish my skin were a darker shade or my hair a curlier texture, but since I've been in college, I have—many times.

Another thing: my Spanish is terrible. Every time I call home, I berate my mama for not teaching me Spanish when I was a child. In fact, not knowing how to speak the language of my home countries is the biggest problem that I have encountered, as have many Latinos. In Mexico there is a term, *pocha,* which is used by native Mexicans to ridicule Mexican-Americans. It expresses a deep-rooted antagonism and dislike for those of us who were raised on the other side of the border. Our failed attempts to speak pure, Mexican Spanish are largely responsible for the dislike. Other Latin American natives have this same attitude. No matter how well a Latino speaks Spanish, it can never be good enough.

Yet Latinos can't even speak Spanish in the U.S. without running the risk of being called "spic" or "wetback." That is precisely why my mother refused to teach me Spanish when I was a child. The fact that she spoke Spanish was constantly used against her: It prevented her from getting good jobs, and it would have placed me in bilingual education—a construct of the Los Angeles public school system that has proved to be more of a hindrance to intellectual development than a help.

To be fully Latina in college, however, I *must* know Spanish. I must satisfy the equation: Latina = Spanish-speaking.

So I'm stuck in this black hole of an identity crisis, and college isn't making my life any easier, as I thought it would. In high school, I was being prepared for an adulthood in which I would be an individual, in which I wouldn't have to wear a Catholic school uniform anymore. But though I led an anonymous adolescence, I knew who I was. I knew I was different from white, black, or Asian people. I knew there was a language other than English that I could call my own if I only knew how to speak it better. I knew there were historical reasons why I was in this country, distinct reasons that make my existence here easier or more difficult than other people's existence. Ultimately, I was content.

Now I feel pushed into a corner, always defining, defending, and proving myself to classmates, professors, or employers. Trying to understand who and why I am, while understanding Plato or Homer, is a lot to ask of myself.

A month ago, I heard three Nuyorican (Puerto Ricans born and raised in New York) writers discuss how New York City has influenced their writing. One problem I have faced as a young writer is finding a voice that is true to my community. I was surprised and reassured to discover that as Latinos, these writers had faced similar pressures and conflicts as myself; some weren't even taught Spanish in childhood. I will never forget the advice that one of them gave me that evening: She said that I need to be true to myself. "Because people will always complain about what you are doing—you're a 'gringa' or a 'spic' no matter what," she explained. "So you might as well do things for yourself and not for them."

I don't know why it has taken 20 years to hear this advice, but I'm going to give it a try. *Soy yo* and no one else. *Punto.*

RESPONDING IN DISCUSSION OR WRITING

1. Did you or any of your acquaintances experience "culture shock and identity crisis" of any kind when you first went to college? If so, what forms did it take?

2. *For Further Research.* Raya made a discovery about herself when she entered college. Survey a few college students or classmates to find out what discoveries and new insights college has given them about themselves and their identities.

3. Who do you see as the audience for this piece of writing? Consider what message Raya wants to convey to that audience and whether or not she succeeds.

4. *Considerations of Style.* In paragraph 9, what effect does the repetition of the phrase "I knew" have on you as the reader?

5. Raya admits to being "stuck in this black hole of an identity crisis." What advice would you give her? Could she have avoided being stuck in a crisis? How?

6. *Considerations of Style.* Raya uses Spanish words at the end of her article. What is the effect of that, and why do you think she chose to end with Spanish words? How does her ending tie in with the title?

WRITING ASSIGNMENTS

1. Raya discusses how in college she is trying to understand Plato or Homer as well as who she is. Do you think that both are goals of a college education? If so, are they equal in importance? How much of the curricular requirements should be devoted to each? Write an essay in which you make a statement about the purposes of a college education, and support your statement by referring to your experiences and to what you have read.

2. Write an essay that begins as Raya's does: "When I entered college, I *discovered* I . . ." and in the essay explain and develop what you mean by that statement and what the discovery has meant for your life.

3. Raya says that her Spanish is terrible because she did not learn it at home. Do you think that children should learn the language of their culture, and, if so, should it be at home or at school? Write an essay in which you consider the arguments people make for and against maintaining native languages in schools and the home. You might want to read the selection by Richard Rodriguez in Unit 6 to give you some more background material to answer this question.

❖

ENGLISH AS A SECOND LANGUAGE

LUCY HONIG

Lucy Honig, born in 1948, has lived in Maine; Brooklyn, New York; and now upstate New York. She teaches English as a Second Language and is the author of many short stories and a novel, Picking Up *(1986). This story was published in the collection* Prize Stories 1992 *and was the winner of an O. Henry Memorial Award.*

INSIDE ROOM 824, MARIA parked the vacuum cleaner, fastened all the locks and the safety chain and kicked off her shoes. Carefully she lay a stack of fluffy towels on the bathroom vanity. She turned the air conditioning up high and the lights down low. Then she hoisted up the skirt of her uniform and settled all the way back on the king-sized bed with her legs straight out in front of her. Her feet and ankles were swollen. She wriggled her toes. She threw her arms out in each direction and still her hands did not come near the edges of the bed. From here she could see, out the picture window, the puffs of green treetops in Central Park, the tiny people circling along the paths below. She tore open a small foil bag of cocktail peanuts and ate them very slowly, turning each one over separately with her tongue until the salt dissolved. She snapped on the TV with the remote control and flipped channels.

The big mouth game show host was kissing and hugging a woman playing on the left-hand team. Her husband and children were right there with her, and *still* he encircled her with his arms. Then he sidled up to the daughter, a girl younger than her own Giuliette, and *hugged* her and kept *holding* her, asking questions. None of his business, if this girl had a boyfriend back in Saginaw!

"Mama, you just don't understand." That's what Jorge always said when she watched TV at home. He and his teenaged friends would sit around in their torn bluejeans dropping potato chips between the cushions of her couch and laughing, writhing with laughter while she sat like a stone.

Now the team on the right were hugging each other, squealing, jumping up and down. They'd just won a whole new kitchen— refrigerator, dishwasher, clothes washer, microwave, *everything*! Maria could win a whole new kitchen too, someday. You just spun a wheel, picked some words. She could do that.

She saw herself on TV with Carmen and Giuliette and Jorge.   5 Her handsome children were so quick to press the buzzers the other team never had a chance to answer first. And they got every single answer right. Her children shrieked and clapped and jumped up and down each time the board lit up. They kissed and hugged that man whenever they won a prize. That man put his hands on her beautiful young daughters. That man pinched and kissed *her,* an old woman, in front of the whole world! Imagine seeing *this* back home! Maria frowned, chewing on the foil wrapper. There was nobody left at home in Guatemala, nobody to care if a strange man squeezed her wrinkled flesh on the TV.

"Forget it, Mama. They don't let poor people on these programs," Jorge said one day.

"But poor people need the money, they can win it here!"

Jorge sighed impatiently. "They don't give it away because you *need* it!"

It was true, she had never seen a woman with her kids say on a show: My husband's dead. Jorge knew. They made sure before they invited you that you were the right kind of people and you said the right things. Where would she put a new kitchen in her cramped apartment anyway? No hookups for a washer, no space for a two-door refrigerator . . .

She slid sideways off the bed, carefully smoothed out the   10 quilted spread, and squeezed her feet into her shoes. Back out in the hall she counted the bath towels in her cart to see if there were enough for the next wing. Then she wheeled the cart down the long corridor, silent on the deep blue rug.

Maria pulled the new pink dress on over her head, eased her arms into the sleeves, then let the skirt slide into place. In the mirror she saw a small dark protrusion from a large pink flower. She struggled to zip up in back, then she fixed the neck, attaching the white collar she had crocheted. She pinned the rhinestone brooch on next. Shaking the pantyhose out of the package, she remembered the phrase: the cow before the horse, wasn't that it?

She should have put these on first. Well, so what. She rolled down the left leg of the nylons, stuck her big toe in, and drew the sheer fabric around her foot, unrolling it up past her knee. Then she did the right foot, careful not to catch the hose on the small flap of scar.

The right foot bled badly when she ran over the broken glass, over what had been the only window of the house. It had shattered from gunshots across the dirt yard. The chickens dashed around frantically, squawking, trying to fly, spraying brown feathers into the air. When she had seen Pedro's head turn to blood and the two oldest boys dragged away, she swallowed every word, every cry, and ran with the two girls. The fragments of glass stayed in her foot for all the days of hiding. They ran and ran and ran and somehow Jorge caught up and they were found by their own side and smuggled out. And still she was silent, until the nurse at the border went after the glass and drained the mess inside her foot. Then she had sobbed and screamed, "Aaiiiee!"

"Mama, stop thinking and get ready," said Carmen.

"It is too short, your skirt," Maria said in Spanish. "What will they say?"

Carmen laughed. "It's what they all wear, except for you old ladies."

"Not to work! Not to school!"

"Yes, to work, to school! And Mama, you are going for an award for your English, for all you've learned, so please speak English!"

Maria squeezed into the pink high heels and held each foot out, one by one, so she could admire the beautiful slim arch of her own instep, like the feet of the American ladies on Fifth Avenue. Carmen laughed when she saw her mother take the first faltering steps, and Maria laughed too. How much she had already practiced in secret, and still it was so hard! She teetered on them back and forth from the kitchen to the bedroom, trying to feel steady, until Carmen finally sighed and said, "Mama, quick now or you'll be late!"

She didn't know if it was a good omen or a bad one, the two Indian women on the subway. They could have been sitting on the dusty ground at the market in San —— , selling corn or clay pots, with the bright-colored striped shawls and full skirts, the black hair pulled into two braids down each back, the deeply furrowed square faces set in those impassive expressions, seeing everything, seeing nothing. They were exactly as they must have been back home, but she was seeing them *here,* on the downtown IRT from the Bronx, surrounded by businessmen in suits, kids with big radio boxes, girls in skin-tight jeans and dark purple lipstick. Above them, advertisements for family planning and TWA. They were like stone-age men sitting on the train in loincloths made from animal skins, so out of place, out of time. Yet timeless. Maria thought, they are timeless guardian spirits, here to accompany me to my honors. Did anyone else see them? As strange as they were, nobody looked. Maria's heart pounded faster. The boys with the radios were standing right over them and never saw them. They were invisible to everyone but her: Maria was utterly convinced of it. The spirit world had come back to life, here on the number 4 train! It was a miracle!

"Mama, look, you see the grandmothers?" said Carmen.   20

"Of course I see them," Maria replied, trying to hide the disappointment in her voice. So Carmen saw them too. They were not invisible. Carmen rolled her eyes and smirked derisively as she nodded in their direction, but before she could put her derision into words, Maria became stern. "Have respect," she said. "They are the same as your father's people." Carmen's face sobered at once.

She panicked when they got to the big school by the river. "Like the United Nations," she said, seeing so much glass and brick, an endless esplanade of concrete.

"It's only a college, Mama. People learn English here, too. And more, like nursing, electronics. This is where Anna's brother came for computers."

"Las Naciones Unidas," Maria repeated, and when the guard stopped them to ask where they were going, she answered in Spanish: to the literacy award ceremony.

"*English,* Mama!" whispered Carmen.   25

But the guard also spoke in Spanish: take the escalator to the third floor.

"See, he knows," Maria retorted.

"That's not the point," murmured Carmen, taking her mother by the hand.

Every inch of the enormous room was packed with people. She clung to Carmen and stood by the door paralyzed until Cheryl, her teacher, pushed her way to them and greeted Maria with a kiss. Then she led Maria back through the press of people to the small group of award winners from other programs. Maria smiled shakily and nodded hello.

"They're all here now!" Cheryl called out. A photographer rushed over and began to move the students closer together for a picture.

"Hey, Bernie, wait for the Mayor!" someone shouted to him. He spun around, called out some words Maria did not understand, and without even turning back to them, he disappeared. But they stayed there, huddled close, not knowing if they could move. The Chinese man kept smiling, the tall black man stayed slightly crouched, the Vietnamese woman squinted, confused, her glasses still hidden in her fist. Maria saw all the cameras along the sides of the crowd, and the lights, and the people from television with video machines, and more lights. Her stomach began to jump up and down. Would she be on television, in the newspapers? Still smiling, holding his pose, the Chinese man next to her asked, "Are you nervous?"

"Oh yes," she said. She tried to remember the expression Cheryl had taught them. "I have worms in my stomach," she said.

He was a much bigger man than she had imagined from seeing him on TV. His face was bright red as they ushered him into the room and quickly through the crowd, just as it was his turn to take the podium. He said hello to the other speakers and called them by their first names. The crowd drew closer to the little stage, the people standing farthest in the back pushed in. Maria tried hard to listen to the Mayor's words. "Great occasion . . . pride of our city . . . ever since I created the program . . . people who have worked so hard . . . overcoming hardship . . . come so far." Was that them? Was he talking about them already? Why were the people out there all starting to laugh? She strained to understand, but still caught only fragments of his words. "My mother used to say . . . and I said, Look, Mama . . ." He was talking about *his* mother now; he called her Mama, just like Maria's kids called *her*. But everyone laughed so hard. At his mother? She forced herself to smile; up front, near the podium, everyone could see her. She should seem to pay attention and understand. Looking out into

the crowd she felt dizzy. She tried to find Carmen among all the
pretty young women with big eyes and dark hair. There she was!
Carmen's eyes met Maria's; Carmen waved. Maria beamed out at
her. For a moment she felt like she belonged there, in this crowd.
Everyone was smiling, everyone was so happy while the Mayor of
New York stood at the podium telling jokes. How happy Maria
felt too!

"Maria Perez grew up in the countryside of Guatemala, the oldest
daughter in a family of 19 children," read the Mayor as Maria
stood quaking by his side. She noticed he made a slight wheezing
noise when he breathed between words. She saw the hairs in his
nostrils, black and white and wiry. He paused. "Nineteen children!" he exclaimed, looking at the audience. A small gasp was
passed along through the crowd. Then the Mayor looked back at
the sheet of paper before him. "Maria never had a chance to learn
to read and write, and she was already the mother of five children
of her own when she fled Guatemala in 1980 and made her way to
New York for a new start."

It was her own story, but Maria had a hard time following. She   35
had to stand next to him while he read it, and her feet had started
to hurt, crammed into the new shoes. She shifted her weight from
one foot to the other.

"At the age of 45, while working as a chambermaid and sending
her children through school, Maria herself started school for the
first time. In night courses she learned to read and write in her
native Spanish. Later, as she was pursuing her G.E.D. in Spanish,
she began studying English as a Second Language. This meant
Maria was going to school five nights a week! Still she worked as
many as 60 hours cleaning rooms at the Plaza Hotel.

"Maria's ESL teacher, Cheryl Sands, says—and I quote—'Maria
works harder than any student I have ever had. She is an inspiration to her classmates. Not only has she learned to read and write
in her new language, but she initiated an oral history project in
which she taped and transcribed interviews with other students,
who have told their stories from around the world.' Maria was also
one of the first in New York to apply for amnesty under the 1986
Immigration Act. Meanwhile, she has passed her enthusiasm for
education to her children: her son is now a junior in high school,
her youngest daughter attends the State University, and her oldest

daughter, who we are proud to have with us today, is in her second year of law school on a scholarship."

Two older sons were dragged through the dirt, chickens squawking in mad confusion, feathers flying. She heard more gunshots in the distance, screams, chickens squawking. She heard, she ran. Maria looked down at her bleeding feet. Wedged tightly into the pink high heels, they throbbed.

The Mayor turned toward her. "Maria, I think it's wonderful that you have taken the trouble to preserve the folklore of students from so many countries." He paused. Was she supposed to say something? Her heart stopped beating. What was folklore? What was preserved? She smiled up at him, hoping that was all she needed to do.

"Maria, tell us now, if you can, what was one of the stories you collected in your project?" 40

This was definitely a question, meant to be answered. Maria tried to smile again. She strained on tiptoes to reach the microphone, pinching her toes even more tightly in her shoes. "Okay," she said, setting off a high-pitched ringing from the microphone.

The Mayor said, "Stand back," and tugged at her collar. She quickly stepped away from the microphone.

"Okay," she said again, and this time there was no shrill sound. "One of my stories, from Guatemala. You want to hear?"

The Mayor put his arm around her shoulder and squeezed hard. Her first impulse was to wriggle away, but he held tight. "Isn't she wonderful?" he asked the audience. There was a low ripple of applause. "Yes, we want to hear!"

She turned and looked up at his face. Perspiration was shining 45 on his forehead and she could see by the bright red bulge of his neck that his collar was too tight. "In my village in Guatemala," she began, "the mayor did not go along—get along—with the government so good."

"Hey, Maria," said the Mayor, "I know exactly how he felt!" The people in the audience laughed. Maria waited until they were quiet again.

"One day our mayor met with the people in the village. Like you meet people here. A big crowd in the square."

"The people liked him, your mayor?"

"Oh, yes," said Maria. "Very much. He was very good. He tried for more roads, more doctors, new farms. He cared very much about his people."

The Mayor shook his head up and down. "Of course," he said, and again the audience laughed.   50

Maria said, "The next day after the meeting, the meeting in the square with all the people, soldiers come and shoot him dead."

For a second there was total silence. Maria realized she had not used the past tense and felt a deep, horrible stab of shame for herself, shame for her teacher. She was a disgrace! But she did not have more than a second of this horror before the whole audience began to laugh. What was happening? They couldn't be laughing at her bad verbs? They couldn't be laughing at her dead mayor! They laughed louder and louder and suddenly flashbulbs were going off around her, the TV cameras swung in close, too close, and the Mayor was grabbing her by the shoulders again, holding her tight, posing for one camera after another as the audience burst into wild applause. But she hadn't even finished! Why were they laughing?

"What timing, huh?" said the Mayor over the uproar. "What d'ya think, the Republicans put her here, or maybe the Board of Estimate?" Everyone laughed even louder and he still clung to her and cameras still moved in close, lights kept going off in her face and she could see nothing but the sharp white poof! of light over and over again. She looked for Carmen and Cheryl, but the white poof! poof! poof! blinded her. She closed her eyes and listened to the uproar, now beginning to subside, and in her mind's eye saw chickens trying to fly, chickens fluttering around the yard littered with broken glass.

He squeezed her shoulders again and leaned into the microphone. "There are ways to get rid of mayors, and ways to get rid of mayors, huh Maria?"

The surge of laughter rose once more, reached a crescendo,   55
and then began to subside again. "But wait," said the Mayor. The cameramen stepped back a bit, poising themselves for something new.

"I want to know just one more thing, Maria," said the Mayor, turning to face her directly again. The crowd quieted. He waited a few seconds more, then asked his question. "It says here 19 children. What was it like growing up in a house with 19 children? How many *bathrooms* did you have?"

Her stomach dropped and twisted as the mayor put his hand firmly on the back of her neck and pushed her toward the microphone again. It was absolutely quiet now in the huge room. Everyone was waiting for her to speak. She cleared her throat and made the microphone do the shrill hum. Startled, she jumped back. Then there was silence. She took a big, trembling breath.

"We had no bathrooms there, Mister Mayor," she said. "Only the outdoors."

The clapping started immediately, then the flashbulbs burning up in her face. The Mayor turned to her, put a hand on each of her shoulders, bent lower and kissed her! Kissed her on the cheek!

"Isn't she terrific?" he asked the audience, his hand on the back of her neck again, drawing her closer to him. The audience clapped louder, faster. "Isn't she just the greatest?"

She tried to smile and open her eyes, but the lights were still going off—poof! poof!—and the noise was deafening.

"Mama, look, your eyes were closed *there*, too," chided Jorge, sitting on the floor in front of the television set.

Maria had watched the camera move from the announcer at the studio desk to her own stout form in bright pink, standing by the Mayor.

"In my village in Guatemala," she heard herself say, and the camera showed her wrinkled face close up, eyes open now but looking nowhere. Then the mayor's face filled the screen, his forehead glistening, and then suddenly all the people in the audience, looking ahead, enrapt, took his place. Then there was her wrinkled face again, talking without a smile. ". . . soldiers come and shoot him dead." Maria winced, hearing the wrong tense of her verbs. The camera shifted from her face to the Mayor. In the brief moment of shamed silence after she'd uttered those words, the Mayor drew his finger like a knife across his throat. And the audience began to laugh.

"Turn it off!" she yelled to Jorge. "Off! This minute!"

Late that night she sat alone in the unlighted room, soaking her feet in Epsom salts. The glow of the television threw shadows across the wall, but the sound was off. The man called Johnny was on the screen, talking. The people in the audience and the men in the band and the movie stars sitting on the couch all had their mouths wide open in what she knew were screams of laughter while Johnny wagged his tongue. Maria heard nothing except brakes squealing below on the street and the lonely clanging of garbage cans in the alley.

She thought about her English class and remembered the pretty woman, Ling, who often fell asleep in the middle of a lesson. The other Chinese students all teased her. Everyone knew that she sewed coats in a sweatshop all day. After the night class she took the subway to the Staten Island Ferry, and after the ferry crossing she had to take a bus home. Her parents were old and sick and she did all their cooking and cleaning late at night. She struggled to keep awake in class; it seemed to take all her energy simply to smile and listen. She said very little and the teacher never forced her, but she fell further and further behind. They called her the Quiet One.

One day just before the course came to an end the Quiet One asked to speak. There was no reason, no provocation—they'd been talking informally about their summer plans—but Ling spoke with a sudden urgency. Her English was very slow. Seeing what a terrible effort it was for her, the classmates all tried to help when she searched for words.

"In my China village there was a teacher," Ling began. "Man teacher." She paused. "All children love him. He teach mathematic. He very—" She stopped and looked up toward the ceiling. Then she gestured with her fingers around her face.

"Handsome!" said Charlene, the oldest of the three Haitian sisters in the class. 70

Ling smiled broadly. "Handsome! Yes, he very handsome. Family very rich before. He have sister go to Hong Kong who have many, many money."

"*Much* money," said Maria.

"Much, much money," repeated Ling thoughtfully. "Teacher live in big house."

"In China? Near you?"

"Yes. Big house with much old picture." She stopped and furrowed her forehead, as if to gather words inside of it. 75

"Art? Paint? Pictures like that?" asked Xavier.

Ling nodded eagerly. "Yes. In big house. Most big house in village."

"But big house, money, rich like that, bad in China," said Fu Wu. "Those year, Government bad to you. How they let him do?"

"In *my* country," said Carlos, "government bad to you if you got *small* house, *no* money."

"Me too," said Maria.

"Me too," said Charlene.

The Chinese students laughed.

Ling shrugged and shook her head. "Don't know. He have big house. Money gone, but keep big house. Then I am little girl." She held her hand low to the floor.

"I *was* a little girl," Charlene said gently.

"I *was*," said Ling. "Was, was." She giggled for a moment, then seemed to spend some time in thought. "We love him. All children love—all children did loved him. He giving tea in house. He was—was—so handsome!" She giggled. All the women in the class giggled. "He very nice. He learn music, he go . . . he went to school far away."

"America?"

Ling shook her head. "Oh no, no. You know, another . . . west."

"Europa!" exclaimed Maria proudly. "Espain!"

"No, no, another."

"France!" said Patricia, Charlene's sister. "He went to school in France?"

"Yes, France," said Ling. Then she stopped again, this time for a whole minute. The others waited patiently. No one said a word. Finally she continued. "But big boys in more old school not like him. He too handsome."

"Oooh!" sang out a chorus of women. "Too handsome!"

"The boys were jealous," said Carlos.

Ling seized the word. "Jealous! Jealous! They very jealous. He handsome, he study France, he very nice to children, he give tea and cake in big house, he show picture on wall." Her torrent of words came to an end and she began to think again, visibly, her brow furrowing. "Big school boys, they . . ." She stopped.

"Jealous!" sang out the others.

"Yes," she said, shaking her head "no". "But more. More bad. Hate. They hate him."

"That's bad," said Patricia.

"Yes, very bad." Ling paused, looking at the floor. "And they heat."

"Hate."

"No, they heat." 100

All the class looked puzzled. Heat? Heat? They turned to Cheryl.

The teacher spoke for the first time. "Hit?" Ling, do you mean hit? They hit him?" Cheryl slapped the air with her hand.

Ling nodded, her face somehow serious and smiling at the same time. "Hit many time. And also so." She scooted her feet back and forth along the floor.

"Oooh," exclaimed Charlene, frowning. "They kicked him with the feet."

"Yes," said Ling. "They kicked him with the feet and hit him 105 with the hands, many many time they hit, they kick."

"Where this happened?" asked Xavier.

"In the school. In classroom like . . ." She gestured to mean their room.

"In the school?" asked Xavier. "But other people were they there? They say stop, no?"

"No. Little children in room. They cry, they . . ." She covered her eyes with her hand, then uncovered them. "Big boys kick and hit. No one stop. No one help."

Everyone in class fell silent. Maria remembered: they could not 110 look at one another then. They could not look at their teacher.

Ling continued. "They break him, very hurt much place." She stopped. They all fixed their stares on Ling, they could bear looking only at her. "Many place," she said. Her face had not changed, it was still half smiling. But now there were drops coming from her eyes, a single tear down each side of her nose. Maria would never forget it. Ling's face did not move or wrinkle or frown. Her body was absolutely still. Her shoulders did not quake. Nothing in the shape or motion of her eyes or mouth changed. None of the things that Maria had always known happen when you cry happened when Ling shed tears. Just two drops rolled slowly down her two pale cheeks as she smiled.

"He very hurt. He *was* very hurt. He blood many place. Boys go away. Children cry. Teacher break and hurt. Later he in hospital. I go there visit him." She stopped, looking thoughtful. "I went there." One continuous line of wetness glistened down each cheek. "My mother, my father say don't go, but I see him. I say, 'You be better?' But he hurt. Doctors no did helped. He alone.

No doctor. No nurse. No medicine. No family." She stopped. They all stared in silence for several moments.

Finally Carlos said, "Did he went home?"

Ling shook her head. "He go home but no walk." She stopped. Maria could not help watching those single lines of tears moving down the pale round face. "A year, more, no walk. Then go."

"Go where?" 115

"End."

Again there was a deep silence. Ling looked down, away from them, her head bent low.

"Oh, no," murmured Charlene. "He died."

Maria felt the catch in her throat, the sudden wetness of tears on her own two cheeks, and when she looked up she saw that all the other students, men and women both, were crying too.

Maria wiped her eyes. Suddenly all her limbs ached, her bones 120 felt stiff and old. She took her feet from the basin and dried them with a towel. Then she turned off the television and went to bed.

RESPONDING IN DISCUSSION OR WRITING

1. What do you learn from the story about Maria's family, values, and economic situation? Which sentences give you information to let you make these judgments?

2. *Considerations of Style.* Honig provides many descriptive details about Maria: what she looks like; what she wears; what she eats, does, and thinks. How do these details affect the way you respond to the story?

3. Events in the story are frequently connected with watching television. How does Honig use television to highlight ideas and contrasts in her story?

4. What effect does the incident of the two Indian women on the subway have on the reader? Why do you think Honig included this incident? What purpose does the incident serve in the story?

5. How are issues of ethnicity and class connected in this story?

6. Why doesn't Maria understand what the people are laughing at when she tells her story about the people in her town shooting the Mayor dead? What is the source of the lack of understanding?

WRITING ASSIGNMENTS

1. Write an essay in which you discuss Maria and Ling as the story's two prominent characters. What connects their two stories, what do they have in common, why is Ling's story included, and how does Honig make the incidents of their lives make comments on society?

2. The incident of the cut foot and the broken glass is referred to a few times. In an essay, assess what purpose the incident serves. Why does Maria remember it at certain points? What effect does it have when it appears at various points in the story? How does Honig present it as related to the life the family leads in New York City?

3. What is the significance of the title of the story, "English as a Second Language"? Discuss in which ways this title is or is not appropriate.

CLASS POEM

AURORA LEVINS MORALES

Aurora Levins Morales now lives and works around San Francisco. She was born in 1954 in Puerto Rico, where she was brought up; she has a Puerto Rican mother and a Jewish father. She is regarded as a "cultural activist." This poem was published in Getting Home Alive *(1986), a volume coauthored with her mother, Rosario Morales.*

This is my poem in celebration of my middle class privilege
This is my poem to say out loud
I'm glad I had food, and shelter, and shoes,
glad I had books and travel, glad there was air and light
and room for poetry.   5

This poem is for Tita, my best friend
who played in the dirt with me

and married at eighteen (which was late) and who was a scientist
but instead she bore six children   and four of them died
Who wanted to know the exact location of color   10
in the hibiscus petal, and patiently peeled away the thinnest,
most translucent layers to find it
and who works in a douche bag factory in Maricao.

This poem is for the hunger of my mother
discovering books at thirteen in the New York Public Library   15
who taught me to read when I was five
and when we lived on a coffee farm
subscribed to a mail-order library,
who read the Blackwell's catalogue
like a menu of delights   20
and when we moved from Puerto Rico to the States
we packed 100 boxes of books and 40 of everything else.

This poem is for my father's immigrant Jewish family.
For my great-grandfather Abe Sackman
who worked in Bridgeport making nurse's uniforms   25
and came home only on weekends, for years, and who painted
on bits of old wooden crates, with housepaint,
birds and flowers for his great-grandchildren
and scenes of his old-country childhood.

This poem celebrates my father the scientist   30
who left the microscope within reach,
with whom I discovered the pomegranate eye of the fruitfly,
and yes, the exact location of color in a leaf.

This poem celebrates my brother the artist
who began to draw when he was two,   35
and so my parents bought him reams of paper
and when he used them up, bought him more,
and today it's a silkscreen workshop
and posters that travel around the world,
and I'm glad for him   and for Pop with his housepaints   40
and Tita staining the cement with crushed flowers
searching for color
and my mother shutting out the cries of her first-born

ten minutes at a time
to sketch the roofs and elevated tracks   45
in red-brown pastels.

This is for Norma
who died of parasites in her stomach when she was four
I remember because her mother wailed her name
screaming and sobbing   50
one whole afternoon in the road in front of our school
and for Angélica
who caught on fire while stealing kerosene for her family
and died in pain
because the hospital she was finally taken to   55
knew she was poor
and would not give her the oxygen she needed to live
but wrapped her in greased sheets
so that she suffocated.

This is a poem against the wrapped sheets,   60
against guilt.
This is a poem to say:
my choosing to suffer gives nothing
to Tita and Norma and Angélica
and that not to use the tongue, the self-confidence, the training 65
my privilege bought me
is to die again for people who are already dead
and who wanted to live.

And in case anyone here confuses the paraphernalia
with the thing itself   70
let me add that I lived with rats and termites
no carpet   no stereo   no TV
that the bath came in buckets and was heated on the stove
that I read by kerosene lamp and had Sears mail-order clothes
and that that has nothing to do   75
with the fact of my privilege.

Understand, I know exactly what I got: protection and choice
and I am through apologizing.
I am going to strip apology from my voice
my posture   80

my apartment
my clothing
my dreams
because the voice that says the only true puertorican
is a dead or dying puertorican   85
is the enemy's voice—
the voice that says
"How can you let yourself shine when Tita, when millions
are daily suffocating in those greased sheets . . ."
I refuse to join them there.   90
I will not suffocate.
I will not hold back.
Yes, I had books and food and shelter and medicine
and I intend to survive.

RESPONDING IN DISCUSSION OR WRITING

1. What is Morales saying in this poem about ethnic affiliation and social class? How do you think she defines "class"?

2. What feeling do you get from the poem? Is it upbeat and optimistic or depressing and pessimistic? What causes those feelings?

3. Do you see this as a poem mostly about class, or is it about family? Do you see the two as separable?

4. Why do you think the author included stanzas about friends as well as family? What do those stories add to the idea of "celebration" that Morales mentions in the first line?

5. Line 61 mentions "guilt" for the first time. What do you think Morales means by guilt? Does she have anything to feel guilty about?

6. Is there a point where the poem appears to change direction and take a new approach? If so, where is that point?

WRITING ASSIGNMENTS

1. Write a poem or an essay in which you celebrate and praise those who have influenced you and describe those less fortunate than yourself.

2. Write a prose account, in your own words, of Morales' experience, and explain why she celebrates her "middle class privilege" and why the poem is called "Class Poem."

Making Connections:
Ethnic Affiliation and Class

1. Both Jones and Jeffries write about having a black father and a white mother, yet they react to the experience in very different ways. Write an essay in which you contrast their reactions and behavior and the way they have written the article describing their experiences.

2. In Unit 1, Mary C. Waters discusses how people choose an ethnic affiliation. Discuss the choices discussed by Jones or Jeffries in light of the points Waters makes.

3. What picture of WASPS as an ethnic group emerges from the articles by Phipps and Graham? Comment on how the authors' different ethnic affiliations and points of view might influence their perceptions.

4. David J. Gordon, Lang Phipps, Gloria Anzaldúa, and Anna Lisa Raya all write about growing up with a precise ethnic affiliation because both parents were of the same race. Select two of these authors, and compare and contrast what they say about their relationship to their ethnic group.

5. In what ways does Graham's working as a busboy connect to the ideas of "passing" in the essays by Waters (Unit 1) and Heilbrun (Unit 3)? As you discuss the concept of passing, you might also want to take into account the movie *Trading Places,* which deals with a destitute black man and a successful white businessman being forced to exchange positions in society and adopt and adapt to each other's roles.

6. Watch five or six situation comedies or soap operas on TV and analyze how people of different ethnic backgrounds are depicted. What conclusions can you draw from your small sample?

7. In "Who I Am," Jeffries mentions (in paragraph 10) the 1954 *Brown v. Topeka* court case and ruling that outlawed racial segregation in the schools. Do library research to find out the

sequence of events that led to the case and how the case was handled. Write an essay in which you inform a reader of the case, and discuss why you think Jeffries could say that it was "a phrase on the lips of many people who lived thousands of miles from Kansas."

8. Jeffries describes writing a composition on "The American Dream" (paragraph 24). In Unit 3 of this book, Ruth Sidel writes about how some young women view the American Dream. What are the differences between the dreams experienced by Jeffries and by the group Sidel describes?

9. Keith Gilyard and Earl Shorris (in Unit 1) and Lawrence Otis Graham and Gloria Anzaldúa (in this unit) discuss language, dialects, and the ways in which they are perceived. In an essay discuss the ways in which their approaches are similar or different and express which author reaches out to you most directly and why.

10. Imagine you are Gloria Anzaldúa writing a letter to Anna Lisa Raya in response to her article. Which issues would you choose to discuss? Write the letter, and in it make references to both Raya's article and to the views expressed by Anzaldúa.

Family Ties

When our relatives are at home, we have to think of all their good points or it would be impossible to endure them. But when they are away, we console ourselves for their absence by dwelling on their vices.

—GEORGE BERNARD SHAW, Heartbreak House, *act 1, 1920*

All happy families resemble one another, but each unhappy family is unhappy in its own way.

—LEO TOLSTOY, Anna Karenina, *1876*

Family Ties

❖

Some aspects of identity are given; we are given, for example, our parents, siblings, sex, basic appearance, physical and mental attributes, ethnicity, and name. Some aspects are chosen and depend on how we interact with our environment; we can choose to change a name, forge a gender role, challenge stereotypes, educate ourselves, and form new family affiliations. In our family ties, we all face both the given and chosen aspects of identity. We are born into a family and immediately have a set of relatives. Usually we interact closely with family members and are greatly influenced by them. Disruptions can be painful, and people spend years searching for lost relatives and their own roots. Sometimes the family interactions themselves are painful, and people spend years trying to reconcile or escape. In addition to these "given" dimensions of family life, however, there is a powerful area of choice connected to family. When we get older we often choose partners and forge new family ties. We decide whom to live with, whether or not to raise children, and what roles within our lives we want to devote time to or deemphasize. Through these and other choices, we can create new families.

In both the given and the chosen dimensions of family life, our identity is shaped by roles. Our roles within our own family structure vary over time. At any one time, for instance, a woman might be daughter, granddaughter, wife, mother, sister, aunt, and niece. Over the course of a lifetime, a person's financial role varies also. One could be dependent, a breadwinner, an equal partner, or completely independent at various times, depending on circumstances. Each of these roles can be extremely gratifying or difficult—or, often, both simultaneously. Just as our roles within our family structure can vary, so, too, can the nature of the family within society. Divorce is more common now than it was fifty years ago. The growth of separation, divorce, and remarriage means that, at least within the traditional marriage culture of North America, it is not unusual for a person to have more than one partner in a lifetime. Family holidays now often feature half brothers and stepbrothers and sisters, stepchildren, adopted children, numerous grandparents, former partners, and couples who at one time or another have been linked to someone else within or outside the group. The extended family used to be a large family of blood relatives: grandparents, aunts, uncles, and cousins; in more recent years, it was supplanted by a nuclear family of adult partners, with or without children. Now the extended family occurs in a new way: an extended family of people connected by former relationships and partnerships, sometimes marriage, sometimes not. The demise and preservation of the nuclear family as a social and historical fact plays a crucial role in shaping the larger culture and individual identities.

The readings in this unit deal with traditional and nontraditional family structures and the roles people play within them. The first two selections present pictures of the members of traditional families interacting with one another. Joan Didion describes her visit to her old family home with her daughter but without her husband. Geoffrey Wolff portrays a father-son relationship and the methods his father used to "disassemble his history" and re-create his own identity. The concerns faced by an adopted child fitting into a family are the subject of an article by psychiatrist James P. Comer.

Two selections explore issues related to family life outside the traditional nuclear family of parents and natural or adopted children. First, Andrew Sullivan in a magazine article makes a case for legalizing gay marriage, which is challenged in an editorial of a more conservative magazine. Then, in a paper for a first-year writing course in college, Marie W. Dallam examines the evidence of the effects on children being brought up by homosexual partners. Two pieces of fiction focus on the expectations set by family members: Jeffery Chan's short story presents a vignette of a family discussing an arranged marriage; Amy Tan's story describes a mother's ambitions for her daughter and the daughter's reactions to those expectations. The unit ends with Jimmy Santiago Baca's poem "Family Ties," which describes a family picnic.

STARTING POINTS [FOR JOURNAL OR FREEWRITING]

Before you read the selections in this unit, write responses to the following questions.

1. How much of your own identity do you think is intimately tied to family connections, and in what ways do your feelings of identity change as you interact with family members?

2. Which people in your family work the hardest to preserve and strengthen family ties? How and why do they do that?

3. How closely are family ties connected with ethnicity? Do you think that a family comprising people of many cultures would be as close and as harmonious as one that is ethnically not diverse?

4. What factors do you think contribute to a harmonious partnership and family life? Does personal identity have to change upon commitment to fidelity to one partner?

5. In what ways does/doesn't your family reflect the stereotypical husband/wife/children model? Does your family include any nontraditional partnerships? Has family identity ever been uncomfortable for you because of ways in which your family differs from a perceived cultural norm?

❖

ON GOING HOME

JOAN DIDION

Joan Didion, a reporter and novelist born in 1934, is the author of many works of fiction and nonfiction, such as Play It as It Lays, The Book of Common Prayer, The White Album, Salvador, *and* After Henry. *She lives in California and is a regular contributor to* The New Yorker *and* The New York Review of Books. *This piece is from her collection of essays* Slouching Towards Bethlehem *(1968).*

I AM HOME FOR my daughter's first birthday. By "home" I do not mean the house in Los Angeles where my husband and I and the baby live, but the place where my family is, in the Central Valley of California. It is a vital although troublesome distinction. My husband likes my family but is uneasy in their house, because once there I fall into their ways, which are difficult, oblique, deliberately inarticulate, not my husband's ways. We live in dusty houses ("D-U-S-T," he once wrote with his finger on surfaces all over the house, but no one noticed it) filled with mementos quite without value to him (what could the Canton dessert plates mean to him? how could he have known about the assay scales, why should he care if he did know?), and we appear to talk exclusively about people we know who have been committed to mental hospitals, about people we know who have been booked on drunk-driving charges, and about property, particularly about property, land, price per acre and C-2 zoning and assessments and freeway access. My brother does not understand my husband's inability to perceive the advantage in the rather common real-estate transaction known as "sale-leaseback," and my husband in turn does not understand why so many of the people he hears about in my father's house have recently been committed to mental hospitals or booked on drunk-driving charges. Nor does he understand that when we talk about sale-leasebacks and right-of-way condemnations we are talking in code about the things we like best, the yellow fields and the cottonwoods and the rivers rising and falling and the mountain roads closing when the heavy snow comes in. We miss each other's points, have another drink and regard the fire. My brother refers to my husband, in his presence, as "Joan's husband." Marriage is the classic betrayal.

Or perhaps it is not any more. Sometimes I think that those of us who are now in our thirties were born into the last generation to carry the burden of "home," to find in family life the source of all tension and drama. I had by all objective accounts a "normal" and a "happy" family situation, and yet I was almost thirty years old before I could talk to my family on the telephone without crying after I had hung up. We did not fight. Nothing was wrong.

And yet some nameless anxiety colored the emotional charges between me and the place that I came from. The question of whether or not you could go home again was a very real part of the sentimental and largely literary baggage with which we left home in the fifties; I suspect that it is irrelevant to the children born of the fragmentation after World War II. A few weeks ago in a San Francisco bar I saw a pretty young girl on crystal take off her clothes and dance for the cash prize in an "amateur-topless" contest. There was no particular sense of moment about this, none of the effect of romantic degradation, of "dark journey," for which my generation strived so assiduously. What sense could that girl possibly make of, say, *Long Day's Journey into Night*? Who is beside the point?

That I am trapped in this particular irrelevancy is never more apparent to me than when I am home. Paralyzed by the neurotic lassitude engendered by meeting one's past at every turn, around every corner, inside every cupboard, I go aimlessly from room to room. I decide to meet it head-on and clean out a drawer, and I spread the contents on the bed. A bathing suit I wore the summer I was seventeen. A letter of rejection from *The Nation*, an aerial photograph of the site for a shopping center my father did not build in 1954. Three teacups hand-painted with cabbage roses and signed "E.M.," my grandmother's initials. There is no final solution for letters of rejection from *The Nation* and teacups hand-painted in 1900. Nor is there any answer to snapshots of one's grandfather as a young man on skis, surveying around Donner Pass in the year 1910. I smooth out the snapshot and look into his face, and do and do not see my own. I close the drawer, and have another cup of coffee with my mother. We get along very well, veterans of a guerrilla war we never understood.

Days pass. I see no one. I come to dread my husband's evening call, not only because he is full of news of what by now seems to me our remote life in Los Angeles, people he has seen, letters which require attention, but because he asks what I have been doing, suggests uneasily that I get out, drive to San Francisco or Berkeley. Instead I drive across the river to a family graveyard. It has been vandalized since my last visit and the monuments are broken, overturned in the dry grass. Because I once saw a rattlesnake in the grass I stay in the car and listen to a country-and-Western station. Later I drive with my father to a ranch he has in the foothills. The man who runs his cattle on it asks us to the roundup, a week from Sunday, and although I know that I will be in Los Angeles I say, in the oblique way my family talks, that I will come. Once home I mention the broken monuments in the graveyard. My mother shrugs.

I go to visit my great-aunts. A few of them think now that I am   5
my cousin, or their daughter who died young. We recall an anecdote about a relative last seen in 1948, and they ask if I still like living in New York City. I have lived in Los Angeles for three years, but I say that I do. The baby is offered a horehound drop, and I am slipped a dollar bill "to buy a treat." Questions trail off, answers are abandoned, the baby plays with the dust motes in a shaft of afternoon sun.

It is time for the baby's birthday party: a white cake, strawberry-marshmallow ice cream, a bottle of champagne saved from another party. In the evening, after she has gone to sleep, I kneel beside the crib and touch her face, where it is pressed against the slats, with mine. She is an open and trusting child, unprepared for and unaccustomed to the ambushes of family life, and perhaps it is just as well that I can offer her little of that life. I would like to give her more. I would like to promise her that she will grow up with a sense of her cousins and of rivers and of her great-grand-mother's teacups, would like to pledge her a picnic on a river with fried chicken and her hair uncombed, would like to give her *home* for her birthday, but we live differently now and I can promise her nothing like that. I give her a xylophone and a sundress from Madeira, and promise to tell her a funny story.

RESPONDING IN DISCUSSION OR WRITING

1. Why do you think Didion makes a distinction between her "home" where she lives with her husband and baby and her family home? What place or places do you regard as "home"?

2. When Didion comments that she and her generation find "in family life the source of all tension and drama," do you agree with her? In what ways does family life provide for drama and tension?

3. Why do you think Didion makes a statement at the end of the first paragraph—"Marriage is the classic betrayal"—and then immediately contradicts it—"Or perhaps it is not any more"? How do you respond to that contradiction?

4. *Considerations of Style.* Didion begins with "home" and ends with it, too. What effect does her return to the idea of "home" in the last paragraph, when she is looking at her daughter sleeping, have on the reader?

5. Does Didion's essay end as you expected? Why does she feel that she cannot offer her daughter "the ambushes of family life" (paragraph 6) and the traditions of "home"? What do you think she means by "the ambushes of family life"?

6. Didion tells stories about incidents and people. Which stories do you find appealing and memorable? What purpose do the stories play in Didion's essay?

WRITING ASSIGNMENTS

1. In a poem by Robert Frost, "The Death of the Hired Man," a man describes home in the following way: "Home is the place where, when you have to go there,/They have to take you in." His wife adds that home is "Something you somehow haven't to deserve." Write an essay in which you reflect on the meaning of the concept of "home" for Frost, Didion, and yourself. Describe some incidents you have experienced to illustrate what "home" means to you.

2. Discuss what it might be like to grow up in a traditional nuclear family (husband, wife, and children), in a nontraditional family (such as with a single parent, homosexual parents, unmarried parents, or other relatives), and in an extended family (parents, children, and many other relatives). Discuss the advantages and disadvantages of each situation. Give examples, and tell stories to let your reader know why you have formed your opinions.

❖❖

MEMORIES OF MY FATHER

GEOFFREY WOLFF

Geoffrey Wolff, born in 1937, lives in Vermont. He is writer in residence at Brandeis University in Massachusetts and the author of biographies and novels. This selection is the first chapter of The Duke of Deception: Memories of My Father *(1979), a memoir of his father, Duke, a charming con man, whom Wolff regarded as "a bad man and a good father." Other works are* The Final Club *(1990),* Day at the Beach Recollections *(1992), and* The Age of Consent *(1995).*

I LISTEN FOR MY father and I hear a stammer. This was explosive and unashamed, not a choking on words but a spray of words. His speech was headlong, edgy, breathless: there was neither room in his mouth nor time in the day to contain what he burned to utter. I have a remnant of that stammer, and I wish I did not; I stammer and blush, my father would stammer and grin. He depended on a listener's good will. My father depended excessively upon people's good will.

As he spoke straight at you, so did he look at you. He could stare down anyone, though this was a gift he rarely practiced. To me, everything about him seemed outsized. Doing a school report on the Easter Islanders I found in an encyclopedia pictures of their huge sculptures, and there he was, massive head and nose, nothing subtle or delicate. He was in fact (and how diminishing those words, *in fact,* look to me now) an inch or two above six feet, full bodied, a man who lumbered from here to there with deliberation. When I was a child I noticed that people were respectful of the cubic feet my father occupied; later I understood that I had confused respect with resentment.

I recollect things, a gentleman's accessories, deceptively simple fabrications of silver and burnished nickel, of brushed Swedish stainless, of silk and soft wool and brown leather. I remember his shoes, so meticulously selected and cared for and used, thin-soled, with cracked uppers, older than I was or could ever be, shining dully and from the depths. Just a pair of shoes? No: I knew before I knew any other complicated thing that for my father there was nothing he possessed that was "just" something. His pocket watch was not "just" a timepiece, it was a miraculous instrument with a hinged front and a representation on its back of porcelain ducks rising from a birch-girt porcelain pond. It struck the hour unassertively, musically, like a silver tine touched to a crystal glass, no hurry, you might like to know it's noon.

He despised black leather, said black shoes reminded him of black attaché cases, of bankers, lawyers, look-before-you-leapers anxious not to offend their clients. He owned nothing black except his dinner jacket and his umbrella. His umbrella doubled as a shooting-stick, and one afternoon at a polo match at Brandywine he was sitting on it when a man asked him what he would do if it rained, sit wet or stand dry? I laughed. My father laughed also, but tightly, and he did not reply; nor did he ever again use this quixotic contraption. He took things, *things,* seriously.

My father, called Duke, taught me skills and manners; he taught me to shoot and to drive fast and to read respectfully and to box and to handle a boat and to distinguish between good jazz music and bad jazz music. He was patient with me, led me to understand for myself why Billie Holiday's understatements were more interesting than Ella Fitzgerald's complications. His codes were not novel, but they were rigid, the rules of decorum that Hemingway prescribed. A gentleman kept his word, and favored simplicity of sentiment; a gentleman chose his words with care, as he chose his friends. A gentleman accepted responsibility for his acts, and welcomed the liberty to act unambiguously. A gentleman was a stickler for precision and punctilio; life was no more than an inventory of small choices that together formed a man's character, entire. A gentleman was this, and not that; a *man* did, did not, said, would not say.

My father could, however, be coaxed to reveal his bona fides. He had been schooled at Groton and passed along to Yale. He was just barely prepared to intimate that he had been tapped for "Bones," and I remember his pleasure when Levi Jackson, the black captain of Yale's 1948 football team, was similarly honored by that secret society. He was proud of Skull and Bones for its hospitality toward the exotic. He did sometimes wince, however, when he pronounced Jackson's Semitic Christian name, and I sensed that his tolerance for Jews was not inclusive; but I never heard him indulge express bigotry, and the first of half a dozen times he hit me was for having called a neighbor's kid a guinea.

There was much luxury in my father's affections, and he hated what was narrow, pinched, or mean. He understood exclusion, mind you, and lived his life believing the world to be divided between a few *us's* and many *thems,* but I was to understand that aristocracy was a function of taste, courage, and generosity. About two other virtues—candor and reticence—I was confused, for my father would sometimes proselytize the one, sometimes the other.

If Duke's preoccupation with bloodlines was finite, this did not cause him to be unmindful of his ancestors. He knew whence he had come, and whither he meant me to go. I saw visible evidence of this, a gold signet ring which I wear today, a heavy bit of business inscribed arsy-turvy with lions and flora and a motto, *nulla vestigium retrorsit.* "Don't look back" I was told it meant.

After Yale—class of late nineteen-twenty something, or early nineteen-thirty something—my father batted around the country, living a high life in New York among school and college chums, flying as a test pilot, marrying my mother, the daughter of a rear admiral. I was born a year after the marriage, in 1937, and three years after that my father went to England as a fighter pilot with Eagle Squadron, a group of American volunteers in the Royal Air Force. Later he transferred to the OSS, and was in Yugoslavia with the partisans; just before the Invasion he was parachuted into Normandy, where he served as a sapper with the Resistance, which my father pronounced *ray-zee-staunce.*

His career following the war was for me mysterious in its particulars; in the service of his nation, it was understood, candor was not always possible. This much was clear: my father mattered in the world, and was satisfied that he mattered, whether or not the world understood precisely why he mattered.

A pretty history for an American clubman. Its fault is that it was not true. My father was a bullshit artist. True, there were many boarding schools, each less pleased with the little Duke than the last, but none of them was Groton. There was no Yale, and by the time he walked from a room at a mention of Skull and Bones I knew this, and he knew that I knew it. No military service would have him; his teeth were bad. So he had his teeth pulled and replaced, but the Air Corps and Navy and Army and Coast Guard still thought he was a bad idea. The ring I wear was made according to his instructions by a jeweler two blocks from Schwab's drugstore in Hollywood, and was never paid for. The motto, engraved backwards so that it would come right on a red wax seal, is dog Latin and means in fact "leave no trace behind," but my father did not believe me when I told him this.

My father was a Jew. This did not seem to him a good idea, and so it was his notion to disassemble his history, begin at zero, and re-create himself. His sustaining line of work till shortly before he died was as a confidence man. If I now find his authentic history more surprising, more interesting, than his counterfeit history, he did not. He would not make peace with his actualities, and so he was the author of his own circumstances, and indifferent to the consequences of this nervy program.

There were some awful consequences, for other people as well as for him. He was lavish with money, with others' money. He preferred to stiff institutions: jewelers, car dealers, banks, fancy hotels. He was, that is, a thoughtful buccaneer, when thoughtfulness was convenient. But people were hurt by him. Much of his mischief was casual enough: I lost a tooth when I was six, and the Tooth Fairy, "financially inconvenienced" or "temporarily out of pocket," whichever was then his locution, left under my pillow an IOU, a sight draft for two bits, or two million.

I wish he hadn't selected from among the world's possible disguises the costume and credentials of a yacht club commodore. Beginning at scratch he might have reached further, tried something a bit more bold and odd, a bit less inexorably conventional, a bit less calculated to please. But it is true, of course, that a confidence man who cannot inspire confidence in his marks is nothing at all, so perhaps his tuneup of his bloodline, educational *vita,* and war record was merely the price of doing business in a culture preoccupied with appearances.

I'm not even now certain what I wish he had made of himself: I once believed that he was most naturally a fictioneer. But for all his preoccupation with make-believe, he never tried seriously to write it. A confidence man learns early in his career that to commit himself to paper is to court trouble. The successful bunco artist does his game, and disappears himself: Who *was* that masked man? No one, no one at all, *nulla vestigium* [*sic*] *retrorsit* [*sic*], not a trace left behind.

Well, I'm left behind. One day, writing about my father with no want of astonishment and love, it came to me that I am his creature as well as his get. I cannot now shake this conviction, that I was trained as his instrument of perpetuation, put here to put him into the record. And that my father knew this, calculated it to a degree. How else explain his eruption of rage when I once gave up what he and I called "writing" for journalism? I had taken a job as the book critic of *The Washington Post,* was proud of myself; it seemed then like a wonderful job, honorable and enriching. My father saw it otherwise: "You have failed me," he wrote, "you have sold yourself at discount" he wrote to me, his prison number stamped below his name.

He was wrong then, but he was usually right about me. He would listen to anything I wished to tell him, but would not tell me only what I wished to hear. He retained such solicitude for his clients. With me he was strict and straight, except about himself. And so I want to be strict and straight with him, and with myself. Writing to a friend about this book, I said that I would not now for anything have had my father be other than what he was, except happier, and that most of the time he was happy enough, cheered on by imaginary successes. He gave me a great deal, and not merely life, and I didn't want to bellyache; I wanted, I told my friend, to thumb my nose on his behalf at everyone who had limited him. My friend was shrewd, though, and said that he didn't believe me, that I couldn't mean such a thing, that if I followed out its implications I would be led to a kind of ripe sentimentality, and to mere piety. Perhaps, he wrote me, you would not have wished him to lie to himself, to lie about being a Jew. Perhaps you would have him fool others but not so deeply trick himself. "In writing about a father," my friend wrote me about our fathers, "one clambers up a slippery mountain, carrying the balls of another in a bloody sack, and whether to eat them or worship them or bury them decently is never cleanly decided."

So I will try here to be exact. I wish my father had done more headlong, more elegant inventing. I believe he would respect my wish, be willing to speak with me seriously about it, find some nobility in it. But now he is dead, and he had been dead two weeks when they found him. And in his tiny flat at the edge of the

Pacific they found no address book, no batch of letters held with a rubber band, no photograph. Not a thing to suggest that he had ever known another human being.

RESPONDING IN DISCUSSION OR WRITING

1. How would you sum up Wolff's feelings for his father? Point to the evidence for your conclusions.

2. Do you know any people who, like Duke, take "things" seriously? If so, what "things" are they especially serious about? Paragraphs 3 and 4 contain detailed descriptions of objects that Duke owned. Why does Wolff include these details? What effect do the details have on the reader?

3. How do you react to the idea of someone who attempts to "disassemble his history" and "re-create himself" in order to be "the author of his own circumstances" (paragraph 12)? Read *her* for *him* if your *someone* is a woman.

4. *Considerations of Style.* In paragraph 5, five sentences begin with "a gentleman." What is the effect of this repetition?

5. At what point in this narrative does Wolff present a turning point for readers, a point at which they begin to see his father in a new light? What was the effect of that turning point on you as you read? How effectively does Wolff preserve the fiction in the first part of this selection?

6. How does the ending of this chapter from Wolff's book make you evaluate the information about his father in the earlier part of the chapter?

WRITING ASSIGNMENTS

1. Write about an action by a member of your family, and discuss how that person could have acted differently and what the results would have been. Paint a written portrait of the person by describing the person's life, appearance, possessions, likes, dislikes, and personality traits.

2. Do you consider the "re-creating" of oneself by lying to others about one's background and achievements to be severely unethical and morally wrong—or can it be seen as merely a set of harmless white lies? What would be your reaction to somebody like Wolff's father?

ADOPTION AND IDENTITY

JAMES P. COMER

James P. Comer, M.D., a psychiatrist and educator, was born in East Chicago, Indiana, in 1934. At present, he is professor of child psychiatry and Dean of the School of Medicine at Yale University. He is the author of Maggie's American Dream: The Life and Times of a Black Family *(1988). This piece appeared in* Parents *magazine in January 1992.*

I ONCE WORKED WITH a parent who felt unappreciated and rejected because her twelve-year-old adopted daughter had become preoccupied with her unknown birth mother. But once the adoptive mother understood the motivation behind the girl's behavior at this stage of development, she was better able to manage her own feelings and to help her daughter.

Children identify with people, places, and ideas that are important to them. Just before adolescence, they begin to have a need to pull it all together and form their own identity, with specific knowledge about their origin and a general sense of where they can go with their life. The question "Who am I?" includes not only "Where did I come from?" but also "Am I adequate, valued, and wanted?" Preadolescents continue to seek the answers to these questions throughout their teenage years, and this process is a normal part of development.

When a child is adopted, she may feel an even stronger need to belong and to know that she is adequate. If these feelings are not addressed, developmental and behavioral problems can occur. Many adopted children face the gnawing question of rejection by their birth mother, thinking, "I must be really bad if she gave me away." Even when the child has addressed this issue at an earlier age, it often returns for reconsideration during preadolescence. But the child's concern is usually driven by a developmental need, not because she is rejecting her parents—as parents often fear— or because the issue was not managed well when she was younger.

Ideally, adoptive parents should introduce their child early on to the concept of adoption in a warm, relaxed way; they should also return periodically to the topic, gradually explaining the child's history in ways that she can understand as she gets older. If your child reexamines everything *but* adoption, it's up to you to bring up the matter again, in an informal way, and to help her cope with her feelings. You can't make it all better and make the pain go away, but you can let her know that it's okay for her to feel sad, that you are not upset by her feelings, and that you are there for her.

It's common for a child this age to question why she was given away. Most likely, the birth parents felt that they couldn't care for her properly and, so, gave her up so that someone else could give her a better life. Don't put down the natural parents; don't build them up; and don't be apologetic. 5

Try not to take it personally if your child expresses interest in her birth parents. This is not a threat to her relationship with you. In fact, knowing that you accept all her feelings—even the "forbidden" ones—can draw her closer to you.

If addressing the issues of adoption and identity get particularly difficult, don't blame yourself, the child, or the birth parents. Instead, seek professional help. Studies show that adopted children are just as successful in life as their nonadopted peers, and feel as close—or even closer—to the parents who raise them.

RESPONDING IN DISCUSSION OR WRITING

1. At what age do you think adopted children should be told they are adopted, and how should they be told?

2. Should unmarried people be allowed/encouraged to adopt children? (In some states, unmarried people are allowed to adopt; in others they are not.) Why or why not?

3. Why do parents give up children for adoption? Do you think that some of the reasons are more "acceptable" to a child than others?

4. Who are Comer's readers for this article? How does he address those specific readers' needs?

5. *Considerations of Style.* Comer is a doctor and an academic. Yet this article is not written in a very formal, academic style, with references and technical language. Why do you think Comer chose a less formal approach to the topic?

6. Comer begins his article with a story of a specific family. After that, he writes more generally about adopted children and their families. If his editor asked him to expand the article, he would probably decide to include more stories of specific cases. Decide where he could add incidents and examples. What stories do you know that could be included in this article?

WRITING ASSIGNMENTS

1. Comer does not touch on the topic of interracial adoption. Write an article on "Adoption and Identity" in which you address adoptive parents of children of a race different from their own.

2. Do you think that adopted children should be encouraged to seek out their birth parents when they reach a certain age? What are your reasons? What could be the advantages and disadvantages of such an action? What circumstances could affect how you might answer the question?

HERE COMES THE GROOM

ANDREW SULLIVAN

Andrew Sullivan, born in 1963 in England, is the editor of The New Republic, *where he writes frequently on current social and political issues. This article was published when he was a doctoral candidate in government at Harvard University. It appeared in* The New Republic *on August 28, 1989.*

[IN JULY, 1989] IN New York, a court ruled that a gay lover had the right to stay in his deceased partner's rent-control apartment because the lover qualified as a member of the deceased's family. The ruling deftly annoyed almost everybody. Conservatives saw judicial activism in favor of gay rent control: three reasons to be appalled. Chastened liberals (such as the *New York Times* editorial page), while endorsing the recognition of gay relationships, also worried about the abuse of already stretched entitlements that the ruling threatened. What neither side quite contemplated is that they both might be right, and that the way to tackle the issue of unconventional relationships in conventional society is to try something both more radical and more conservative than putting courts in the business of deciding what is and is not a family. That alternative is the legalization of civil gay marriage.

The New York rent-control case did not go anywhere near that far, which is the problem. The rent-control regulations merely stipulated that a "family" member had the right to remain in the apartment. The judge ruled that to all intents and purposes a gay lover is part of his lover's family, inasmuch as a "family" merely means an interwoven social life, emotional commitment, and some level of financial interdependence.

It's a principle now well established around the country. Several cities have "domestic partnership" laws, which allow relationships that do not fit into the category of heterosexual marriage to be registered with the city and qualify for benefits that up till now have been reserved for straight married couples. San Francisco, Berkeley, Madison, and Los Angeles all have legislation, as does the politically correct Washington, D.C., suburb, Takoma Park. In these cities, a variety of interpersonal arrangements qualify for health insurance, bereavement leave, insurance, annuity and pension rights, housing rights (such as rent-control apartments), adoption and inheritance rights. Eventually, according to gay lobby groups, the aim is to include federal income tax and veterans' benefits as well. A recent case even involved the right to use a family member's accumulated frequent-flier points. Gays are not the only beneficiaries; heterosexual "live-togethers" also qualify.

There's an argument, of course, that the current legal advantages extended to married people unfairly discriminate against people who've shaped their lives in less conventional arrangements. But it doesn't take a genius to see that enshrining in the law a vague principle like "domestic partnership" is an invitation to qualify at little personal cost for a vast array of entitlements otherwise kept crudely under control.

To be sure, potential DPs have to prove financial interdependence, shared living arrangements, and a commitment to mutual caring. But they don't need to have a sexual relationship or even closely mirror old-style marriage. In principle, an elderly woman and her live-in nurse could qualify. A couple of uneuphemistically confirmed bachelors could be DPs. So could two close college students, a pair of seminarians, or a couple of frat buddies. Left as it is, the concept of domestic partnership could open a Pandora's box of litigation and subjective judicial decision-making about who qualifies. You either are or are not married; it's not a complex question. Whether you are in a "domestic partnership" is not so clear.

More important, the concept of domestic partnership chips away at the prestige of traditional relationships and undermines the priority we give them. This priority is not necessarily a product of heterosexism. Consider heterosexual couples. Society has good reason to extend legal advantages to heterosexuals who choose the formal sanction of marriage over simply living together. They make a deeper commitment to one another and to society; in exchange, society extends certain benefits to them. Marriage provides an anchor, if an arbitrary and weak one, in the chaos of sex and relationships to which we are all prone. It provides a mechanism for emotional stability, economic security, and the healthy rearing of the next generation. We rig the law in its favor not because we disparage all forms of relationship other than the nuclear family, but because we recognize that not to promote marriage would be to ask too much of human virtue. In the context of the weakened family's effect upon the poor, it might also invite social disintegration. One of the worst products of the New Right's "family values" campaign is that its extremism and hatred of diversity has disguised this more measured and more convincing case for the importance of the marital bond.

The concept of domestic partnership ignores these concerns, indeed directly attacks them. This is a pity, since one of its most important objectives—providing some civil recognition for gay relationships—is a noble cause and one completely compatible with the defense of the family. But the way to go about it is not to undermine straight marriage; it is to legalize old-style marriage for gays.

The gay movement has ducked this issue primarily out of fear of division. Much of the gay leadership clings to notions of gay life as essentially outsider, anti-bourgeois, radical. Marriage, for them, is co-optation into straight society. For the Stonewall generation, it is hard to see how this vision of conflict will ever fundamentally change. But for many other gays—my guess, a majority—while they don't deny the importance of rebellion 20 years ago and are grateful for what was done, there's now the sense of a new opportunity. A need to rebel has quietly ceded to a desire to belong. To be gay and to be bourgeois no longer seems such an absurd proposition. Certainly since AIDS, to be gay and to be responsible has become a necessity.

Gay marriage squares several circles at the heart of the domestic partnership debate. Unlike domestic partnership, it allows for recognition of gay relationships, while casting no aspersions on traditional marriage. It merely asks that gays be allowed to join in. Unlike domestic partnership, it doesn't open up avenues for heterosexuals to get benefits without the responsibilities of marriage, or a nightmare of definitional litigation. And unlike domestic partnership, it harnesses to an already established social convention the yearnings for stability and acceptance among a fast-maturing gay community.

Gay marriage also places more responsibilities upon gays: it says 10 for the first time that gay relationships are not better or worse than straight relationships, and that the same is expected of them. And it's clear and dignified. There's a legal benefit to a clear, common symbol of commitment. There's also a personal benefit. One of the ironies of domestic partnership is that it's not only more complicated than marriage, it's more demanding, requiring an elaborate statement of intent to qualify. It amounts to a substantial invasion of privacy. Why, after all, should gays be required to prove commitment before they get married in a way we would never dream of asking of straights?

Legalizing gay marriage would offer homosexuals the same deal society now offers heterosexuals: general social approval and specific legal advantages in exchange for a deeper and harder-to-extract-yourself-from commitment to another human being. Like straight marriage, it would foster social cohesion, emotional security, and economic prudence. Since there's no reason gays should not be allowed to adopt or be foster parents, it could also help nurture children. And its introduction would not be some sort of radical break with social custom. As it has become more acceptable for gay people to acknowledge their loves publicly, more and more have committed themselves to one another for life in full view of their families and their friends. A law institutionalizing gay marriage would merely reinforce a healthy social trend. It would also, in the wake of AIDS, qualify as a genuine public health measure. Those conservatives who deplore promiscuity among some homosexuals should be among the first to support it. Burke could have written a powerful case for it.

The argument that gay marriage would subtly undermine the unique legitimacy of straight marriage is based upon a fallacy. For heterosexuals, straight marriage would remain the most significant—and only legal—social bond. Gay marriage could only delegitimize straight marriage if it were a real alternative to it, and this is clearly not true. To put it bluntly, there's precious little evidence that straights could be persuaded by any law to have sex with—let alone marry—someone of their own sex. The only possible effect of this sort would be to persuade gay men and women who force themselves into heterosexual marriage (often at appalling cost to themselves and their families) to find a focus for their family instincts in a more personally positive environment. But this is clearly a plus, not a minus: gay marriage could both avoid a lot of tortured families and create the possibility for many happier ones. It is not, in short, a denial of family values. It's an extension of them.

Of course, some would claim that any legal recognition of homosexuality is a de facto attack upon heterosexuality. But even the most hardened conservatives recognize that gays are a permanent minority and aren't likely to go away. Since persecution is not an option in a civilized society, why not coax gays into traditional values rather than rail incoherently against them?

There's a less elaborate argument for gay marriage: it's good for gays. It provides role models for young gay people who, after the exhilaration of coming out, can easily lapse into short-term relationships and insecurity with no tangible goal in sight. My own guess is that most gays would embrace such a goal with as much (if not more) commitment as straights. Even in our society as it is, many lesbian relationships are virtual textbook cases of monogamous commitment. Legal gay marriage could also help bridge the gulf often found between gays and their parents. It could bring the essence of gay life—a gay couple—into the heart of the traditional straight family in a way the family can most understand and the gay offspring can most easily acknowledge. It could do as much to heal the gay-straight rift as any amount of gay rights legislation.

If these arguments sound socially conservative, that's no accident. It's one of the richest ironies of our society's blind spot toward gays that essentially conservative social goals should have the appearance of being so radical. But gay marriage is not a radical step. It avoids the mess of domestic partnership; it is humane; it is conservative in the best sense of the word. It's also practical. Given the fact that we already allow legal gay relationships, what possible social goal is advanced by framing the law to encourage those relationships to be unfaithful, undeveloped, and insecure?

RESPONDING IN DISCUSSION OR WRITING

1. What does the title lead you to expect this article to be about? How did you react as you read the article and discovered Sullivan's thesis?

2. What entitlements is Sullivan referring to in paragraphs 1 and 4 when he says that domestic partnerships would stretch "a vast array of entitlements" too far?

3. In his opening paragraph, Sullivan uses the terms "radical" and "conservative" when discussing gay marriage. In what ways does the rest of his article pick up on and explain what he means by that paradox? When Sullivan returns to those issues in his final paragraph, how does he justify the legalization of gay marriage as both a conservative and a radical step?

4. Sullivan mentions the "legalization of civil gay marriage" at the end of his first paragraph. What points in his article show why he is in favor of the legalization of gay marriage? List points for and against Sullivan's proposal.

5. Sullivan devotes a large part of the beginning of his article to opposing what some might propose as a solution to the problem he poses. He opposes the idea of a "domestic partnership" law. What reasons does he give? What effect does he hope to have on his readers by first challenging what they might propose?

6. When Sullivan says in paragraph 11 that "there's no reason gays should not be allowed to adopt or be foster parents," how do you react? Do you agree with him? Why or why not?

WRITING ASSIGNMENTS

1. Discuss Sullivan's statement that "gay marriage . . . places more responsibilities upon gays" (paragraph 10). What do you think he means by that? Do you agree with him? Why?

2. The following guest editorial was published in *National Review* (September 15, 1989) in response to Sullivan's article. Write a letter to *The New Republic* or to *National Review* in support of either Sullivan or Van den Haag.

GUEST EDITORIAL: CONFIRMED BUT NOT BACHELORS?

Andrew Sullivan urges (*The New Republic*, Aug. 28) that homosexuals be enabled to marry one another. His essay was prompted by a New York court's decision that let the survivor live in the rent-controlled apartment he had shared with his deceased lover, because the homosexual couple constituted a "family." Mr. Sullivan rightly objects to the court's flexible and arbitrary definition of "family." But his proposal is bizarre. It assumes that the New York rent-control laws will last forever and should be broadened to benefit homosexual cohabitants as well as widows.

Why should landlords forever be compelled to rent apartments at less than market prices to tenants or their heirs, of whatever sex? If one wants an apartment for a surviving lover one should buy one, just as one would buy a car for him or her. The benefit should be granted at one's own expense, not that of a landlord. Nor should pensions become available to a surviving homosexual partner, as Mr. Sullivan advocates. They were instituted to provide for children and widows incapable of earning a living. How does this apply to surviving homosexual lovers?

All societies have marriage, polygynous, polyandrous, monogamous, or serially polygamous (as with us). None, to my knowledge, has homosexual marriage. Ancient Greece and Rome did not, despite acceptance of homosexuality. Since there is no possibility of offspring, the major raison d'être for marriage is lacking. Homosexual marriage could serve only to morally legitimize a homosexual relationship. Indeed, this is what Mr. Sullivan aims at.

He sees other benefits as well: "[Homosexual marriage] would also in the wake of AIDS qualify as a general public-health measure." Hardly. Young homosexuals are far more promiscuous than their heterosexual coevals. How would marriage make them monogamous? On the other hand, the few monogamous and stable homosexual couples do not need marriage to avoid promiscuity. Mr. Sullivan also argues that marriage would facilitate adoption by homosexual couples. Perhaps. There is no evidence, however, that such adoption would be consistent with the interests of the adoptees. The presumption is against it.

The "general social approval" of homosexual unions which Mr. 5
Sullivan wants is neither possible nor desirable. Societies approve of values shared by the majority. A society that does not support and defend its widely shared values will lack the cohesion needed to function. Although willing to tolerate values they do not share and sexual relations they do not care for, most Americans are unwilling to grant "general social approval" to homosexual unions and to regard them as morally equal to heterosexual ones. No reason to deny homosexuals the right to practice privately, or to place them at a disadvantage when their homosexuality is irrelevant. But no reason either to give social sanction to their relationships any more than to polyandry. Most of us actually disapprove of homosexuality for religious, moral, traditional, or psychological reasons. We are entitled to our judgments. Wherefore we will not and should not institute homosexual marriage, or grant "general social approval" to homosexual unions. They are, and should remain, a private affair.

—*Ernest van den Haag*

❖

AN AX TO GRIND

MARIE W. DALLAM

Marie W. Dallam, born in Philadelphia in 1971, is a religion major at Hunter College, a member of the Honors program, and a lead singer for a band. After graduation, she plans to enter a Ph.D. program. She wrote this research paper for a required first-year composition course in college. The assignment was to select a contemporary, controversial debate and, after presenting the issues clearly, to draw conclusions. Dallam uses the MLA (Modern Language Association) system of documentation, citing author and page number in her essay and including a list of works cited at the end. This paper has not been previously published.

THREE EXPERTS SET THE scene of a widespread controversy. On a National Public Radio (NPR) talk show, *Talk of the Nation,* one of these experts Robert Knight of the Family Research Council in Washington, DC, remarked on the studies that show homosexuals are perfectly capable parents: "The studies are done by gay researchers with an ax to grind."

In an earlier, completely unrelated interview, Dr. Michael Lamb of the National Institute of Child Health and Human Development said that early studies showing homosexuals were bad parents looked only at children with psychological problems, and were done by "researchers with an ax to grind" (qtd. in Goleman). Despite what Knight has since said, science writer Daniel Goleman confidently asserts that the "scientific consensus" that homosexual parents damage children's development "is based on anecdotal reports and biased research rather than scientifically gathered evidence."

The challenge to the tradition of the nuclear family that occupies the talk show experts goes hand in hand with the rapidly changing culture and lifestyle in twentieth century America. One particularly heated issue is the place occupied by families in which the parents are gay or lesbian. As the number of these families increases, so do the claims that homosexuals make inappropriate parents. Studies have shown that there are between one and three million gay fathers and between one and five million lesbian mothers in the United States (Patterson 1026). A 1985 study claims that these parents have at least six million children (Gottman 177), and that number may even be as high as fourteen million (Patterson 1026). It is perhaps the strength of these numbers that provokes conservative forces to insist that gays and lesbians are unfit parents, referring to what Goleman calls "biased research." Careful scrutiny of the literature and research, however, reveals that overall, gay fathers and lesbian mothers do not have negative effects on the children they raise, and can create better home lives in some ways than do some heterosexual parents.

Three basic questions arise when sorting out the facts of this matter from mere prejudice. First, what impact do these nontraditional family forms have on the psychological development of children? Second, what have studies on the families shown, in terms of the children's mental and emotional lives, as well as their sexual orientation? Finally, how does the American legal system figure into the controversy? All of these questions address various fears often articulated about these families. The most commonly mentioned fears surround the psychological health and sexual orientation of the children, but also arising frequently are fears of sexual abuse and social ostracism. But attention to the research can do a great deal to allay these fears.

One thing to keep in mind about families, whether they are   5
nuclear, single-parent, heterosexual, homosexual, or otherwise, is that they do not all function well. Some people will refuse to accept this fact, however. In the NPR interview, Knight asserted that two-parent heterosexual homes are "the cornerstone of civilization, and any time we depart from that, we end up with a lot of social pathologies." But the traditional family structure does not guarantee stability. There is no reason to conclude, as many do, that homosexual parents will automatically raise gay children or other social minorities, especially when one admits that heterosexual parents can raise drug addicts, criminals and, most importantly, the majority of the American homosexual population (Bigner and Bozett 169).

Established theories of social development recommend having both genders in the home to serve as role models (Patterson 1028). Knight has said that a healthy sexual identity (by which he means heterosexuality) is brought about by the children's "most important" role models: their parents. He adds, "We didn't dream up the two-parent family. . . . This is natural sexuality; it follows natural law." Virginia Casper of the Infant and Parent Development Program at Bank Street College, New York City, in the same interview, opposes Knight's view by pointing out another commonly held belief: that children learn from many different people of both sexes, not merely the parental figure(s) in their home. Casper also questions the term "role model." In reality, one cannot know or decide whom a child will model him or herself after, or in what aspects. As for parents being role models for sexual identity, recent studies have shown a possibility of genetic causes for homosexuality, in which case the role model factor of parenting is slim to nonexistent (Henry 71). To date, however, studies are inconclusive. What is clear is that the influence parents have on sexual orientation, if any, will vary, possibly even in accord with their own sexuality. But whether one views this influence as positive or detrimental depends on one's own perspective of sexuality.

In the past twenty-five years, extensive scholarly research has been done on gay men, lesbians, and their children. According to Gottman, researchers have mainly examined social adjustment, self esteem, sexual orientation, gender role, and gender identity (179). She explains gender role as the display of behavior that society at large has determined as belonging to one of the particular sexes; and gender identity as one's concept of oneself as inherently male or female (Gottman 180). Across the board, the studies of personal development in children of lesbians and gays (including intelligence, morals, self-control, and self-concept) show no significant differences when they are compared to children of straight parents (Patterson 1033).

Significant studies of children of lesbians done in 1981, 1983, and 1987 have shown that they are more likely to have regular contact with their fathers than are children of heterosexual divorced or single mothers (Patterson 1024). One could certainly say that this behavior on the part of lesbian-headed families is socially healthy and responsible, and even Mr. Knight would surely have to agree that in terms of seeking out new role models, it appears the lesbians are doing a better job than heterosexual mothers.

The children of gay fathers also suffer no obvious disadvantage in terms of role models within the family. Bigner and Bozett point to a 1985 study that clearly shows gay fathers "trying harder to create stable home lives and positive relationships than what would be expected among traditional heterosexual parents" (163). Knight insists that boys need fathers present in their lives to understand "what manhood is all about," which is akin to the institutional viewpoint that weak or absent fathers encourage the development of a male's homosexuality (Bigner and Bozett 169). Knight claims, in addition, that "recovering homosexuals" say the seeds of their gayness were planted when they had no father figure to bond with in their early years. "Warm, accessible, nurturing fathers promote the development of masculinity in sons," says Lamb (qtd. in Bigner and Bozett 169).

Side-stepping the implicit assumption that male homosexuality
is opposed to masculine identity, these statements all assume that
a loving, present father theoretically will produce heterosexual
sons; and as was shown in the 1985 study (Bigner and Bozett 163),
gay men make more attempts to create that type of loving home-
life than do heterosexual parents. This is extremely significant
because even if one accepts the conservatives' logic, it can still be
demonstrated that homosexuals make appropriate parents. Gays
and lesbians do not automatically breed homosexual children.

One of the biggest challenges for homosexuals is the coming
out process: openly telling people that they are lesbian or gay.
Homosexual parents often hesitate to tell their children, especially if they are still involved in a heterosexual marriage because,
as many researchers have seen, they fear being rejected by their
children. Paul's 1986 study shows that the greatest number of negative responses from children occur when they are told during
adolescence (qtd. in Gottman 185). Multiple studies of children
of gay men, however, have shown that responses are usually positive, possibly because the men tend to "teach their children to
be accepting of variations in human behavior" (Bigner and
Bozett 161).

In an interview, Sharon McConnell, the 13-year-old daughter of
a lesbian, reports that it took her a few years to actually notice that
her mother's situation was any different from that of her peer's
parents. "It's not like she ever came out to me and said, 'Sharon,
I'm gay.' It was just always normal," says McConnell.

Normality is important for adolescents. Bigner and Bozett
notice that during adolescence children often fear telling their
friends in case they too will be viewed as gay and will be teased
(162). But even if this actually were to happen, it seems a weak
defense for saying that gay-parented homes are inappropriate.
Children will always be teased by one another, and whether it is
"Your mom's ugly," or "Your dad's a garbage man," or "Your dad's
a fag," it happens to all children. McConnell reports that other
than a brief six-month period of fear about teasing, it has never
mattered to her whether people know about her mother or not.
In fact, she claims, "They're too scared to tease me," alluding to
her confidence and ease in these situations. And indeed, according to Gottman, children are more likely to choose friends that

will accept their family rather than "attempting to make their family fit their friends" (186), which displays a healthy acceptance of and identity with one's parents.

Mainstream culture frequently suggests there is a possibility of sexual abuse of children raised in gay homes. Kircheimer, for example, cites statements of people who believe that all homosexuals are promiscuous; that they have all-night orgies; and that friends of the parents may abuse the child (qtd. in Bigner and Bozett 156). However, most research has shown that the majority of sexual abuse is committed by heterosexual men on little girls (Patterson 1034), which would virtually eliminate gay homes from this possibility. Casper points out that more than sixty studies done in the past 25 years show no mental or physical damage to children raised by gay and lesbian parents. Even lacking evidence that there is physical risk to these children, conservatives still tend to assume that the very existence of obscure groups like NAMBLA (North American Man-Boy Love Association) proves risk. This is one of the difficult problems the gay community must contend with, particularly in issues of custody rights and adoption.

The psychological effects of being brought up in a homosexual [15] family have been thoroughly examined. A 1985 study comparing daughters of lesbians to daughters of heterosexual women shows no detrimental psychological effects on lesbians' daughters as a result of their mothers' sexual orientation (Gottman 190). And about a dozen studies in the 1980's show, according to Patterson, no significant differences between children of gay and straight homes in the categories of gender role, gender identity, and sexual orientation (1030–31). Three studies show that the most severe emotional disturbances in children, whether of gay or straight parents, are a direct result of troublesome divorces, and here most of the children affected come from families with heterosexual parents (Gottman 182). McConnell says she feels better off for having grown up in the gay community, adding that she is more open and understanding than her peers. "It makes life easier," she says, simply summing up her situation.

The final factor, and perhaps the most important, is the role the U.S. courts have taken in insuring that homosexuals are legally able to care for children. Liz Hendrikson of the National Center for Lesbian Rights said on the NPR talk show that the courts are supposed to uphold a person's right to "have, raise, and keep children" unless there is extreme neglect or abuse involved. But as Patterson says

> both in resolution of custody disputes and in administration of adoption and foster-care policies, the legal system in the United States has frequently operated under strong but unverified assumptions about difficulties faced by children of lesbians and gay men, and there are important questions about the veridicality of such assumptions. (1026)

Often courts have taken children away from homosexual parents without proving risk to the child, so many parents fear losing their children (Gottman 179). Four states—Arkansas, Missouri, North Dakota, and Virginia—have legal precedents that deem homosexuals "unfit" as parents (Henry 67). But since so many gays and lesbians go out of their way to have and keep their children, they must care a great deal about them. Why should they be seen as unfit, inappropriate, or harmful?

A recent Virginia case involves Sharon Bottoms and April Wade. They lost their son Tyler to Bottoms' mother, who took them to court because she disapproved of their lesbian lifestyle and its potential influence on the child (Henry 66). Tyler moved from a two-parent lesbian home to a home in which the grandmother lived with another woman. Casper points to the slim differences in the two homes Tyler has now occupied, and says the case implies that a "heterosexual nonparent is simply better" than a homosexual natural parent. The case is now on appeal with Bottoms claiming, "I'm a good mother. I'm a good person. I don't understand why, if you're gay or lesbian, you don't have the same rights as anyone else" (Henry 67). Her confusion echoes worldwide, as millions of homosexuals are subject to bias on social and legal levels.

The studies so far have shown no evidence that living with a gay or lesbian parent will have negative effects on a child's development. Until ignorance about this fact and the lives of gays and lesbians in general is dispelled, the stigma will continue to interfere with their daily lives. Additionally, people will continue to hear remarks like the one my unsuspecting co-worker recently made: "If gay people have kids, the kids will grow up gay." Even among the educated and well informed, doubts about the soundness of nontraditional families abound. Therefore the conservative powers that attack them gain momentum because an ignorant public provides fuel. This is also why they can have influence, with almost no scholarly research to support their claims, in courts of law, schools, and American culture as a whole. The seeds of change lie in the evidence of research studies and in the families of gays and lesbians who go ahead and raise their children, ignoring the taboos that many try to put on them.

Works Cited

Bigner, Jerry J., and Frederick W. Bozett. "Parenting by Gay Fathers." *Marriage and Family Review* 14 (1989): 155–75.

Goleman, Daniel. "Studies Find No Disadvantage in Growing Up in a Gay Home." *New York Times* 2 Dec. 1992: C14.

Gottman, Julie Schwartz. "Children of Gay and Lesbian Parents." *Marriage and Family Review* 14 (1989): 177–93.

Henry, William A., III. "Gay Parents: Under Fire and On the Rise." *Time* 20 Sept. 1993: 66–71.

Knight, Robert, Virginia Casper, and Liz Hendrikson. Interview with Derrick McGinty. *Talk of the Nation*. Natl. Public Radio. WNYC, New York City. 8 Sept. 1993.

McConnell, Sharon. Personal interview. 3 Dec. 1993.

Patterson, Charlotte J. "Children of Lesbian and Gay Parents." *Child Development* 63 (1992): 1025–42.

RESPONDING IN DISCUSSION OR WRITING

1. *Considerations of Style.* Dallam's first two paragraphs present similar quotations used to comment on disparate situations. What is the effect of beginning an essay with startling quotations?

2. Which sentence or sentences would you identify as presenting Dallam's thesis? Once you have read the thesis, what do you expect to read in the rest of the essay? Does Dallam fulfill your expectations?

3. Dallam uses articles in professional journals, magazines, and newspapers as well as radio interviews and a personal interview. What impact does the variety of source material have on the persuasiveness of her arguments?

4. Which of Dallam's points or examples do you find most convincing and which the least convincing? Why?

5. What questions and suggestions would you have for Dallam concerning her paper?

WRITING ASSIGNMENTS

1. At one point in her paper, Dallam asserts that "normality is important for adolescents" (paragraph 13). Discuss this issue in relation to the case she makes for gay-parent households.

2. Do you think that public school systems should include in their curriculum information about homosexuality and gay parents? Or should the traditional family be the only model talked about and read about in school? Present your reasons for your opinion.

❖

FAMILY RESEMBLANCE

JEFFERY CHAN

Jeffery Chan is professor of Asian American Studies at San Francisco State University, where he also teaches writing. He is coeditor of Aiiieeeee! An Anthology of Asian American Writers *(1974). Chan has criticized "the white racist imagination" that has permeated some popular Asian American works of literature. This essay appeared in volume 15 of* Amerasia Journal *in 1989.*

My Auntie May who has just become a great-grandmama for the third time was watching Michael Chang take the weekend's fourth round Davis Cup match against Paraguay's Hugo Chapacu she'd taped on her VCR when I stopped by for a New Year's week visit clutching what I could conveniently shop between the public parking garage and her third-floor walk-up, oranges, pork buns, peanuts; and, as usual, she fed them to me, dividing the piled peanuts on yesterday's newspaper, quartering the oranges, pouring tea from her trusty thermos, leaving the buns in the bag to keep warm.

Chang wins his service in the first game of the second set after dropping the first set 5-7. Auntie leans over the newspaper to sweep peanut debris from her sweater. "He's going to get him, now, you watch."

"I did watch. On Sunday. It was a great win," I said.

"Me, too. His mother and his father are so proud. Did you see his ma looks just like your ma in the picture waving the flag in the parade?"

"What picture?" I ask, tea steaming my glasses. Auntie thinks   5
she has a sharp eye for family resemblances. Everybody looks like somebody she knows. "She doesn't look like Ma."

"No, she doesn't look exactly like your ma. She looks like the picture of your ma, the one where she's holding the flag in her face, just after the war, I think, at the New Year parade. You know the one. I showed you before."

"You want a bun?"

"No, no. You eat it."

Because she was born and raised in Chinatown and has lived east of the Stockton Tunnel her entire life, Auntie's ability to recognize perfect strangers and make family of them comes from Chinatown habit. The neighborhood she walked was filled with family. Every Chinese person she ever saw was related. These days, Chinatown is filled with strangers but she still savors the resemblance.

Chang's service. 4-0 in the second.   10

Auntie bends over the table, clapping a prayerful full of peanuts between both hands, peering intently as Chang cracks a second service ace, wide to Chapacu's backhand. The peanuts snap their mild applause as she rubs her hands to separate the nuts from the shell. "The first time I saw him, I said he looks just like my bachelor nephews, especially your big brother, Andy Boy, when he used to play tennis at Chinese playground."

An accountant in LA, my brother Andy's fifty-one and bald. So it's hard to tell. And after forty years?

Auntie stops the tape when Chang breaks to take the second set at love. She scoots to the edge of the sofa to pour more tea. Lovers on the Kowloon Ferry in a Hong Kong soap fill the screen. "I've noticed you gained just a little bit of weight, but I want you to know that it's very becoming." She rubs the lobes of her ears for luck. "And I've found a woman to be your wife."

"What did you say?"

"She looks like your Auntie Rose's girlfriend did when she was 15 young. Long-haired Janet, remember her? You were probably too young. Anyway, there were two Janets and one Veronica that worked with Auntie Rose as salesgirls downtown. Well, long-haired Janet worked at Emporium until she retired, finally, just like me. But this one's an FOB."

"I'm too old to fall in love, Auntie May."

"Who said anything about love? You marry for love, you divorce for the same thing. Besides," she adds, spitting a melon seed, "You ain't no spring chicken kiddo."

"You have a picture of her?"

"Picture? You think I got you a picture bride? I'm not selling girls. I'm arranging a marriage so you can have a family."

"I'm fifty years old. I don't want kids." 20

"She's just a little bit older. Fifty-three, I think, maybe fifty-two. But that doesn't make any difference. She's got kids already. Very nice kids, two girls. Both the same age too. Sixteen."

"They're both sixteen?"

"Yeah. Twins. And they're very smart. Both scored 100 percent on the PSAT. Merit scholars. You don't have to support their college. And cute too."

"So you got me a Chinese bride?"

"Pretty lucky huh? Of course, the whole family won't be 25 Chinese. Not all Chinese anyway."

"Why?"

"The girls are only half Chinese. In a way, they make one whole one if you count in halfs."

"What's the other half?"

"African American."

"I beg your pardon?" 30

"Whatsamatta, you deaf now? Black. Negro. What do you want me to say, *see yow gai*? Soy sauce chicken?" She was breathing hard, her face flushed, her voice catching. "You are a fifty-year-old, never married, Chinese American, who could never get a girl to marry you for love. You're damn right I'm serious. What good are you if you can't help even yourself?"

"You're serious."

"Damn right."

"I see."

"So, okay?"   35

"If you say so."

"Good. Don't forget your blood test." She was calm now. "Gung Hay Fat Choy. You want to watch the last set with me?"

"Of course."

It's late when I hit the streets. The ghosts of men in Derby jackets and dark raincoats gather at the corner of Brenham alley and Washington, resting against the warm sandstone brick facade to take the night's perfume and bathe in the neon glow of two restaurants and the nightlight from the Poultry Market across the street. A salty breeze wells up from the traffic corridors around the base of the bay bridge and carries across the scrub lawn, the cement planters of the Square. The sewer stink rises, a rich smell of rot and nightsoil, burnt oil, blackening garlic smoke, the neighborhood exhaling the wok breath of a thousand kitchens to fill the evening redolent, the air thick as fermenting bean cheese. They hawk and spit like cannon fire lobbing sputum at the iron grating and pat their lips with linen.

What I couldn't grow with just a whiff of that stuff.   40

RESPONDING IN DISCUSSION OR WRITING

1. Why does Chan think it is important to mention that Auntie May is a "great-grandmama"?

2. Why is the narrator particularly surprised when he discovers that the woman his aunt found to be his wife has two children who are half Chinese American and half African American?

3. How do you respond to Chan's description of Auntie May as someone with the "ability to recognize perfect strangers and make family of them"? Would you see that as an endearing or an annoying trait?

4. What can you say about the fact that the story takes place against a taped replay of a tennis match? Do you think Chan was making a point with that? In an introductory note to the story, Russell Leong writes: "Reading this story—as an avid ex-student of Jeff's 1968 writing classes—I sense his unspoken questions: 'How much does each generation resemble that of its mothers and fathers?' Closely followed by, 'Is this all play, or replay?'" Does Chan's story begin to answer those questions?

5. What effect do the descriptions of food have on the reader? What do they contribute to the story?

6. The story ends with a description of the sights, sounds, and smells of the Chinatown neighborhood. How satisfactory an ending is this for you as the reader? How did you expect the story to end?

WRITING ASSIGNMENTS

1. Would you advise the narrator of Chan's story to take up his aunt's offer to arrange a marriage for him? Why or why not?

2. *For Further Research.*   Do research to find out as much as you can about arranged marriages. Write an essay informing readers about where in the world arranged marriages are still common and the procedures that are established for them.

TWO KINDS

AMY TAN

Amy Tan, born in Oakland, California, in 1952, is the author of The Joy Luck Club *(1989), now also a motion picture, and* The Kitchen God's Wife *(1991). This short story was published in the* Atlantic Monthly *in February 1989 and forms one chapter of* The Joy Luck Club.

MY MOTHER BELIEVED YOU could be anything you wanted to be in America. You could open a restaurant. You could work for the government and get good retirement. You could buy a house with almost no money down. You could become rich. You could become instantly famous.

"Of course, you can be prodigy, too," my mother told me when I was nine. "You can be best anything. What does Auntie Lindo know? Her daughter, she is only best tricky."

America was where all my mother's hopes lay. She had come to San Francisco in 1949 after losing everything in China: her mother and father, her family home, her first husband, and two daughters, twin baby girls. But she never looked back with regret. Things could get better in so many ways.

We didn't immediately pick the right kind of prodigy. At first my mother thought I could be a Chinese Shirley Temple. We'd watch Shirley's old movies on TV as though they were training films. My mother would poke my arm and say, "*Ni kan.* You watch." And I would see Shirley tapping her feet, or singing a sailor song, or pursing her lips into a very round O while saying "Oh, my goodness."

"*Ni kan,*" my mother said, as Shirley's eyes flooded with tears. 5
"You already know how. Don't need talent for crying!"

Soon after my mother got this idea about Shirley Temple, she took me to the beauty training school in the Mission District and put me in the hands of a student who could barely hold the scissors without shaking. Instead of getting big fat curls, I emerged with an uneven mass of crinkly black fuzz. My mother dragged me off to the bathroom and tried to wet down my hair.

"You look like Negro Chinese," she lamented, as if I had done this on purpose.

The instructor of the beauty training school had to lop off these soggy clumps to make my hair even again. "Peter Pan is very popular these days," the instructor assured my mother. I now had hair the length of a boy's, with curly bangs that hung at a slant two inches above my eyebrows. I liked the haircut, and it made me actually look forward to my future fame.

In fact, in the beginning I was just as excited as my mother, maybe even more so. I pictured this prodigy part of me as many different images, and I tried each one on for size. I was a dainty ballerina girl standing by the curtain, waiting to hear the music that would send me floating on my tiptoes. I was like the Christ child lifted out of the straw manger, crying with holy indignity. I was Cinderella stepping from her pumpkin carriage with sparkly cartoon music filling the air.

In all of my imaginings I was filled with a sense that I would   10
soon become perfect. My mother and father would adore me. I
would be beyond reproach. I would never feel the need to sulk, or
to clamor for anything.

But sometimes the prodigy in me became impatient. "If you
don't hurry up and get me out of here, I'm disappearing for
good," it warned. "And then you'll always be nothing."

Every night after dinner my mother and I would sit at the
Formica-topped kitchen table. She would present new tests, taking
her examples from stories of amazing children that she had read
in *Ripley's Believe It or Not* or *Good Housekeeping, Reader's Digest,* or
any of a dozen other magazines she kept in a pile in our bathroom. My mother got these magazines from people whose houses
she cleaned. And since she cleaned many houses each week, we
had a great assortment. She would look through them all, searching for stories about remarkable children.

The first night she brought out a story about a three-year-old
boy who knew the capitals of all the states and even of most of the
European countries. A teacher was quoted as saying that the little
boy could also pronounce the names of the foreign cities correctly. "What's the capital of Finland?" my mother asked me, looking at the story.

All I knew was the capital of California, because Sacramento
was the name of the street we lived on in Chinatown. "Nairobi!" I
guessed, saying the most foreign word I could think of. She
checked to see if that might be one way to pronounce *Helsinki*
before showing me the answer.

The tests got harder—multiplying numbers in my head, finding   15
the queen of hearts in a deck of cards, trying to stand on my head
without using my hands, predicting the daily temperatures in Los
Angeles, New York, and London. One night I had to look at a
page from the Bible for three minutes and then report everything
I could remember. "Now Jehoshaphat had riches and honor in
abundance and . . . that's all I remember, Ma," I said.

And after seeing, once again, my mother's disappointed face,
something inside me began to die. I hated the tests, the raised
hopes and failed expectations. Before going to bed that night I
looked in the mirror above the bathroom sink, and when I saw
only my face staring back—and understood that it would always

be this ordinary face—I began to cry. Such a sad, ugly girl! I made high-pitched noises like a crazed animal, trying to scratch out the face in the mirror.

And then I saw what seemed to be the prodigy side of me—a face I had never seen before. I looked at my reflection, blinking so that I could see more clearly. The girl staring back at me was angry, powerful. She and I were the same. I had new thoughts, willful thoughts—or, rather, thoughts filled with lots of won'ts. I won't let her change me, I promised myself. I won't be what I'm not.

So now when my mother presented her tests, I performed listlessly, my head propped on one arm. I pretended to be bored. And I was. I got so bored that I started counting the bellows of the foghorns out on the bay while my mother drilled me in other areas. The sound was comforting and reminded me of the cow jumping over the moon. And the next day I played a game with myself, seeing if my mother would give up on me before eight bellows. After a while I usually counted only one bellow, maybe two at most. At last she was beginning to give up hope.

Two or three months went by without any mention of my being a prodigy. And then one day my mother was watching the *Ed Sullivan Show* on TV. The TV was old and the sound kept shorting out. Every time my mother got halfway up from the sofa to adjust the set, the sound would come back on and Sullivan would be talking. As soon as she sat down, Sullivan would go silent again. She got up—the TV broke into loud piano music. She sat down— silence. Up and down, back and forth, quiet and loud. It was like a stiff, embraceless dance between her and the TV set. Finally, she stood by the set with her hand on the sound dial.

She seemed entranced by the music, a frenzied little piano piece with a mesmerizing quality, which alternated between quick, playful passages and teasing, lilting ones.

"*Ni kan,*" my mother said, calling me over with hurried hand gestures. "Look here."

I could see why my mother was fascinated by the music. It was being pounded out by a little Chinese girl, about nine years old, with a Peter Pan haircut. The girl had the sauciness of a Shirley Temple. She was proudly modest, like a proper Chinese child. And she also did a fancy sweep of a curtsy, so that the fluffy skirt of her white dress cascaded to the floor like the petals of a large carnation.

In spite of these warning signs, I wasn't worried. Our family had no piano and we couldn't afford to buy one, let alone reams of sheet music and piano lessons. So I could be generous in my comments when my mother badmouthed the little girl on TV.

"Play note right, but doesn't sound good!" my mother complained. "No singing sound."

"What are you picking on her for?" I said carelessly. "She's 25 pretty good. Maybe she's not the best, but she's trying hard." I knew almost immediately that I would be sorry I had said that.

"Just like you," she said. "Not the best. Because you not trying." She gave a little huff as she let go of the sound dial and sat down on the sofa.

The little Chinese girl sat down also, to play an encore of "Anitra's Tanz," by Grieg. I remember the song, because later on I had to learn how to play it.

Three days after watching the *Ed Sullivan Show* my mother told me what my schedule would be for piano lessons and piano practice. She had talked to Mr. Chong, who lived on the first floor of our apartment building. Mr. Chong was a retired piano teacher, and my mother had traded housecleaning services for weekly lessons and a piano for me to practice on every day, two hours a day, from four until six.

When my mother told me this, I felt as though I had been sent to hell. I whined, and then kicked my foot a little when I couldn't stand it anymore.

"Why don't you like me the way I am?" I cried. "I'm *not* a 30 genius! I can't play the piano. And even if I could, I wouldn't go on TV if you paid me a million dollars!"

My mother slapped me. "Who ask you to be genius?" she shouted. "Only ask you be your best. For you sake. You think I want you to be genius? Hnnh! What for! Who ask you!"

"So ungrateful," I heard her mutter in Chinese. "If she had as much talent as she has temper, she'd be famous now."

Mr. Chong, whom I secretly nicknamed Old Chong, was very strange, always tapping his fingers to the silent music of an invisible orchestra. He looked ancient in my eyes. He had lost most of the hair on the top of his head, and he wore thick glasses and had eyes that always looked tired. But he must have been younger than I thought, since he lived with his mother and was not yet married.

I met Old Lady Chong once, and that was enough. She had a peculiar smell, like a baby that had done something in its pants, and her fingers felt like a dead person's, like an old peach I once found in the back of the refrigerator; its skin just slid off the flesh when I picked it up.

I soon found out why Old Chong had retired from teaching piano. He was deaf. "Like Beethoven!" he shouted to me. "We're both listening only in our head!" And he would start to conduct his frantic silent sonatas.

Our lessons went like this. He would open the book and point to different things, explaining their purpose: "Key! Treble! Bass! No sharps or flats! So this is C major! Listen now and play after me!"

And then he would play the C scale a few times, a simple chord, and then, as if inspired by an old unreachable itch, he would gradually add more notes and running trills and a pounding bass until the music was really something quite grand.

I would play after him, the simple scale, the simple chord, and then just play some nonsense that sounded like a cat running up and down on top of garbage cans. Old Chong would smile and applaud and say, "Very good! But now you must learn to keep time!"

So that's how I discovered that Old Chong's eyes were too slow to keep up with the wrong notes I was playing. He went through the motions in half time. To help me keep rhythm, he stood behind me and pushed down on my right shoulder for every beat. He balanced pennies on top of my wrists so that I would keep them still as I slowly played scales and arpeggios. He had me curve my hand around an apple and keep that shape when playing chords. He marched stiffly to show me how to make each finger dance up and down, staccato, like an obedient little soldier.

He taught me all these things, and that was how I also learned I could be lazy and get away with mistakes, lots of mistakes. If I hit the wrong notes because I hadn't practiced enough, I never corrected myself. I just kept playing in rhythm. And Old Chong kept conducting his own private reverie.

So maybe I never really gave myself a fair chance. I did pick up the basics pretty quickly, and I might have become a good pianist at that young age. But I was so determined not to try, not to be anybody different, that I learned to play only the most ear-splitting preludes, the most discordant hymns.

Over the next year I practiced like this, dutifully in my own way. And then one day I heard my mother and her friend Lindo Jong both talking in a loud, bragging tone of voice so that others could hear. It was after church, and I was leaning against a brick wall, wearing a dress with stiff white petticoats. Auntie Lindo's daughter, Waverly, who was my age, was standing farther down the wall, about five feet away. We had grown up together and shared all the closeness of two sisters, squabbling over crayons and dolls. In other words, for the most part, we hated each other. I thought she was snotty. Waverly Jong had gained a certain amount of fame as "Chinatown's Littlest Chinese Chess Champion."

"She bring home too many trophy," Auntie Lindo lamented that Sunday. "All day she play chess. All day I have no time do nothing but dust off her winnings." She threw a scolding look at Waverly, who pretended not to see her.

"You lucky you don't have this problem," Auntie Lindo said with a sigh to my mother.

And my mother squared her shoulders and bragged: "Our 45 problem worser than yours. If we ask Jing-mei wash dish, she hear nothing but music. It's like you can't stop this natural talent."

And right then I was determined to put a stop to her foolish pride.

A few weeks later old Chong and my mother conspired to have me play in a talent show that was to be held in the church hall. By then my parents had saved up enough to buy me a secondhand piano, a black Wurlitzer spinet with a scarred bench. It was the showpiece of our living room.

For the talent show I was to play a piece called "Pleading Child," from Schumann's *Scenes from Childhood*. It was a simple, moody piece that sounded more difficult than it was. I was supposed to memorize the whole thing. But I dawdled over it, playing a few bars and then cheating, looking up to see what notes followed. I never really listened to what I was playing. I daydreamed about being somewhere else, about being someone else.

The part I liked to practice best was the fancy curtsy: right foot out, touch the rose on the carpet with a pointed foot, sweep to the side, bend left leg, look up, and smile.

My parents invited all the couples from their social club to   50
witness my debut. Auntie Lindo and Uncle Tin were there.
Waverly and her two older brothers had also come. The first two
rows were filled with children either younger or older than I was.
The littlest ones got to go first. They recited simple nursery
rhymes, squawked out tunes on miniature violins, and twirled
hula hoops in pink ballet tutus, and when they bowed or curtsied,
the audience would sigh in unison, "*Awww,*" and then clap
enthusiastically.

When my turn came, I was very confident. I remember my
childish excitement. It was as if I knew, without a doubt, that the
prodigy side of me really did exist. I had no fear whatsoever, no
nervousness. I remember thinking, This is it! This is it! I looked
out over the audience, at my mother's blank face, my father's
yawn, Auntie Lindo's stiff-lipped smile, Waverly's sulky expression.
I had on a white dress, layered with sheets of lace, and a pink bow
in my Peter Pan haircut. As I sat down, I envisioned people jumping to their feet and Ed Sullivan rushing up to introduce me to
everyone on TV.

And I started to play. Everything was so beautiful. I was so
caught up in how lovely I looked that I wasn't worried about how I
would sound. So I was surprised when I hit the first wrong note.
And then I hit another, and another. A chill started at the top of
my head and began to trickle down. Yet I couldn't stop playing, as
though my hands were bewitched. I kept thinking my fingers
would adjust themselves back, like a train switching to the right
track. I played this strange jumble through to the end, the sour
notes staying with me all the way.

When I stood up, I discovered my legs were shaking. Maybe I
had just been nervous, and the audience, like Old Chong, had
seen me go through the right motions and had not heard anything wrong at all. I swept my right foot out, went down on my
knee, looked up, and smiled. The room was quiet, except for Old
Chong, who was beaming and shouting, "Bravo! Bravo! Well
done!" But then I saw my mother's face, her stricken face. The
audience clapped weakly, and as I walked back to my chair, with
my whole face quivering as I tried not to cry, I heard a little boy
whisper loudly to his mother, "That was awful," and the mother
whispered back, "Well, she certainly tried."

And now I realized how many people were in the audience—
the whole world, it seemed. I was aware of eyes burning into my

back. I felt the shame of my mother and father as they sat stiffly through the rest of the show.

We could have escaped during intermission. Pride and some strange sense of honor must have anchored my parents to their chairs. And so we watched it all: The eighteen-year-old boy with a fake moustache who did a magic show and juggled flaming hoops while riding a unicycle. The breasted girl with white makeup who sang an aria from *Madame Butterfly* and got an honorable mention. And the eleven-year-old boy who won first prize playing a tricky violin song that sounded like a busy bee.

After the show the Hsus, the Jongs, and the St. Clairs, from the Joy Luck Club, came up to my mother and father.

"Lots of talented kids," Auntie Lindo said vaguely, smiling broadly.

"That was somethin' else," my father said, and I wondered if he was referring to me in a humorous way, or whether he even remembered what I had done.

Waverly looked at me and shrugged her shoulders. "You aren't a genius like me," she said matter-of-factly. And if I hadn't felt so bad, I would have pulled her braids and punched her stomach.

But my mother's expression was what devastated me: a quiet, blank look that said she had lost everything. I felt the same way, and everybody seemed now to be coming up, like gawkers at the scene of an accident, to see what parts were actually missing.

When we got on the bus to go home, my father was humming the busy-bee tune and my mother was silent. I kept thinking she wanted to wait until we got home before shouting at me. But when my father unlocked the door to our apartment, my mother walked in and went straight to the back, into the bedroom. No accusations. No blame. And in a way, I felt disappointed. I had been waiting for her to start shouting, so that I could shout back and cry and blame her for all my misery.

I had assumed that my talent-show fiasco meant that I would never have to play the piano again. But two days later, after school, my mother came out of the kitchen and saw me watching TV.

"Four clock," she reminded me, as if it were any other day. I was stunned, as though she were asking me to go through the talent-show torture again. I planted myself more squarely in front of the TV.

"Turn off TV," she called from the kitchen five minutes later.

I didn't budge. And then I decided. I didn't have to do what my mother said anymore. I wasn't her slave. This wasn't China. I had listened to her before, and look what happened. She was the stupid one.

She came out from the kitchen and stood in the arched entryway of the living room. "Four clock," she said once again, louder.

"I'm not going to play anymore," I said nonchalantly. "Why should I? I'm not a genius."

She stood in front of the TV. I saw that her chest was heaving up and down in an angry way.

"No!" I said, and I now felt stronger, as if my true self had finally emerged. So this was what had been inside me all along.

"No! I won't!" I screamed.

She snapped off the TV, yanked me by the arm and pulled me off the floor. She was frighteningly strong, half pulling, half carrying me toward the piano as I kicked the throw rugs under my feet. She lifted me up and onto the hard bench. I was sobbing by now, looking at her bitterly. Her chest was heaving even more and her mouth was open, smiling crazily as if she were pleased that I was crying.

"You want me to be someone that I'm not!" I sobbed. "I'll never be the kind of daughter you want me to be!"

"Only two kinds of daughters," she shouted in Chinese. "Those who are obedient and those who follow their own mind! Only one kind of daughter can live in this house. Obedient daughter!"

"Then I wish I weren't your daughter. I wish you weren't my mother," I shouted. As I said these things I got scared. It felt like worms and toads and slimy things crawling out of my chest, but it also felt good, that this awful side of me had surfaced, at last.

"Too late change this," my mother said shrilly.

And I could sense her anger rising to its breaking point. I wanted to see it spill over. And that's when I remembered the babies she had lost in China, the ones we never talked about. "Then I wish I'd never been born!" I shouted. "I wish I were dead! Like them."

It was as if I had said magic words. Alakazam!—her face went blank, her mouth closed, her arms went slack, and she backed out of the room, stunned, as if she were blowing away like a small brown leaf, thin, brittle, lifeless.

It was not the only disappointment my mother felt in me. In the years that followed, I failed her many times, each time asserting my will, my right to fall short of expectations. I didn't get straight As. I didn't become class president. I didn't get into Stanford. I dropped out of college.

Unlike my mother, I did not believe I could be anything I wanted to be. I could only be me.

And for all those years we never talked about the disaster at the recital or my terrible declarations afterward at the piano bench. Neither of us talked about it again, as if it were a betrayal that was now unspeakable. So I never found a way to ask her why she had hoped for something so large that failure was inevitable.

And even worse, I never asked her about what frightened me the most: Why had she given up hope? For after our struggle at the piano, she never mentioned my playing again. The lessons stopped. The lid to the piano was closed, shutting out the dust, my misery, and her dreams.

So she surprised me. A few years ago she offered to give me the piano, for my thirtieth birthday. I had not played in all those years. I saw the offer as a sign of forgiveness, a tremendous burden removed.

"Are you sure?" I asked shyly. "I mean, won't you and Dad miss it?"

"No, this your piano," she said firmly. "Always your piano. You only one can play."

"Well, I probably can't play anymore," I said. "It's been years."

"You pick up fast," my mother said, as if she knew this was certain. "You have natural talent. You could be genius if you want to."

"No, I couldn't."

"You just not trying," my mother said. And she was neither angry nor sad. She said it as if announcing a fact that could never be disproved. "Take it," she said.

But I didn't, at first. It was enough that she had offered it to me. And after that, every time I saw it in my parents' living room, standing in front of the bay window, it made me feel proud, as if it were a shiny trophy that I had won back.

Last week I sent a tuner over to my parents' apartment and had the piano reconditioned, for purely sentimental reasons. My mother had died a few months before, and I had been getting things in order for my father, a little bit at a time. I put the jewelry in special silk pouches. The sweaters she had knitted in yellow, pink, bright orange—all the colors I hated—I put in moth-proof boxes. I found some old Chinese silk dresses, the kind with little slits up the sides. I rubbed the old silk against my skin, and then wrapped them in tissue and decided to take them home with me.

After I had the piano tuned, I opened the lid and touched the keys. It sounded even richer than I remembered. Really, it was a very good piano. Inside the bench were the same exercise notes with handwritten scales, the same secondhand music books with their covers held together with yellow tape.

I opened up the Schumann book to the dark little piece I had played at the recital. It was on the left-hand page, "Pleading Child." It looked more difficult than I remembered. I played a few bars, surprised at how easily the notes came back to me.

And for the first time, or so it seemed, I noticed the piece on the right-hand side. It was called "Perfectly Contented." I tried to play this one as well. It had a lighter melody but with the same flowing rhythm and turned out to be quite easy. "Pleading Child" was shorter but slower; "Perfectly Contented" was longer but faster. And after I had played them both a few times, I realized they were two halves of the same song.

RESPONDING IN DISCUSSION OR WRITING

1. Parents often talk about what they hope their children will be or will do. What expectations did your parents have for you while you were growing up?

2. How many instances can you find of the differences between Jing-mei and her mother? Which differences seem to arise from different perceptions of identity?

3. Who do you feel more sympathy for, Jing-mei or her mother? What does Tan do in the story to make you feel that sympathy? Or does it come more from your own experience than from anything in the story? Which one do you have more in common with?

4. *Considerations of Style.*   Find examples of similes that Tan uses to make her descriptions more vivid and more specific, for example, Jing-mei played "some nonsense that sounded like a cat running up and down on top of garbage cans."

5. How would you explain the story's ending? Why does Tan end the story with "two halves of the same song"?

WRITING ASSIGNMENTS

1. Jing-mei says: "I did not believe I could be anything I wanted to be" (paragraph 79). How does that cause conflict in her family and in herself? Is it better to be realistic or to strive for something that seems impossible?

2. Discuss the ways in which this story, while it is about Chinese Americans, can be seen as primarily an American story. How could a similar story be written about other protagonists, such as Italian Americans, Greek Americans, Irish Americans, Mexican Americans, or any other groups?

❖

FAMILY TIES

JIMMY SANTIAGO BACA

The poems of Jimmy Santiago Baca, who was born in 1952, have their roots in the families and communities of the American Southwest. Baca won a 1988 American Book Award for his verse autobiography Martin and Meditations in the South Valley *(1987). Recent essays are collected in* Working in the Dark: Reflections of a Poet of the Barrio *(1992). This poem is from* Black Mesa Poems *(1986).*

Mountain barbecue.
They arrive, young cousins singly,
older aunts and uncle in twos and threes,
like trees. I play with a new generation
of children, my hands in streambed silt
of their lives, a scuba diver's hands, dusting
surface sand for buried treasure.
Freshly shaved and powdered faces
of uncles and aunts surround taco

5

and tamale tables. Mounted elk head on wall,   10
brass rearing horse cowboy clock
on fireplace mantle. Sons and daughters
converse round beer and whiskey table.
Tempers ignite on land grant issues.
Children scurry round my legs.   15
Old bow-legged men toss horseshoes on lawn,
other farmhands from Mexico sit on a bench,
broken lives repaired for this occasion.
I feel no love or family tie here. I rise
to go hiking, to find abandoned rock cabins   20
in the mountains. We come to a grass clearing,
my wife rolls her jeans up past ankles,
wades ice cold stream, and I barefooted,
carry a son in each arm and follow.
We cannot afford a place like this.   25
At the party again, I eat bean and chile
burrito, and after my third glass of rum,
we climb in the car and my wife drives
us home. My sons sleep in the back,
dream of the open clearing,   30
they are chasing each other with cattails
in the sunlit pasture, giggling,
as I stare out the window
at no trespassing signs white flashing past.

RESPONDING IN DISCUSSION OR WRITING

1. In what way can the title be said to contain the gist of the poem? In what ways would you say it is a poem "about" family ties?

2. What feelings does the poem leave you with as it ends? What causes those feelings?

3. How many "scenes" appear in the poem? Which one comes across to you as the most vivid and why?

4. What is the effect of the last line, with its mention of "no trespassing signs"? Is it unexpected after the first line: "Mountain barbecue"? What is there in the poem that prepares the reader for this ending and for the word "white" in the last line?

5. Consider the meaning and the impact of the line "broken lives repaired for this occasion." What point is Baca making here?

6. What does the poem reveal about Baca's views on family and identity?

WRITING ASSIGNMENTS

1. Write an essay or a poem discussing an event that shows your own attitude to family ties.

2. Discuss why you think Baca, even though he is with cousins, aunts, and uncles, can say, "I feel no love or family tie here." Why do you think he leaves the barbecue to go hiking? What generalizations can you make about individuals and families from what he says about himself and his family in this poem?

Making Connections: Family Ties

1. Write a detailed account of the ways in which family ties have shaped and changed your own identities over time and how they have shaped and changed the identities of other family members.

2. Do library research to investigate the changing nature of the family in the United States or Canada in the last twenty years. You might begin by looking for census statistics on divorce, single parents, and same-sex guardians. Then turn to articles that discuss changes in the family. What do your sources say about the impact of the changes on children?

3. Investigate the status of legal "domestic partnership" arrangements in some states. What has been written about how those laws are working? What recommendations have been made on the issue of legalizing gay marriage?

4. Do research to learn about the reasons why an adopted child might be taken from his or her adoptive parents and returned to the birth parents. Write an essay presenting your findings and drawing conclusions.

5. Compare and contrast the ways in which any two of the following authors in this book perceive their relationship with their fathers: Ferraro, Kim, Gordon, and Wolff. Or compare and contrast the relationship between mothers and daughters in the selections of two of the following authors: Walker, hooks, Jong, Jones, and Didion.

6. Taking Wolff's description of his con man father as a starting point, examine the portrayal of other con artists. You could focus on literature: Melville's *The Confidence Man,* for example, or on films such as *The Sting, Dirty Rotten Scoundrels,* or *House of Games.*

7. If complicated situations about identity arise because of adoption, consider the problems caused by surrogate parenting (the situation in which, with a financial arrangement, one

woman, impregnated with a man's sperm, bears a child and then gives up the child to the man and his family) or the situation in which a woman uses artificial insemination, against the man's wishes, to conceive and bear a child whom she then keeps. Describe actual cases in which disputes occurred about which family a child belonged to, and discuss the outcomes of those disputes.

8. Read James P. Comer's *Maggie's American Dream: The Life and Times of a Black Family,* and connect it to the pictures of families presented in this unit.

9. See the film *The Joy Luck Club*. Write an essay in which you show how the events described in "Two Kinds" are presented in the film and how they relate to the other family stories in the film.

10. Psychologist Kenneth Gergen, in an interview published in *U.S. News & World Report* on July 1, 1991, said this about the family: "As we develop an array of relationships outside the family, it will become difficult to sustain the notion of the family as a central nesting place. It is more and more a gas station where we drop by, fill up and go on out." Is that how you view the family? Explain your response, and support it with examples.

Education

What sculpture is to a block of marble, education is to an human soul.

—JOSEPH ADDISON, Spectator, *6 November 1711*

What does education often do? It makes a straight-cut ditch of a free, meandering brook.

—HENRY DAVID THOREAU, Journals, *1906, entry for October/November, 1850*

Education

❖

WHILE OUR EDUCATION MIGHT be influenced by our psychological makeup, socioeconomic status, and the abilities and disabilities we have inherited, it becomes progressively more under our own control, at least after we reach a certain age. Choice of elementary and middle school is frequently made by our parents, but after that we veer increasingly toward our own choice of educational experience. Still, society and culture influence us. Whatever path we choose, we become subject both to the way our culture and society view education and to local educational policies. Policies such as bilingual education, tracking, vocational schooling, gifted classes, vouchers in place of public education, affirmative action, self-directed learning, special education for the disabled, mainstreaming, and multicultural curricula—all have effects on learners and their identities.

Education effectively delivered has the power to shape identities, change lives, and extend opportunities, transcending the social and political boundaries imposed by gender, race, class, family customs, and ethnic affiliation. When people speak and write about education, they often speak and write about how it changed them. After years in prison, for example, Malcolm X was able to say, "Reading had changed forever the course of my life." Denying an effective education can also have significant effects on individuals, resulting in what Jonathan Kozol sees as "savage inequalities" in our system.

This unit includes selections that deal with educational issues from kindergarten through college. The unit begins with accounts of elementary school days and then moves on to high school and college. Shirley Jackson's story describes a young child's first few weeks of finding his identity in school; the

personal experience of his own monolingual schooling in
California leads Richard Rodriguez to criticize the principles of
bilingual education programs. Polly Pui-Yee Lai, in an essay written for a college writing class, describes in an autobiographical
reminiscence how she took charge of her own education when
she opposed her family's choice of school and insisted on one
particular high school that matched her needs. Mike Rose, now a
college writing instructor, describes his high school experiences
and, in doing so, moves from a personal account to an evaluation
of tracking systems.

The last four readings take up the topic of education through
college. Stephen L. Carter takes a close look at affirmative action
policies and their effects on college applications, individual feelings, and the balance of society. In considering the actual college
curriculum, a newspaper opinion exchange between Henry Louis
Gates, Jr., and Donald Kagan offers opposing points of view on
multicultural education requirements in college. The unit ends
with a fitting return to the classroom, with Langston Hughes's
poem about his experience as a black student in an English class
with a white instructor.

STARTING POINTS [FOR JOURNAL OR FREEWRITING]

Before you turn to the readings, reflect in writing on the links
between identity and education by responding to the following
questions.

1. What would you like to have done differently about your education up to this point? Why? How might different decisions or
opportunities have influenced your identity?

2. How is education viewed in your family? What levels of education have various members of your family reached?

3. Which of the following statements do you most identify with
and why?

   a. Children should concentrate on learning about the lan-
      guage, literature, and culture of their own ethnic group.
   b. Children should concentrate on learning about the lan-
      guage, literature, and culture of a wide range of ethnic
      groups.

4. How were you placed in your high school classes—by choice,
by a counselor, by teacher recommendation, by tests? Did your

school include different tracks, such as a vocational track and a college-bound track? If so, how were students placed in these tracks? How did the students feel about them?

5. Do you think that students have a private identity (at home) and a public identity (in school)? In what ways was this true or not true for you and your fellow students in school?

CHARLES

SHIRLEY JACKSON

Shirley Jackson was born in San Francisco in 1919. She wrote many short stories and novels, often setting horrifying events in a background of everyday life. Jackson died in 1965. Her novels include The Sundial *(1958) and* We Have Always Lived in the Castle *(1962). One of her best-known short stories is "The Lottery" (1949). "Charles" first appeared in a collection of Jackson's short stories called* The Lottery, *published in 1949.*

THE DAY MY SON Laurie started kindergarten he renounced corduroy overalls with bibs and began wearing blue jeans with a belt. I watched him go off the first morning with the older girl next door, seeing clearly that an era of my life was ended, my sweet-voiced nursery-school tot replaced by a long-trousered, swaggering character who forgot to stop at the corner and wave good-bye to me.

He came home the same way, the front door slamming open, his hat on the floor, and the voice suddenly become raucous shouting, "Isn't anybody *here?*"

At lunch he spoke insolently to his father, spilled his baby sister's milk, and remarked that his teacher said we were not to take the name of the Lord in vain.

"How *was* school today?" I asked, elaborately casual.

"All right," he said.   5

"Did you learn anything?" his father asked.

Laurie regarded his father coldly. "I didn't learn nothing," he said.

"Anything," I said. "Didn't learn anything."

"The teacher spanked a boy, though," Laurie said, addressing his bread and butter. "For being fresh," he added, with his mouth full.

"What did he do?" I asked. "Who was it?"   10

Laurie thought. "It was Charles," he said. "He was fresh. The teacher spanked him and made him stand in a corner. He was awfully fresh."

"What did he do?" I asked again, but Laurie slid off his chair, took a cookie, and left, while his father was still saying, "See here, young man."

The next day Laurie remarked at lunch, as soon as he sat down, "Well, Charles was bad again today." He grinned enormously and said, "Today Charles hit the teacher."

"Good heavens," I said, mindful of the Lord's name. "I suppose he got spanked again?"

"He sure did," Laurie said. "Look up," he said to his father.   15

"What?" his father said, looking up.

"Look down," Laurie said. "Look at my thumb. Gee, you're dumb." He began to laugh insanely.

"Why did Charles hit the teacher?" I asked quickly.

"Because she tried to make him color with red crayons," Laurie said. "Charles wanted to color with green crayons so he hit the teacher and she spanked him and said nobody play with Charles but everybody did."

The third day—it was Wednesday of the first week—Charles   20
bounced a see-saw on the head of a little girl and made her bleed, and the teacher made him stay inside all during recess. Thursday Charles had to stand in a corner during story-time because he kept pounding his feet on the floor. Friday Charles was deprived of blackboard privileges because he threw chalk.

On Saturday I remarked to my husband, "Do you think kindergarten is too unsettling for Laurie? All this toughness and bad grammar, and this Charles boy sounds like such a bad influence."

"It'll be all right," my husband said reassuringly. "Bound to be people like Charles in the world. Might as well meet them now as later."

On Monday Laurie came home late, full of news. "Charles," he shouted as he came up the hill; I was waiting anxiously on the front steps. "Charles," Laurie yelled all the way up the hill, "Charles was bad again."

"Come right in," I said, as soon as he came close enough. "Lunch is waiting."

"You know what Charles did?" he demanded, following me through the door. "Charles yelled so in school they sent a boy in from first grade to tell the teacher she had to make Charles keep quiet, and so Charles had to stay after school. And so all the children stayed to watch him."

"What did he do?" I asked.

"He just sat there," Laurie said, climbing into his chair at the table. "Hi, Pop, y'old dust mop."

"Charles had to stay after school today," I told my husband. "Everyone stayed with him."

"What does this Charles look like?" my husband asked Laurie. "What's his other name?"

"He's bigger than me," Laurie said. "And he doesn't have any rubbers and he doesn't ever wear a jacket."

Monday night was the first Parent-Teachers meeting, and only the fact that the baby had a cold kept me from going; I wanted passionately to meet Charles's mother. On Tuesday Laurie remarked suddenly, "Our teacher had a friend come to see her in school today."

"Charles's mother?" my husband and I asked simultaneously.

"Naaah," Laurie said scornfully. "It was a man who came and made us do exercises, we had to touch our toes. Look." He climbed down from his chair and squatted down and touched his toes. "Like this," he said. He got solemnly back onto his chair and said, picking up his fork, "Charles didn't even *do* exercises."

"That's fine," I said heartily. "Didn't Charles want to do the exercises?"

"Naaah," Laurie said. "Charles was so fresh to the teacher's friend he wasn't *let* do exercises."

"Fresh again," I said.

"He kicked the teacher's friend," Laurie said. "The teacher's friend told Charles to touch his toes like I just did and Charles kicked him."

"What are they going to do about Charles, do you suppose?" Laurie's father asked him.

Laurie shrugged elaborately. "Throw him out of school, I guess," he said.

Wednesday and Thursday were routine; Charles yelled during story hour and hit a boy in the stomach and made him cry. On Friday Charles stayed after school again and so did all the other children. 40

With the third week of kindergarten Charles was an institution in our family; the baby was being a Charles when he filled his wagon full of mud and pulled it through the kitchen; even my husband, when he caught his elbow in the telephone cord and pulled telephone, ashtray, and a bowl of flowers off the table, said, after the first minute, "Looks like Charles."

During the third and fourth weeks it looked like a reformation in Charles; Laurie reported grimly at lunch on Thursday of the third week, "Charles was so good today the teacher gave him an apple."

"What?" I said, and my husband added warily, "You mean Charles?"

"Charles," Laurie said. "He gave the crayons around and he picked up the books afterward and the teacher said he was her helper."

"What happened?" I asked incredulously. 45

"He was her helper, that's all," Laurie said, and shrugged.

"Can this be true, about Charles?" I asked my husband that night. "Can something like this happen?"

"Wait and see," my husband said cynically. "When you've got a Charles to deal with, this may mean he's only plotting."

He seemed to be wrong. For over a week Charles was the teacher's helper; each day he handed things out and he picked things up; no one had to stay after school.

"The PTA meeting's next week again," I told my husband one evening. "I'm going to find Charles's mother there." 50

"Ask her what happened to Charles," my husband said. "I'd like to know."

"I'd like to know myself," I said.

On Friday of that week things were back to normal. "You know what Charles did today?" Laurie demanded at the lunch table, in a voice slightly awed. "He told a little girl to say a word and she said it and the teacher washed her mouth out with soap and Charles laughed."

"What word?" his father asked unwisely, and Laurie said, "I'll have to whisper it to you, it's so bad." He got down off his chair and went around to his father. His father bent his head down and Laurie whispered joyfully. His father's eyes widened.

"Did Charles tell the little girl to say *that?*" he asked respectfully. 55

"She said it *twice,*" Laurie said. "Charles told her to say it *twice.*"

"What happened to Charles?" my husband asked.

"Nothing," Laurie said. "He was passing out the crayons."

Monday morning Charles abandoned the little girl and said the evil word himself three or four times, getting his mouth washed out with soap each time. He also threw chalk.

My husband came to the door with me that evening as I set out 60 for the PTA meeting. "Invite her over for a cup of tea after the meeting," he said. "I want to get a look at her."

"If only she's there," I said prayerfully.

"She'll be there," My husband said. "I don't see how they could hold a PTA meeting without Charles's mother."

At the meeting I sat restlessly, scanning each comfortable matronly face, trying to determine which one hid the secret of Charles. None of them looked to me haggard enough. No one stood up in the meeting and apologized for the way her son had been acting. No one mentioned Charles.

After the meeting I identified and sought out Laurie's kindergarten teacher. She had a plate with a cup of tea and a piece of chocolate cake; I had a plate with a cup of tea and a piece of marshmallow cake. We maneuvered up to one another cautiously, and smiled.

"I've been so anxious to meet you," I said. "I'm Laurie's 65 mother."

"We're all so interested in Laurie," she said.

"Well, he certainly likes kindergarten," I said. "He talks about it all the time."

"We had a little trouble adjusting, the first week or so," she said primly, "but now he's a fine little helper. With occasional lapses, of course."

"Laurie usually adjusts very quickly," I said. "I suppose this time it's Charles's influence."

"Charles?"

"Yes," I said, laughing, "you must have your hands full in that kindergarten, with Charles." 70

"Charles?" she said. "We don't have any Charles in the kindergarten."

RESPONDING IN DISCUSSION OR WRITING

1. As you were reading the story, what was your reaction to Charles's exploits?

2. What does the story about Laurie and Charles have to say about identity as related to family life and education? How are the two "people" different in the two settings?

3. How do you imagine Laurie's parents reacted after they heard the news that there was no Charles in the class? What do you think they said to Laurie? What would you say if you were one of the parents?

4. How do you imagine the other parents at the meeting reacted when they saw Laurie's mother?

5. What alternative endings could you devise for the story from the point at which the PTA meeting begins?

WRITING ASSIGNMENTS

1. Tell the story of the first four weeks of Laurie's school from the point of view of another child in the class talking to his or her parents.

2. Discuss what purpose Charles serves for Laurie and why you think he needs this other identity to help him cope with school.

SCHOOL AND HOME: PUBLIC
AND PRIVATE IDENTITY

RICHARD RODRIGUEZ

Richard Rodriguez was born in 1944, the son of Mexican American immigrants, and won acclaim for his book Hunger of Memory: The Education of Richard Rodriguez *(1981). This excerpt is from chapter one, "Aria," in which Rodriguez takes a firm stand against the policy of bilingual education in schools, which allows students to take subject courses such as history and science in their native language until they have acquired enough English to be "mainstreamed" into the curriculum with monolingual (English-speaking) students. Rodriguez's latest book is* Days of Obligation: An Argument with My Mexican Father *(1992).*

I REMEMBER TO START with that day in Sacramento—a California now nearly thirty years past—when I first entered a classroom, able to understand some fifty stray English words.

The third of four children, I had been preceded to a neighborhood Roman Catholic school by an older brother and sister. But neither of them had revealed very much about their classroom experiences. Each afternoon they returned, as they left in the morning, always together, speaking in Spanish as they climbed the five steps of the porch. And their mysterious books, wrapped in shopping-bag paper, remained on the table next to the door, closed firmly behind them.

An accident of geography sent me to a school where all my classmates were white, many the children of doctors and lawyers and business executives. All my classmates certainly must have been uneasy on that first day of school—as most children are uneasy—to find themselves apart from their families in the first institution of their lives. But I was astonished.

The nun said, in a friendly but oddly impersonal voice, "Boys and girls, this is Richard Rodriguez." (I heard her sound out: *Rich-heard Road-ree-guess.*) It was the first time I had heard anyone name me in English. "Richard," the nun repeated more slowly, writing my name down in her black leather book. Quickly I turned to see my mother's face dissolve in a watery blur behind the pebbled glass door.

Many years later there is something called bilingual education—a   5
scheme proposed in the late 1960s by Hispanic-American social activists, later endorsed by a congressional vote. It is a program that seeks to permit non-English-speaking children, many from lower-class homes, to use their family language as the language of school. (Such is the goal its supporters announce.) I hear them and am forced to say no: It is not possible for a child—any child—ever to use his family's language in school. Not to understand this is to misunderstand the public uses of schooling and to trivialize the nature of intimate life—a family's "language."

Memory teaches me what I know of these matters; the boy reminds the adult. I was a bilingual child, a certain kind—socially disadvantaged—the son of working-class parents, both Mexican immigrants.

In the early years of my boyhood, my parents coped very well in America. My father had steady work. My mother managed at home. They were nobody's victims. Optimism and ambition led them to a house (our home) many blocks from the Mexican south side of town. We lived among *gringos* and only a block from the biggest, whitest houses. It never occurred to my parents that they couldn't live wherever they chose. Nor was the Sacramento of the fifties bent on teaching them a contrary lesson. My mother and father were more annoyed than intimidated by those two or three neighbors who tried initially to make us unwelcome. ("Keep your brats away from my sidewalk!") But despite all they achieved, perhaps because they had so much to achieve, any deep feeling of ease, the confidence of "belonging" in public was withheld from them both. They regarded the people at work, the faces in crowds, as very distant from us. They were the others, *los gringos*. That term was interchangeable in their speech with another, even more telling, *los americanos*. . . .

Today I hear bilingual educators say that children lose a degree of "individuality" by becoming assimilated into public society. (Bilingual schooling was popularized in the seventies, that decade when middle-class ethnics began to resist the process of assimilation—the American melting pot.) But the bilingualists simplistically scorn the value and necessity of assimilation. They do not seem to realize that there are *two* ways a person is individualized. So they do not realize that while one suffers a diminished sense of *private* individuality by becoming assimilated into public society, such assimilation makes possible the achievement of *public* individuality.

The bilingualists insist that a student should be reminded of his difference from others in mass society, his heritage. But they equate mere separateness with individuality. The fact is that only in private—with intimates—is separateness from the crowd a prerequisite for individuality. (An intimate draws me apart, tells me that I am unique, unlike all others.) In public, by contrast, full individuality is achieved, paradoxically, by those who are able to consider themselves members of the crowd. Thus it happened for me: Only when I was able to think of myself as an American, no longer an alien in *gringo* society, could I seek the rights and opportunities necessary for full public individuality. The social and political advantages I enjoy as a man result from the day that I came to believe that my name, indeed, is *Rich-heard Road-ree-guess*. It is true that my public society today is often impersonal. (My public society is usually mass society.) Yet despite the anonymity of the crowd and despite the fact that the individuality I achieve in public is often tenuous—because it depends on my being one in a crowd—I celebrate the day I acquired my new name. Those middle-class ethnics who scorn assimilation seem to me filled with decadent self-pity, obsessed by the burden of public life. Dangerously, they romanticize public separateness and they trivialize the dilemma of the socially disadvantaged.

My awkward childhood does not prove the necessity of bilingual education. My story discloses instead an essential myth of childhood—inevitable pain. If I rehearse here the changes in my private life after my Americanization, it is finally to emphasize the public gain. The loss implies the gain: The house I returned to each afternoon was quiet. Intimate sounds no longer rushed to the door to greet me. There were other noises inside. The telephone rang. Neighborhood kids ran past the door of the bedroom where I was reading my schoolbooks—covered with shopping-bag paper. Once I learned public language, it would

10

never again be easy for me to hear intimate family voices. More and more of my day was spent hearing words. But that may only be a way of saying that the day I raised my hand in class and spoke loudly to an entire roomful of faces, my childhood started to end.

RESPONDING IN DISCUSSION OR WRITING

1. How did you feel on your first day of school? Did you feel either "uneasy" or "astonished"? Can you recall at what point you felt that your own childhood "started to end"?

2. Rodriguez makes a distinction between family language and "the public uses of schooling" (paragraph 5). How might these contrasts be reflected in the experience of a native speaker of the language of instruction in the schools—or do they not apply? How do these issues connect to the issue of identity?

3. *Considerations of Style.* Note how strongly Rodriguez makes a commitment to his point in paragraph 5. He mentions bilingual education, explains how it came about historically, and discusses what the program aims to do. Then he says, "I hear them and am forced to say no: It is not possible for a child—any child—ever to use his family's language in school." Examine some of your own pieces of writing. At what point have you made a commitment to expressing an opinion? How firmly have you made that commitment?

4. When Rodriguez tells a story about his first day at school, what is his purpose in telling that story? Does telling the story help him make his point effectively?

5. Rodriguez uses his memory to make a point about the principles of education. Recall incidents from your education that have led you to make generalizations and recommendations about educational principles and practices.

WRITING ASSIGNMENTS

1. When Rodriguez says that childhood means "inevitable pain," what do you think he means? Do you agree with him? Write an essay in which you give examples that illustrate your point of view. Let your reader see why you hold this point of view by providing evidence in stories and examples. Your readers need to know not only what opinion you hold but also what circumstances have led you to form that opinion.

2. *For Further Research.* Do a periodical and newspaper index search (on a CD-ROM database or in reference books) to find two articles that present opposing points of view on the effectiveness of bilingual education. Discuss how each side makes its case and what methods are used to convince the readers.

M AND A

POLLY PUI-YEE LAI

Polly Pui-Yee Lai, born in 1957 in Hong Kong, wrote this essay in a freshman writing class at Hunter College, City University of New York. She majored in studio art, specializing in black and white photography, particularly portraits and interiors. She graduated in 1995 and intends to go to graduate school. At the High School of Music and Art (M and A) she also played the harp. The part of the essay about education and choice of school serves as a frame for personal memories of family hardship, adoption, and coming to terms with decision making. "M and A" is published here for the first time.

I WAS THINKING TO myself: "I can't wait until I get the hell out of Junior High School #22." Even though I hated the school, I did not have a choice because of where I lived. It had to be the worst school in the entire city. As I approached my senior year there, I expected I would have to go to the neighborhood high school. I was not overjoyed.

One Sunday afternoon in church, someone told me about M and A. I had to ask to find out that M and A was an abbreviation for the High School of Music and Art, a highly specialized school for students with exceptional musical and artistic talents. An electric buzz went through my body at the thought that such a school existed. And auditions were open to students from all five boroughs.

When I got home that night, feeling intense and excited, I told my parents I was going to try out for a high school on 145th Street in Harlem. They dropped their chopsticks and looked at me in disbelief. "Harlem! Harlem!" they both hollered. "No! You're not going anywhere," my father George said. "You're going to Seward Park High School and that's final." Pui Chun, my stepmother, added, "Seward Park is only two blocks away and they have a lot of Chinese students there. It's close to home, so you can walk home for lunch, not to mention saving money." Then they made the point that it was unsafe for a girl to travel early mornings on the trains. Harlem was one of the most dangerous areas in the city because there were so many black ghosts living there who were on drugs. I could get raped or killed, they feared. Besides, according to my parents, studying music was impractical and unrealistic.

Whenever I got upset, I would sit at the piano and bang on it for two or three hours. That night, I played into the night. I needed Beethoven because of his sense of tragedy. I wanted Mozart because his spirit was light and animated, but most of all, I needed to play to unleash my anger.

My relationship with my parents was like the black and white   5 keys on the keyboard. Never was there a medium tone or a shade of gray in between.

As I played louder and louder, faster and faster, my thoughts drifted. I felt my dreams fading, dissolving, and finally vanishing. Traumatized, I inhabited a world where memories of pain intruded, where tears flooded my eyes, where a cracked vase sat in the center of my heart. The realities of the past came back to me as if it were yesterday.

At a fairly young age, I knew I was different. I knew I was unique and had little in common with others. The children I grew up with came from normal backgrounds. I did not. Their lives were conventional. Mine was not. The fundamental difference was pain. I was basically a living mystery, not knowing my roots, my genealogy, or my birth. I had once imagined that I exploded out of a solid mass; or I was a traveling space alien and the mother ship had deliberately taken off without me. No matter how imaginative I became and how endlessly I re-created the scenario of my own life story, I could not escape the truth. The truth lay deep and was painful to confront.

In the fall of 1957, I was found in front of the Precious Blood Hospital on Hong Kong Island. There I lay on the front steps of the hospital entrance, wrapped in a padded Chinese cotton jacket. A morning worker had found me and reported the incident to the police. No identification had been left with me, so a social worker at a local orphanage was called in. With my umbilical cord still fresh with blood and attached to my belly, I was taken to the Po Leung Kok Orphanage.

My health was very poor, and I nearly died before my first birthday. The doctors thought I was born blind because my eyes were so small. They later found that I had a condition known as "distended eyelid," in which the muscles of the eyes did not function. This birth defect and my general ill health prevented several potential adoptions. Only when I was nine was I notified that a couple from overseas was interested in filing for my adoption. In less than six months, I was on my way to New York.

Kum Chuen, my adopted mother, originally came from Guangdong in China. She completed grammar school and then, as both her parents were dead, she had to work to support her eight siblings. At the age of twenty-six, she made the journey to Hong Kong in the hope of making a better living. She found a job as a midwife in a hospital; there, she became acquainted with influential people and taught herself manners, social etiquette, tailoring, and gourmet cooking. She adapted to a more leisurely way of life.

My adopted father, George, was the oldest of three children. When his father died, he was only thirteen. He had a widowed mother and two siblings to support. He left China and became a busboy on a big luxurious British cruise liner, traveling between Hong Kong, South East Asia, Europe, South America, and North America. One night, when the cruise liner docked at a port in New Jersey he managed to jump ship and became an illegal alien. Working as a waiter, he was able to send money home. Not until World War II broke out did he seize the opportunity to become a United States citizen by enlisting in the army. After the war, George and a few friends went into the restaurant business.

When George was vacationing in Hong Kong, mutual friends introduced him to Kum Chuen. After a year of courtship and romance, they married and came to New York to start their lives together.

I became their daughter. I thought they were good parents. Kum Chuen was strict and George was lenient, a perfect balance. Five months after my adoption, during a routine physical, Kum

Chuen was told she had cancer of the lymph nodes. For three brief years I watched her deterioration, helpless and hopeless. Chemotherapy, radiation and the so-called advanced treatments of the time took their toll on her. She looked like a skeleton even as she lay dying. At the funeral, I remember vividly not crying. The family members called me heartless, barbarian, wild beast. My logic was, if I withheld my tears, she might come back. I had for a long time wondered about the "death" word. I did not understand. I only knew I missed her terribly.

Life became harder and harder. George married another woman—Pui Chun. His new wife was to be my new mother. From the very first, I instinctively disliked her. Every fiber in my body resisted her. George explained that she was a hard-working woman and a faithful Christian and that she would look after me. He wanted nothing less from me than total respect for the new mother. There was no way I could give it.

On day one, I knew she was trouble. She dragged me into the sweat-shop where I had to work stitching window shades every day after school, including weekends. The factory was filthy. Dust permeated everything. The smell of urine filled the room. Rats and cockroaches roamed the assembly lines. Along the walls and baseboards, flakes of white lead paint spread on the floor like snow. Children picked them up and put them in their mouths. I saw workers hurt themselves by accidentally running needles into the fleshy part of their fingers. I got boils from sitting ten hours a day next to the steam press machine.

Pui Chun did her preaching at least once a week in the factory. She spoke of Jesus' love and salvation to those who believed. The workers would dart a glance my way, silently expressing empathy. They probably thought that the little girl's mother was nothing but a Jesus freak. Sunday was supposed to be a day of rest and a day of worship. But when money came knocking on Pui Chun's door, even Jesus had to be put on hold.

I played my last chord. The apartment was quiet, the night still. I knew what I had to do. Only I could do it.

I knew that despite everything my parents were good hardworking people who tried in one way or another to make me someone of importance. They struggled courageously in hard times, and survived as best they knew how, in Chinatown, in Mott Street, in the Chinese sweat-shop.

I wanted to experience life on my own terms. I did not believe in compromise. From birth, I was abandoned. From Kum Chuen's death, I experienced loss. From Pui Chun's rigidity, I experienced misery. I needed to come to grips with my own reality and my own worth, break away, and take charge. M and A would be the first step.

RESPONDING IN DISCUSSION OR WRITING

1. *For Further Research.*   Conduct a survey in your class. How many students chose their own high school, and how many went to one in their neighborhood or one their parents recommended?

2. Lai's parents make a case for a local school; they say it would be closer to home and no traveling would be involved, so Polly would be safer and could go home for lunch. They also oppose the other school because they think music will not be practical and lead later to a job. How would you try to convince them if you were Polly Lai?

3. What questions would you like to ask Polly Lai about the details of her life? Do you wish she had included more of the story of her early life?

4. Lai discusses the fact that her poor health and a birth defect prevented people from adopting her. How can people be encouraged to adopt children with special needs?

5. At one point, Lai says that her parents were a "perfect balance," one lenient and the other strict. Do you agree that that is perfect? What problems could it cause?

6. *Considerations of Style.*   Lai's essay was written for a first-year writing course in college. What suggestions could you make to her for revision?

WRITING ASSIGNMENTS

1. Retell Polly Lai's story about her choice of high school from the point of view of either George or Pui Chun.

2. Polly Lai describes how her parents thought that studying music was "impractical and unrealistic." Do you think that students should select a course of study that is practical and leads to a specific type of job? Or should undergraduate years be a time for exploration? Describe the arguments on each side, and

explain which ones are ultimately the most convincing for you
and why.

❖

TRACKING

MIKE ROSE

*Mike Rose grew up in Los Angeles, the son of immigrant Italian parents.
He is now associate director of the writing programs at the University of
California, Los Angeles, and publishes articles on teaching and writing.
One of his areas of research is writer's block. This excerpt is taken from
Lives on the Boundary (1989), his autobiographical account of mak-
ing it through school and then helping others fight against illiteracy. His
most recent book is Possible Lives.*

Entrance to school brings with it forms and releases and assessments. Mercy [Rose's new high school: Our Lady of Mercy] relied
on a series of tests, mostly the Stanford-Binet, for placement, and
somehow the results of my tests got confused with those of
another student named Rose. The other Rose apparently didn't
do very well, for I was placed in the vocational track, a euphemism
for the bottom level. Neither I nor my parents realized what this
meant. We had no sense that Business Math, Typing, and English-
Level D were dead ends. The current spate of reports on the
schools criticizes parents for not involving themselves in the education of their children. But how would someone like Tommy
Rose, with his two years of Italian schooling, know what to ask?
And what sort of pressure could an exhausted waitress apply? The
error went undetected, and I remained in the vocational track for
two years. What a place.

My homeroom was supervised by Brother Dill, a troubled and
unstable man who also taught freshman English. When his class
drifted away from him, which was often, his voice would rise in
paranoid accusations, and occasionally he would lose control and

shake or smack us. I hadn't been there two months when one of
his brisk, face-turning slaps had my glasses sliding down the aisle.
Physical education was also pretty harsh. Our teacher was a stubby
ex-lineman who had played old-time pro ball in the Midwest. He
routinely had us grabbing our ankles to receive his stinging pad-
dle across our butts. He did that, he said, to make men of us.
"Rose," he bellowed on our first encounter; me standing geeky in
line in my baggy shorts. "'Rose'? What the hell kind of name
is that?"

"Italian, sir," I squeaked.

"Italian! Ho. Rose, do you know the sound a bag of shit makes
when it hits the wall?"

"No, sir."   5

"Wop!"

Sophomore English was taught by Mr. Mitropetros. He was a
large, bejeweled man who managed the parking lot at the Shrine
Auditorium. He would crow and preen and list for us the stars
he'd brushed against. We'd ask questions and glance knowingly
and snicker, and all that fueled the poor guy to brag some more.
Parking cars was his night job. He had little training in English, so
his lesson plan for his day work had us reading the district's
required text, *Julius Caesar,* aloud for the semester. We'd finish
the play way before the twenty weeks was up, so he'd have us
switch parts again and again and start again: Dave Snyder, the
fastest guy at Mercy, muscling through Caesar to the breathless
squeals of Calpurnia, as interpreted by Steve Fusco, a surfer who
owned the school's most envied paneled wagon. Week ten and
Dave and Steve would take on new roles, as would we all, and ren-
der a water-logged Cassius and a Brutus that are beyond my powers of description.

Spanish I—taken in the second year—fell into the hands of a
new recruit. Mr. Montez was a tiny man, slight, five foot six at the
most, soft-spoken and delicate. Spanish was a particularly rowdy
class, and Mr. Montez was as prepared for it as a doily maker at a
hammer throw. He would tap his pencil to a room in which Steve
Fusco was propelling spitballs from his heavy lips, in which Mike
Dweetz was taunting Billy Hawk, a half-Indian, half-Spanish, reed-
thin, quietly explosive boy. The vocational track at Our Lady of
Mercy mixed kids traveling in from South L.A. with South Bay
surfers and a few Slavs and Chicanos from the harbors of San

Pedro. This was a dangerous miscellany: surfers and hodads and South-Central blacks all ablaze to the metronomic tapping of Hector Montez's pencil.

One day Billy lost it. Out of the corner of my eye I saw him strike out with his right arm and catch Dweetz across the neck. Quick as a spasm, Dweetz was out of his seat, scattering desks, cracking Billy on the side of the head, right behind the eye. Snyder and Fusco and others broke it up, but the room felt hot and close and naked. Mr. Montez's tenuous authority was finally ripped to shreds, and I think everyone felt a little strange about that. The charade was over, and when it came down to it, I don't think any of the kids really wanted it to end this way. They had pushed and pushed and bullied their way into a freedom that both scared and embarrassed them.

Students will float to the mark you set. I and the others in the vocational classes were bobbing in pretty shallow water. Vocational education has aimed at increasing the economic opportunities of students who do not do well in our schools. Some serious programs succeed in doing that, and through exceptional teachers—like Mr. Gross in *Horace's Compromise*—students learn to develop hypotheses and troubleshoot, reason through a problem, and communicate effectively—the true job skills. The vocational track, however, is most often a place for those who are just not making it, a dumping ground for the disaffected. There were a few teachers who worked hard at education; young Brother Slattery, for example, combined a stern voice with weekly quizzes to try to pass along to us a skeletal outline of world history. But mostly the teachers had no idea of how to engage the imaginations of us kids who were scuttling along at the bottom of the pond.

And the teachers would have needed some inventiveness, for none of us was groomed for the classroom. It wasn't just that I didn't know things—didn't know how to simplify algebraic fractions, couldn't identify different kinds of clauses, bungled Spanish translations—but that I had developed various faulty and inadequate ways of doing algebra and making sense of Spanish. Worse yet, the years of defensive tuning out in elementary school had given me a way to escape quickly while seeming at least half alert. During my time in Voc. Ed., I developed further into a mediocre student and a somnambulant problem solver, and that affected the subjects I did have the wherewithal to handle: I detested Shakespeare; I got bored with history. My attention flitted here and there. I fooled around in class and read my books indifferently—the intellectual equivalent of playing with your food. I did what I had to do to get by, and I did it with half a mind.

But I did learn things about people and eventually came into my own socially. I liked the guys in Voc. Ed. Growing up where I did, I understood and admired physical prowess, and there was an abundance of muscle here. There was Dave Snyder, a sprinter and halfback of true quality. Dave's ability and his quick wit gave him a natural appeal, and he was welcome in any clique, though he always kept a little independent. He enjoyed acting the fool and could care less about studies, but he possessed a certain maturity and never caused the faculty much trouble. It was a testament to his independence that he included me among his friends— I eventually went out for track, but I was no jock. Owing to the Latin alphabet and a dearth of *R*s and *S*s, Snyder sat behind Rose, and we started exchanging one-liners and became friends.

There was Ted Richard, a much-touted Little League pitcher. He was chunky and had a baby face and came to Our Lady of Mercy as a seasoned street fighter. Ted was quick to laugh and he had a loud, jolly laugh, but when he got angry he'd smile a little smile, the kind that simply raises the corner of the mouth a quarter of an inch. For those who knew, it was an eerie signal. Those who didn't found themselves in big trouble, for Ted was very quick. He loved to carry on what we would come to call philosophical discussions: What is courage? Does God exist? He also loved words, enjoyed picking up big ones like *salubrious* and *equivocal* and using them in our conversations—laughing at himself as the word hit a chuckhole rolling off his tongue. Ted didn't do all that well in school—baseball and parties and testing the courage he'd speculated about took up his time. His textbooks were *Argosy* and *Field and Stream,* whatever newspapers he'd find on the bus stop—from *The Daily Worker* to pornography—conversations with uncles or hobos or businessmen he'd meet in a coffee shop, *The Old Man and the Sea.* With hindsight, I can see that Ted was developing into one of those rough-hewn intellectuals whose sources are a mix of the learned and the apocryphal, whose discussions are both assured and sad.

And then there was Ken Harvey. Ken was good-looking in a
puffy way and had a full and oily ducktail and was a car enthusiast
. . . a hodad. One day in religion class, he said the sentence that
turned out to be one of the most memorable of the hundreds of
thousands I heard in those Voc. Ed. years. We were talking about
the parable of the talents, about achievement, working hard,
doing the best you can do, blah-blah-blah, when the teacher
called on the restive Ken Harvey for an opinion. Ken thought
about it, but just for a second, and said (with studied, minimal
affect), "I just wanna be average." That woke me up. Average?!
Who wants to be average? Then the athletes chimed in with the
clichés that make you want to laryngectomize them, and the
exchange became a platitudinous melee. At the time, I thought
Ken's assertion was stupid, and I wrote him off. But his sentence
has stayed with me all these years, and I think I am finally coming
to understand it.

Ken Harvey was gasping for air. School can be a tremendously   15
disorienting place. No matter how bad the school, you're going to
encounter notions that don't fit with the assumptions and beliefs
that you grew up with—maybe you'll hear these dissonant notions
from teachers, maybe from the other students, and maybe you'll
read them. You'll also be thrown in with all kinds of kids from all
kinds of backgrounds, and that can be unsettling—this is especially true in places of rich ethnic and linguistic mix, like the L.A.
basin. You'll see a handful of students far excel you in courses that
sound exotic and that are only in the curriculum of the elite:
French, physics, trigonometry. And all this is happening while
you're trying to shape an identity, your body is changing, and
your emotions are running wild. If you're a working-class kid in
the vocational track, the options you'll have to deal with this will
be constrained in certain ways: You're defined by your school as
"slow"; you're placed in a curriculum that isn't designed to liber-
ate you but to occupy you, or, if you're lucky, train you, though
the training is for work the society does not esteem; other students are picking up the cues from your school and your curriculum and interacting with you in particular ways. If you're a kid
like Ted Richard, you turn your back on all this and let your mind
roam where it may. But youngsters like Ted are rare. What Ken
and so many others do is protect themselves from such suffocating madness by taking on with a vengeance the identity implied in

the vocational track. Reject the confusion and frustration by openly defining yourself as the Common Joe. Champion the average. Rely on your own good sense. Fuck this bullshit. Bullshit, of course, is everything you—and the others—fear is beyond you: books, essays, tests, academic scrambling, complexity, scientific reasoning, philosophical inquiry.

The tragedy is that you have to twist the knife in your own gray matter to make this defense work. You'll have to shut down, have to reject intellectual stimuli or diffuse them with sarcasm, have to cultivate stupidity, have to convert boredom from a malady into a way of confronting the world. Keep your vocabulary simple, act stoned when you're not or act more stoned than you are, flaunt ignorance, materialize your dreams. It is a powerful and effective defense—it neutralizes the insult and the frustration of being a vocational kid and, when perfected, it drives teachers up the wall, a delightful secondary effect. But like all strong magic, it exacts a price.

My own deliverance from the Voc. Ed. world began with sophomore biology. Every student, college prep to vocational, had to take biology, and unlike the other courses, the same person taught all sections. When teaching the vocational group, Brother Clint probably slowed down a bit or omitted a little of the fundamental biochemistry, but he used the same book and more or less the same syllabus across the board. If one class got tough, he could get tougher. He was young and powerful and very handsome, and looks and physical strength were high currency. No one gave him any trouble.

I was pretty bad at the dissecting table, but the lectures and the textbook were interesting: plastic overlays that, with each turned page, peeled away skin, then veins and muscle, then organs, down to the very bones that Brother Clint, pointer in hand, would tap out on our hanging skeleton. Dave Snyder was in big trouble, for the study of life—versus the living of it—was sticking in his craw. We worked out a code for our multiple-choice exams. He'd poke me in the back: once for the answer under *A*, twice for *B*, and so on; and when he'd hit the right one, I'd look up to the ceiling as though I were lost in thought. Poke: cytoplasm. Poke, poke: methane. Poke, poke, poke: William Harvey. Poke, poke, poke, poke: islets of Langerhans. This didn't work out perfectly, but

Dave passed the course, and I mastered the dreamy look of a guy on a record jacket. And something else happened. Brother Clint puzzled over this Voc. Ed. kid who was racking up 98s and 99s on his tests. He checked the school's records and discovered the error. He recommended that I begin my junior year in the College Prep program. According to all I've read since, such a shift, as one report put it, is virtually impossible. Kids at that level rarely cross tracks. The telling thing is how chancy both my placement into and exit from Voc. Ed. was; neither I nor my parents had anything to do with it. I lived in one world during spring semester, and when I came back to school in the fall, I was living in another.

RESPONDING IN DISCUSSION OR WRITING

1. Recall the kinds of tests you had to take in school. What action was taken as a result of those tests? Did you ever feel that a test did not get at your real abilities?

2. Rose describes how one teacher had the students read aloud all semester. What do you think are the advantages and disadvantages of students reading aloud in class?

3. *Considerations of Style.* In paragraph 8, Rose uses a colorful simile: He says that Mr. Montez was as prepared for the Spanish class "as a doily maker at a hammer throw." What images does the simile conjure up? How does it help you see Rose's point about Mr. Montez? Think up other similes that would convey the same meaning.

4. At the end of paragraph 16, Rose says that defining oneself as average builds a defense but "exacts a price." What do you think he means by that? What price would someone pay?

5. In your own high school years, were "looks and physical strength . . . high currency," as Rose says was the case in his school? Whichever way you answer that, how does your answer play out in some of the events you remember from your high school years?

WRITING ASSIGNMENTS

1. When Rose says "Students will float to the mark you set" (paragraph 10), how does he illustrate that from his own experience? What can you add to that from your own experience? Explain why you agree or do not agree with Rose's statement.

2. When you read Ken Harvey's statement, "I just wanna be average" (paragraph 14), how do you react? What is your understanding of why he says that and what it implies about the educational system? (If you read Bruce Bower's article "Average Attractions" in Unit 2, you might want to comment on how both that article and this excerpt perceive the concept of being average.)

❖

AFFIRMATIVE ACTION BABY

STEPHEN L. CARTER

Stephen L. Carter, born in 1954, served as law clerk for Justice Thurgood Marshall of the Supreme Court of the United States and is now professor of law at Yale University. He is the author of The Culture of Disbelief *(1993) and* The Confirmation Mess: Cleaning Up the Federal Appointments Process *(1994). This excerpt is from the first chapter of his book* Reflections of an Affirmative Action Baby *(1991), a scholarly work in which he documents his references in endnotes. The affirmative action policy he discusses is a policy that aims at providing equal opportunity in college admissions and in employment hiring for members of previously disadvantaged groups, such as women and minorities.*

I GOT INTO LAW school because I am black.

As many black professionals think they must, I have long suppressed this truth, insisting instead that I got where I am the same way everybody else did. Today I am a professor at the Yale Law School. I like to think that I am a good one, but I am hardly the most objective judge. What I am fairly sure of, and can now say without trepidation, is that were my skin not the color that it is, I would not have had the chance to try.

For many, perhaps most, black professionals of my generation, the matter of who got where and how is left in a studied and, I think, purposeful ambiguity. Some of us, as they say, would have made it into an elite college or professional school anyway. (But, in my generation, many fewer than we like to pretend, even though one might question the much-publicized claim by Derek Bok, the president of Harvard University, that in the absence of preferences, only 1 percent of Harvard's entering class would be black.)[1] Most of us, perhaps nearly all of us, have learned to bury the matter far back in our minds. We are who we are and where we are, we have records of accomplishment or failure, and there is no rational reason that anybody—employer, client, whoever— should care any longer whether racial preference played any role in our admission to a top professional school.

When people in positions to help or hurt our careers *do* seem to care, we tend to react with fury. Those of us who have graduated professional school over the past fifteen to twenty years, and are not white, travel career paths that are frequently bumpy with suspicions that we did not earn the right to be where we are. We bristle when others raise what might be called the qualification question—"Did you get into school or get hired because of a special program?"—and that prickly sensitivity is the best evidence, if any is needed, of one of the principal costs of racial preferences. Scratch a black professional with the qualification question, and you're likely to get a caustic response, such as this one from a senior executive at a major airline: "Some whites think I've made it because I'm black. Some blacks think I've made it only because I'm an Uncle Tom. The fact is, I've made it because I'm good."[2]

Given the way that so many Americans seem to treat receipt of the benefits of affirmative action as a badge of shame, answers of this sort are both predictable and sensible. In the professional world, moreover, they are very often true: relatively few corporations are in a position to hand out charity. The peculiar aspect of the routine denial, however, is that so many of those who will bristle at the suggestion that they themselves have gained from racial preferences will try simultaneously to insist that racial preferences be preserved and to force the world to pretend that no one benefits from them. That awkward balancing of fact and fiction explains the frequent but generally groundless cry that it is racist to suggest that some individual's professional accomplishments would be fewer but for affirmative action; and therein hangs a tale.

For students at the leading law schools, autumn brings the recruiting season, the idyllic weeks when law firms from around the country compete to lavish upon them lunches and dinners and other attentions, all with the professed goal of obtaining the students' services—perhaps for the summer, perhaps for a longer term. The autumn of 1989 was different, however, because the nation's largest firm, Baker & McKenzie, was banned from interviewing students at the University of Chicago Law School, and on probation—that is, enjoined to be on its best behavior—at some others.

The immediate source of Baker & McKenzie's problems was a racially charged interview that a partner in the firm had conducted the previous fall with a black third-year student at the school. The interviewer evidently suggested that other lawyers might call her "nigger" or "black bitch" and wanted to know how she felt about that. Perhaps out of surprise that she played golf, he observed that "there aren't too many golf courses in the ghetto." He also suggested that the school was admitting "foreigners" and excluding "qualified" Americans.[3]

The law school reacted swiftly, and the firm was banned from interviewing on campus. Other schools contemplated taking action against the firm, and some of them did.[4] Because I am black myself, and teach in a law school, I suppose the easiest thing for me to have done would have been to clamor in solidarity for punishment. Yet I found myself strangely reluctant to applaud the school's action. Instead, I was disturbed rather than excited by this vision of law schools circling the wagons, as it were, to defend their beleaguered minority students against racially insensitive remarks. It is emphatically not my intention to defend the interviewer, most of whose reported questions and comments were inexplicable and inexcusable. I am troubled, however, by my suspicion that there would still have been outrage—not as much, but some—had the interviewer asked only what I called at the beginning of the chapter the qualification question.

I suspect this because in my own student days, something over a decade ago, an interviewer from a prominent law firm addressed this very question to a Yale student who was not white, and the student voices—including my own—howled in protest. "Racism!" we insisted. "Ban them!" But with the passing years, I have come to wonder whether our anger might have been misplaced.

To be sure, the Yale interviewer's question was boorish. And because the interviewer had a grade record and résumé right in front of him, it was probably irrelevant as well. (It is useful here to dispose of one common but rather silly anti-affirmative action bromide: the old question, "Do you really want to be treated by a doctor who got into medical school because of skin color?" The answer is, or ought to be, that the patient doesn't particularly care how the doctor got *into* school; what matters is how the doctor got *out*. The right question, the sensible question, is not "What medical school performance did your grades and test scores predict?" but "What was your medical school performance?") But irrelevance and boorishness cannot explain our rage at the qualification question, because lots of interviewers ask questions that meet the tests of boorishness and irrelevance.

The controversy is not limited to outsiders who come onto campus to recruit. In the spring of 1991, for example, students at Georgetown Law School demanded punishment for a classmate who argued in the school newspaper that affirmative action is unfair because students of color are often admitted to law school on the basis of grades and test scores that would cause white applicants to be rejected. Several universities have considered proposals that would deem it "racial harassment" for a (white?) student to question the qualifications of nonwhite classmates. But we can't change either the truths or the myths about racial preferences by punishing those who speak them.

This clamor for protection from the qualification question is powerful evidence of the terrible psychological pressure that racial preferences often put on their beneficiaries. Indeed, it sometimes seems as though the programs are not supposed to have any beneficiaries—or, at least, that no one is permitted to suggest that they have any.

And that's ridiculous. If one supports racial preferences in professional school admissions, for example, one must be prepared to treat them like any other preference in admission and believe that they make a difference, that some students would not be admitted if the preferences did not exist. This is not a racist observation. It is not normative in any sense. It is simply a fact. A good deal of emotional underbrush might be cleared away were the fact simply conceded, and made the beginning, not the end, of any discussion of preferences. For once it is conceded that the programs have beneficiaries, it follows that some of us who are professionals and are not white must be among them. Supporters of preferences must stop pretending otherwise. Rather, some large segment of us must be willing to meet the qualification question head-on, to say, "Yes, I got into law school because of racial preferences. So what?"—and, having said it, must be ready with a list of what we have made of the opportunities the preferences provided.

Now, this is a costly concession, because it carries with it all the baggage of the bitter rhetorical battle over the relationship between preferences and merit. But bristling at the question suggests a deep-seated fear that the dichotomy might be real. Indeed, if admitting that racial preferences make a difference leaves a funny aftertaste in the mouths of proponents, they might be more comfortable fighting against preferences rather than for them.

So let us bring some honesty as well as rigor to the debate, and begin at the beginning. I have already made clear my starting point: I got into a top law school because I am black. Not only am I unashamed of this fact, but I can prove its truth.

As a senior at Stanford back in the mid-1970s, I applied to about half a dozen law schools. Yale, where I would ultimately enroll, came through fairly early with an acceptance. So did all but one of the others. The last school, Harvard, dawdled and dawdled. Finally, toward the end of the admission season, I received a letter of rejection. Then, within days, two different Harvard officials and a professor contacted me by telephone to apologize. They were quite frank in their explanation for the "error." I was told by one official that the school had initially rejected me because "we assumed from your record that you were white." (The words have always stuck in my mind, a tantalizing reminder of what is expected of me.) Suddenly coy, he went on to say that the school had obtained "additional information that should have been counted in your favor"—that is, Harvard had discovered the color of my skin. And if I had already made a deposit to confirm my decision to go elsewhere, well, that, I was told, would "not be allowed" to stand in my way should I enroll at Harvard.

Naturally, I was insulted by this miracle. Stephen Carter, the white male, was not good enough for the Harvard Law School; Stephen Carter, the black male, not only was good enough but rated agonized telephone calls urging him to attend. And Stephen Carter, color unknown, must have been white: How else could he have achieved what he did in college? Except that my college achievements were obviously not sufficiently spectacular to merit acceptance had I been white. In other words, my academic record was too good for a black Stanford University undergraduate, but not good enough for a white Harvard law student. Because I turned out to be black, however, Harvard was quite happy to scrape me from what it apparently considered somewhere nearer the bottom of the barrel.

My objective is not to single out Harvard for special criticism; on the contrary, although my ego insists otherwise, I make no claim that a white student with my academic record would have been admitted to any of the leading law schools. The insult I felt came from the pain of being reminded so forcefully that in the judgment of those with the power to dispose, I was good enough for a top law school only because I happened to be black.

Naturally, I should not have been insulted at all; that is what racial preferences are for—racial preference. But I was insulted and went off to Yale instead, even though I had then and have now absolutely no reason to imagine that Yale's judgment was based on different criteria than Harvard's. Hardly anyone granted admission at Yale is denied admission at Harvard, which admits a far larger class; but several hundreds of students who are admitted at Harvard are denied admission at Yale. Because Yale is far more selective, the chances are good that I was admitted at Yale for essentially the same reason I was admitted at Harvard—the color of my skin made up for what were evidently considered other deficiencies in my academic record. I may embrace this truth as a matter of simple justice or rail against it as one of life's great evils, but being a member of the affirmative action generation means that the one thing I cannot do is deny it. I will say it again: I got into law school because I am black. So what?

One answer to the "So what?" question is that someone more deserving than I—someone white—may have been turned away. I hardly know what to make of this argument, for I doubt that the mythical white student on the cusp, the one who almost made it to Yale but for my rude intervention, would have done better than I did in law school. Nor am I some peculiar case: the Yale Law School of my youth trained any number of affirmative action babies who went on to fine academic performances and are now in the midst of stellar careers in the law.

Even in the abstract, what I call the "fairness story" has never struck me as one of the more convincing arguments against preferential policies. The costs of affirmative action differ from the costs of taxation only in degree, not in kind. People are routinely taxed for services they do not receive that are deemed by their government necessary to right social wrongs they did not commit. The taxpayer-financed "bailout" of the weak or collapsed savings-and-loan institutions is one example. Another is the provision of tax dollars for emergency disaster assistance after a hurricane devastates a coastal community. The people who bear the costs of these programs are not the people who caused the damage, but they still have to pay.[5]

Like many, perhaps most, of America's domestic policies, affirmative action programs are essentially redistributive in nature. They transfer resources from their allocation in the market to other recipients, favored for social policy reasons. Much of the attack on affirmative action is fueled by the same instinct—the same American dream—that stands as a bulwark against any substantial redistribution of wealth. In America, most people like to think, it is possible for anyone to make it, and those who do not have been victims principally of their own sloth or lack of talent or perhaps plain bad luck—but not of anybody else's sinister plottings. Seymour Martin Lipset, among others, has argued plausibly that a stable democracy is possible only when an economically secure middle class exists to battle against radical economic reforms that the wealthier classes would otherwise resist by using means outside the system.[6] In America, that middle class plainly exists, and racial preferences are among the radical reforms it is willing to resist.

Sometimes the fervent opposition of the great majority of white Americans to affirmative action is put down to racism, or at least racial resentment, and I do not want to argue that neither motivation is *ever* present. But affirmative action programs are different from other social transfers, and the way they differ is in the basis on which the favored and disfavored groups are identified. The basis is race, and sometimes sex—and that makes all the difference.

I say that race is different not because I favor the ideal of a color-blind society; indeed . . . I fear that the rhetoric of color blindness conflates values that are best kept separate. Race is different for obvious historical reasons: the world in general, and this nation in particular, should know well the risks of encouraging powerful institutions to categorize by such immutable characteristics as race. Besides, even were race as a category less controversial, there is still the further fairness argument, that the sins for which the programs purportedly offer compensation are not sins of the current generation.

Many proponents of preferential policies, however, insist that the current generation of white males deserves to bear the costs of affirmative action. "White males," we are told, "have had exclusive access to certain information, education, experience, and contacts through which they have gained unfair advantage."[7] In the words of a leading scholar, "[W]e have to say to whites, 'Listen, you have benefited in countless ways from racism, from its notions of beauty [and] its exclusion of minorities in jobs and schools.'"[8] The argument has a second step, too: "For most of this country's history," wrote one commentator, "the nation's top universities practiced the most effective form of affirmative action ever; the quota was for 100 percent white males."[9] The analogy is fair— indeed, it is so fair that it wins the endorsement of opponents as well as supporters of affirmative action[10]—but what does it imply? For proponents of preferences, the answer is clear: if white males have been for centuries the beneficiaries of a vast and all-encompassing program of affirmative action, today's more limited programs can be defended as simply trying to undo the most pernicious effects of that one. That is how, in the contemporary rhetoric of affirmative action, white males turn out to deserve the disfavored treatment that the programs accord.

But there is risk in this rhetoric. To make race the determining factor not simply of the favored group but of the disfavored one encourages an analytical structure that seeks and assigns reasons in the present world for disfavoring one group. The simplest structure—and the one that has come, with mysterious force, to dominate the terms of intellectual and campus debate—is what Thomas Sowell has called "social irredentism," an insistence that all members of the disfavored dominant group bear the mantle of oppressor.[11] Affirmative action, then, becomes almost a punishment for the sin of being born the wrong color and the wrong sex.

All of this carries a neat historical irony. The personalization of affirmative action, the specification of white males as the villains, has diluted the message of the black left of the 1960s and early 1970s, which often (but by no means always) joined forces with the white left to insist that the problems were systemic, not individual. In those halcyon days of campus radicalism, the race struggle was widely described as hand-in-glove with the class struggle. Racial justice was said to be impossible under capitalism, and the principal debate among radical students was over what form of socialism was best for black people—a separate society or an integrated one, central planning or local communities?

As for affirmative action, well, sophisticated nationalists understood that it was part of the problem. By funneling the best and brightest young black men and women into the white-dominated system of higher education, the critics argued, the programs would simply skim the cream from our community, co-opting into the (white) mainstream those who should have been our leaders. An attack on efforts to substitute enhanced educational opportunities for racial justice was a principal focus of Robert Allen's provocative 1969 book *Black Awakening in Capitalist America*. "The black student," Allen warned, "is crucial to corporate America's neocolonial plans."[12] The best and brightest among black youth, he argued, instead of criticizing capitalism from the outside, would be trained to serve it from the inside. Nationalist reviewers agreed. For example, Anne Kelley wrote in *The Black Scholar* that "the emphasis on higher education for black students" was part of a "neo-colonialist scheme" that was "designed to stabilize the masses."[13]

But the language of protest is quite different now, and the success of affirmative action is one of the reasons; to paraphrase John le Carré, it is hard to criticize the system when it has brought you inside at its own expense. Affirmative action programs in education are designed to move people of color into productive roles in capitalist society, and the best sign that they are working is the way the argument has shifted. White males have replaced "the society" or "the system" or "the establishment" in the rhetoric of racial justice, perhaps because the rhetoric of justice is no longer under the control of genuine radicals. The modern proponents of preferences rarely plan to spend their lives in community organizing as they await the revolutionary moment, and there is no particular reason that they should. They are liberal reformers, not radical revolutionaries; with the collapse of communism as a force in the world, nobody seems to think any longer that the solution is to burn everything down and start over. On campuses nowadays, especially in the professional schools, the students of color seem about as likely as their white classmates to be capitalists to their very fingertips; they have no desire to kill the golden goose that the (white male) establishment has created. Or, to switch metaphors, today's affirmative action advocates want mainly to share in the pie, not to see it divided up in some scientific socialist redistribution.

Notes

1. Derek Bok, "Admitting Success," *New Republic,* 4 February 1985, p. 14. For the past several years, Scholastic Aptitude Test scores and scores on other standardized tests taken by black candidates have been improving both in absolute terms and relative to scores of white candidates. (National Research Council, *A Common Destiny: Blacks and American Society* [Washington, D.C.: National Academy Press, 1989], pp. 348–52.)

2. Quoted in Colin Leinster, "Black Executives: How They're Doing," *Fortune,* 18 January 1988, p. 109.

3. Anthony Borden, "Baker & McKenzie Gives a Lesson in Damage Control," *American Lawyer* (April 1989): 30.

4. For discussions of the aftermath, see, for example, Lisa Green Markoff, "Employers Learn the Hard Way About What Campuses Will Allow," *National Law Journal,* 13 March 1989, p. 4; Lisa Green Markoff, "Stanford Bars Firm," *National Law Journal,* 24 April 1989, p. 4.

5. The legal scholar Charles Black suggested long ago that the personal sacrifice entailed by preferential policies is an obligation of citizenship, just as taxes are: everyone has a role to play in reducing the debts that the society has undertaken, and the debts may be moral as well as financial. See Charles Black, "Civil Rights in Times of Economic Stress—Jurisprudential and Philosophic Aspects," *University of Illinois Law Forum* (1976): 559. According to Black, this line of argument also answers the claim that white immigrants and their children should not be made to suffer a detriment for wrongs done before their arrival in America. One who takes up the benefits of citizenship, says Black, takes up the burdens as well.

To be sure, Black's thesis is not a perfect one. The costs of preferential admissions, for example, may fall with special force on relatively disadvantaged whites, which would make the programs in some sense regressive. Moreover, in economic terms, if the resources transferred through preferential programs are less valuable (that is, less productive) in the hands of the favored than the disfavored group, there will be a net societal loss from the transfer. (I take no position here on who will put the resources to a more productive use.) Those distinctions, however, at best make affirmative action an extreme case of a form of social transfer that takes place all the time; so even if it appears that the singling out of white males (or subgroups of white males) for special disfavoring is in a sense less fair than some other societal transfers, the similarities may outweigh the differences.

6. Seymour Martin Lipset, *Political Man: The Bases of Politics,* rev. ed. (Baltimore: Johns Hopkins University Press, 1981). For my own views on this proposition, see Carter, "The Constitution, the Uniqueness Puzzle, and the Economic Conditions of Democracy," *George Washington Law Review* 56 (1987): 136.

7. Maria Markham Thompson, letter to the editor, *Bond Buyer,* 18 June 1990, p. 22.

8. Randall Kennedy, quoted in Ethan Bronner, "High Court's Split on Affirmative Action Echoes Nation's Division," *Boston Globe,* 29 June 1990, p. 1.

9. R. Richard Banks, "Affirmative Action—The Blacks' 'Burden,'" *San Francisco Chronicle,* 26 July 1990, p. A19. For further examples of this line of argument, see, for example, Richard Wasserstrom, "One Way to Understand and Defend Programs of Preferential Treatment," in *The Moral Foundations of Civil Rights,* ed. Robert K. Fullinwider and Claudia Mills (Totowa, N. J.: Rowman & Littlefield, 1986), p. 46; Ian Waldon, letter to the editor, *Newsday,* 19 August 1988, p. 82; Rosenfeld, "Decoding Richmond: Affirmative Action and the Elusive Meaning of Constitutional Equality," *Michigan Law Review* 87 (1989): 1729.

10. See, for example, Thomas Sowell, *Preferential Policies: An International Perspective* (New York: William Morrow, 1990).

11. Ibid., page 160.

12. Robert L. Allen, *Black Awakening in Capitalist America* (New York: Anchor, 1970), p. 262.

13. Anne Kelley, "Book Review," *Black Scholar* (October 1971): 50, 52.

RESPONDING IN DISCUSSION OR WRITING

1. What causes the "terrible psychological pressure" that "racial preferences often put on their beneficiaries" (paragraph 12)?

2. Do you think Carter's recommendation that the beneficiaries of racial preferences admit that they received priority and demand "So what?" is a good idea? Why or why not?

3. How do you react to Carter's story about his own admission to law school?

4. *Considerations of Style.*   What effect do Carter's short sentences have on the reader, particularly the one-sentence first paragraph and the first sentence of paragraph 13?

5. *Considerations of Style.*   Carter includes endnotes in his book and documents his sources. In what ways does he make an academic book into one that is accessible to the general public and not just to academic specialists? What kind of words and sentences does he use?

6. In the introduction to his book, Carter claims that "the affirmative action era has been a decidedly mixed blessing." He asserts that the prospect that it will end "should be a challenge and a chance; it does not portend disaster." Where in this excerpt does he amplify these views for the reader?

WRITING ASSIGNMENTS

1. In what ways is the "qualification question" at the heart of the debate about affirmative action policies? What makes it such a crucial question?

2. Discuss Carter's point that affirmative action programs are "essentially redistributive in nature" (paragraph 22). How might that cause problems?

3. Speculate on the connections between an affirmative action policy, the people who are accepted or rejected from colleges as a result of such a policy, and how acceptance or rejection would play a role in shaping their identity. To what conclusions does your exploration lead?

❖

IT'S NOT JUST ANGLO-SAXON

HENRY LOUIS GATES, JR.

Henry Louis Gates, Jr., born in 1950 in Keyser, West Virginia, is professor of humanities at Harvard University. He has also taught at Cornell and Duke. He is the author of The Signifying Monkey: Toward a

Theory of Afro-American Literary Criticism *(1988), which won both a National Book Award and an American Book Award. He is coeditor of* The Dictionary of Global Culture *(1995). The following article was published under the heading "Whose Culture Is It, Anyway?" in* The New York Times *on May 4, 1991.*

I RECENTLY ASKED THE dean of a prestigious liberal arts college if his school would ever have, as Berkeley has, a 70 percent non-white enrollment. "Never," he replied. "That would completely alter our identity as a center of the liberal arts."

The assumption that there is a deep connection between the shape of a college's curriculum and the ethnic composition of its students reflects a disquieting trend in education. Political representation has been confused with the "representation" of various ethnic identities in the curriculum.

The cultural right wing, threatened by demographic changes and the ensuing demands for curricular change, has retreated to intellectual protectionism, arguing for a great and inviolable "Western tradition," which contains the seeds, fruit and flowers of the very best thought or uttered in history. (Typically, Mortimer Adler has ventured that blacks "wrote no good books.") Meanwhile, the cultural left demands changes to accord with population shifts in gender and ethnicity. Both are wrongheaded.

I am just as concerned that so many of my colleagues feel that the rationale for a diverse curriculum depends on the latest Census Bureau report as I am that those opposed see pluralism as forestalling the possibility of a communal "American" identity. To them, the study of our diverse cultures must lead to "tribalism" and "fragmentation."

The cultural diversity movement arose partly because of the 5 fragmentation of society by ethnicity, class and gender. To make it the culprit for this fragmentation is to mistake effect for cause. A curriculum that reflects the achievement of the world's great cultures, not merely the West's, is not "politicized"; rather it situates the West as one of a community of civilizations. After all, culture is always a conversation among different voices.

To insist that we "master our own culture" before learning others—as Arthur Schlesinger Jr. has proposed—only defers the vexed question: What gets to count as "our" culture? What has passed as "common culture" has been an Anglo-American regional culture, masking itself as universal. Significantly different cultures sought refuge underground.

Writing in 1903, W.E.B. Du Bois expressed his dream of a high culture that would transcend the color line: "I sit with Shakespeare and he winces not." But the dream was not open to all. "Is this the life you grudge us," he concluded, "O knightly America?" For him, the humanities were a conduit into a republic of letters enabling escape from racism and ethnic chauvinism. Yet no one played a more crucial role than he in excavating the long buried heritage of Africans and African-Americans.

The fact of one's ethnicity, for any American of color, is never neutral: One's public treatment, and public behavior, are shaped in large part by one's perceived ethnic identity, just as by one's gender. To demand that Americans shuck their cultural heritages and homogenize themselves into a "universal" WASP culture is to dream of an America in cultural white face, and that just won't do.

So it's only when we're free to explore the complexities of our hyphenated culture that we can discover what a genuinely common American culture might actually look like.

Is multiculturalism un-American? Herman Melville didn't think   10
so. As he wrote: "We are not a narrow tribe, no. . . . We are not a nation, so much as a world." We're all ethnics; the challenge of transcending ethnic chauvinism is one we all face.

We've entrusted our schools with the fashioning and refashioning of a democratic polity. That's why schooling has always been a matter of political judgment. But in a nation that has theorized itself as plural from its inception, schools have a very special task.

Our society won't survive without the values of tolerance, and cultural tolerance comes to nothing without cultural understanding. The challenge facing America will be the shaping of a truly common public culture, one responsive to the long-silenced cultures of color. If we relinquish the ideal of America as a plural nation, we've abandoned the very experiment America represents. And that is too great a price to pay.

RESPONDING IN DISCUSSION OR WRITING

1. In what ways does the curriculum of your college or university ask students to explore diversity and pluralism in the culture?

What is the enrollment percentage of minorities and foreign students at your college or university?

2. What comment does Gates have about the connection between the two queries in question number one? What does he say about the relationship between curriculum and the ethnic composition of the students?

3. Gates mentions (in paragraph 8) a "'universal' WASP culture." What would be the features of such a culture? How would that culture look similar to or different from any other culture? You might refer to the articles by Lang Phipps and Lawrence Otis Graham in Unit 4 to find out more about their perceptions of WASP culture.

4. Gates takes issue with both the cultural right wing and the cultural left. How does he define the position of these two wings? Do you see evidence of either of these wings on your campus?

5. What is the significance of the term "hyphenated culture"? What does the term convey to readers?

6. What is the force of the question "Is multiculturalism un-American" (paragraph 10)? Is Gates asking it as a real question, one that he does not know the answer to, or is he asking it to make a point—as a rhetorical question?

WRITING ASSIGNMENTS

1. Describe your college or university in terms of its students and their ethnic heritage, its curriculum, and what you think Gates might have to say about its approach to multiculturalism.

2. Discuss the following comment made by Gates: "One's public treatment, and public behavior, are shaped in large part by one's perceived ethnic identity, just as by one's gender." Do you agree with that statement or not? Why? Include support for your opinion in specific examples from college life and experience.

❖

WESTERN VALUES ARE CENTRAL

DONALD KAGAN

*Donald Kagan, born in 1932, was dean of Yale College when he wrote
this article, which was originally part of a speech to first-year students.
After that speech, Yale received $20 million for a new course of studies in
Western civilization, which it has since returned to the donor because the
college and the donor could not agree on the terms and conditions of the
endowment. This article was published in the* New York Times *on May
4, 1991, as a counterpoint to the preceding article by Gates. Kagan is the
author of numerous texts on facets of Western civilization.*

AMERICANS DO NOT SHARE a common ancestry and a common
blood. What they have in common is a system of laws and beliefs
that shaped the establishment of the country, a system developed
within the context of Western civilization.

It should be obvious, then, that all Americans need to learn
about that civilization to understand our country's origins and
share in its heritage, purposes and character.

At present, however, the study of Western civilization is under
attack. We are told we should not give a privileged place in the
curriculum to the great works of its history and literature. At the
extremes of this onslaught, the civilization, and its study, is
attacked because of its history of slavery, imperialism, racial prejudice, addiction to war, its exclusion of women and people not of
the white race from its rights and privileges.

Some criticize its study as narrow, limiting, arrogant and discriminatory, asserting that it has little or no value for those of different cultural origins. Others concede the value of the Western
heritage but regard it as only one among many, all of which have
equal claim to our attention.

These attacks are unsound. It is necessary to place Western civi-   5
lization and the culture to which it has given rise at the center of

our studies, and we fail to do so at the peril of our students, country and the hopes for a democratic, liberal society.

The assault on Western civilization badly distorts history. Its flaws are real enough, but they are common to almost all the civilizations on any continent at any time in history.

What is remarkable about the Western heritage is the important ways in which it has departed from the common experience. More than any other, it has asserted the claims of the individual against those of the state, limiting its power and creating a realm of privacy into which it cannot penetrate.

By means of the philosophical, scientific, agricultural and industrial revolutions in the West, human beings have been able to produce and multiply the things needed for life so as to make survival and prosperity possible for ever-increasing numbers, without rapacious wars and at a level that permits dignity and independence. It is the champion of representative democracy as the normal way for human beings to govern themselves. It has produced the theory and practice of the separation of church from state, protecting each from the other and creating a free and safe place for the individual conscience.

At its core is a tolerance and respect for diversity unknown in most cultures. One of its most telling characteristics is its encouragement of criticism of itself and its ways. The university itself, a specially sheltered place for such self-examination, is a Western phenomenon only partially assimilated in other cultures.

Western culture and institutions are the most powerful paradigm in the world. As they increasingly become the objects of emulation by peoples everywhere, their study becomes essential for those of all nations who wish to understand their nature and origins.

Happily, student bodies have grown vastly more diverse. Less happily, students see themselves increasingly as parts of groups, distinct from other groups. They often feel pressure to communicate mainly with others like themselves in the group and to pursue intellectual interests that are of particular importance to it. But a liberal education needs to bring about a challenge to the ideas, habits and attitudes students bring with them.

Take pride in your family and in the culture they and your forebears have brought to our shores. Learn as much as you can about that culture. Learn as much as you can of what the particular cultures of others have to offer. But do not fail to learn the great traditions that are the special gifts of Western civilization.

RESPONDING IN DISCUSSION OR WRITING

1. Why do you think the ideas in this article prompted a gift to Yale University of funds for courses in Western civilization? What assumptions would you make about the background and views of the person who provided the funds?

2. Examine your own education in high school and beyond. How much of it has been devoted to Western civilization (history, art, literature, and social studies) and how much to other cultures? Think in terms of percentages.

3. This article appeared on the same page as the article by Gates under a common heading that linked them: "Whose Culture Is It, Anyway?" When Kagan says that some people criticize the study of Western civilization as "narrow, limiting, arrogant and discriminatory," do you think those concepts apply to Gates's criticisms? Why or why not?

4. *Considerations of Style.*   In what ways does Kagan take note of opposing ideas and try to refute them?

5. How does Kagan include the concept of diversity within the concept of the Western heritage? Do you find his point convincing?

6. Kagan ends with a list of commands and exhortations. Consider that list. Does it provide an effective ending to the article? Do you find his arguments convincing? Why or why not?

WRITING ASSIGNMENTS

1. Kagan states that "a liberal education needs to bring about a challenge to the ideas, habits and attitudes students bring with them." Do you agree with him? What kind of curriculum would such a principle lead to in your college or university? What kinds of challenges do you think Kagan has in mind? How does he want ideas, habits, and attitudes to change?

2. Argue for or against Kagan's point that "it is necessary to place Western civilization and the culture to which it has given rise at the center of our studies" in college since to him, a major contri-

bution of the Western heritage is that "it has asserted the claims of the individual against those of the state."

❖

THEME FOR ENGLISH B

LANGSTON HUGHES

Langston Hughes, born in Joplin, Missouri, in 1902, was a driving force in the Harlem Renaissance. His poetry reflects African American urban life and deals with social issues and injustice. In addition to poetry, he also wrote novels, plays, and children's books. He died in 1967. "Theme for English B" appears in Selected Poems of Langston Hughes *(1959). It was first published in 1950.*

The instructor said,

> Go home and write
> a page tonight.
> And let that page come out of you—
> Then, it will be true.   5

I wonder if it's that simple?
I am twenty-two, colored, born in Winston-Salem.
I went to school there, then Durham, then here
to this college on the hill above Harlem.
I am the only colored student in my class.   10
The steps from the hill lead down into Harlem,
through a park, then I cross St. Nicholas,
Eighth Avenue, Seventh, and I come to the Y,
the Harlem Branch Y, where I take the elevator
up to my room, sit down, and write this page: 15

It's not easy to know what is true for you or me
at twenty-two, my age. But I guess I'm what

I feel and see and hear, Harlem, I hear you:
hear you, hear me—we two—you, me, talk on this page.
(I hear New York, too.) Me—who? 20
Well, I like to eat, sleep, drink, and be in love.
I like to work, read, learn, and understand life.
I like a pipe for a Christmas present,
or records—Bessie, bop, or Bach.
I guess being colored doesn't make me *not* like 25
the same things other folks like who are other races.
So will my page be colored that I write?
Being me, it will not be white.
But it will be
a part of you, instructor. 30
You are white—
yet a part of me, as I am a part of you.
That's American.
Sometimes perhaps you don't want to be a part of me.
Nor do I often want to be a part of you. 35
But we are, that's true!
As I learn from you,
I guess you learn from me—
although you're older—and white—
and somewhat more free. 40

This is my page for English B.

RESPONDING IN DISCUSSION OR WRITING

1. What experiences, good and bad, have you had in English classes when you had to write? Have you been told to "let that page come out of you"? What kind of writing do you think Hughes's instructor wants?

2. When Hughes says "I am the only colored student in my class," what connections does he make between that fact and the paper he has to write? Has your race ever affected the way you perceive and handle a writing assignment?

3. How is going to college at age twenty-two different from going right after high school?

4. What effect does the last line of the poem have on the reader?

5. *Considerations of Style.* Some lines in the poem rhyme. What effect does the rhyme have? Does the rhyme seem contrived, or is it part of natural-sounding speech?

6. What is Hughes's attitude to the assignment and to his white instructor? How does he convey his feelings?

WRITING ASSIGNMENTS

1. In what ways can "Theme for English B" be regarded as a poem about identity?

2. What effects do you think occur in students' learning and performance when they are taught by people who are of the same race and/or ethnic affiliation as the students themselves? What are the advantages and disadvantages in having teachers with the same background as the students?

Making Connections: Education

❖

1. What connections can you make between the selections in
   this unit and the views about identity expressed in the selections in Unit 4, "Ethnic Affiliation and Class"? What are the
   connections between education and class and ethnicity?

2. Both Keith Gilyard's experience ("Keith and Raymond," in
   Unit 1) and Jackson's short story describe a boy assigning
   himself different names. Discuss in which ways the selections
   are similar and in which ways they are different. Which story
   relates more directly to your own experience and why?

3. Richard Rodriguez is not in favor of bilingual education in
   elementary schools. Do library research to discover what the
   views of those in favor of and opposed to bilingual education
   are. On what evidence do they base their views? Which side
   presents the most convincing case?

4. Read Rodriguez's *Hunger of Memory,* from which this excerpt
   is taken, and summarize what position he takes on the issue of
   affirmative action in college admissions and job applications.
   How does his position on affirmative action compare to
   Stephen L. Carter's? Do you agree with Rodriguez or not?
   Why?

5. Polly Pui-Yee Lai writes about the attractions of a specialized
   public school that accepts students who pass a test. Do you
   think that public education should provide special schools for
   special students, or should all students go to their local neighborhood school? Discuss the issues involved in such a
   decision.

6. Do research to find articles written for and against the use of
   affirmative action principles in college admissions. One
   famous lawsuit involving affirmative action is the Bakke case,
   which you might want to explore. Summarize the arguments
   you find in your reading for and against an affirmative action
   policy, and draw your own conclusions.

7. If you had to design a course that taught students in your college or university about the main features of the culture with which you identify, what would you include in that course? Explain why you make those choices and how what you have chosen will be of interest to other students and teach them about a culture other than their own.

8. Write an account of the issues in the controversy around multicultural education as introduced in the selections by Gates and Kagan. Express your own point of view on the issues, and support it with examples from your reading and experience. You might choose to write this in the form of a letter to *The New York Times* responding to the articles by Gates and Kagan.

9. Gates refers to the work of W.E.B. Du Bois. Do research to find out about his life, work, and views on culture.

10. Do research to discover why some people choose to educate their children at home. Include in your essay specific examples.

11. The selections by Gilyard, Kim, Jackson, Rodriguez, Rose, and Hughes depict students and teachers in classrooms. How are the pictures similar, and how are they different? Together, what picture do they present of our educational system?

Beliefs and Religion

Religion is love; in no case is it logic.

—BEATRICE POTTER WEBB, My Apprenticeship, *Introduction, 1926*

Every religion is good that teaches man to be good; and I know of none that instructs him to be bad.

—THOMAS PAINE, The Rights of Man, *part 2, chapter 5, 1792*

Beliefs and Religion

❖

AN IMPORTANT PART OF the identity of an individual, society, or culture is the system of beliefs that determines behavior. Moral and ethical codes, organized religion, and value systems contribute to the positions we take on a wide range of serious issues. Think, for example, of issues such as drugs, gun control, divorce, abortion, gays in the military, condom distribution in schools, censorship, libel, surrogate motherhood, and corporal and capital punishment. When we discuss issues like these, we confront our beliefs about human life, liberty, right, and wrong. Sometimes we form these beliefs from our experience and interactions; sometimes we derive them from what we read or accept from the teachings of a group.

Beliefs and religion can seem almost like an inherent part of us, passed on by family, community, and educational institutions and characterizing both individuals and cultures. When beliefs and religion are adopted later in life, they provide the means by which we rebel against cultural tradition and initiate a process of change, putting distance between a prior and current identity.

In everyday life, even when controversial issues are not subjects for discussion, beliefs lead to differing views of food, activities, dress, appearance, education, and transportation. Orthodox Jews do not eat pork, Hindus do not eat beef, the Amish do not travel in cars or use zippers, Muslim women cover their heads and faces, teenagers follow fashion, schools and colleges revise their curricular offerings to fit current theories—and those theories are often based on beliefs rather than on proven facts. Beliefs can bind people together in cohesive groups; they also divide people and form the basis of conflict and war.

People seem to need something to believe in. A cover story in *Time* magazine in December 1993 described people's beliefs in

403

angels. In a poll, 69 percent of the respondents said they believed that angels existed. "We are born believing. A man bears beliefs as a tree bears apples," says Ralph Waldo Emerson. What beliefs we hold and why we hold them, however, are matters for dispute, as psychiatrist Carl Jung acknowledges when he says, "The word *belief* is a difficult thing for me. I don't *believe*. I must have a reason for a certain hypothesis. Either I *know* a thing, and then I know it—I don't need to believe it." The scientific method sets out to form knowledge based on observable, replicable facts, not on beliefs. Still, most people and most scholars hold beliefs that they try to support and justify, and justifying beliefs, values, and opinions is a scholarly task, often addressed in writing.

The selections in this unit mirror the variety of beliefs and approaches to religion that concern people today. Anna Quindlen takes a personal approach and discusses what it means to her to be a Catholic. Two essays take up important topics associated with religion: the beginning of life—evolution or creationism—is the topic of Stephen Jay Gould's strongly argued article, while Alice Trillin confronts cancer and the fear of death. A connection with Unit 6's focus on education is made by Ellen Goodman's article on religion in school textbooks. From Ari Goldman, we learn about his experience with a religion unfamiliar to him, Buddhism; in contrast, Robert Bellah and his coeditors depict religion in America through local congregations in a Presbyterian church and an evangelical church near San Jose, California. The fact that religious beliefs are not fixed but change as we change is the topic of the selection by Harold Bryant, an African American veteran of the Vietnam War, who shows and tells us what the devastation of a land in war did to his religious beliefs. The connections between the land, people, and religion are the topic of Leslie Marmon Silko's short story. Gary Snyder ends the unit with a poem in the form of a prayer.

STARTING POINTS [FOR JOURNAL OR FREEWRITING]

Before you read, write your own responses to the questions that follow.

1. Do you see any problems with reconciling American individualism with the tenets of an organized religion?

2. What do you believe happens to people when they die? On what do you base this belief?

3. What role has organized religion played in your life?

4. Do you think that religious principles are worth fighting and dying for? Why or why not?

❖

I AM A CATHOLIC

ANNA QUINDLEN

Anna Quindlen, born in 1952, has written regular columns for The New York Times. *She is the author of two collections of her newspaper columns,* Living Out Loud *(1988) and* Thinking Out Loud *(1993), and received a Pulitzer Prize for Commentary in 1992. She is also the author of two novels,* Object Lessons *(1991) and* One True Thing *(1994). Quindlen frequently combines public and private issues in her newspaper columns, writing about herself and her family and friends alongside issues of national and local policy. She acknowledges that "it is impossible to write an honest column about your own life without somehow involving your family and your friends." The following selection appeared as an op-ed piece (opposite the editorial page) in* The New York Times *on June 18, 1986.*

DOMINUS VOBISCUM. ET CUM *spiritu tuo.* These are my bona fides: a word, a phrase, a sentence in a language no one speaks anymore. *Kyrie eleison. Confiteor dei.* I am a Catholic. Once at a nursing home for retired clergy, I ate lunch with a ninety-year-old priest, a man who still muttered the Latin throughout the English Mass and ate fish on Fridays. When he learned how old I was, he said with some satisfaction, "You were a Catholic when being a Catholic still meant something."

What does it mean now? For myself, I cannot truly say. Since the issue became material to me, I have not followed the church's teaching on birth control. I disagree with its stand on abortion. I believe its resistance to the ordination of women as priests is a manifestation of a misogyny that has been with us much longer than the church has. Yet it would never have occurred to my husband and me not to be married in a Catholic church, not to have our children baptized. On hospital forms and in political polls, while others leave the space blank or say "none of your business," I have no hesitation about giving my religion.

We are cultural Catholics. I once sneered at that expression, used by Jewish friends at college, only because I was not introspective enough to understand how well it applied to me. Catholicism is to us now not so much a system of beliefs or a set of laws but a shared history. It is not so much our faith as our past. The tenets of the church which I learned as a child have ever since been at war with the facts of my adult life. The Virgin Birth. The Trinity. The Resurrection. Why did God make me? God made me to know Him, to love Him, and to serve Him in this world and to be happy with Him forever in the next. I could recite parts of the Baltimore Catechism in my sleep. Do I believe those words? I don't know. What I do believe are those guidelines that do not vary from faith to faith, that are as true of Judaism or Methodism as they are of Catholicism: that people should be kind to one another, that they should help those in need, that they should respect others as they wish to be respected.

And I believe in my own past. I was educated by nuns, given absolution by priests. My parents were married in a Catholic church, my grandparents and mother buried from one. Saturday afternoons kneeling on Leatherette pads in the dim light of the confessional, listening for the sound of the priest sliding back the grille on his side. Sunday mornings kneeling with my face in my hands, the Communion wafer stuck to the roof of my dry mouth. These are my history. I could no more say I am not Catholic than say I am not Irish, not Italian. Yet I have never been to Ireland or Italy.

Some of our Jewish friends have returned to the ways of their past, to Shabbat without automobiles and elevators, to dietary laws and the study of Hebrew. We cannot do the same. There is no longer a Latin Mass, no Communion fast from midnight on. Even the inn is gone from the Bible; now Mary and Joseph are turned away from "the place where travelers lodged."

The first time my husband and I went to midnight mass on Christmas Eve in our parish church, we arrived a half-hour early so we would get a seat. When the bells sounded twelve and the priest came down the center aisle, his small acolytes in their child-size cassocks walking before him, the pews were still half empty. We were thinking of a different time, when the churches were packed, when missing Mass was a sin, when we still believed that that sort of sin existed—sins against rules, victimless sins.

There are more families coming to that church now, families like us with very small children who often have to leave before the Gospel because of tears, fatigue, temper tantrums. (I remember that, when I was growing up, my family's parish church was shaped like a cross, and one of the short arms was for the women with babies. It had a sheet of glass walling it off and was sound-proof. And through the glass you could see the babies, as though in a movie with no audio, their little mouths round, their faces red. Inside that room, the noise was dreadful. But missing Mass was a sin.)

I think perhaps those families are people like us, people who believe in something, although they are not sure what, people who feel that in a world of precious little history or tradition, this is theirs. We will pass down the story to our children: There was a woman named Mary who was visited by an angel. And the angel said, "Do not be afraid" and told her that though she was a virgin she would have a child. And He was named Jesus and was the Son of God and He rose from the dead. Everything else our children learn in America in the late twentieth century will make this sound like a fairy tale, like tales of the potato famines in Ireland and the little ramshackle houses with grape arbors on hillsides in Italy. But these are my fairy tales, and so, whether or not they are fact, they are true.

I was born a Catholic and I think I will die one. I will ask for a priest to give me Extreme Unction, as it was given to my mother, and to her mother before her. At the end, as in the beginning, I will ask for the assistance of the church, which is some fundamental part of my identity. I am a Catholic.

RESPONDING IN DISCUSSION OR WRITING

1. What words or phrases are meaningful to you as symbols of some of the important things you believe in?

2. If you are asked to indicate your religion on a form, what do you write? Why?

3. Explain how you understand Quindlen's view of Catholicism as "a shared history" (paragraph 3).

4. When you were growing up, did you regard any kinds of actions as "sins against rules," as Quindlen says? If so, what were they and why were they sins? How is a sinner expected to atone for the sins?

5. Quindlen's article about her beliefs states her position clearly in the title: "I Am a Catholic." If you were to write a similar article about your beliefs, what would the title of your article be and what points would you make about your beliefs?

WRITING ASSIGNMENTS

1. Write a short essay that outlines your own belief system and explains to readers why you hold your beliefs and what attracts you to that system of beliefs.

2. Write an essay in response to Quindlen's statement that belief is a set of guidelines: "that people should be kind to one another, that they should help those in need, that they should respect others as they wish to be respected." Do you think that these guidelines form the basis of most religions and value systems?

EVOLUTION AS FACT AND THEORY

STEPHEN JAY GOULD

Stephen Jay Gould, born in 1941, is a paleontologist, geologist, zoologist, and biologist, who writes on scientific issues for the general public, often in Natural History *magazine, frequently arguing against biological determinism. His many books include* Ever Since Darwin *(1977);* Panda's Thumbs *(1980);* Hen's Teeth and Horse's Toes *(1983), in which this essay was published after its initial publication in* Discover; Wonderful Life *(1989); and* Bully for the Brontosaurus *(1991). He is Professor of Geology and History of Science at Harvard University. In this essay, he argues for evolution, the scientific theory formulated by the great naturalist and scientist Charles Darwin that states that living things have developed from previously existing forms of life through gradual change and adaptation; simultaneously, he argues against creationism, the belief that God created all living things in their present form.*

KIRTLEY MATHER, WHO DIED last year at age ninety, was a pillar of both science and Christian religion in America and one of my dearest friends. The difference of a half-century in our ages evaporated before our common interests. The most curious thing we shared was a battle we each fought at the same age. For Kirtley had gone to Tennessee with Clarence Darrow to testify for evolution at the Scopes trial of 1925. When I think that we are enmeshed again in the same struggle for one of the best documented, most compelling and exciting concepts in all of science, I don't know whether to laugh or cry.

According to idealized principles of scientific discourse, the arousal of dormant issues should reflect fresh data that give renewed life to abandoned notions. Those outside the current debate may therefore be excused for suspecting that creationists have come up with something new, or that evolutionists have generated some serious internal trouble. But nothing has changed; the creationists have presented not a single new fact or argument. Darrow and Bryan were at least more entertaining than we lesser antagonists today. The rise of creationism is politics, pure and simple; it represents one issue (and by no means the major concern) of the resurgent evangelical right. Arguments that seemed kooky just a decade ago have reentered the mainstream.

The basic attack of modern creationists falls apart on two general counts before we even reach the supposed factual details of their assault against evolution. First, they play upon a vernacular misunderstanding of the word "theory" to convey the false impression that we evolutionists are covering up the rotten core of our edifice. Second, they misuse a popular philosophy of science to argue that they are behaving scientifically in attacking evolution. Yet the same philosophy demonstrates that their own belief is not science, and that "scientific creationism" is a meaningless and self-contradictory phrase, an example of what Orwell called "newspeak."

In the American vernacular, "theory" often means "imperfect fact"—part of a hierarchy of confidence running downhill from fact to theory to hypothesis to guess. Thus, creationists can (and do) argue: evolution is "only" a theory, and intense debate now rages about many aspects of the theory. If evolution is less than a fact, and scientists can't even make up their minds about the theory, then what confidence can we have in it? Indeed, President Reagan echoed this argument before an evangelical group in Dallas when he said (in what I devoutly hope was campaign rhetoric): "Well, it is a theory. It is a scientific theory only, and it has in recent years been challenged in the world of science—that is, not believed in the scientific community to be as infallible as it once was."

Well, evolution *is* a theory. It is also a fact. And facts and theo-   5
ries are different things, not rungs in a hierarchy of increasing certainty. Facts are the world's data. Theories are structures of ideas that explain and interpret facts. Facts do not go away while scientists debate rival theories for explaining them. Einstein's theory of gravitation replaced Newton's, but apples did not suspend themselves in mid-air pending the outcome. And human beings evolved from apelike ancestors whether they did so by Darwin's proposed mechanism or by some other, yet to be discovered.

Moreover, "fact" does not mean "absolute certainty." The final proofs of logic and mathematics flow deductively from stated premises and achieve certainty only because they are *not* about the empirical world. Evolutionists make no claim for perpetual truth, though creationists often do (and then attack us for a style of argument that they themselves favor). In science, "fact" can only mean "confirmed to such a degree that it would be perverse to withhold provisional assent." I suppose that apples might start to rise tomorrow, but the possibility does not merit equal time in physics classrooms.

Evolutionists have been clear about this distinction between fact and theory from the very beginning, if only because we have always acknowledged how far we are from completely understand-ing the mechanisms (theory) by which evolution (fact) occurred. Darwin continually emphasized the difference between his two great and separate accomplishments: establishing the fact of evolution, and proposing a theory—natural selection—to explain the mechanism of evolution. He wrote in *The Descent of Man:* "I had two distinct objects in view; firstly, to show that species had not been separately created, and secondly, that natural selection had been the chief agent of change . . . Hence if I have erred in . . . having exaggerated its [natural selection's] power . . . I have at least, as I hope, done good service in aiding to overthrow the dogma of separate creations."

Thus Darwin acknowledged the provisional nature of natural selection while affirming the fact of evolution. The fruitful theoretical debate that Darwin initiated has never ceased. From the 1940s through the 1960s, Darwin's own theory of natural selection did achieve a temporary hegemony that it never enjoyed in his lifetime. But renewed debate characterizes our decade, and, while no biologist questions the importance of natural selection, many now doubt its ubiquity. In particular, many evolutionists argue that substantial amounts of genetic change may not be subject to natural selection and may spread through populations at random. Others are challenging Darwin's linking of natural selection with gradual, imperceptible change through all intermediary degrees; they are arguing that most evolutionary events may occur far more rapidly than Darwin envisioned.

Scientists regard debates on fundamental issues of theory as a sign of intellectual health and a source of excitement. Science is—and how else can I say it?—most fun when it plays with interesting ideas, examines their implications, and recognizes that old information may be explained in surprisingly new ways. Evolutionary theory is now enjoying this uncommon vigor. Yet amidst all this turmoil no biologist has been led to doubt the fact that evolution occurred; we are debating *how* it happened. We are all trying to explain the same thing: the tree of evolutionary descent linking all organisms by ties of genealogy. Creationists pervert and caricature this debate by conveniently neglecting the common conviction that underlies it, and by falsely suggesting that we now doubt the very phenomenon we are struggling to understand.

Secondly, creationists claim that "the dogma of separate creations," as Darwin characterized it a century ago, is a scientific theory meriting equal time with evolution in high school biology curricula. But a popular viewpoint among philosophers of science belies this creationist argument. Philosopher Karl Popper has argued for decades that the primary criterion of science is the falsifiability of its theories. We can never prove absolutely, but we can falsify. A set of ideas that cannot, in principle, be falsified is not science.

The entire creationist program includes little more than a rhetorical attempt to falsify evolution by presenting supposed contradictions among its supporters. Their brand of creationism, they claim, is "scientific" because it follows the Popperian model in trying to demolish evolution. Yet Popper's argument must apply in both directions. One does not become a scientist by the simple act of trying to falsify a rival and truly scientific system; one has to present an alternative system that also meets Popper's criterion—it too must be falsifiable in principle.

"Scientific creationism" is a self-contradictory, nonsense phrase precisely because it cannot be falsified. I can envision observations and experiments that would disprove any evolutionary theory I know, but I cannot imagine what potential data could lead creationists to abandon their beliefs. Unbeatable systems are dogma, not science. Lest I seem harsh or rhetorical, I quote creationism's leading intellectual, Duane Gish, Ph.D., from his recent (1978) book, *Evolution? The Fossils Say No!* "By creation we mean the bringing into being by a supernatural Creator of the basic kinds of plants and animals by the process of sudden, or fiat, creation. We do not know how the Creator created, what processes He used, *for He used processes which are not now operating anywhere in the natural universe* [Gish's italics]. This is why we refer to creation as special creation. We cannot discover by scientific investigations anything about the creative processes used by the Creator." Pray tell, Dr. Gish, in the light of your last sentence, what then is "scientific" creationism?

Our confidence that evolution occurred centers upon three general arguments. First, we have abundant, direct, observational evidence of evolution in action, from both field and laboratory. This evidence ranges from countless experiments on change in nearly everything about fruit flies subjected to artificial selection in the laboratory to the famous populations of British moths that became black when industrial soot darkened the trees upon which the moths rest. (Moths gain protection from sharp-sighted bird predators by blending into the background.) Creationists do not deny these observations; how could they? Creationists have tightened their act. They now argue that God only created "basic kinds," and allowed for limited evolutionary meandering within them. Thus toy poodles and Great Danes come from the dog kind and moths can change color, but nature cannot convert a dog to a cat or a monkey to a man.

The second and third arguments for evolution—the case for major changes—do not involve direct observation of evolution in action. They rest upon inference, but are no less secure for that reason. Major evolutionary change requires too much time for direct observation on the scale of recorded human history. All historical sciences rest upon inference, and evolution is no different from geology, cosmology, or human history in this respect. In principle, we cannot observe processes that operated in the past. We must infer them from results that still surround us: living and fossil organisms for evolution, documents and artifacts for human history, strata and topography for geology.

The second argument—that the imperfection of nature reveals evolution—strikes many people as ironic, for they feel that evolution should be most elegantly displayed in the nearly perfect adaptation expressed by some organisms—the camber of a gull's wing, or butterflies that cannot be seen in ground litter because they mimic leaves so precisely. But perfection could be imposed by a wise creator or evolved by natural selection. Perfection covers the tracks of past history. And past history—the evidence of descent—is the mark of evolution.

Evolution lies exposed in the *imperfections* that record a history of descent. Why should a rat run, a bat fly, a porpoise swim, and I type this essay with structures built of the same bones unless we all inherited them from a common ancestor? An engineer, starting from scratch, could design better limbs in each case. Why should all the large native mammals of Australia be marsupials, unless they descended from a common ancestor isolated on this island continent? Marsupials are not "better," or ideally suited for Australia; many have been wiped out by placental mammals imported by man from other continents. This principle of imperfection extends to all historical sciences. When we recognize the etymology of September, October, November, and December (seventh, eighth, ninth, and tenth), we know that the year once started in March, or that two additional months must have been added to an original calendar of ten months.

The third argument is more direct: transitions are often found in the fossil record. Preserved transitions are not common—and should not be, according to our understanding of evolution—but they are not entirely wanting, as creationists often claim. The lower jaw of reptiles contains several bones, that of mammals only one. The non-mammalian jawbones are reduced, step by step, in mammalian ancestors until they become tiny nubbins located at the back of the jaw. The "hammer" and "anvil" bones of the mammalian ear are descendants of these nubbins. How could such a transition be accomplished? the creationists ask. Surely a bone is either entirely in the jaw or in the ear. Yet paleontologists have discovered two transitional lineages of therapsids (the so-called mammal-like reptiles) with a double jaw joint—one composed of the old quadrate and articular bones (soon to become the hammer and anvil), the other of the squamosal and dentary bones (as in modern mammals). For that matter, what better transitional form could we expect to find than the oldest human, *Australopithecus afarensis,* with its apelike palate, its human upright stance, and a cranial capacity larger than any ape's of the same body size but a full 1,000 cubic centimeters below ours? If God made each of the half-dozen human species discovered in ancient rocks, why did he create in an unbroken temporal sequence of progressively more modern features—increasing cranial capacity, reduced face and teeth, larger body size? Did he create to mimic evolution and test our faith thereby?

Faced with these facts of evolution and the philosophical bankruptcy of their own position, creationists rely upon distortion and innuendo to buttress their rhetorical claim. If I sound sharp or bitter, indeed I am—for I have become a major target of these practices.

I count myself among the evolutionists who argue for a jerky, or episodic, rather than a smoothly gradual, pace of change. In 1972 my colleague Niles Eldredge and I developed the theory of punctuated equilibrium. We argued that two outstanding facts of the fossil record—geologically "sudden" origin of new species and failure to change thereafter (stasis)—reflect the predictions of evolutionary theory, not the imperfections of the fossil record. In most theories, small isolated populations are the source of new species, and the process of speciation takes thousands or tens of thousands of years. This amount of time, so long when measured against our lives, is a geological microsecond. It represents much less than 1 per cent of the average lifespan for a fossil invertebrate species—more than ten million years. Large, widespread, and well established species, on the other hand, are not expected to change very much. We believe that the inertia of large populations explains the stasis of most fossil species over millions of years.

We proposed the theory of punctuated equilibrium largely to [20] provide a different explanation for pervasive trends in the fossil record. Trends, we argued, cannot be attributed to gradual transformation within lineages, but must arise from the differential success of certain kinds of species. A trend, we argued, is more like climbing a flight of stairs (punctuations and stasis) than rolling up an inclined plane.

Since we proposed punctuated equilibria to explain trends, it is infuriating to be quoted again and again by creationists—whether through design or stupidity, I do not know—as admitting that the fossil record includes no transitional forms. Transitional forms are generally lacking at the species level, but they are abundant between larger groups. Yet a pamphlet entitled "Harvard Scientists Agree Evolution Is a Hoax" states: "The facts of punctuated equilibrium which Gould and Eldredge . . . are forcing Darwinists to swallow fit the picture that Bryan insisted on, and which God has revealed to us in the Bible."

Continuing the distortion, several creationists have equated the theory of punctuated equilibrium with a caricature of the beliefs of Richard Goldschmidt, a great early geneticist. Goldschmidt argued, in a famous book published in 1940, that new groups can arise all at once through major mutations. He referred to these suddenly transformed creatures as "hopeful monsters." (I am attracted to some aspects of the non-caricatured version, but Goldschmidt's theory still has nothing to do with punctuated equilibrium—see my explicit essay on Goldschmidt in *The Panda's Thumb*.) Creationist Luther Sunderland talks of the "punctuated equilibrium hopeful monster theory" and tells his hopeful readers that "it amounts to tacit admission that anti-evolutionists are correct in asserting there is no fossil evidence supporting the theory that all life is connected to a common ancestor." Duane Gish writes, "According to Goldschmidt, and now apparently according to Gould, a reptile laid an egg from which the first bird, feathers and all, was produced." Any evolutionist who believed such nonsense would rightly be laughed off the intellectual stage; yet the only theory that could ever envision such a scenario for the origin of birds is creationism—with God acting in the egg.

I am both angry at and amused by the creationists; but mostly I am deeply sad. Sad for many reasons. Sad because so many people who respond to creationist appeals are troubled for the right reason, but venting their anger at the wrong target. It is true that scientists have often been dogmatic and elitist. It is true that we have often allowed the white-coated, advertising image to represent us—"Scientists say that Brand X cures bunions ten times faster than . . ." We have not fought it adequately because we derive benefits from appearing as a new priesthood. It is also true that faceless and bureaucratic state power intrudes more and more into our lives and removes choices that should belong to individuals and communities. I can understand that school curricula, imposed from above and without local input, might be seen as one more insult on all these grounds. But the culprit is not, and cannot be, evolution or any other fact of the natural world. Identify and fight your legitimate enemies by all means, but we are not among them.

I am sad because the practical result of this brouhaha will not be expanded coverage to include creationism (that would also make me sad), but the reduction or excision of evolution from high school curricula. Evolution is one of the half dozen "great ideas" developed by science. It speaks to the profound issues of genealogy that fascinate all of us—the "roots" phenomenon writ large. Where did we come from? Where did life arise? How did it develop? How are organisms related? It forces us to think, ponder, and wonder. Shall we deprive millions of this knowledge and once again teach biology as a set of dull and unconnected facts, without the thread that weaves diverse material into a supple unity?

But most of all I am saddened by a trend I am just beginning to   25
discern among my colleagues. I sense that some now wish to mute the healthy debate about theory that has brought new life to evolutionary biology. It provides grist for creationist mills, they say, even if only by distortion. Perhaps we should lie low and rally round the flag of strict Darwinism, at least for the moment—a kind of old-time religion on our part.

But we should borrow another metaphor and recognize that we too have to tread a straight and narrow path, surrounded by roads to perdition. For if we ever begin to suppress our search to understand nature, to quench our own intellectual excitement in a misguided effort to present a united front where it does not and should not exist, then we are truly lost.

RESPONDING IN DISCUSSION OR WRITING

1. *Considerations of Style.* How would you describe the tone of paragraph 2 of Gould's essay? How do you evaluate his use of the term *kooky*?

2. *Considerations of Style.* Gould devotes the first part of his essay to examining and criticizing the fundamentalists' beliefs in "scientific creationism." He then moves on to proposing three arguments for evolution. The last part of his essay is devoted to pointing out the distortions that creationists rely on to support their claims. Make an outline of the essay that shows its structure.

3. *Considerations of Style.* In paragraphs 23–25, Gould repeats the word *sad*. What is the effect of the repetition?

4. How would you describe Gould's audience and his methods of argument? Whom is he trying to convince? Do you think he is convincing? Is he likely to win over a creationist? Why or why not?

5. Select three sentences that you find particularly striking. What made you select them?

6. Note how Gould uses the definition of his basic terms as a crucial part of the argument in his essay. He defines *theory* and *fact*. How does he use the definitions to further his argument?

WRITING ASSIGNMENTS

1. Write an essay explaining why Gould will not accept the term *scientific creationism*. Write it for a reader who has not read Gould's essay, a reader who needs a clear and accessible explanation of why Gould takes exception to the phrase itself.

2. *For Further Research.* Take an issue in which you believe strongly and for which you think you have empirical evidence and argue for it in a convincing way, with reasons and with refutations of opposing arguments. Do additional research as necessary.

❖

OF DRAGONS AND GARDEN PEAS:
A CANCER PATIENT TALKS TO DOCTORS

ALICE TRILLIN

Alice Trillin, born in 1939, teacher, educational consultant, and film-maker, had a lung removed in 1977 when she was thirty-eight years old. She gave this talk to medical students, and it was published in 1981 in one of the country's leading medical journals, The New England Journal of Medicine. *She lives in New York City and continues to spend time in Nova Scotia.*

WHEN I FIRST REALIZED that I might have cancer, I felt immediately that I had entered a special place, a place I came to call "The Land of the Sick People." The most disconcerting thing, however, was not that I found that place terrifying and unfamiliar, but that I found it so ordinary, so banal. I didn't feel different, didn't feel that my life had radically changed at the moment the word *cancer* became attached to it. The same rules still held. What had changed, however, was other people's perceptions of me. Unconsciously, even with a certain amount of kindness, everyone—with the single rather extraordinary exception of my husband—regarded me as someone who had been altered irrevo-cably. I don't want to exaggerate my feeling of alienation or to give the impression that it was in any way dramatic. I have no hor-ror stories of the kind I read a few years ago in the *New York Times*; people didn't move their desks away from me at the office or refuse to let their children play with my children at school because they thought that cancer was catching. My friends are all too sophisticated and too sensitive for that kind of behavior. Their distance from me was marked most of all by their inability to understand the ordinariness, the banality of what was happening to me. They marveled at how well I was "coping with cancer." I had become special, no longer like them. Their genuine concern for what had happened to me, and their complete separateness from it, expressed exactly what I had felt all my life about anyone I had ever known who had experienced tragedy.

When asked to speak to a group of doctors and medical students about what it was like to be a cancer patient, I worried for a long time about what I should say. It was a perfect opportunity— every patient's fantasy—to complain about doctors' insensitivity, nurses who couldn't draw blood properly, and perhaps even the awful food in hospitals. Or, instead, I could present myself as the good patient, full of uplifting thoughts about how much I had learned from having cancer. But, unlike many people, I had had very good experiences with doctors and hospitals. And the role of the brave patient troubled me, because I was afraid that all the brave things I said might no longer hold if I got sick again. I had to think about this a great deal during the first two years after my operation as I watched my best friend live out my own worst nightmares. She discovered that she had cancer several months after I did. Several months after that, she discovered that it had metastasized; she underwent eight operations during the next year and a half before she died. All my brave talk was tested by her illness as it has not yet been tested by mine.

And so I decided not to talk about the things that separate those of us who have cancer from those who do not. I decided that the only relevant thing for me to talk about was the one thing that we all have most in common. We are all afraid of dying.

Our fear of death makes it essential to maintain a distance between ourselves and anyone who is threatened by death. Denying our connection to the precariousness of others' lives is a way of pretending that we are immortal. We need this deception—it is one of the ways we stay sane—but we also need to be prepared for the times when it doesn't work. For doctors, who confront death when they go to work in the morning as routinely as other people deal with balance sheets and computer printouts, and for me, to whom a chest x-ray or a blood test will never again be a simple, routine procedure, it is particularly important to face the fact of death squarely, to talk about it with one another.

Cancer connects us to one another because having cancer is an embodiment of the existential paradox that we all experience: we feel that we are immortal, yet we know that we will die. To Tolstoy's Ivan Ilyich, the syllogism he had learned as a child, "'Caius is a man, men are mortal, therefore Caius is mortal,' had always seemed . . . correct as applied to Caius but certainly not as applied to himself." Like Ivan Ilyich, we all construct an elaborate set of defense mechanisms to separate ourselves from Caius. To anyone who has had cancer, these defense mechanisms become talismans that we invest with a kind of magic. These talismans are essential to our sanity, and yet they need to be examined.

First of all, we believe in the magic of doctors and medicine. The purpose of a talisman is to give us control over the things we are afraid of. Doctors and patients are accomplices in staging a kind of drama in which we pretend that doctors have the power to keep us well. The very best doctors—and I have had the very best—share their power with their patients and try to give us the information that we need to control our own treatment. Whenever I am threatened by panic, my doctor sits me down and tells me something concrete. He draws a picture of my lung, or my lymph nodes; he explains as well as he can how cancer cells work and what might be happening in my body. Together, we approach my disease intelligently and rationally, as a problem to be solved, an exercise in logic to be worked out. Of course, through knowledge, through medicine, through intelligence, we do have some control. But at best this control is limited, and there is always the danger that the disease I have won't behave rationally and respond to the intelligent argument we have constructed. Cancer cells, more than anything else in nature, are likely to behave irrationally. If we think that doctors and medicine can always protect us, we are in danger of losing faith in doctors and medicine when their magic doesn't work. The physician who fails to keep us well is like an unsuccessful witch doctor; we have to drive him out of the tribe and look for a more powerful kind of magic.

The reverse of this, of course, is that the patient becomes a kind of talisman for the doctor. Doctors defy death by keeping people alive. To a patient, it becomes immediately clear that the best way to please a doctor is to be healthy. If you can't manage that, the next best thing is to be well-behaved. (Sometimes the difference between being healthy and being well-behaved becomes blurred in a hospital, so that it almost seems as if being sick were being badly behaved.) If we get well, we help our doctors succeed; if we are sick, we have failed. Patients often say that their doctors seem angry with them when they don't respond to treatment. I think that this phenomenon is more than patients' paranoia or the result of overdeveloped medical egos. It is the fear of death again. It is necessary for doctors to become a bit angry with patients who are dying, if only as a way of separating themselves from someone in whom they have invested a good bit of time and probably a good bit of caring. We all do this to people who are sick. I can remember being terribly angry with my mother, who was prematurely senile, for a long time. Somehow I needed to think that it was her fault that she was sick, because her illness frightened me so much. I was also angry with my friend who died of cancer. I felt that she had let me down, that perhaps she hadn't fought hard enough. It was important for me to find reasons for her death, to find things that she might have done to cause it, as a way of separating myself from her and as a way of thinking that I would somehow have behaved differently, that I would somehow have been able to stay alive.

So, once we have recognized the limitations of the magic of doctors and medicine, where are we? We have to turn to our own magic, to our ability to "control" our bodies. For people who don't have cancer, this often takes the form of jogging and exotic diets and transcendental meditation. For people who have cancer, it takes the form of conscious development of the will to live. For a long time after I found out that I had cancer, I loved hearing stories about people who had simply decided that they would not be sick. I remember one story about a man who had a lung tumor and a wife with breast cancer and several children to support; he said, "I simply can't afford to be sick." Somehow the tumor went away. I think I suspected that there was a missing part to this story when I heard it, but there was also something that sounded right to me. I knew what he meant. I also found the fact that I had cancer unacceptable; the thought that my children might grow up without me was as ridiculous as the thought that I might forget to make appointments for their dental checkups and polio shots. I simply had to be there. Of course, doctors give a lot of credence to the power of the will over illness, but I have always suspected that the stories in medical books about this power might also have missing parts. My friend who died wanted to live more than anyone I have ever known. The talisman of will didn't work for her.

The need to exert some kind of control over the irrational forces that we imagine are loose in our bodies also results in what

I have come to recognize as the "brave act" put on by people who have cancer. We all do it. The blood-count line at Memorial Hospital can be one of the cheeriest places in New York on certain mornings. It was on this line, during my first visit to Memorial, that a young leukemia patient in remission told me, "They treat lung cancer like the common cold around here." (Believe me, that was the cheeriest thing anyone had said to me in months.) While waiting for blood counts, I have heard stories from people with lymphoma who were given up for dead in other hospitals and who are feeling terrific. The atmosphere in that line suggests a gathering of knights who have just slain a bunch of dragons. But there are always people in the line who don't say anything at all, and I always wonder if they have at other times felt the exhilaration felt by those of us who are well. We all know, at least, that the dragons are never quite dead and might at any time be aroused, ready for another fight. But our brave act is important. It is one of the ways we stay alive, and it is the way that we convince those who live in "The Land of the Well People" that we aren't all that different from them.

As much as I rely on the talisman of the will, I know that believ- 10
ing in it too much can lead to another kind of deception. There has been a great deal written (mostly by psychiatrists) about why people get cancer and which personality types are most likely to get it. Susan Sontag has pointed out that this explanation of cancer parallels the explanations for tuberculosis that were popular before the discovery of the tubercle bacillus. But it is reassuring to think that people get cancer because of their personalities, because that implies that we have some control over whether we get it. (On the other hand, if people won't give up smoking to avoid cancer, I don't see how they can be expected to change their personalities on the basis of far less compelling evidence.) The trouble with this explanation of cancer is the trouble with any talisman: it is only useful when its charms are working. If I get sick, does that mean that my will to live isn't strong enough? Is being sick a moral and psychological failure? If I feel successful, as if I had slain a dragon, because I am well, should I feel guilty, as if I have failed, if I get sick?

One of the ways that all of us avoid thinking about death is by concentrating on the details of our daily lives. The work that we do every day and the people we love—the fabric of our lives—

convince us that we are alive and that we will stay alive. William Saroyan said in a recent book, "Why am I writing this book? To save my life, to keep from dying, of course. That is why we get up in the morning." Getting up in the morning seems particularly miraculous after having seriously considered the possibility that these mornings might be limited. A year after I had my lung removed, my doctors asked me what I cared about most. I was about to go to Nova Scotia, where we have a summer home, and where I had not been able to go the previous summer because I was having radiation treatments, and I told him that what was most important to me was garden peas. Not the peas themselves, of course, though they were particularly good that year. What was extraordinary to me after that year was that I could again think that peas were important, that I could concentrate on the details of when to plant them and how much mulch they would need instead of thinking about platelets and white cells. I cherished the privilege of thinking about trivia. Thinking about death can make the details of our lives seem unimportant, and so, paradoxically, they become a burden—too much trouble to think about. This is the real meaning of depression: feeling weighed down by the concrete, unable to make the effort to move objects around, overcome by ennui. It is the fear of death that causes that ennui, because the fear of death ties us too much to the physical. We think too much about our bodies, and our bodies become too concrete—machines not functioning properly.

The other difficulty with the talisman of the moment is that it is often the very preciousness of these moments that makes the thought of death so painful. As my friend got closer to death she became rather removed from those she loved the most. She seemed to have gone to some place where we couldn't reach her—to have died what doctors sometimes call a "premature death." I much preferred to think of her enjoying precious moments. I remembered the almost ritualistic way she had her hair cut and tied in satin ribbons before brain surgery, the funny, somehow joyful afternoon that we spent trying wigs on her newly shaved head. Those moments made it seem as if it wasn't so bad to have cancer. But of course it was bad. It was unspeakably bad, and toward the end she couldn't bear to speak about it or to be too close to the people she didn't want to leave. The strength of my love for my children, my husband, my life, even my garden peas has probably been more important than anything else in keeping me alive. The intensity of this love is also what makes me so terrified of dying.

For many, of course, a response to the existential paradox is religion—Kierkegaard's irrational leap toward faith. It is no coincidence that such a high number of conversions take place in cancer hospitals; there is even a group of Catholic nurses in New York who are referred to by other members of their hospital staff as "the death squad." I don't mean to belittle such conversions or any help that religion can give to anyone. I am at this point in my life simply unqualified to talk about the power of this particular talisman.

In considering some of the talismans we all use to deny death, I don't mean to suggest that these talismans should be abandoned. However, their limits must be acknowledged. Ernest Becker, in *The Denial of Death,* says that "skepticism is a more radical experience, a more manly confrontation of potential meaninglessness than mysticism." The most important thing I know now that I didn't know four years ago is that this "potential meaninglessness" can in fact be confronted. As much as I rely on my talismans—my doctors, my will, my husband, my children, and my garden peas— I know that from time to time I will have to confront what Conrad described as "the horror." I know that we can—all of us—confront that horror and not be destroyed by it, even, to some extent, be enhanced by it. To quote Becker again: "I think that taking life seriously means something such as this: that whatever man does on this planet has to be done in the lived truth of the terror of creation, of the grotesque, of the rumble of panic underneath everything. Otherwise it is false."

It astonishes me that having faced the terror, we continue to   15 live, even to live with a great deal of joy. It is commonplace for people who have cancer—particularly those who feel as well as I do—to talk about how much richer their lives are because they have confronted death. Yes, my life is very rich. I have even begun to understand that wonderful line in *King Lear,* "Ripeness is all." I suppose that becoming ripe means finding out that none of the really important questions have answers. I wish that life had devised a less terrifying, less risky way of making me ripe. But I wasn't given any choice about this.

William Saroyan said recently, "I'm growing old! I'm falling apart! And it's VERY INTERESTING!" I'd be willing to bet that

Mr. Saroyan, like me, would much rather be young and all in one piece. But somehow his longing for youth and wholeness doesn't destroy him or stop him from getting up in the morning and writing, as he says, to save his life. We will never kill the dragon. But each morning we confront him. Then we give our children breakfast, perhaps put a bit more mulch on the peas, and hope that we can convince the dragon to stay away for a while longer.

RESPONDING IN DISCUSSION OR WRITING

1. *Considerations of Style.* How effective is the title of this essay? Why do you think Trillin chose this title rather than just "A Cancer Patient Talks to Doctors"?

2. Trillin discusses finding the world of sickness ordinary and banal. What leads her to draw those conclusions? Do you agree with her that banality is a feature of being sick?

3. Trillin states her main point very clearly, "We are all afraid of dying" (paragraph 3), and then discusses the defense mechanisms, the talismans, that we inevitably set up when we are sick to deny the fact of death. These talismans Trillin sees as a set of beliefs, quite distinct from belief in a religion, which she briefly alludes to in paragraph 13. What is your view of the efficacy of each of the defense mechanisms she discusses? Would you add any of your own? You might want to make connections to the talisman Leonard Kriegel describes in paragraph 4 of his essay in Unit 2.

4. Trillin's paragraph on the talisman of religion is short. Why do you think she does not discuss this in much detail? What conclusions would you draw about her attachment to organized religion?

5. Trillin uses several incidents and anecdotes to support her points. Which of the stories she includes interests you the most and makes the strongest point?

6. Assemble as much information as you can on how various religious belief systems regard death and how they prepare their believers for it. What common threads emerge?

WRITING ASSIGNMENTS

1. Trillin writes: "We will never kill the dragon. But each morning we confront him." Write a short story or an essay that begins with those two sentences. You don't have to write about sickness. You can make "the dragon" represent anything that is threatening or

frightening in a person's life, anything against which people set up defense mechanisms.

2. Do you agree with the people Trillin describes who think that their lives become richer once they have confronted death? Write an essay in which you give the arguments that could be used for and against this view.

❖

RELIGION IN THE TEXTBOOKS

ELLEN GOODMAN

Ellen Goodman, born in 1941, won the Pulitzer Prize in 1980 for Distinguished Commentary. She writes a syndicated column, "At Large," for the Boston Globe, *where she is now also an associate editor. She frequently writes about politics, women's issues, and the movies. Goodman publishes collections of her articles. This article, originally published in the* Washington Post *in 1986, appears in her collection* Making Sense *(1989). Her most recent book is* Value Judgments *(1993).*

THERE WAS A TIME when people who wanted to keep the peace and keep the crockery intact held to a strict dinner-table rule: Never argue about politics or religion. I don't know how well it worked in American dining rooms, but it worked pretty well in our schools. We dealt with religion by not arguing about it.

Children who came out of diverse homes might carve up the turf of their neighborhood and turn the playgrounds into a religious battlefield, but the public classroom was common ground. Intolerance wasn't tolerated.

In place of teaching one religion or another, the schools held to a common denominator of values. It was, in part, the notion of Horace Mann, the nineteenth-century father of the public-school system. He believed that the way to avoid religious conflicts was to extract what all religions agreed upon and allow this "non-religious" belief system into schools.

I wonder what Mann would think of that experiment now. Was it naive or sophisticated? Was it a successful or a failed attempt to avoid conflict in a pluralistic society?

Today, textbooks are the texts of public-school education and their publishers are, if anything, controversy-phobic. Textbooks are written and edited by publishing committees that follow elaborate guidelines to appease state and local education committees. They must avoid alienating either atheist or fundamentalist. And still these books have become centerpieces, controversial sources of evidence in courtrooms.

A judge in Tennessee recently allowed a group of students to "opt out" of reading class because the textbooks violated their religious beliefs. Their parents had managed to read religious subtexts, even witchcraft, into such tales as "Goldilocks," "Cinderella" and "The Three Little Pigs." Nothing was safe enough or bland enough to please them.

At the same time, a group of parents in Alabama went to court protesting that textbooks are teaching a state religion masquerading as "secular humanism." Not to teach about God is to teach about no God. The attempt to keep religion out of the textbooks was no guarantee against controversy either.

There is still a third argument about religion in the public schools that doesn't come from fanatics but from educators. They maintain that the attempt to avoid conflict has pushed textbook publishers to excise religion altogether, even from history class. It is not just the teaching *of* religion that has become taboo, they claim. It is teaching *about* religion.

Sources as diverse as William Bennett's Department of Education and Norman Lear's People for the American Way have reported in the past year on the distortions that result. There is a history book that tells about Joan of Arc without mentioning her religious motives. Others explain Thanksgiving without discussing the religious beliefs of the Puritans or to Whom they were giving thanks.

"The result of wanting to avoid controversy is a kind of censorship," maintains Diane Ravitch of Columbia University. "It becomes too controversial to write about Christianity and Judaism." Ravitch is involved in creating a new history curriculum for California that would incorporate teaching about people's belief systems and their impact on society. It may be tricky, she admits, to teach about religion without teaching religion, but then all good teaching is risky. So is learning. And that's what is at stake.

The common ground of values, neutral turf in the religious strife, threatens to shrink to the size of a postage stamp. In Tennessee, the court agreed to protect the religious beliefs of a set of parents whose own beliefs included intolerance of other religions and the importance of binding a child's imagination. These are ideas that are profoundly hostile to the American concept of education.

If textbook publishers keep retreating to a shrinking patch of safe ground, they will end up editing chunks out of "The Three Little Pigs." The task is not to shy away from our diversity, but to teach it to our children, and proudly. The strength of our system, what's worth telling the young, is not that Americans deny their differences or always resolve them, but that we have managed, until now, to live with them.

RESPONDING IN DISCUSSION OR WRITING

1. What topics does your family like to discuss and to avoid discussing? To what extent do discussions of politics and religion figure in your family's conversations?

2. The issue of whether prayers should be said in public schools is often hotly debated. What is your view on the issue? What do you see as the main points in opposition to your point of view?

3. Goodman says that textbooks in schools must avoid alienating "either atheist or fundamentalist." Can you recall how such issues were treated in the textbooks you had in high school?

4. Do you think that students should be allowed to decide not to read books that are assigned in school? Why or why not?

5. Goodman provides examples to illustrate how textbooks avoid even discussing religion. Are her examples convincing? What other examples could Goodman use?

6. Do you agree with Goodman when she says that the strength of the educational system is "not that Americans deny their differences or always resolve them, but that we have managed, until now, to live with them"? What examples can you provide to support your opinion?

WRITING ASSIGNMENTS

1. Describe your own religious upbringing at home and at school. Did the systems match, or were they in conflict?

2. Write a response to Diane Ravitch's comment: "The result of wanting to avoid controversy is a kind of censorship." How do you interpret that comment, and what does it mean for educational policies?

BUDDHISM

ARI L. GOLDMAN

Ari L. Goldman, born in 1949, is religion correspondent for the New York Times. *His book,* The Search for God at Harvard *(1992), describes his experience when he, an Orthodox Jew aged thirty-five, was sent by the* New York Times *to spend a year as a graduate student at Harvard Divinity School studying comparative religion. He writes about his encounters with other religions, as he learned about other faiths and more about his own. This excerpt is a chapter from his account. It describes what he learned in the lectures on Buddhism and compares Buddhism to his own religion, Judaism.*

IN A MATTER OF lectures we went from Hinduism, with its millions of gods, to Buddhism, with none. "None" is an even harder concept for Westerners to swallow. Professor Eck recalled one former student's reaction to Buddhism: "You mean they don't even believe in God? That really grosses me out. And they don't want to live forever? You call *that* a religion?"

Yes, we do. And in so doing I am introduced to the idea that a belief in God may not even be a prerequisite for a religion. After all, we are talking about Buddhism as a religion (from "binding back") rather than in the God-talk of theology. And Buddhism binds the believer back to a period some five hundred years before Jesus.

The Buddha, Siddhartha Gautama, was a human being, a seeker, who became free. He was born to a privileged family in the north of India and was raised a prince. His father, the raja of Kapilavastu, had a vision in which he saw that his son would be either a beggar or a king. He sought to protect the youth from the harsh realities of life. The prince lived comfortably in the palace, took a wife of his father's choosing, who bore him a son. His privileged life insulated him from the realities of the world, realities he only glimpsed when his coachman drove him through the streets.

On one journey the prince saw old age. Then he saw disease and then, in the figure of a corpse, death. On his final trip, he saw a mendicant, a man who had renounced worldly goods to go through life begging for alms in the streets. The prince returned home, kissed his wife and son as they slept and told his servant to prepare his white horse. The prince galloped to the outskirts of town, dismounted, set his horse free and became a seeker.

At first, he searched for knowledge in the traditional Hindu way, striving through rigorous yoga exercise to unite himself with the world. But this failed. He continued through harsh physical denial, living on one sesame seed a day, until he was near death. Ultimately, he rejected the ascetic life and turned to meditation. Sitting under a fig tree, he gained Enlightenment.

The cause of all unhappiness, the Buddha reasoned, is desire. The ills of life all flow from the lust for power, success, sex and material pleasures. Give up the desire and one can attain truth. In Leviticus, the God of the Hebrews declares that one must love one's neighbor as oneself. To Buddha, one need not love even oneself.

Even after the story, the question remains, what kind of religion is this? In class, we read Walpola Rahula's *What the Buddha Taught*. Rahula describes Buddhism as more of a therapy than a philosophy and Buddha as "a physician not a metaphysician."

In one three-word saying of the Buddha I find an entire lesson in comparative religion. "Come and see," the Buddha tells his followers. It is not the "Come, follow me" of Jesus and it is not the "Come and learn" of the rabbis of the Talmud. For Buddhists, it is come and see . . . for yourself.

My first reporting experience with Buddhism, which came soon after I left the Div School, seemed a long way from the ideals described in the Harvard classroom. I journeyed to a clearing in the Vermont woods for the cremation of a Tibetan teacher who had helped bring Buddhism to the West. His name was Chogyam Trungpa Rinpoche, and he died at the age of forty-seven of what his critics described as excess. Too much food, too much liquor, too much sex. His American followers saw his great appetite for life as a virtue and attributed his death to a heart attack. Although AIDS was never mentioned in connection with Trungpa's death, the man who succeeded him as leader of the sect, Osel Tendzin, died of the disease in 1990, also at the age of forty-seven.

On the spring morning of the cremation, there was a mood of restrained celebration. The followers preparing for the rite were an interesting assortment of 1980s yuppies, people who had been attracted to Trungpa in the tumultuous sixties and remained under his influence even as they settled down and prospered.

The ceremony, to which several thousand followers flocked, gave me an opportunity to write about Trungpa's life, how he fled from Tibet in 1959 and became a major exponent of Buddhism in the West, and about the dramatic cremation rite, complete with ringing handbells and Zen archers performing a choreographed ceremony around the burning pyre. In my piece, I was also able to give a sense that, although a funeral, this was a kind of Woodstock for grown-ups, noting the blankets, insect repellent, lunch coolers and backpacks for toddlers. But my favorite, if whimsical, quote fell prey to one of my straitlaced editors: "This is not a wake," I had quoted one follower, "it is awake."

"Awake" is the goal of every Buddhist, and that is what Trungpa's death meant. In death, Trungpa came into full enlightenment and shared that spirit with his followers. "Although the body of the teacher has died and will be consumed by flames, his mind still exists and pervades all space," David Rome, an aide to the holy man, explained at a press briefing the day before the cremation. The moment of the cremation, he added, would be a propitious moment during which the followers could "connect with the mind of the teacher and accomplish a greater realization of ourselves."

Aside from his Buddhist connections, the fortyish Rome was a descendant of Salman Schocken, a department store owner in

Germany who in 1932 became a book publisher. When, under Hitler, Aryan companies could no longer publish books by Jewish writers, Schocken acquired the rights to Kafka's works, which the company still holds. Like most of the two thousand people who gathered for the Buddhist funeral rite, Rome was born Jewish.

In my article, I did not mention the large Jewish presence at the Buddhist leader's cremation. (The *Times*'s policy is not to note religion or race unless it is "relevant" to the article, a judgment call exercised by editors.) Nor could I relate what Emily Wolitzky, another devotee of Trungpa in her forties, told me: "I always wanted to be awakened by Judaism, but as a woman there was nothing there for me." Emily was not just another woman in the crowd; she had been my older brother's girlfriend some fifteen years earlier.

Emily's complaints about Judaism were something I had heard   15 from other Jewish women. At a Buddhist study center in western New Jersey, a woman who grew up in an Orthodox Jewish home told me: "If I were twenty today, I'd probably want to become a rabbi, but I'm forty and a Buddhist." The first women were admitted to the Reform rabbinate in the early 1970s. The Conservatives began to ordain women in 1985; the Orthodox still do not and probably never will.

While some Jewish women were drawn to Buddhism because they felt excluded from Judaism, Buddhism holds other attractions for Jews. It is a faith that makes few demands on its adherents; you don't even have to be a Buddhist to participate. An outsider is welcome to draw what spiritual nourishment he or she wants from the faith and leave the rest. For Jews alienated from Judaism, Buddhism provides an alternative that isn't Christianity. As disillusioned as many of these Jews were with their own faith, they had been conditioned by their upbringing to seeing Christianity not merely as a substitute for but as a repudiation of Judaism.

For this reason, Buddhism is especially attractive to Jewish-Christian couples. Instead of setting up a struggle over who, the Jew or the Christian, should give in, it offers a third alternative— take on a new faith that is broadminded enough to encompass the practices of the old ones.

Not long after the Trungpa cremation, I covered the first dialogue between the Dalai Lama, the leader of Tibetan Buddhism, and a group of Jewish scholars. The meeting was held at the impetus of the Dalai Lama, who lives in exile from his native Tibet and makes frequent visits to the United States. The Dalai Lama said that he wanted to better understand "the secret" of Jewish survival through two thousand years of exile. He also wanted to learn more about Judaism, he said, since so many of his American followers were Jews. I spent some time with the Buddhist organizers of the event, all of whom were born Jewish. Then I met their wives, virtually all of whom were born Christian.

With my Orthodox background, however, I felt alienated from Buddhism. I could neither bow nor light candles to a statue. At the cremation in Vermont, though, I was clearly in the minority. No one, it seemed, was as hung up about these things as I. I was surrounded by people with names as Jewish as my own who were using Tibetan words to describe their spiritual life (*dharma, samsara, nirvana*) and meditating on their knees before the burning stupa of their teacher, who had been preserved in salt, covered in purified butter and wrapped in silk.

I thought back to the time when Shalom and Emily had dated. I cannot picture Shalom alone during those years, only with Emily at his side. He was tall and bearded, his red hair in a ponytail. She was petite and curly haired and favored loose-fitting peasant dresses. Once on a visit to the brownstone Emily and Shalom shared in Brooklyn's Park Slope section (to the horror of my parents), I saw Emily kneeling silently in a darkened room as she lit a candle at an altar in front of a corpulent wooden Buddha. As someone who then knew just one religion—Judaism—I wondered what was wrong with her. But now, in Vermont, with a basic understanding of Buddhism, I wondered what was wrong with me. After all, was lighting candles before the Buddha all that different from lighting candles to welcome the Sabbath on Friday night?

20

RESPONDING IN DISCUSSION OR WRITING

1. *Considerations of Style.* Goldman ends his opening paragraph with a series of questions. What is the effect on the reader of these questions? And what is the effect of Goldman's reply: "Yes, we do"?

2. *For Further Research.* How do you react to Goldman's idea that "a belief in God may not even be a prerequisite for a religion" (paragraph 2)? Survey others to find out how they react to that.

3. What examples could be used to illustrate the Buddhist belief that "the ills of life all flow from the lust for power, success, sex and material pleasures"?

4. Explain how an emphasis on "Come and see" could lead to a different religious experience from "Come, follow me" or "Come and learn."

5. *Considerations of Style.* Goldman uses some direct quotations. What are they, and which ones add something particularly memorable to his piece?

WRITING ASSIGNMENTS

1. Describe in detail a religious ceremony you have attended and the behavior of the participants.

2. *For Further Research.* Do research to find out about the life and teaching of a religious leader in a religion to which you have not been connected.

❖

THE LOCAL CONGREGATION

ROBERT N. BELLAH, RICHARD MADSEN, WILLIAM M. SULLIVAN, ANN SWIDLER, AND STEVEN M. TIPTON

In their book Habits of the Heart: Individualism and Commitment in American Life *(1985), Robert Bellah, Richard Madsen, William Sullivan, Ann Swidler, and Steven Tipton have provided a penetrating analysis of American society. They begin the preface with these questions: "How ought we to live? How do we think about how to live? Who are we, as Americans? What is our character?" The fundamental question they pose as they interview and observe over two hundred white, middle-class Americans in groups or communities is "how to preserve or create a morally coherent life." They probe the essence of American individualism in the context of cultural traditions in both private and public life. This excerpt is from the section on public life, the chapter on "Religion."*

We MAY BEGIN A closer examination of how religion operates in the lives of those to whom we talked by looking at the local congregation, which traditionally has a certain priority. The local church is a community of worship that contains within itself, in small, so to speak, the features of the larger church, and in some Protestant traditions can exist autonomously. The church as a community of worship is an adaptation of the Jewish synagogue. Both Jews and Christians view their communities as existing in a covenant relationship with God, and the Sabbath worship around which religious life centers is a celebration of that covenant. Worship calls to mind the story of the relationship of the community with God: how God brought his chosen people out of Egypt or gave his only begotten son for the salvation of mankind. Worship also reiterates the obligations that the community has undertaken, including the biblical insistence on justice and righteousness, and on love of God and neighbor, as well as the promises God has made that make it possible for the community to hope for the future. Though worship has its special times and places, especially on the Sabbath in the house of the Lord, it functions as a model or pattern for the whole of life. Through reminding the people of their relationship to God, it establishes patterns of character and virtue that should operate in economic and political life as well as in the context of worship. The community maintains itself as a community of memory, and the various religious traditions have somewhat different memories.

The very freedom, openness, and pluralism of American religious life makes this traditional pattern hard for Americans to understand. For one thing, the traditional pattern assumes a certain priority of the religious community over the individual. The community exists before the individual is born and will continue after his or her death. The relationship of the individual to God is ultimately personal, but it is mediated by the whole pattern of community life. There is a givenness about the community and the tradition. They are not normally a matter of individual choice.

For Americans, the traditional relationship between the individual and the religious community is to some degree reversed. On the basis of our interviews, we are not surprised to learn that a 1978 Gallup poll found that 80 percent of Americans agreed that "an individual should arrive at his or her own religious beliefs independent of any churches or synagogues."[1] From the traditional point of view, this is a strange statement—it is precisely within church or synagogue that one comes to one's religious beliefs—but to many Americans it is the Gallup finding that is normal.

Nan Pfautz, raised in a strict Baptist church, is now an active member of a Presbyterian congregation near San Jose. Her church membership gives her a sense of community involvement, of engagement with issues at once social and moral. She speaks of her "commitment" to the church, so that being a member means being willing to give time, money, and care to the community it embodies and to its wider purposes. Yet, like many Americans, she feels that her personal relationship to God transcends her involvement in any particular church. Indeed, she speaks with humorous disdain of "churchy people" such as those who condemn others for violations of external norms. She says, "I believe I have a commitment to God which is beyond church. I felt my relationship with God was O.K. when I wasn't with the church."

For Nan, the church's value is primarily an ethical one. [5] "Church to me is a community, and it's an organization that I belong to. They do an awful lot of good." Her obligations to the church come from the fact that she has chosen to join it, and "just like any organization that you belong to, it shouldn't be just to have another piece of paper in your wallet." As with the Kiwanis or any other organization, "you have a responsibility to do something or don't be there," to devote time and money, and especially to "care about the people." It is this caring community, above all, that the church represents. "I really love my church and what they have done for me, and what they do for other people, and the community that's there." Conceived as an association of loving individuals, the church acquires its value from "the caring about people. What I like about my church is its community."

This view of the church as a community of empathetic sharing is related to another aspect of Nan's thought. Despite her fundamentalist upbringing, her religiousness has developed a mystical cast. She sees the Christian tradition as only one, and perhaps not even the best, expression of our relationship to what is sacred in the universe. It is this mysticism and her sense of empathy with others, rather than any particularly Christian vision, that seems to motivate Nan's extraordinary range of social and political commitments. "I feel we have a commitment to the world, to animals, to the environment, to the water, to the whole thing. It all, in my opinion, is the stewardship of what God has loaned us. The American Indian religion is so fantastic, I think. All those Bible-pounding people came and told them that they were pagans, when they have such a better concept of what religion is all about." For Nan, empathy creates a sense of responsibility because she feels kinship, equality, perhaps even a kind of fusion with all others in the world, and so she suffers for their suffering. Her credo is, "We're all on this earth. Just because I was fortunate to be born in America and white doesn't make me any better than someone that's born in Africa and is black. They deserve to eat just as much as I deserve to eat. The boat people have the same feelings that I do. The same feelings—how can we say no to them?"

In talking to Art Townsend, the pastor of Nan's church, we found views quite consonant with hers. Art is not unaware of the church as a community of memory, though he is as apt to tell a story from the Maharishi or a Zen Buddhist text as from the New Testament. But what excites him are the individuals themselves: "The church is really a part of me and I am a part of the church, and my shift professionally has gone from 'how can I please them and make them like me so that I can keep my job and get a promotion' to 'how can I love them, how can I help these beautiful, special people to experience how absolutely wonderful they are.'" It is the self—both his and those of others—that must be the source of all religious meaning. In Art's optimistic vision, human beings need to learn to "lighten up" as "one of the steps to enlightenment." His job in turn is to "help them take the scales from their eyes and experience and see their magnificence." Difficulties between people are misunderstandings among selves who are ultimately in harmony. If a couple who are angry or disappointed or bored with each other really share their feelings, "you get into a deeper level, and what happens is that feelings draw together, and you actually, literally feel the feeling the same way the other person feels it. And when you do, there is a shift, there is a zing, and it is like the two become one."

For Art Townsend, God becomes the guarantee of what he has "experienced in my life, that there is nothing that happens to me that is not for the fulfillment of my higher self." His cheery mysticism eliminates any real possibility of sin, evil, or damnation, since "if I thought God were such a being that he would waste a human soul on the basis of its mistakes, that would be a little limiting." In consonance with this primarily expressive individualist ethos, Art's philosophy is remarkably upbeat. Tragedy and sacrifice are not what they seem. "Problems become the playground of consciousness" and are to be welcomed as opportunities for growth.

Such a view can justify high levels of social activism, and Art Townsend's church engages in a wide variety of activities, volunteering as a congregation to care for Vietnamese refugee families, supporting broader understanding of the homosexual minority, and visiting the sick or distressed in the congregation. A member such as Nan Pfautz carries her sense of responsibility further, participating through the church in a range of activities from environmental protection to fighting multinational corporations marketing infant formula in the Third World. But it is clear for her, as for Art Townsend, that the ultimate meaning of the church is an expressive-individualist one. Its value is as a loving community in which individuals can experience the joy of belonging. As the church secretary says, "Certainly all the things that we do involve caring about people in a loving manner, at least I hope that we do." She puts it succinctly when she says, "For the most part, I think this community is a safe place for a lot of people."

Art Townsend's Presbyterian church would be viewed as theologically liberal. A look at a nearby conservative church brings out many differences but also many similarities. Pastor Larry Beckett describes his church as independent, conservative, and evangelical, and as neither liberal nor fundamentalist. At first glance, this conservative evangelical church is more clearly a community of memory than Art Townsend's. Larry Beckett indicates that its central beliefs are the divinity of Christ and the authority of scripture. A great deal of time is given to the study and exposition of scripture. Larry even gave a brief course on New Testament Greek so that the original text would be to some degree available to the congregation. While Larry insists that the great commandment to love God and one's neighbor is the essence of biblical teaching, his church tries to follow the specific commandments as much as possible. It is, for example, strongly against divorce because of Jesus' injunction (Matt. 19:6) against putting asunder what God has joined together. The firm insistence on belief in God and in the divinity of Christ, the importance of Christ as a model for how to act, and the attempt to apply specific biblical injunctions as far as possible provide the members of this church with a structure of external authority that might make the members of Art Townsend's congregation uneasy. Not so different socially and occupationally from the nearby Presbyterian church, and subject to many of the same insecurities and tensions, the members of this evangelical church have found a faith that is secure and unchanging. As Larry Beckett says, "God doesn't change. The values don't change. Jesus Christ doesn't change. In fact, the Bible says He is the same yesterday, today, and forever. Everything in life is always changing, but God doesn't change."

Despite his religious conservatism, Larry Beckett mixes a liberal dose of humanistic psychology with his strong biblical imagery, telling church members that God's love can be a source of "self-worth." Because God has created them in his image, because he loves them and sent his son to redeem them, they have infinite worth and value. "No matter how a person is performing, no matter how many friends they have, no matter how handsome or ugly, or no matter how much money they have, they have an inherent value base that cannot be changed or altered." But this attempt to make people feel good about themselves is only a first step in persuading them to enter an exclusive Christian community. He distances himself from the view that "basically everybody in America and everybody in Western culture is Christian. That's not what Evangelicals mean. It is that I have made a personal identification with the historic person of Christ in a very simple way. I did that about ten years ago, and before that I was non-Christian."

The community of Larry Beckett's church is a warm and loving one. There is freshly baked zucchini bread sitting out on the counter of the church's modest kitchen, and the whole community has the feeling of a family. Here members practice the virtues of their biblical ethic, learning to put the needs of others before their own. For Larry Beckett and the members of his congregation, biblical Christianity provides an alternative to the utilitarian individualist values of this world. But that alternative, appealing precisely because it is "real clear," does not go very far in helping them understand their connection to the world or the society in which they live. The Bible provides unambiguous moral answers about "the essential issues—love, obedience, faith, hope," so that "killing or, say, murdering is never right. Or adultery. A relationship outside of your marriage is never right. The Bible says that real simple." To "follow the Scriptures and the words of Jesus" provides a clear, but narrow, morality centered on family and personal life. One must personally, as an individual, resist temptation and put the good of others ahead of one's own. Christian love applies to one-to-one relationships—I may not cheat my neighbor, or exploit him, or sell him something I know he can't afford. But outside this sphere of personal morality, the evangelical church has little to say about wider social commitments. Indeed, the sect draws together those who have found a personal relationship to Christ into a special loving community, and while it urgently seeks to have everyone make the same commitment, it separates its members off from attachment to the wider society. Morality becomes personal, not social; private, not public.

Both Larry Beckett's conservative church and Art Townsend's liberal one stress stable, loving relationships, in which the intention to care outweighs the flux of momentary feelings, as the ideal pattern in marriage, family, and work relationships. Thus both attempt to counter the more exploitative tendencies of utilitarian individualism. But in both cases, their sense of religious community has trouble moving beyond an individualistic morality. In Art Townsend's faith, a distinctively religious vision has been absorbed into the categories of contemporary psychology. No autonomous standard of good and evil survives outside the needs of individual psyches for growth. Community and attachment come not from the demands of a tradition, but from the empathetic sharing of feelings among therapeutically attuned selves.

Larry Beckett's evangelical church, in contrast, maintains a vision of the concrete moral commitments that bind church members. But the bonds of loyalty, help, and responsibility remain oriented to the exclusive sect of those who are "real" Christians. Direct reliance on the Bible provides a second language with which to resist the temptations of the "world," but the almost exclusive concentration on the Bible, especially the New Testament, with no larger memory of how Christians have coped with the world historically, diminishes the capacity of their second language to deal adequately with current social reality. There is even a tendency visible in many evangelical circles to thin the biblical language of sin and redemption to an idea of Jesus as the friend who helps us find happiness and self-fulfillment.[2] The emphasis on love, so evident within the community, is not shared with the world, except through missionary outreach.

There are thousands of local churches in the United States, representing an enormous range of variation in doctrine and worship. Yet most define themselves as communities of personal support. A recent study suggests that what Catholics look for does not differ from the concerns of the various types of Protestants we have been discussing. When asked the direction the church should take in future years, the two things that a national sample of Catholics most asked for were "personal and accessible priests" and "warmer, more personal parishes."[3] The salience of these needs for personal intimacy in American religious life suggests why the local church, like other voluntary communities, indeed like the contemporary family, is so fragile, requires so much energy to keep it going, and has so faint a hold on commitment when such needs are not met.

Notes

1. Dean R. Hoge, *Converts, Dropouts, Returnees: A Study of Religious Change Among Catholics* (Washington, D.C.: United States Catholic Conference; New York: Pilgrim Press, 1981), p. 167.

2. James Davison Hunter has documented an important shift in conservative evangelical piety through a study of books published by the eight largest publishers of evangelical literature. He finds a phenomenon he calls "psychological Christocentrism" beginning in the 1960s and reaching dominance in the 1970s. This literature consists of many variations on such statements as "Jesus meant for the Christian life to be an exciting, abundant adventure." Suffering and sacrifice are downplayed and happiness, fulfillment, and "a new zest for living" are promised. Hunter summarizes: "Subjectivism has displaced the traditional asceticism as the dominant attitude in theologically conservative Protestant culture. There is some variability, but in mainstream contemporary American Evangelicalism, an austere instrumentalism has been replaced by a malleable expressivity" (James Davison Hunter, *American Evangelicalism* [New Brunswick, N.J.: Rutgers University Press, 1983], 91–101).

3. Hoge, *Converts, Dropouts, Returnees,* p. 171.

RESPONDING IN DISCUSSION OR WRITING

1. Would you agree or disagree with the Gallup poll statement that "an individual should arrive at his or her own religious beliefs independent of any churches or synagogues"? Explain your reasons.

2. Do you feel a sense of community involvement? If so, what fosters it? If not, what inhibits it?

3. Do you regard belonging to a religious group as forming "a community of empathetic sharing"?

4. When Nan Pfautz talks about "a commitment to the world, to animals, to the environment, to the water, to the whole thing," she talks about a responsibility that is broader than a commitment to just one church or one community. Do you agree with her that a religious commitment also involves a political and social commitment to work for the improvement of our environment?

5. Do you think a person can have a social and moral commitment to a community outside of a religious institution?

WRITING ASSIGNMENTS

1. Write an essay in which you explain the similarities and differences between Larry Beckett's conservative church and Art Townsend's liberal church. What types of people is each one likely to appeal to?

2. Comment on the summary at the end of paragraph 12: "Morality becomes personal, not social; private, not public." In which ways do you agree or disagree with a religious focus on such sentiments? Can there ever be conflict between private and public morality?

BLOODS

HAROLD "LIGHT BULB" BRYANT

Bloods, *published in 1984, is a collection of oral histories told by black veterans of the Vietnam War. These excerpts are from the contribution of Harold "Light Bulb" Bryant from East St. Louis, Illinois, who was a combat engineer in the 1st Cavalry Division of the U.S. Army and who was stationed in Vietnam from February 1966 to February 1967. Bryant's account describes the inhumanities of war that soldiers experienced while fighting in Vietnam: the atrocities, the disregard for human life, the racism, and the lack of trust.*

I WAS SENT TO An Khe, 8th Engineers Battalion, and attached to the 1st of the 9th of the Cav. It was in February, after the first battle of the Ia Drang Valley, when 300 Cav troops got wiped out in the first real fight anybody had with the NVA. I was one of those replacements.

We probed for mines, blew up mines, disarmed and blew up booby traps. If you saw a trip wire, you could take a look at what was happening. You could see where the booby trap was, then throw a grenade at the beginning of the booby trap. Or shoot up the trail to make 'em go off. The land mines, ones you had to dig up, was the big problem, 'cause they could have another one planted somewhere next to it.

And you had to worry about crimping right and taking your time. You squeeze the blasting cap and the fuse together so they won't come apart. Crimping, right. But if you don't crimp right, like an inch high from the bottom of the cap, it will blow you up. And you can't be rushed by some second lieutenant, telling you, "Hurry up, hurry up, so we can move on." If you rush, something wrong would happen. We lost three guys from rushing or crimping wrong.

One time I had to get a guy off a mine. It looked like it was impossible.

This infantry unit was on a little trail, west of Pleiku, makin' a   5
sweep towards the Ia Drang Valley. This white dude had stepped
on a mine. And knew it. He felt the plunger go down. Everybody
moved away from him, about 20 meters. So they called for the
engineers, and somebody asked for Light Bulb.

I have a nickname from the streets of East St. Louis. Light Bulb.
Came from a friend of mine when we were growing up, 'cause he
said I was always full of ideas.

When I got there on the chopper, he's been standin' there for
over an hour. He really wasn't in any panic. He was very calm. He
knew if he alleviated any of the pressure, both of us would have
got destroyed.

I dug all around the mine with my bayonet and found out that
it was a Bouncin' Betty. I told him I was gonna try to defuse it. But
the three-prong primer on the Bouncin' Betty had gotten in
between the cleats on his jungle boots, so there wasn't any way I
could deal with it. So I said let's see if we could kind of change the
pressure by him takin' his foot out of his boot and me keepin' the
pressure by holding his boot down. That way he could get out
uninjured. But when he started doin' that, I thought I was seein'
the plunger rise, so I told him to stop.

I guess maybe I'd been working with him for maybe an hour
now.

Then I got the idea. I knew when the plunger would depress,   10
the Bouncin' Betty would bounce up about 3 feet and then
explode. So I got the other members of his team together, and I
tied a rope around his waist. And everybody, including me, moved
off about 20 yards from the mine and him. And when I counted
to three, everyone would pull on the rope and snatch him about
15 feet off the mine. And it would bounce up its 3 feet and then
explode. And it did that. And the only damage that he received
was the heel of his jungle boot was blown off. No damage to him.

This was somethin' that they never taught us in school.

This guy thanked me for saving his life and the life of his squad.
And whenever we were back in base camp, I would always go with
them. And since a platoon would always carry three or four combat engineers with them in the bush, I would always go with them.

When I came to Vietnam, I thought we were helping another
country to develop a nation. About three or four months later I
found out that wasn't the case. In high school and in the papers I

had been hearing about Indochina, but I couldn't find Indochina on the map. I didn't know anything about the country, about the people. Those kinds of things I had to learn on myself while I was there.

We had a Vietnamese interpreter attached to us. I would always be asking him questions. He had told me this war in Vietnam had been going on for hundreds of years. Before the Americans, they had been fighting for hundreds of years against the Chinese aggressors. I thought we had got into the beginning of a war. But I found out that we were just in another phase of their civil wars.

And we weren't gaining any ground. We would fight for a hill all day, spend two days or two nights there, and then abandon the hill. Then maybe two, three months later, we would have to come back and retake the same piece of territory. Like this Special Forces camp outside Dak To. The camp was attacked one evening. Maybe two or three platoons flew up to give them some assistance. Then somehow headquarters decided we should close down that camp. So they ended up closing down. Two or three months later, we went back to the same area to retake it. We lost 20 men the first time saving it, 30 or 40 men the next time retaking it.

And they had a habit of exaggerating a body count. If we killed 7, by the time it would get back to base camp, it would have gotten to 28. Then by the time it got down to Westmoreland's office in Saigon, it done went up to 54. And by the time it left from Saigon going to Washington, it had went up to about 125. To prove we were really out there doing our jobs, doing, really, more than what we were doing.

I remember a place called the Ashau Valley. The 7th went in there and got cut up real bad. They had underestimated the enemy's power. So they sent in the 9th, and we cleared the Ashau Valley out. All we was doing was making contact, letting the gunships know where they were, and then we would draw back. We had 25 gunships circling around, and jet strikes coming in to drop napalm. We did that all day, and the next day we didn't receive any other fire.

Stars and Stripes said we had a body count of 260 something. But I don't think it was true.

By then I had killed my first VC. It was two or three o'clock in the afternoon, somewhere in the Central Highlands. I was point man. I was blazing my own trail. I was maybe 40 meters in front of the rest of the squad. And I just walked up on him. He just stepped out of the bush. I didn't see him until he moved. I'd say maybe 50 meters. And then he saw me. We both had a look of surprise. And I cracked him, because it just ran through my mind it would be either him or me. I just fired from the hip. And he hadn't even brought his weapon down from port arms.

But what really got to me from the beginning was not really having any information, not knowing what I was gonna be doin' next. We might be pullin' guard for some artillery one night. Then the next day some choppers would come and get us. We would never know where we were going until in the air. Then we would get word that we were going to the LZ that was really hot. Or something ignorant, like the time we went over in Cambodia to pull guard on a helicopter that had been shot down. And we got stuck there. [20]

It was in the latter part of '66, late in the afternoon. I think it got shot down probably in 'Nam and just ended up in Cambodia. So they sent out a squad of us combat engineers to cut around the shaft so a Chinook could come in, hook up, and pull it out. We didn't get there until six or seven, and it was getting dark. So the Chinook couldn't come in, so we had to stay there all night. The chopper had one door gunner and two pilots, and they were all dead. It wasn't from any rounds. They died from the impact of the chopper falling. I thought it made a lot more sense for us to get out of there and bring the bodies back with us.

When it got dark, we could see a fire maybe half a mile from us. We knew it had to be a VC camp. In the bamboo thicket right up on us we kept hearing this movement, these small noises. We thought if we fired, whoever was out there would attack us. We were so quiet that none of us moved all night. Matter of fact, one of the guy's hair turned stone gray. Because of the fear. He was just nineteen. He was a blond-headed kid when the sun went down, and when the sunlight came up, his hair was white.

We didn't find out they were monkeys until that morning.

That was about as crazy as the time we tryin' to take a shower in a monsoon rain. We had no shower for maybe ten days in the bush. We was standin' out there in the middle of a rice paddy, soapin' up. By the time all of us got soaped up, it stopped rainin'.

So we had to lay down and roll around in the rice paddy to get the soap off of us. We never did call that a shower. . . .

Today I'm constantly thinking about the war. I walk down streets different. I look at places where individuals could hide. Maybe assault me or rob me or just harass me. I hear things that other people can't hear. My wife, she had a habit at one time of buying cheap watches and leaving them on top of the dresser. I could hear it ticking, so she would put it in a drawer. I could still hear it ticking. And I dream of helicopters coming over my house, comin' to pick me up to take me to a fire fight. And when we get to the fire fight, they were dropping napalm on our own men. And I have to shoot our own soldiers to put them out of their misery. After my discharge, I lived off my unemployment until it ran out, which was about 18 months. Then I decided to go back to school. I went two years, and then I got involved in veterans affairs. I was noticing that in my city, which is 95 percent black, that there were a lot of black combat veterans coming back not able to find any employment because of bad discharges, or killing theirselves or dopin' up. We started the Wasted Men Project at the university, and I have been counseling at veterans centers ever since.

In 1982 I transferred to the Vet Center in Tucson because I wanted to do some research on the Buffalo Soldiers. In 'Nam I didn't know they were part of the original 9th Cav. These are black boys who had just received their freedom from the United States government, and they had to go to the West and suppress the freedom from another race of people who were the Indians. I think they won 13 or 14 Congressional Medals of Honor. But they were really policing other people, just like we were in Vietnam.

When my son, Ronnie, turned sixteen, I had him sit down and watch all thirteen hours of this film documentary about the Vietnam War so he could have an understanding of what war really was about. He had asked had I did any killing. I told him, "Yes. I had to do it. I had to do it to keep myself alive."

I wouldn't want him to go and fight an unpopular war like I did. I wouldn't want him to go down to El Salvador. And if that means that I would have to pick up me and my family baggage and move somewhere out of the country, then I would do that.

America should have won the war. But they wouldn't free us to fight. With all the American GIs that were in Vietnam, they could have put us all shoulder to shoulder and had us march from Saigon all the way up to the DMZ. Just make a sweep. We had enough GIs, enough equipment to do that.

When I came to Washington to see the Vietnam Veterans Memorial, I looked through the book and there were about 15 guys from my hometown who were killed. And six of them I knew.

But I looked up the memorial for James Plummer first.

Plummer was a black guy from Cincinnati. We were the same age. Twenty. We were at Camp Alpha together. That's where they assign you when you first come to 'Nam. I was in C Company, a line company. He was a truck driver, so he was in Headquarters Company, where they had all the heavy equipment.

I liked Plummer's style. He was just so easygoing. We'd sit down and just rap. Rap about music, the girls, what was happening in the world. Get high. Plummer was a John Coltrane fan. And I'm bein' a Miles Davis fan, we just automatically fell in with each other.

He was my best friend.

One day we were at the airfield at the LZ. Plummer was out of the truck, over by the ammo dump. And the ammo dump received a mortar round. It blew him up.

It freaked me out. I mean that here I saw him, and five minutes later he's instantaneously dead.

Me and two other guys ran and grabbed what we could. We pulled on the jungle fatigues, which was full of blood. It looked like maybe a dog after it crossed the street and got hit by a truck. His head was gone, both his legs from about the knee down were both gone. One arm was gone. The other was a stump left. We finally got his trunk together. The rest of it we really couldn't find, 'cause that one mortar round, it started the ammo dump to steady exploding. It constantly blew up for about an hour.

What we found was probably sent back to the States. They probably had a closed-casket funeral.

I kind of cried. I was sayin' to myself that this was such a waste because we weren't really doin' anything at the time. And him just being such a nice fella, why did he have to go this way? Go in pieces?

Everybody knew that me and him was tight, so a couple of guys took me up over to a bunker and we rapped about him all night. 'Cause we were out in the bush, I really couldn't get no booze. But when I did get back, I bought me a half gallon of gin, and I knocked it off. And that didn't make me feel any better.

When I got back, I called his mother. His mother knew me from him writing to her. I told her I was close by when he did get killed. I just told her a ammo dump blew up. I'm pretty sure she didn't have no idea what that was.

Every year I send her a Christmas card. I just sign my name.

When I saw Plummer on the memorial, I kind of cried again.

I guess deep down in my head now I can't really believe in God like I did because I can't really see why God would let something like this happen. Specially like to my friend Plummer. Why He would take such a good individual away from here.

Before I went to Vietnam, I was very active in the church, because of my mother's influence. She sent me a Bible, and I carried it in my pocket everywhere I went. When I couldn't find any *Playboy*s or something like that, I would read it. Matter of fact, I read it from cover to cover, starting from Genesis.

I guess I got kind of really unreligious because of my Vietnam experience. Oh, I went to church once in my uniform to please my mother. But I haven't been back since except for a funeral. I've talked to chaplains, talked to preachers about Vietnam. And no one could give me a satisfactory explanation of what happened overseas.

But each year since I've been back I have read the Bible from cover to cover. I keep looking for the explanation.

I can't find it. I can't find it.

RESPONDING IN DISCUSSION OR WRITING

1. Bryant says he thought the U.S. was "helping another country to develop a nation." Do you think most people in the armed services in wartime have idealistic motives?

2. What situations, if any, do you feel justify declaring war?

3. *Considerations of Style.* What features of this excerpt show that it is a transcribed oral account and not an edited literary piece? What are the advantages of reading oral histories?

4. What point does Bryant make about combat when he relates the first two incidents? What other points do you think he made in the rest of his story?

5. Bryant says he has turned away from religion because it cannot provide a satisfactory explanation of what happened in the war. Do you think it is the job of a religion to offer rational explanations? Why or why not?

WRITING ASSIGNMENTS

1. Describe and explain your belief system in relation to human life. Discuss one of the following issues: abortion, capital punishment, euthanasia, assisted suicide.

2. Write an essay in which you discuss what circumstances would justify going to war and killing other people. Can a decision to go to war be compatible with a belief in the sanctity of human life?

❖

THE MAN TO SEND RAIN CLOUDS

LESLIE MARMON SILKO

A Native American writer, Leslie Marmon Silko, born in 1948, was raised on the Laguna Pueblo Reservation in New Mexico. She writes fiction and poetry and is the author of Ceremony *(1977), which won an American Book Award in 1980,* Almanac of the Dead *(1991), and* Yellow Woman *(1993). This story shows the conflict between Native American and Christian cultural ceremonies. It was first published in 1974 in an anthology of short stories called* The Man to Send Rain Clouds.

THEY FOUND HIM UNDER a big cottonwood tree. His Levi jacket and pants were faded light blue so that he had been easy to find. The big cottonwood tree stood apart from a small grove of winterbare cottonwoods which grew in the wide, sandy arroyo. He had been dead for a day or more, and the sheep had wandered and scattered up and down the arroyo. Leon and his brother-in-law, Ken, gathered the sheep and left them in the pen at the sheep camp before they returned to the cottonwood tree. Leon waited under the tree while Ken drove the truck through the deep sand to the edge of the arroyo. He squinted up at the sun and unzipped his jacket—it sure was hot for this time of year. But high and northwest the blue mountains were still in snow. Ken came sliding down the low, crumbling bank about fifty yards down, and he was bringing the red blanket.

Before they wrapped the old man, Leon took a piece of string out of his pocket and tied a small gray feather in the old man's long white hair. Ken gave him the paint. Across the brown wrinkled forehead he drew a streak of white and along the high cheekbones he drew a strip of blue paint. He paused and watched Ken throw pinches of corn meal and pollen into the wind that fluttered the small gray feather. Then Leon painted with yellow under the old man's broad nose, and finally, when he had painted green across the chin, he smiled.

"Send us rain clouds, Grandfather." They laid the bundle in the back of the pickup and covered it with a heavy tarp before they started back to the pueblo.

They turned off the highway onto the sandy pueblo road. Not long after they passed the store and post office they saw Father Paul's car coming toward them. When he recognized their faces he slowed his car and waved for them to stop. The young priest rolled down the car window.

"Did you find old Teofilo?" he asked loudly.

Leon stopped the truck. "Good morning, Father. We were just out to the sheep camp. Everything is O.K. now."

"Thank God for that. Teofilo is a very old man. You really shouldn't allow him to stay at the sheep camp alone."

"No, he won't do that any more now."

"Well, I'm glad you understand. I hope I'll be seeing you at Mass this week—we missed you last Sunday. See if you can get old Teofilo to come with you." The priest smiled and waved at them as they drove away.

Louise and Teresa were waiting. The table was set for lunch, and   10
the coffee was boiling on the black iron stove. Leon looked at
Louise and then at Teresa.

"We found him under a cottonwood tree in the big arroyo near
sheep camp. I guess he sat down to rest in the shade and never
got up again." Leon walked toward the old man's bed. The red
plaid shawl had been shaken and spread carefully over the bed,
and a new brown flannel shirt and pair of stiff new Levi's were
arranged neatly beside the pillow. Louise held the screen door
open while Leon and Ken carried in the red blanket. He looked
small and shriveled, and after they dressed him in the new shirt
and pants he seemed more shrunken.

It was noontime now because the church bells rang the
Angelus. They ate the beans with hot bread, and nobody said anything until after Teresa poured the coffee.

Ken stood up and put on his jacket. "I'll see about the gravediggers. Only the top layer of soil is frozen. I think it can be ready
before dark."

Leon nodded his head and finished his coffee. After Ken had
been gone for a while, the neighbors and clanspeople came quietly to embrace Teofilo's family and to leave food on the table
because the gravediggers would come to eat when they were
finished.

The sky in the west was full of pale yellow light. Louise stood out-   15
side with her hands in the pockets of Leon's green army jacket
that was too big for her. The funeral was over, and the old men
had taken their candles and medicine bags and were gone. She
waited until the body was laid into the pickup before she said anything to Leon. She touched his arm, and he noticed that her
hands were still dusty from the corn meal that she had sprinkled
around the old man. When she spoke, Leon could not hear her.

"What did you say? I didn't hear you."

"I said that I had been thinking about something."

"About what?"

"About the priest sprinkling holy water for Grandpa. So he
won't be thirsty."

Leon stared at the new moccasins that Teofilo had made for   20
the ceremonial dances in the summer. They were nearly hidden

by the red blanket. It was getting colder, and the wind pushed gray dust down the narrow pueblo road. The sun was approaching the long mesa where it disappeared during the winter. Louise stood there shivering and watching his face. Then he zipped up his jacket and opened the truck door. "I'll see if he's there."

Ken stopped the pickup at the church, and Leon got out; and then Ken drove down the hill to the graveyard where people were waiting. Leon knocked at the old carved door with its symbols of the Lamb. While he waited he looked up at the twin bells from the king of Spain with the last sunlight pouring around them in their tower.

The priest opened the door and smiled when he saw who it was. "Come in! What brings you here this evening?"

The priest walked toward the kitchen, and Leon stood with his cap in his hand, playing with the earflaps and examining the living room—the brown sofa, the green armchair, and the brass lamp that hung down from the ceiling by links of chain. The priest dragged a chair out of the kitchen and offered it to Leon.

"No thank you, Father. I only came to ask you if you would bring your holy water to the graveyard."

The priest turned away from Leon and looked out the window at the patio full of shadows and the dining-room windows of the nuns' cloister across the patio. The curtains were heavy, and the light from within faintly penetrated; it was impossible to see the nuns inside eating supper. "Why didn't you tell me he was dead? I could have brought the Last Rites anyway."

Leon smiled. "It wasn't necessary, Father."

The priest stared down at his scuffed brown loafers and the worn hem of his cassock. "For a Christian burial it was necessary."

His voice was distant, and Leon thought that his blue eyes looked tired.

"It's O.K. Father, we just want him to have plenty of water."

The priest sank down into the green chair and picked up a glossy missionary magazine. He turned the colored pages full of lepers and pagans without looking at them.

"You know I can't do that, Leon. There should have been the Last Rites and a funeral Mass at the very least."

Leon put on his green cap and pulled the flaps down over his ears. "It's getting late, Father. I've got to go."

When Leon opened the door Father Paul stood up and said, "Wait." He left the room and came back wearing a long brown overcoat. He followed Leon out the door and across the dim churchyard to the adobe steps in front of the church. They both stopped to fit through the low adobe entrance. And when they started down the hill to the graveyard only half of the sun was visible above the mesa.

The priest approached the grave slowly, wondering how they had managed to dig into the frozen ground; and then he remembered that this was New Mexico, and saw the pile of cold loose sand beside the hole. The people stood close to each other with little clouds of steam puffing from their faces. The priest looked at them and saw a pile of jackets, gloves, and scarves in the yellow, dry tumbleweeds that grew in the graveyard. He looked at the red blanket, not sure that Teofilo was so small, wondering if it wasn't some perverse Indian trick—something they did in March to ensure a good harvest—wondering if maybe old Teofilo was actually at sheep camp corralling the sheep for the night. But there he was, facing into a cold dry wind and squinting at the last sunlight, ready to bury a red wool blanket while the faces of his parishioners were in shadow with the last warmth of the sun on their backs.

His fingers were stiff, and it took him a long time to twist the lid off the holy water. Drops of water fell on the red blanket and soaked into dark icy spots. He sprinkled the grave and the water disappeared almost before it touched the dim, cold sand; it reminded him of something—he tried to remember what it was, because he thought if he could remember he might understand this. He sprinkled more water; he shook the container until it was empty, and the water fell through the light from sundown like August rain that fell while the sun was still shining, almost evaporating before it touched the wilted squash flowers.

The wind pulled at the priest's brown Franciscan robe and swirled away the corn meal and pollen that had been sprinkled on the blanket. They lowered the bundle into the ground, and they didn't bother to untie the stiff pieces of new rope that were tied around the ends of the blanket. The sun was gone, and over on the highway the eastbound lane was full of headlights. The priest walked away slowly. Leon watched him climb the hill, and when he had disappeared within the tall, thick walls, Leon turned to look up at the high blue mountains in the deep snow that reflected a faint red light from the west. He felt good because it was finished, and he was happy about the sprinkling of the holy water; now the old man could send them big thunderclouds for sure.

RESPONDING IN DISCUSSION OR WRITING

1. *Considerations of Style.* Silko begins her story talking about *he* and *him*. At what point does the reader learn who *he* is? Why do you think Silko does not begin with the identification?

2. Note when mention is made of the red blanket. What would you say its significance is?

3. List the parts of the story where Native American and Christian rituals differ. Do you find that any of these rituals overlap?

4. Leon and Ken do not tell Father Paul about Teofilo's death right away. Why do you think they withhold the information? How does Father Paul react when he finds out?

5. At first Father Paul refuses to sprinkle holy water. Then he does so. What do you think makes him change his mind? How does Leon interpret the ceremony?

WRITING ASSIGNMENTS

1. Discuss in what ways people can incorporate rituals into their behavior without accepting the culture that prescribes those rituals. What purposes do the rituals serve? Can they be separated from the culture's beliefs?

2. Analyze the ways in which the story describes the Christian and the Native American ways of life. Which words and thoughts, characters, descriptions, and events reflect the two different cultures?

❖

PRAYER FOR THE GREAT FAMILY

GARY SNYDER

Gary Snyder, born in 1930, is a poet, environmentalist, and philosopher who lives in the Sierra Nevada Mountains. He won the Pulitzer Prize for Poetry in 1975 for Turtle Island, *from which the following poem is taken. The protection of the environment has increasingly become a theme in his work. His most recent books are* The Practice of the Wild *(1990) and* No Nature: New and Selected Poems *(1992).*

Gratitude to Mother Earth, sailing through night and day—
    and to her soil: rich, rare, and sweet
        in our minds so be it.

Gratitude to Plants, the sun-facing light-changing leaf
    and fine root-hairs; standing still through wind   5
    and rain; their dance is in the flowing spiral grain
        in our minds so be it.

Gratitude to Air, bearing the soaring Swift and the silent
    Owl at dawn. Breath of our song
    clear spirit breeze   10
        in our minds so be it.

Gratitude to Wild Beings, our brothers, teaching secrets,
    freedoms, and ways; who share with us their milk;
    self-complete, brave, and aware
        in our minds so be it.   15

Gratitude to Water: clouds, lakes, rivers, glaciers;
    holding or releasing; streaming through all
    our bodies salty seas
        in our minds so be it.

Gratitude to the Sun: blinding pulsing light through   20
    trunks of trees, through mists, warming caves where
    bears and snakes sleep—he who wakes us—
        in our minds so be it.

Gratitude to the Great Sky
    who holds billions of stars—and goes yet beyond that—   25
    beyond all powers, and thoughts
    and yet is within us—
    Grandfather Space.
    The Mind is his Wife.

    so be it.   30
        after a Mohawk prayer

RESPONDING IN DISCUSSION OR WRITING

1. What is the effect of the refrain on the reader? And what is the impact of the change in the refrain at the end of the poem?

2. *Considerations of Style.*   How important are the typographical formats, such as the indentations and the italics, to the poem's meaning? How would the impact change if there were no indentations or italics?

3. Consider the relationship between the *Family* of the title and each stanza. What family is Snyder concerned with in this poem?

4. *Considerations of Style.*   What descriptive words about the poem's tone come to mind as you read it?

5. The poem was modeled after a Mohawk prayer. What features of a prayer does it retain?

WRITING ASSIGNMENTS

1. Write a poem or a prose poem in which you take a cynical and pessimistic view of the world, pointing out faults and human foibles.

2. *For Further Research.*   Snyder's concern for the environment comes across in this poem. What two environmental issues do you feel are the most important ones facing us today? Do further research to explore the topic, and write an essay describing the issues and what can be done about them.

Making Connections: Beliefs and Religion

❖

1. The issue of our attitude to death goes hand in hand with the issue of euthanasia. Explain your position on the moral issues involved in euthanasia, determining that someone should die rather than continue to suffer without hope of recovery.

2. At the beginning of his essay, Gould mentions the 1925 Scopes trial. Do research to find out about the trial. Write a speech that you would make either for Darrow's or Bryan's position in the trial.

3. See the film *Inherit the Wind* and write about the connections you see with the arguments Gould makes in his essay.

4. In paragraph 14 of her essay, Trillin discusses Ernest Becker's statement that skepticism is "a more manly confrontation of potential meaninglessness than mysticism." Discuss what this means in the light of what Trillin says about sickness and death. Where do you stand when you consider Becker's views as expressed in paragraph 14?

5. Discuss your reactions to the idea of religious instruction and prayer being a mandated part of a school curriculum.

6. Use the library to find out about one of the following religions that is new to you: Judaism, Hinduism, Quakerism, Shakerism, Islam, Buddhism, Shintoism, Episcopalianism, Methodism, the Baptist religion, Mormonism, Mennonitism, the religion of the Jehovah's Witnesses, or the Nuer religion in the Sudan. Write a companion piece to Quindlen's "I Am a Catholic" with a title such as "I Am an Orthodox Jew," "I Am a Mennonite," and so on. Write it in the first person, describing the religion for your readers. Comment on how the religion differs from other religions you know, and describe how the religion perceives sickness and death.

7. The last two selections in this unit address Native American rituals and prayers. What commonalities do you find in these selections?

8. Do research to find out about one species of wildlife whose existence is being threatened by human beings as they "develop" the land and the waterways. How important is it to you that the environment be protected? What informs your beliefs and opinions on this issue?

9. Read three articles on the Vietnam War, one written during the involvement of the United States in the war (1961–1973), one at the end (1968–1975), and one in 1995. Compare the perspectives in the articles, and relate the waging of the war to beliefs in principles.

10. Compare Bryant's depiction of the Vietnam War to the depiction in Louise Erdrich's short story in Unit 2. Which account has a more powerful effect on the reader, the nonfictional or the fictional? Discuss your reasons for answering the way you do.

Nationality

A nation is the same people living in the same place.

—JAMES JOYCE, Ulysses, *chapter 12, 1922*

I do not call the sod under my feet my country; but language—religion—government—blood—identity in these makes men of one country.

—SAMUEL TAYLOR COLERIDGE, Table Talk, *1830*

Nationality

❖

THE UNITS OF THIS book have collected readings on facets of identity, parts of our lives that contribute to the total picture of who we are at various times in our lives, in various contexts. These components of identity—name, appearance, gender, ethnic affiliation, family ties, education, and beliefs—are fluid, not fixed, and when associated with nationality, they can be intertwined or even in conflict with each other.

In some parts of the world, a reference to nationality would imply homogeneity—people with the same race, color, and ethnic affiliation and people with similar names, appearance, and values. In a multicultural society, though, the multiplicity of cultures occurs across divisions of society and within each individual. In such a society, diversity and not homogeneity holds sway, within individuals and across groups. To say, "I am American," or "I am a Canadian," for instance, means many different things to different people.

In America, some of the questions frequently raised that address the issue of nationality include the following: Are there uniquely American ideals that hold this country together despite the many contradictions in our society? How are those ideals different from, say, those of Canada or Mexico? What are the factors that affect a collective sense of a national identity? Is there, in fact, a collective sense of national identity?

Mary Antin, who wrote *The Promised Land* (1912), describes leaving Russia and settling in 1894 in the environs of Boston. The beginning of her moving autobiography addresses the issues of immigration, nationality, and identity in a concise way:

I was born, I have lived, and I have been made over. Is it not time to write my life's story? I am just as much out of the way as if I were dead,

463

for I am absolutely other than the person whose story I have to tell. Physical continuity with my earlier self is no disadvantage. I could speak in the third person and not feel that I was masquerading. I can analyze my subject, I can reveal everything; for *she,* and not *I,* is my real heroine. My life I have still to live; her life ended when mine began.

New beginnings and new identities are not uncommon in North America. Historian Perry Miller (1905–1963) succinctly sums up how nationality relates to identity when he says that "being an American is not something to be inherited so much as something to be achieved."

The readings in this unit look at the complicated issue of nationality, what it means, and how much we ourselves determine what it means. The unit begins with facts and figures taken from the census that describe what might be a "typical" American. Horace Miner presents a broader, anthropological study of culture, the ties that bind people, and the beliefs and practices that are shared. A senior citizen student, Helen Skoratowicz, presents a series of vignettes of what it means to be American. Ishmael Reed and Andy Warhol bring different perspectives to bear on the issue of nationality: Reed discusses diversity, and Warhol takes a humorous look at equality.

Since the American continent is so vast and varied, and since being American is so often intimately connected with belonging to a specific region or a part of the country, a sense of place often figures largely in how we shape our identity. David Lamb describes how a sense of place helps define us and our feelings of belonging, and William Least Heat Moon illustrates this sense of place by describing a place he visited and liked in Georgia. Contrasting the comfort of a firm sense of one's own place with the fact of homelessness, Sonia Sanchez's short story shows us women without a place to attach their identity to, with no place to call their own. The unit—and the readings—conclude with a poem by Maya Angelou that fittingly extends the notion of identity from belonging to a nation to the idea of belonging to one human family.

STARTING POINTS [FOR JOURNAL OR FREEWRITING]

Before you read the selections, respond to the following questions.

1. How important is your nationality to your own feelings of identity? Consider the relationship between your nationality and your name, appearance, gender, ethnic affiliation, family, education, and beliefs. Is the relationship always a harmonious one? Does conflict ever arise?

2. People often talk about "the American dream." What is it? Is it only a dream? Is it ever a nightmare? Does it ever become reality?

3. What two things would you pick out as the best and the worst features of the country of which you are a citizen?

4. How much does the actual place where we live contribute to our feelings about our nation and our nationality?

❖

A TYPICAL AMERICAN AS SEEN THROUGH THE EYES OF THE CENSUS BUREAU

HARRY A. SCARR

This essay was written by Dr. Harry A. Scarr, Deputy Director of the Bureau of the Census. Scarr, who was born in 1934, bases his conclusions on data collected for the 1990 census. The essay appeared in The World Almanac 1995.

I AM OFTEN ASKED to describe a typical American: What do we do? Where do we live? How much money do we make? According to Census Bureau data, typical America is a patchwork of cultures, lifestyles, and economic groups. Let's look at that typical American and at some not-so-typical Americans.

Who We Are

Typical America is composed of many racial and ethnic groups. On April 1, 1994, almost 26 million of us (9.9%) were of Hispanic origin, and more than 9 million of us (3.5%) identified ourselves as Asian-Pacific Islanders. Blacks numbered 32.5 million, or 12.5% of the population, and the American Indian/Eskimo/Aleut populations made up about 2.2 million (0.8%). An estimated 192.5 million people (74.1%) considered themselves to be white non-Hispanic.

According to the 1990 Census, nearly 20 million of us were not born in America, but call it home. In 1993, about 33% of our population growth came from net international migration.

America speaks many *languages:* More than 31 million of us speak a language other than English at home; more than half this number speaks Spanish.

We are also aging: since 1980 our *median age* has risen from 30.0   5
to 34.0 in 1994 (the median for blacks is 28.9, and the median for whites is 35.0). More than 26% of us are under 18 years of age, and more than 12.7% are 65 and older.

Females outnumber males in America by 6.1 million; 51% of the total population was female, as of April 1, 1994.

There were 96.4 million *households* in our nation in March 1993; 70% of them contained families. Of all households, 55% are maintained by married couples, and 74% of all households with children under 18 include a married couple. In about one-fourth of all households, one person lives alone.

What We Do

About 66% of Americans 16 years and older were in the labor force in 1993: almost 76% of men and nearly 58% of women. The unemployment rate was 6.7%.

Our top three *occupations* are administrative support, including clerical; professional specialty; and executive, administrative, and managerial. There are 20.2 million persons employed in the retail sales industry.

More than 8 million working-age Americans are prevented   10
from working because of a disability, but 16 million persons with a disability work at a job or business.

Of the more than 115.1 million employed workers, 73.2% drive to work alone, and 13.4% are in car pools. About 76.1% of us work in the county in which we live, and our *commuting time* averages about 22.4 minutes (one way).

Where We Live

At least half of our population (56.4%) lives in the South and West regions of the country. Between 1980 and 1990, the West grew by 22.3%, and the South grew by 13.4%, well above the U.S. average of 9.8%. From 1990 to 1993, the trend continued (West, 6.2%; South, 4.7%; U.S. 3.7%).

Since 1990, we have been increasing by about 2.8 million persons a year. Our 5 most populous states are California (31.2 million), New York (18.2 million), Texas (18.0 million), Florida (13.7 million), and Pennsylvania (12 million). The 5 states at the other end of the spectrum are Delaware (700,000), North Dakota (635,000), Alaska (599,000), Vermont (576,000), and Wyoming (470,000).

Most of us—79.5%—live in *metropolitan areas,* and more than half of us (53.7%) live in one of the 41 metropolitan areas with populations of at least 1 million.

Our 5 largest metropolitan areas are scattered across the map: New York/Northern New Jersey/Long Island (19.7 million), Los Angeles/Riverside/Orange County (15.0 million), Chicago/Gary/Kenosha Counties (8.4 million), Washington/Baltimore (6.9 million), and San Francisco/Oakland/San Jose (6.4 million). Although the New York area remains in first position, the Los Angeles area is growing at a much faster rate (3.6 versus 0.6% since 1990).

How We Live

Typical Americans live in a household with others. The average number of people living in a household in the U.S. was 2.63 in 1993.

We have a total of about 105 million *housing units* nationwide; nearly 93 million of them are occupied. The vast majority of housing units have public water and sewer service, and our top 2 house heating fuel sources are utility gas (51 million units) and electricity (27 million units). About 3 million units lack complete plumbing facilities, and 4 million lack complete kitchen facilities.

Almost two-thirds (64%) of us are *homeowners.* Of the 60 million owner units, nearly 35 million have mortgages. The median monthly costs for all owner units is $455. The median for mortgage units is $761, and the median for non-mortgage units is $222. The median value of owner homes is $80,000.

If you live in one of the 33 million *renter-occupied housing units,* your housing costs are $462 per month.

Quality of Life

Education: Typical America has more high school graduates than at any other time in U.S. history: more than 80.2% of all Americans age 25 and older. About 21.9% of this same group have a bachelor's degree or higher. [20]

Educational attainment has a direct impact on many aspects of life, but most directly on earnings. Average annual earnings for persons without a high school diploma are $14,391; with a diploma, $20,036; with a bachelor's degree, $34,096; with a doctorate, $54,982; and with a professional degree, $74,725. We spend an average of $4,700 annually per student in our public elementary and secondary schools.

Health insurance: Nearly 85% of us have health insurance. Those most likely to be insured are the elderly, the employed, and those with at least a high school diploma.

Poverty: In 1992, 36.9 million persons had income below the official government poverty level, up from 35.7 million in 1991 and 31.5 million in 1989. The 1992 poverty rate was 14.5%—not statistically different from the 1991 poverty rate of 14.2%, but different from the 1989 rate of 12.8%.

Child care: Families with working mothers and preschool children spend about 7% of their family income on child care for their children. Most care for preschoolers takes place in a home environment, such as with relatives or neighbors (67%); about 23% of child care for preschoolers is in organized facilities, such as nursery schools and day-care centers; 9% are cared for by the mother while she works; and 1% are in a school-based activity.

Child support: Of the 5.7 million women awarded child support, 5.0 million were supposed to receive payments in 1989. Of the women due payments, about half received the full amount they were due. The average amount of child support received in 1989 was $2,995. The aggregate amount of child support received in 1989 was $11.2 billion, 69% of $16.3 billion due. [25]

RESPONDING IN DISCUSSION OR WRITING

1. Scarr's essay ends without a conclusion. What would you write in a concluding paragraph for this essay?

2. Scarr states in paragraph 1 that he sees typical America as "a patchwork of cultures, lifestyles, and economic groups." Does he provide evidence for that statement in his essay? Where? How well do his details support his thesis?

3. Do any of the figures in the essay surprise you? If so, which ones? Why are they surprising?

4. How useful is it to collect census data every ten years? How are the data useful?

5. What questions would you like Dr. Scarr to find the answers to? Why do you think these questions are important?

6. This essay is filled with figures and data. Do you see any problems in drawing conclusions about a typical person from data collected from so many people? What might the problems be?

WRITING ASSIGNMENTS

1. Basing your conclusions on people you have met and your own experience, write an essay describing what you regard as a "typical American." Consider whether you know anyone you could describe as a "typical" American. What makes that person typical? Use descriptions of individuals rather than facts and figures gathered from surveys. That is, base your analysis on observation rather than numbers. Support your conclusions with individual examples.

2. Scarr includes five headings in his section "Quality of Life." Do these five headings adequately cover the topic? A previous version of this article included ten headings, including also "Assets," "Pensions," "Assistance," "Voting," "Federal Aid" and "Lotteries." Discuss whether you think the most recent classification works, and if you don't think it does, which other categories would you like to see included? Discuss what issues you regard as important for their contribution to the quality of life.

❖

BODY RITUAL AMONG THE NACIREMA

HORACE MINER

Horace Miner, who was born in 1912, was professor of sociology and anthropology at the University of Michigan. He died in 1993. Much of his research and writing was devoted to the cultures of West and Central Africa. This article was published in The American Anthropologist *in 1956. For this professional journal, Miner writes an academic documented paper, citing date and page numbers of his sources in his text and attaching a complete bibliographical list of the references cited.*

THE ANTHROPOLOGIST HAS BECOME so familiar with the diversity of ways in which different peoples behave in similar situations that he is not apt to be surprised by even the most exotic customs. In fact, if all of the logically possible combinations of behavior have not been found somewhere in the world, he is apt to suspect that they must be present in some yet undescribed tribe. This point has, in fact, been expressed with respect to clan organization by Murdock (1949:71). In this light, the magical beliefs and practices of the Nacirema present such unusual aspects that it seems desirable to describe them as an example of the extremes to which human behavior can go.

Professor Linton first brought the ritual of the Nacirema to the attention of anthropologists twenty years ago (1936:326), but the culture of this people is still very poorly understood. They are a North American group living in the territory between the Canadian Cree, the Yaqui and Tarahumare of Mexico, and the Carib and Arawak of the Antilles. Little is known of their origin, although tradition states that they came from the east. According to Nacirema mythology, their nation was originated by a culture hero, Notgnihsaw, who is otherwise known for two great feats of strength—the throwing of a piece of wampum across the river Pa-To-Mac and the chopping down of a cherry tree in which the Spirit of Truth resided.

Nacirema culture is characterized by a highly developed market economy which has evolved in a rich natural habitat. While much of the people's time is devoted to economic pursuits, a large part of the fruits of these labors and a considerable portion of the day are spent in ritual activity. The focus of this activity is the human body, the appearance and health of which loom as a dominant concern in the ethos of the people. While such a concern is certainly not unusual, its ceremonial aspects and associated philosophy are unique.

The fundamental belief underlying the whole system appears to be that the human body is ugly and that its natural tendency is to debility and disease. Incarcerated in such a body, man's only hope is to avert these characteristics through the use of the powerful influences of ritual and ceremony. Every household has one or more shrines devoted to this purpose. The more powerful individuals in the society have several shrines in their houses and, in fact, the opulence of a house is often referred to in terms of the number of such ritual centers it possesses. Most houses are of wattle and daub construction, but the shrine rooms of the more wealthy are walled with stone. Poorer families imitate the rich by applying pottery plaques to their shrine walls.

While each family has at least one such shrine, the rituals associated with it are not family ceremonies but are private and secret. The rites are normally only discussed with children, and then only during the period when they are being initiated into these mysteries. I was able, however, to establish sufficient rapport with the natives to examine these shrines and to have the rituals described to me.

The focal point of the shrine is a box or chest which is built into the wall. In this chest are kept the many charms and magical potions without which no native believes he could live. These preparations are secured from a variety of specialized practitioners. The most powerful of these are the medicine men, whose assistance must be rewarded with substantial gifts. However, the medicine men do not provide the curative potions for their clients, but decide what the ingredients should be and then write them down in an ancient and secret language. This writing is understood only by the medicine men and by the herbalists who, for another gift, provide the required charm.

The charm is not disposed of after it has served its purpose, but is placed in the charm-box of the household shrine. As these magical materials are specific for certain ills, and the real or imagined maladies of the people are many, the charm-box is usually full to overflowing. The magical packets are so numerous that people forget what their purposes were and fear to use them again. While the natives are very vague on this point, we can only assume that the idea in retaining all the old magical materials is that their presence in the charm-box, before which the body rituals are conducted, will in some way protect the worshipper.

Beneath the charm-box is a small font. Each day every member of the family, in succession, enters the shrine room, bows his head before the charm-box, mingles different sorts of holy water in the font, and proceeds with a brief rite of ablution. The holy waters are secured from the Water Temple of the community, where the priests conduct elaborate ceremonies to make the liquid ritually pure.

In the hierarchy of magical practitioners, and below the medicine men in prestige, are specialists whose designation is best translated "holy-mouth-men." The Nacirema have an almost pathological horror of and fascination with the mouth, the condition of which is believed to have a supernatural influence on all social relationships. Were it not for the rituals of the mouth, they believe that their teeth would fall out, their gums bleed, their jaws shrink, their friends desert them, and their lovers reject them. They also believe that a strong relationship exists between oral and moral characteristics. For example, there is a ritual ablution of the mouth for children which is supposed to improve their moral fiber.

The daily body ritual performed by everyone includes a mouth-rite. Despite the fact that these people are so punctilious about care of the mouth, this rite involves a practice which strikes the uninitiated stranger as revolting. It was reported to me that the ritual consists of inserting a small bundle of hog hairs into the mouth, along with certain magical powders, and then moving the bundle in a highly formalized series of gestures.

In addition to the private mouth-rite, the people seek out a holy-mouth-man once or twice a year. These practitioners have an impressive set of paraphernalia, consisting of a variety of augers, awls, probes, and prods. The use of these objects in the exorcism of the evils of the mouth involves almost unbelievable ritual torture of the client. The holy-mouth-man opens the client's mouth and, using the above mentioned tools, enlarges any holes which decay may have created in the teeth. Magical materials are put into these holes. If there are no naturally occurring holes in the teeth, large sections of one or more teeth are gouged out so that the supernatural substance can be applied. In the client's view, the purpose of these ministrations is to arrest decay and to draw friends. The extremely sacred and traditional character of the rite is evident in the fact that the natives return to the holy-mouth-men year after year, despite the fact that their teeth continue to decay.

It is to be hoped that, when a thorough study of the Nacirema is made, there will be careful inquiry into the personality structure of these people. One has but to watch the gleam in the eye of a holy-mouth-man, as he jabs an awl into an exposed nerve, to suspect that a certain amount of sadism is involved. If this can be established, a very interesting pattern emerges, for most of the population shows definite masochistic tendencies. It was to these that Professor Linton referred in discussing a distinctive part of the daily body ritual which is performed only by men. This part of the rite involves scraping and lacerating the surface of the face with a sharp instrument. Special women's rites are performed only four times during each lunar month, but what they lack in frequency is made up in barbarity. As part of this ceremony, women bake their heads in small ovens for about an hour. The theoretically interesting point is that what seems to be a preponderantly masochistic people have developed sadistic specialists.

The medicine men have an imposing temple, or *latipso,* in every community of any size. The more elaborate ceremonies required to treat very sick patients can only be performed at this temple. These ceremonies involve not only the thaumaturge but a permanent group of vestal maidens who move sedately about the temple chambers in distinctive costume and headdress.

The *latipso* ceremonies are so harsh that it is phenomenal that a fair proportion of the really sick natives who enter the temple ever recover. Small children whose indoctrination is still incomplete have been known to resist attempts to take them to the temple because "that is where you go to die." Despite this fact, sick adults are not only willing but eager to undergo the protracted ritual purification, if they can afford to do so. No matter how ill the supplicant or how grave the emergency, the guardians of many temples will not admit a client if he cannot give a rich gift to the custodian. Even after one has gained admission and survived the ceremonies, the guardians will not permit the neophyte to leave until he makes still another gift.

The supplicant entering the temple is first stripped of all his or her clothes. In every-day life the Nacirema avoids exposure of his body and its natural functions. Bathing and excretory acts are performed only in the secrecy of the household shrine, where they are ritualized as part of the body-rites. Psychological shock results from the fact that body secrecy is suddenly lost upon entry into the *latipso*. A man, whose own wife has never seen him in an excretory act, suddenly finds himself naked and assisted by a vestal maiden while he performs his natural functions into a sacred vessel. This sort of ceremonial treatment is necessitated by the fact that the excreta are used by a diviner to ascertain the course and nature of the client's sickness. Female clients, on the other hand, find their naked bodies are subjected to the scrutiny, manipulation and prodding of the medicine men.

Few supplicants in the temple are well enough to do anything but lie on their hard beds. The daily ceremonies, like the rites of the holy-mouth-men, involve discomfort and torture. With ritual precision, the vestals awaken their miserable charges each dawn and roll them about on their beds of pain while performing ablutions, in the formal movements of which the maidens are highly trained. At other times they insert magic wands in the supplicant's mouth or force him to eat substances which are supposed to be healing. From time to time the medicine men come to their clients and jab magically treated needles into their flesh. The fact that these temple ceremonies may not cure, and may even kill the neophyte, in no way decreases the people's faith in the medicine men.

There remains one other kind of practitioner, known as a "listener." This witch-doctor has the power to exorcise the devils that lodge in the heads of people who have been bewitched. The Nacirema believe that parents bewitch their own children. Mothers are particularly suspected of putting a curse on children while teaching them the secret body rituals. The counter-magic of the witch-doctor is unusual in its lack of ritual. The patient simply tells the "listener" all his troubles and fears, beginning with the earliest difficulties he can remember. The memory displayed by the Nacirema in these exorcism sessions is truly remarkable. It is not uncommon for the patient to bemoan the rejection he felt upon being weaned as a babe, and a few individuals even see their troubles going back to the traumatic effects of their own birth.

In conclusion, mention must be made of certain practices which have their base in native esthetics but which depend upon the pervasive aversion to the natural body and its functions. There are ritual fasts to make fat people thin and ceremonial feasts to make thin people fat. Still other rites are used to make women's breasts larger if they are small, and smaller if they are large. General dissatisfaction with breast shape is symbolized in the fact that the ideal form is virtually outside the range of human variation. A few women afflicted with almost inhuman hypermammary development are so idolized that they make a handsome living by simply going from village to village and permitting the natives to stare at them for a fee.

Reference has already been made to the fact that excretory functions are ritualized, routinized, and relegated to secrecy. Natural reproductive functions are similarly distorted. Intercourse is taboo as a topic and scheduled as an act. Efforts are made to avoid pregnancy by the use of magical materials or by limiting intercourse to certain phases of the moon. Conception is actually very infrequent. When pregnant, women dress so as to hide their condition. Parturition takes place in secret, without friends or relatives to assist, and the majority of women do not nurse their infants.

Our review of the ritual life of the Nacirema has certainly shown them to be a magic-ridden people. It is hard to understand how they have managed to exist so long under the burdens which they have imposed upon themselves. But even such exotic customs as these take on real meaning when they are viewed with the insight provided by Malinowski when he wrote (1948:70):

> Looking from far and above, from our high places of safety in the developed civilization, it is easy to see all the crudity and irrelevance of magic. But without its power and guidance early man could not have mastered his practical difficulties as he has done, nor could man have advanced to the higher stages of civilization.

References

Linton, Ralph. 1936. *The Study of Man.* New York, D. Appleton-Century Co.

Malinowski, Bronislaw. 1948. *Magic, Science, and Religion.* Glencoe, The Free Press.

Murdock, George P. 1949. *Social Structure.* New York, The Macmillan Co.

RESPONDING IN DISCUSSION OR WRITING

1. What kind of people do you think the Nacirema are? Would you like to live among them? Why or why not?

2. What inferences can you make about other habits of the Nacirema, for instance, what they wear and eat, how they organize a household and family life, and how they spend their time?

3. Which custom of the Nacirema do you find (a) the most interesting and (b) the most repellent? Why?

4. Examine some of Miner's words: Nacirema (paragraph 1); Notgnihsaw (paragraph 2); *latipso* (paragraph 13). Read them backward. Does this create any change in the way you read Miner's article?

5. At what point did you discover that Miner is writing about Americans? (Of course, if you had read all these questions first, you would have known from the beginning.) Given that fact, reread the article and make a list in which you relate each name, fact, and ceremony to the rituals of everyday life. Which parts of the article now become humorous?

6. *Considerations of Style.* How does Miner manage to preserve the illusion of a serious academic article? What techniques does he use? What audience does the author envision for this article?

WRITING ASSIGNMENTS

1. Write a parallel article in the form of a parody about some other rituals of the Nacirema, for example, education and attending school, playing and/or watching a sport, listening to music and dancing, playing music and singing, shopping, or watching television.

2. Describe the picture Miner paints of his subjects and discuss in which ways you think the picture is accurate, exaggerated, or inaccurate. What do you think Miner's purpose in this essay is? Is it just to be humorous, or does he have an anthropological purpose

in mind?

❖

WHAT IT MEANS TO BE AMERICAN

HELEN SKORATOWICZ

Helen Skoratowicz, whose parents were immigrants from Poland, is from New Jersey and worked for many years as a buyer for the department store Henri Bendel. It was not until she retired in 1990 that she found the time to attend college full time. She is a senior citizen working toward her degree in studio art. She wrote this essay, previously unpublished, in 1994, in one of her first courses, a first-year writing class.

AFTER ENJOYING A PERFORMANCE of Puccini's opera *La Bohème,* the friends I was with commented that the tenor was "too American." Oh? This implies that there are degrees of being American—or any other nationality. When I asked what the comment meant, I was told the tenor did not have the tall, dark, handsome looks of an Italian, nor was he emotional enough for the role of Rodolfo. The response was thought-provoking for me, but I did not argue. Every performer can give only an interpretation of the character portrayed. I suggested that if this same performance took place in Italy, and we had no knowledge that the tenor was American, we might simply accept the fact that he was a less emotional Italian.

While I might contest the idea that we can calculate degrees of intensity of the nationality a person holds, it is clear that in this country, the boundaries separating nationalities and ethnic groups are in flux. In our society, people cross boundaries all the time. In America, an advertisement tells us that we don't have to be Jewish to enjoy Jewish rye bread. In big cities, where people of many different backgrounds congregate, we can enjoy the best breads and the best food and customs of all nations. It is only when we travel to other nations that we can appreciate what benefits are available here because so many diverse people live and work together.

We don't have to be Polish to dance the polka or eat kielbasy— and after eating kielbasy, we really need to dance the polka to work off the calories. And we don't have to be American to love square dancing. In the summer, a group meets regularly in Central Park for folk dancing, and these are Greek, Jewish, Polish and other dances.

On St. Patrick's Day, a national transformation occurs. Everyone American becomes Irish. Everyone wears something green. Flower-sellers make money dying carnations green. Bar owners make money selling green beer. For some reason, corned beef and cabbage taste better on St. Patrick's Day than any other time of year.

National and religious boundaries can be so expanded that we don't have to be Christian to celebrate Christmas in a traditional American way. Businesses and offices close for a long holiday. Many people, whatever their belief, decorate a tree, invite friends and family for a party, and give gifts. Of course, this coming together of multicultural groups at Christmas time is fuelled by the retail businesses in the urge to make profits. They sell, and people buy.

In fact, money is the measure of success in many fields. Aiming for success is seen as an American virtue. When people strive to do something well, they also expect to be rewarded financially. Unfortunately, however, sometimes the urge for success takes over and becomes almost a national characteristic. Americans away from home are eager to establish immediately where one lives, where one works, and whom one knows. This is their touch-stone for finding out who one is, their way of deciding whether to continue the conversation and prolong the acquaintance. For many Americans, identity is linked to money and success. For Europeans, casual conversation is more likely to be about the weather, the skiing or other sports, and good places for lunch. It is conversation, not a quiz.

Being American means not only loving success, it also means being familiar with the products of a rich capitalistic society. Once an American and an Asian were having tea. The Asian tore the tea bag open and dropped the loose tea in the hot water. The American told him to place the entire tea bag in his cup. The

Asian then dropped the sugar packet in his cup and the American told him he had to rip open the packet and drop the sugar in the cup. Culture is reflected in how we treat everyday objects.

What does it mean to be American? It means coming in contact with other cultures and taking on some of their exotic customs, words, and foods. It means absorbing some common customs and making them one's own. It means being ambitious, valuing success, money, and the goods and services that go along with a capitalist economy. If there are degrees of holding a nationality, surely being "too American" will be a value judgement referring to looks and to the love of individual success. Anyone who is "too American" in absorbing the features of other cultures may find that others regard him or her as not American enough!

RESPONDING IN DISCUSSION OR WRITING

1. React to Skoratowicz's idea that there are degrees of being American or any other nationality. How valid is that observation? On a scale of 1 to 10 (with 10 being *very* and 1 being *hardly at all*), rate yourself according to your nationality. Then consider why you rate yourself in that way.

2. Skoratowicz describes how people celebrate some holidays and customs specific to nationalities and ethnic groups that are not their own. What examples can you add of such practices? Do you perceive these practices as a broadening of culture or a watering down?

3. *Considerations of Style.* Skoratowicz included this essay in a portfolio of her writing submitted for evaluation in a first-year college writing course. What questions, comments, or suggestions would you have for her as a reader of this essay? Are there things you would suggest she do in a subsequent draft?

4. Make an outline of Skoratowicz's essay, paragraph by paragraph. What is Skoratowicz's thesis? Which points support that thesis directly?

5. Skoratowicz makes observations about how Americans and Europeans conduct casual conversations. Deborah Tannen in Unit 3 makes observations about talk between men and women. Consider differences you have noticed in the ways in which various groups of people conduct conversations.

WRITING ASSIGNMENTS

1. Describe the ways in which Skoratowicz's view of America differs from that of Horace Miner. Why do you think their perspectives differ? Which perspective most closely resembles your own? What do you think causes the resemblance?

2. Using Skoratowicz's idea about degrees of nationality, write a short story or a nonfiction account of two people with widely disparate degrees of national characteristics. You can choose American or any other nationality as the basis for your story or essay.

❖

AMERICA: THE MULTINATIONAL SOCIETY

ISHMAEL REED

Ishmael Reed was born Emmett Coleman in Chattanooga, Tennessee, in 1938 and grew up in Buffalo, New York. He is a prolific writer, contributing frequently to the New York Times, Los Angeles Times, *and* Ramparts. *He writes essays, novels, poetry, and plays and is also a television producer, publisher, songwriter, and editor. At present he teaches at the University of California at Berkeley. His novels include* The Free-Lance Pall Bearers *(1967),* Mumbo Jumbo *(1972),* Flight to Canada *(1976), and* Japanese by Spring *(1993). Reed is one of the founders of BCF (Before Columbus Foundation), which awards its own version of the American Book Award. Winners of this award include Sandra Cisneros, Henry Louis Gates, Jr., Linda Hogan, Jimmy Santiago Baca, Sonia Sanchez, Gary Snyder, and Leslie Marmon Silko, all of whom appear in this book. This essay appeared in* Writin' Is Fightin' *(1990).*

At the annual Lower East Side Jewish Festival yesterday, a Chinese woman ate a pizza slice in front of Ty Thuan Duc's Vietnamese grocery store. Beside her a Spanish-speaking family patronized a cart with two signs: "Italian Ices" and "Kosher by Rabbi Alper." And after the pastrami ran out, everybody ate knishes.

(New York Times, 23 June 1983)

On the day before Memorial Day, 1983, a poet called me to describe a city he had just visited. He said that one section included mosques, built by the Islamic people who dwelled there. Attending his reading, he said, were large numbers of Hispanic people, forty thousand of whom lived in the same city. He was not talking about a fabled city located in some mysterious region of the world. The city he'd visited was Detroit.

A few months before, as I was leaving Houston, Texas, I heard it announced on the radio that Texas's largest minority was Mexican American, and though a foundation recently issued a report critical of bilingual education, the taped voice used to guide the passengers on the air trams connecting terminals in Dallas Airport is in both Spanish and English. If the trend continues, a day will come when it will be difficult to travel through some sections of the country without hearing commands in both English and Spanish; after all, for some western states, Spanish was the first written language and the Spanish style lives on in the western way of life.

Shortly after my Texas trip, I sat in an auditorium located on the campus of the University of Wisconsin at Milwaukee as a Yale professor—whose original work on the influence of African cultures upon those of the Americas has led to his ostracism from some monocultural intellectual circles—walked up and down the aisle, like an old-time southern evangelist, dancing and drumming the top of the lectern, illustrating his points before some serious Afro-American intellectuals and artists who cheered and applauded his performance and his mastery of information. The professor was "white." After his lecture, he joined a group of Milwaukeeans in a conversation. All of the participants spoke Yoruban, though only the professor had ever traveled to Africa.

One of the artists told me that his paintings, which included African and Afro-American mythological symbols and imagery, were hanging in the local McDonald's restaurant. The next day I went to McDonald's and snapped pictures of smiling youngsters

eating hamburgers below paintings that could grace the walls of
any of the country's leading museums. The manager of the local
McDonald's said, "I don't know what you boys are doing, but
I like it," as he commissioned the local painters to exhibit in
his restaurant.

Such blurring of cultural styles occurs in everyday life in the   5
United States to a greater extent than anyone can imagine and is
probably more prevalent than the sensational conflict between
people of different backgrounds that is played up and often
encouraged by the media. The result is what the Yale professor,
Robert Thompson, referred to as a cultural bouillabaisse, yet
members of the nation's present educational and cultural Elect
still cling to the notion that the United States belongs to some
vaguely defined entity they refer to as "Western civilization," by
which they mean, presumably, a civilization created by the people
of Europe, as if Europe can be viewed in monolithic terms. Is
Beethoven's Ninth Symphony, which includes Turkish marches, a
part of Western civilization, or the late nineteenth- and twentieth-
century French paintings, whose creators were influenced by
Japanese art? And what of the cubists, through whom the influence of African art changed modern painting, or the surrealists,
who were so impressed with the art of the Pacific Northwest
Indians that, in their map of North America, Alaska dwarfs the
lower forty-eight in size?

Are the Russians, who are often criticized for their adoption of
"Western" ways by Tsarist dissidents in exile, members of Western
civilization? And what of the millions of Europeans who have
black African and Asian ancestry, black Africans having occupied
several countries for hundreds of years? Are these "Europeans"
members of Western civilization, or the Hungarians, who originated across the Urals in a place called Greater Hungary, or the
Irish, who came from the Iberian Peninsula?

Even the notion that North America is part of Western civilization because our "system of government" is derived from Europe
is being challenged by Native American historians who say that
the founding fathers, Benjamin Franklin especially, were actually
influenced by the system of government that had been adopted by
the Iroquois hundreds of years prior to the arrival of large numbers of Europeans.

Western civilization, then, becomes another confusing category like Third World, or Judeo-Christian culture, as man attempts to impose his small-screen view of political and cultural reality upon a complex world. Our most publicized novelist recently said that Western civilization was the greatest achievement of mankind, an attitude that flourishes on the street level as scribbles in public restrooms: "White Power," "Niggers and Spics Suck," or "Hitler was a prophet," the latter being the most telling, for wasn't Adolph Hitler the archetypal monoculturalist who, in his pig-headed arrogance, believed that one way and one blood was so pure that it had to be protected from alien strains at all costs? Where did such an attitude, which has caused so much misery and depression in our national life, which has tainted even our noblest achievements, begin? An attitude that caused the in-carceration of Japanese-American citizens during World War II, the persecution of Chicanos and Chinese Americans, the near-extermination of the Indians, and the murder and lynchings of thousands of Afro-Americans.

Virtuous, hardworking, pious, even though they occasionally would wander off after some fancy clothes, or rendezvous in the woods with the town prostitute, the Puritans are idealized in our schoolbooks as "a hardy band" of no-nonsense patriarchs whose discipline razed the forest and brought order to the New World (a term that annoys Native American historians). Industrious, responsible, it was their "Yankee ingenuity" and practicality that created the work ethic. They were simple folk who produced a number of good poets, and they set the tone for the American writing style, of lean and spare lines, long before Hemingway. They worshiped in churches whose colors blended in with the New England snow, churches with simple structures and ornate lecterns.

The Puritans were a daring lot, but they had a mean streak. They hated the theater and banned Christmas. They punished people in a cruel and inhuman manner. They killed children who disobeyed their parents. When they came in contact with those whom they considered heathens or aliens, they behaved in such a bizarre and irrational manner that this chapter in the American history comes down to us as a late-movie horror film. They exter-minated the Indians, who taught them how to survive in a world unknown to them, and their encounter with the calypso culture of Barbados resulted in what the tourist guide in Salem's Witches' House refers to as the Witchcraft Hysteria.

The Puritan legacy of hard work and meticulous accounting led to the establishment of a great industrial society; it is no wonder that the American industrial revolution began in Lowell, Massachusetts, but there was the other side, the strange and paranoid attitudes toward those different from the Elect.

The cultural attitudes of that early Elect continue to be voiced in everyday life in the United States: the president of a distinguished university, writing a letter to the *Times,* belittling the study of African civilizations; the television network that promoted its show on the Vatican art with the boast that this art represented "the finest achievements of the human spirit." A modern up-tempo state of complex rhythms that depends upon contacts with an international community can no longer behave as if it dwelled in a "Zion Wilderness" surrounded by beasts and pagans.

When I heard a schoolteacher warn the other night about the invasion of the American educational system by foreign curriculums, I wanted to yell at the television set, "Lady, they're already here." It has already begun because the world is here. The world has been arriving at these shores for at least ten thousand years from Europe, Africa, and Asia. In the late nineteenth and early twentieth centuries, large numbers of Europeans arrived, adding their cultures to those of the European, African, and Asian settlers who were already here, and recently millions have been entering the country from South America and the Caribbean, making Yale Professor Bob Thompson's bouillabaisse richer and thicker.

One of our most visionary politicians said that he envisioned a time when the United States could become the brain of the world, by which he meant the repository of all of the latest advanced information systems. I thought of that remark when an enterprising poet friend of mine called to say that he had just sold a poem to a computer magazine and that the editors were delighted to get it because they didn't carry fiction or poetry. Is that the kind of world we desire? A humdrum homogenous world of all brains but no heart, no fiction, no poetry; a world of robots with human attendants bereft of imagination, of culture? Or does North America deserve a more exciting destiny? To become a place where the cultures of the world crisscross. This is possible because the United States is unique in the world: The world is here.

RESPONDING IN DISCUSSION OR WRITING

1. Why do you think Reed chooses to include the quotation from *The New York Times* at the head of his essay?

2. How is Robert Thompson's image of a "cultural bouillabaisse" different from the idea of the "melting pot" that used to be often used to describe the cultural diversity in the United States?

3. In paragraph 8, Reed discusses his view of Western civilization. What associations can you make between his views and those expressed in the exchange between Henry Louis Gates, Jr., and Donald Kagan in Unit 6?

4. Reed expresses the opinion that the idea that Western civilization is "the greatest achievement of mankind" has led to "misery and depression" (paragraph 8). What examples does he give to explain what he means? Do the examples help you appreciate his idea?

5. When Reed proposes the quite startling view that "[t]he Puritans were a daring lot, but they had a mean streak" (paragraph 10), what does he do to make sure we know why he has formed such an opinion? What evidence does he present? Do you find the evidence convincing? Why or why not?

WRITING ASSIGNMENTS

1. Following the style of the first four paragraphs of Reed's essay, describe a series of scenes you see in your environment (people and places, newspapers, magazines, TV, movies, advertisements, and so forth) that *show* a "cultural bouillabaisse," and then comment on your reactions.

2. Reed discusses a "blurring of cultural styles in everyday life in the United States" (paragraph 5). What examples does he give of this "blurring"? How does he view such "blurring"? Do you agree with his views? Why or why not? How do you feel about such blurring?

WHAT'S GREAT ABOUT THIS COUNTRY

ANDY WARHOL

Andy Warhol, born in Pittsburgh in 1928 as Andrew Warhola, was a leading Pop artist who presented images of everyday objects such as soup cans and soap-pad boxes as well as Marilyn Monroe, Elizabeth Taylor, and other popular cultural icons. He chose silk-screen painting for its ability to produce multiple images, not just unique works of art. He also made many films, including The Chelsea Girls *(1966) and* Andy Warhol's Dracula *(1974), and published a magazine,* Andy Warhol's Interview. *He died in 1987. This excerpt appears in* The Philosophy of Andy Warhol: From A to B and Back Again *(1975).*

WHAT'S GREAT ABOUT THIS country is that America started the tradition where the richest consumers buy essentially the same things as the poorest. You can be watching TV and see Coca-Cola, and you can know that the President drinks Coke, Liz Taylor drinks Coke, and just think, you can drink Coke, too. A Coke is a Coke and no amount of money can get you a better Coke than the one the bum on the corner is drinking. All the Cokes are the same and all the Cokes are good. Liz Taylor knows it, the President knows it, the bum knows it, and you know it.

In Europe the royalty and the aristocracy used to eat a lot better than the peasants—they weren't eating the same things at all. It was either partridge or porridge, and each class stuck to its own food. But when Queen Elizabeth came here and President Eisenhower bought her a hot dog I'm sure he felt confident that she couldn't have had delivered to Buckingham Palace a better hot dog than that one he bought her for maybe twenty cents at the ballpark. Because there *is* no better hot dog than a ballpark hot dog. Not for a dollar, not for ten dollars, not for a hundred thousand dollars could she get a better hot dog. She could get one for twenty cents and so could anybody else.

Sometimes you fantasize that people who are really up-there and rich and living it up have something you don't have, that their things must be better than your things because they have more money than you. But they drink the same Cokes and eat the same hot dogs and wear the same ILGWU clothes and see the same TV shows and the same movies. Rich people can't see a sillier version of *Truth or Consequences,* or a scarier version of *The Exorcist.* You can get just as revolted as they can—you can have the same nightmares. All of this is really American.

The idea of America is so wonderful because the more equal something is, the more American it is. For instance, a lot of places give you special treatment when you're famous, but that's not really American. The other day something *very* American happened to me. I was going into an auction at Parke-Bernet and they wouldn't let me in because I had my dog with me, so I had to wait in the lobby for the friend I was meeting there to tell him I'd been turned away. And while I was waiting in the lobby I signed autographs. It was a really American situation to be in.

(Also, by the way, the "special treatment" sometimes works in reverse when you're famous. Sometimes people are mean to me because I'm Andy Warhol.)   5

RESPONDING IN DISCUSSION OR WRITING

1. How do you react to Warhol's first sentence? Does he explain what he means? Do you understand his point of view? Is he being entirely serious?

2. Warhol's art depicts everyday objects such as soup cans, supermarket soap-pad boxes, and portraits of people like Elizabeth Taylor and Marilyn Monroe. What connections can you make between what he chooses to paint and what he chooses to write about?

3. What examples can you think of to refute the points Warhol makes in paragraph 3? Your examples should show that rich people actually do "have something you don't have."

4. What voice is Warhol using here? Is it the voice of a famous, wealthy artist? Or is it more the voice of an ordinary person? What makes you answer as you do?

5. *Considerations of Style.* Warhol uses some colloquial language in this excerpt. What colloquialisms can you find? What is their

effect on the reader? How would the effect change if an editor had changed them into formal prose?

6. Which parts of this excerpt make you smile or laugh? What does Warhol do to produce that reaction in you as a reader?

WRITING ASSIGNMENTS

1. Write a short essay beginning with the same words Warhol used: "What's great about this country is that . . ." Select a tone: formal, informal, serious, humorous, informative, satirical, or argumentative, and make sure you maintain consistency as you write.

2. Warhol argues that the rich and the poor buy and experience the same things, and that is equality. Do you agree with him? Argue for or against his point with your own concrete and specific examples and stories.

A SENSE OF PLACE

DAVID LAMB

David Lamb, born in 1940 in Boston, is a journalist for the Los Angeles Times *and United Press International who covers topics ranging from the U.S. involvement in Rwanda to baseball. He has lived in Egypt, Kenya, Australia, Vietnam, and in many cities in the United States. As a* Los Angeles Times *reporter, he traveled through forty-eight countries in four years. He is the author of* The Africans *(1983),* The Arabs: Journeys Beyond the Mirage *(1987), and* Stolen Season: A Journey Through America and Baseball's Minor Leagues *(1991). This selection is an excerpt from the introduction to a recent book,* A Sense of Place: Listening to Americans, *which was published in 1993.*

I HAVE BEEN WANDERING the country, more often than not on back roads, since the early 1970s for the *Los Angeles Times* and still cannot adequately answer, What is America? or Who are the Americans? Our country and our people are too diverse to abide easy definition. America is more about the quality of an idea than it is about a place. It is, in the ideal, about being young and confident, finding new frontiers, having the freedom to live and speak and move as one chooses. "For me, more than anything else, I guess," Evan Armstrong said the day he and his wife took the oath of citizenship at the courthouse in Thief River Falls, Minnesota, "America has meant the opportunity to grow."

France is a civilization and England is a people, but what is America? In a geographic sense, America isn't even a singular place; it's two continents, North and South, yet unlike, say, Canadians or Mexicans, we call ourselves Americans as though we had laid claim to everything from Barrow, Alaska, to Tierra del Fuego, Argentina. But when you travel abroad and tell inquirers you are an American, they know exactly what you mean. Your skin could be of any color, your religion of any persuasion, your financial means of either extreme, but . . . "Ah, yes, *American*," cabdrivers used to say when I lived in Egypt, "America a very good country."

The French traveler Alexis de Tocqueville wrote after his journey through the United States in 1831–32: "The time will therefore come when one hundred and fifty million men will be living in North America, equal in condition, all belonging to one family, owing their origin to the same cause, and preserving the same civilization, the same language, the same religion, the same habits, the same manners, and imbued with the same opinions, propagated under the same forms. The rest is uncertain, but this is certain; and it is a fact new to the world, a fact that the imagination strives in vain to grasp."

Could that be us he was talking about? What Tocqueville didn't foresee was that our commonality would be our differences, not our similarities. Americans would be bound not by language or color or opinions but by sharing a dream and a universal sense of place. America, F. Scott Fitzgerald said, is "a willingness of the heart," and that says it pretty well. Though pop cynics would have us believe such sentiments are antiquated these days, the strength of the American character remains a striking and provable thing. I have seen it on the battlefields of Vietnam and the Middle East, in the prairie towns of the Dakotas and along the long, lonely byways that cut through the heartland of a great nation. From all these places I came away convinced that, however wrenching our problems, the America of the 1990s is an achievement to be celebrated, not lamented.

I may well be out of sync with common sentiment, but the pessimism I hear expressed when learned people gather to discuss our country mystifies me. The self-indulgence of the sixties and the trickle-down indifference of the eighties are behind us, and what the doomsayers tend to ignore are the Americans themselves. I did not find in my travels a defeated people looking backward. Most of the Americans I met had rolled up their sleeves and gotten on with life. They accepted any honorable man as a neighbor and knew that the best social program was a good job. It wasn't very glamorous stuff, and I doubt that Oprah would have booked many of them, but still, they always left me heartened and reminded me that there was a lot to feel good about in America.

Coming home from a trip, I often felt the America I read about and the one I had seen were two different places—the former teetering on the brink, the latter muddling along, as we always do, with hopes of making this a better place. I heard anxiety expressed about our problems but surprisingly little cynicism (except when the subject was political leadership) about our future. An honest day's labor, decency and a faith in tomorrow are no less in vogue than they had been a hundred years ago. Though we may speak many languages—ninety in the Los Angeles Unified School District alone—the American personality remains distinct, shaped by the persuasion of opportunity and, yes, sacrifice. "Work seems to very slowly, but steadily, improve," John Laban, a B-52 pilot during the Vietnam War and now an underemployed Maine forester, wrote me not long ago. "One of the nice things about starting from scratch is that whatever does come along seems like a bonus. Gets you back to basics, and I am silly enough to think that's good."

Laban lives by pride, with his dreams detained, not lost, and I do not find his attitude untypical. We remain a young nation, though we are no longer youthful. Our exuberance has been tempered by caution. In countless conversations from Maine to Alaska, Americans spoke of a bittersweet longing for the past, as though no one knew quite what to make of the social and economic upheavals that have swept across the land. "I'll tell you, this was some town awhile back," a miner said one night at the bar of the Elks Lodge in Sheridan, Wyoming. "You could walk down Main Street and, all in a block and a half, you could buy a saddle, a Pendleton shift, the best fillet you ever tasted. Outside of First Avenue over in Billings [Montana], Main Street in Sheridan was as fine a place as a man'd ever want to go." Yet I don't think the miner or anyone else I met meant they wanted to turn back the clock. They were talking about community and holding on to all that is good and searching for what one New England mill worker calls "the comfort zone" of life.

It had been a long time since I had watched Johnny Carson regularly, but when he left our living rooms in the spring of 1992, I, like millions of Americans, stayed up late for his final shows and found myself saddened that time had claimed another icon. Carson had started on *The Tonight Show* before there was a war in Vietnam and ended after our troops had come home from war in the Persian Gulf. During his nightly visits with us, the Peace Corps had been born and the Soviet Union had disintegrated. John Kennedy had lived and died. The Washington Senators had become the Texas Rangers and Rhodesia had given way to Zimbabwe. Nothing was as it had been—except for Johnny. It was reassuring to know he was there, connecting us to the past, and as we showered him with fond attention before the curtain closed, I wondered whether we were saying good-bye to Johnny Carson, or to ourselves.

Certainly entering the last decade of the twentieth century has given us cause for nostalgia. We went to the polls to choose between two men for President: One likened himself to Harry S Truman (but had voted for Thomas Dewey in 1948); the other had smoked marijuana (but hadn't inhaled). Our prisons are full, our welfare ranks swollen, our budget deficit out of control. If you watch television in almost any major city, you would swear Armageddon is upon us. Life is all 911 calls, and in an era of "infotainment," fact and fiction have become mysteriously intertwined. We talk about "the good old days" without defining what they were. Yes, life was simpler then, but was it better? Do we really want to eat at soda fountains again and travel west at 40 mph on Route 66? Probably not, except in the recesses of our selective memories. Americans are not a people who take their guidance from the past. We push ahead and seldom look back, and our collective national memory is short. We crow in triumph when we prove we are mighty but seem unwilling to take credit for our simple accomplishments in being the most tolerant, generous, prosperous and multicultural society on earth.

From my earliest days as a journalist, I have been drawn not to the cities or to the rich and powerful, but to the towns and ranches and factories where everyday Americans are living everyday lives. I feel at ease with these people. They have taught me about courage and stamina and tradition. From them I have learned the meaning of place—where you belong and not necessarily where you are. When I asked Red Garretson, Wyoming's chief brand inspector, why he wore the working clothes of the range—Stetson, jeans and boots—and kept his .45 revolver tucked out of sight in his Chevy pickup, he explained: "In these parts, you knock on a man's door wearing a uniform and carrying a gun, and, oh, sure, he'll give you respect, but you'll do your talking on his doorstep. You won't get invited in to eat his wife's pie at the kitchen table and you won't really find out what's going on like you have to in this job." In that brief reply Garretson defined, I think, the essence of *place* as eloquently as a poet.

RESPONDING IN DISCUSSION OR WRITING

1. When Lamb says that "America is more about the quality of an idea than it is about a place" (paragraph 1), how does that connect with his search for a sense of place as "where you belong and not necessarily where you are" (paragraph 10)?

2. What, if anything, do you think binds Americans and provides a commonality?

3. What could make you agree with Lamb that the "America of the 1990s is an achievement to be celebrated, not lamented"?

4. *For Further Research.* Find out who Alexis de Tocqueville is. Why do you think Lamb quotes from Alexis de Tocqueville, and what use does he make of the quotation?

5. *Considerations of Style.* What use does Lamb make of questions in this excerpt? Examine each question and the effect it has on the reader.

6. What is Lamb's purpose in discussing Johnny Carson on "The Tonight Show"? How does he make the connection between that show and America and a sense of place?

WRITING ASSIGNMENTS

1. Lamb discusses the fact that Americans share "a dream and a universal sense of place." Describe a place that crystallizes for you the feeling and experience of living in a country and feeling a real part of it.

2. Do you agree or disagree with Lamb's statement that for most Americans "the best social program [is] a good job"? What does he mean by that? Explain your reasons for agreeing or disagreeing.

SWAMP GUINEA'S FISH LODGE

WILLIAM LEAST HEAT MOON

William Least Heat Moon, born in 1939, is a Native American writer, a member of the Sioux. He was born William Lewis Trogdon in Kansas City, Missouri, and now lives in Columbia, Missouri. His book Blue Highways: A Journey into America, *published in 1982, resulted from his decision after losing his job to "set out on a long (equivalent to half the circumference of the earth), circular trip over the back roads of the United States." This excerpt describes one of the places he visited in Georgia and the impression it made on him. His most recent work is* PrairyErth: A Deep Map *(1991), which describes the local history of Chase County in rural Kansas, with lists of travelers, portraits of inhabitants, and a detailed two-hundred-item inventory of the contents of a covered wagon.*

IN THE LAND OF "Coke-Cola" it was hot and dry. The artesian water was finished. Along route 72, an hour west of Ninety Six, I tried not to look for a spring; I knew I wouldn't find one, but I kept looking. The Savannah River, dammed to an unnatural wideness, lay below, wet and cool. I'd come into Georgia. The sun seemed to press on the roadway, and inside the truck, hot light bounced off chrome, flickering like a torch. Then I saw what I was trying not to look for: in a coppice, a long-handled pump.

I stopped and took my bottles to the well. A small sign: WATER UNSAFE FOR DRINKING. I drooped like warm tallow. What fungicide, herbicide, nematicide, fumigant, or growth regulant—potions that rebuilt Southern agriculture—had seeped into the ground water? In the old movie Westerns there is commonly a scene where a dehydrated man, crossing the barren waste, at last comes to a water hole; he lies flat to drink the tepid stuff. Just as lips touch water, he sees on the other side a steer skull. I drove off thirsty but feeling a part of mythic history.

The thirst subsided when hunger took over. I hadn't eaten since morning. Sunset arrived west of Oglesby, and the air cooled. Then a roadsign:

> SWAMP GUINEA'S FISH LODGE
> ALL YOU CAN EAT!

An arrow pointed down a county highway. I would gorge myself. A record would be set. They'd ask me to leave. An embarrassment to all.

The road through the orange earth of north Georgia passed an old, three-story house with a thin black child hanging out of every window like an illustration for "The Old Woman Who Lived in a Shoe"; on into hills and finally to Swamp Guinea's, a conglomerate of plywood and two-by-fours laid over with the smell of damp pine woods.

Inside, wherever an oddity or natural phenomenon could hang, one hung: stuffed rump of a deer, snowshoe, flintlock, hornet's nest. The place looked as if a Boy Scout troop had decorated it. Thirty or so people, black and white, sat around tables almost foundering under piled platters of food. I took a seat by the reproduction of a seventeenth-century woodcut depicting some Rabelaisian banquet at the groaning board.

The diners were mostly Oglethorpe County red-dirt farmers. In Georgia tones they talked about their husbandry in terms of rain and nitrogen and hope. An immense woman with a glossy picture of a hooked bass leaping the front of her shirt said, "I'm gonna be sick from how much I've ate."

I was watching everyone else and didn't see the waitress standing quietly by. Her voice was deep and soft like water moving in a cavern. I ordered the $4.50 special. In a few minutes she wheeled up a cart and began off-loading dinner: ham and eggs, fried catfish, fried perch fingerlings, fried shrimp, chunks of bar-becued beef, fried chicken, French fries, hush puppies, a broad bowl of cole slaw, another of lemon, a quart of ice tea, a quart of ice, and an entire loaf of factory-wrapped white bread. The table was covered.

"Call me if y'all want any more." She wasn't joking. I quenched the thirst and then—slowly—went to the eating. I had to stand to reach plates across the table, but I intended to do the supper in. It was all Southern fried and good, except the Southern-style sweetened ice tea; still I took care of a quart of it. As I ate, making up for meals lost, the Old-Woman-in-the-Shoe house flashed before me, lightning in darkness. I had no moral right to eat so much. But I did. Headline: STOMACH PUMP FAILS TO REVIVE TRAVELER.

The loaf of bread lay unopened when I finally abandoned the meal. At the register, I paid a man who looked as if he'd been chipped out of Georgia chert. The Swamp Guinea. I asked about the name. He spoke of himself in the third person like the Wizard of Oz. "The Swamp Guinea only tells regulars."

"I'd be one, Mr. Guinea, if I didn't live in Missouri."   10

"Y'all from the North? Here, I got somethin' for you." He went to the office and returned with a 45 rpm record. "It's my daughter singin'. A little promotion we did. Take it along." Later, I heard a husky north Georgia voice let go a down-home lyric rendering of Swamp Guinea's menu:

> *That's all you can eat*
> *For a dollar fifty,*
> *Hey! The barbecue's nifty!*

And so on through the fried chicken and potatoes.

As I left, the Swamp Guinea, a former antique dealer whose name was Rudell Burroughs, said, "The nickname don't mean anything. Just made it up. Tried to figure a good one so we can franchise someday."

The frogs, high and low, shrilled and bellowed from the trees and ponds. It was cool going into Athens, a city suffering from a nasty case of the sprawls. On the University of Georgia campus, I tried to walk down Swamp Guinea's supper. Everywhere couples entwined like moonflower vines, each waiting for the blossom that opens only once.

RESPONDING IN DISCUSSION OR WRITING

1. Do you know of restaurants and cafés where you and all the customers feel very relaxed and at home? What are the characteristics that give the place that special quality?

2. How would you summarize Heat Moon's feelings about Swamp Guinea's Fish Lodge? What kind of impression does he intend the reader to take away?

3. How do you think the local people felt about Swamp Guinea's Fish Lodge? What clues do you find in the reading?

4. *Considerations of Style.*   In paragraph 2, what is the effect of the analogy to a scene in old movie Westerns? Why do you think Heat Moon refers to that scene?

5. *Considerations of Style.*   What details does Heat Moon include that are not necessary for the events of the story but provide background details about the place and the setting? What do those details add to his account?

6. *Considerations of Style.*   How would the effect of the story have been different if Heat Moon had written only this in paragraph 7, omitting the details about the food:

> I ordered the $4.50 special. In a few minutes she wheeled up a cart and began off-loading dinner. The table was covered.

WRITING ASSIGNMENTS

1. Write a description of a place and an incident that once helped you to feel better when you were feeling hungry, upset, lonely, or depressed. Describe the place in detail, and show how it helped your mood improve.

2. If you had to describe to a visitor from overseas a place that seemed to you to be quintessentially American, what place would that be? What is it about it that makes it American?

3. Imagine that you visit Swamp Guinea's Fish Lodge the day after Heat Moon was there. Write a story about what you saw and what happened. Try to give your reader more details about the place and the people.

BLUEBIRDBLUEBIRDTHRUMYWINDOW

SONIA SANCHEZ

Sonia Sanchez, born in Birmingham, Alabama, in 1934, poet, essayist, playwright, and author of children's books, is also professor of English at Temple University, Philadelphia. She is the winner of two American Book Awards, for homegirls and handgrenades *(1984), in which the following story appeared, and* Under a Soprano Sky *(1987). She also won the American Book Award's lifetime achievement award in 1990. Recently, she contributed to* Double Stitch: Black Women Write about Mothers and Daughters *(1993).*

> denn die einen sind im Dunkeln
> (some there are who live in darkness)
> und die andern sind im Licht
> (while the others live in light)
> und man siehet die im Lichte
> (we see those who live in daylight)
> die im Dunkeln sieht man nicht
> (those in darkness out of sight)
>
> —*Bertolt Brecht*

And the Supreme Court said housing and welfare are not fundamental rights.

The right to vote, marry and procreate are the only fundamental rights.

Question: What rights are considered fundamental?

Answer: Only those rights essential to our concept of ordered liberty.

Question: What do you mean? Make it plain, girl. Make it plain.   5

Answer: In other words, a democratic society without these rights would not be considered civilized. If you don't have 'em, you ain't civilized.

Isn't it lovely to be civilized?

You've seen her. You know you have. She sits on cardboard at Broad and Columbia in front of Zavelle's. Four coats layer her body. Towels are wrapped with a rope around her feet to keep them warm. A plastic bag full of her belongings stands in formation next to her. She's anywhere between 40 and 70 years-old. A grey Black woman of North Philadelphia. Sitting sharply. Watching the whirl of people pass by, she sits through winter, spring, summer, fall and law students keeping time to memory.

You've seen her. You know you have. The old woman walking her ulcerated legs down Market street; the old harridan mumbling pieces of a dead dream as she examines garbage can after garbage can.

"Hey there, girlie. Can you spare me a quarter? I ain't eaten in four days. C'mon now, honey. Just one little quarter."

So you give her a quarter and keep on walking to your apartment. So you hand her the money that relieves you of her past, present and future. Onward Christian country marching off as to war, with your cross behind you, going as before.

She was turning the corner of the rest room at Pennsylvania Station as I came out of the stall. It was 10:59 P.M., and I was waiting for the 11:59 P.M. to Philadelphia. She entered the bathroom, walking her swollen black feet, dragging her polkadot feet in blue house slippers. Her cape surrounded her like a shroud. She grunted herself down underneath one of the hand dryers.

I watched her out of the corner of my eyes as I washed and dried my hands. What did she remind me of? This cracked body full of ghosts. This beached black whale. This multilayered body gathering dust.

Whose mother are you? Whose daughter were you for so many years? What grandchild is standing still in your eyes? What is your name, old black woman of bathrooms and streets?

She opened her dirty sheet of belongings and brought out an old plastic bowl. She looked up and signaled to me.

"Hey you. There. Yeah. You. Miss. Could you put some water in this here bowl for me please? It's kinda hard for me to climb back up once I sits down here for the night."

I took the bowl and filled it with water. There was no hot water, only cold. I handed it to her, and she turned the bowl up to her mouth and drank some of the water. Then she began the slow act of taking off her slippers and socks. The socks numbered six. They were all old and dirty. But her feet. A leper's feet. Cracked. Ulcerated. Peeling with dirt and age.

She baptized one foot and then the other with water. Yes. Wash the "souls" of your feet, my sister. Baptize them in bathroom water. We're all holy here.

You've seen her. You know you have. Sitting in the lower chambers of the garage. Guarding the entering and exiting cars. Old black goddess of our American civilization at its peak.

She sits still as a Siamese. Two shopping bags surround her like constant lovers. She sits on two blankets. A heavy quilt is wrapped around her body.

"Good morning, sister." I scream against the quiet. Her eyes. Closed. Open into narrow slits. Yellow sleep oozes out of her eyes. Then a smile of near-recognition. A smile of gratitude perhaps. Here I am, her smile announces, in the upper sanctum of Manhattan. A black Siamese for these modern monuments. Let those who would worship at my shrine come now or forever hold their peace. Hee. Hee. Hee.

She leans toward me and says, "Glorious morning, ain't it?" You has something for yo' ole sister today? For yo' old mother?"

The blue and white morning stretches her wings across the dying city. I lean forward and give her five dollars. The money disappears under her blanket as she smiles a lightning smile. Her eyes open and for the first time I see the brown in her eyes. Brown-eyed woman. She looks me in the eye and says, "Don't never go to sleep on the world, girl. Whiles you sleeping the world scrambles on. Keep yo' eyes open all the time."

Then she closes her eyes and settles back into a sinister stillness. I stand waiting for more. After all, we have smiled at each other for years. I have placed five dollars regularly into her hand. I wait. She does not move, and finally I walk on down the street. What were you waiting for girl? What more could she possibly say to you that you don't already know? Didn't you already know who and what she was from her voice, from her clothes? Hadn't you seen her for years on the streets and in the doorways of America? Didn't you recognize her?

I walk the long block to my apartment. It will be a long day. I feel exhausted already. Is it the New York air? My legs become uncoordinated. Is it the rhythm of the city that tires me so this morning? I must find a chair, or curb, a doorway to rest on. My legs are going every which way but up.

I find a doorway on Broadway. I lean. Close my eyes to catch my morning breath. Close my mouth to silence the screams moving upward like vomit.

She was once somebody's mama. I ain't playing the dozens. She was once someone's child toddling through the playgrounds of America in tune to bluebirdbluebird thru my window, bluebird-bluebird thru my window.

Where do the bluebirds go when they're all used up?

RESPONDING IN DISCUSSION OR WRITING

1. *Considerations of Style.*   Consider your reactions to the title and the quotation before the story. What do they lead you to expect? Are your expectations met?

2. Several women make an appearance in the story, including the narrator. How many? In which ways are they similar? In which ways are they different?

3. The story shifts from place to place. What is the effect on the reader of the shifts in place? Why do you think Sanchez chose to set the story in a variety of places?

4. *Considerations of Style.*   Sanchez uses many intentional sentence fragments, such as "Sitting sharply." Select three of the fragments, write what form a revision to a nonfragment would take, and discuss which version fits better in the story and why. Why do you think Sanchez elected to write a fragment in each case?

5. Which people does Sanchez want to reach with her story? What makes you answer the way you do?

WRITING ASSIGNMENTS

1. Sanchez begins her story by mentioning the fundamental rights of a citizen of a civilized nation, a democratic society. Explore the issue of human fundamental rights with reference both to Sanchez's story and to your own views. What does the story say about the fundamental rights of an American? How closely does it touch on reality? What kind of statement is Sanchez making? You might want to consider the following questions:

What does Sanchez's story tell about her view of fundamental rights? Does her story present these views in a persuasive way? What would you add to the initial discussion of fundamental rights, and what story would you tell to make your own point?

2. *Considerations of Style.*   Analyze how stylistic features contribute to the story's effectiveness. Consider features such as repetition, sentence fragments, slang and colloquial language, figurative language such as simile and metaphor, the absence of names for the characters, and references to songs and popular culture.

❖

HUMAN FAMILY

MAYA ANGELOU

Maya Angelou was born Marguerite Johnson in 1928 in St. Louis, Missouri, and grew up in Arkansas. She has held numerous college teaching positions, holds more than thirty honorary degrees, and is a poet, playwright, director, and actress. She is particularly well known for her autobiography, I Know Why the Caged Bird Sings *(1970), as well as for the fact that she wrote and read a poem for the inauguration of President Bill Clinton on January 20, 1993. Maya Angelou now teaches at Wake Forest University, Winston-Salem, North Carolina. Her most recent books are a volume of poetry,* Life Doesn't Frighten Me *(1993), and a collection of essays,* Wouldn't Take Nothing for My Journey Now *(1993). "Human Family" is from* I Shall Not Be Moved *(1990).*

> I note the obvious differences
> in the human family.
> Some of us are serious,
> some thrive on comedy.
>
> Some declare their lives are lived   5
> as true profundity,

and others claim they really live
the real reality.
The variety of our skin tones
can confuse, bemuse, delight,   10
brown and pink and beige and purple,
tan and blue and white.

I've sailed upon the seven seas
and stopped in every land,
I've seen the wonders of the world,   15
not yet one common man.

I know ten thousand women
called Jane and Mary Jane,
but I've not seen any two
who really were the same.   20

Mirror twins are different
although their features jibe,
and lovers think quite different thoughts
while lying side by side.

We love and lose in China,   25
we weep on England's moors,
and laugh and moan in Guinea,
and thrive on Spanish shores.

We seek success in Finland,
are born and die in Maine.   30
In minor ways we differ,
in major we're the same.

I note the obvious differences
between each sort and type,
but we are more alike, my friends,   35
than we are unalike.

We are more alike, my friends,
than we are unalike.

We are more alike, my friends,
than we are unalike.   40

RESPONDING IN DISCUSSION OR WRITING

1. How do you react to the poem as a whole? What kind of feelings do you have as you read and after you finish reading?

2. Do you know people who claim to live "the real reality"? How
do you think Angelou perceives these types of people?

3. *Considerations of Style.* The rhymes in the poem of the second
and fourth line in each stanza are usually not exact rhymes. In
fact, only one is: *delight* and *white* in stanza 3. How do you react to
the rhyme? Why do you think Angelou chose to rhyme and then
to rhyme only approximately?

4. Where would you put yourself in the two types mentioned in
stanza 1: among the serious or among those who "thrive on comedy"? Do you reconsider your answer when you read the definitions of comedy and tragedy given by the filmmaker and comic
actor Mel Brooks: "Tragedy is when I cut my finger. Comedy is
when you fall into an open sewer and die"?

5. *Considerations of Style.* The last two stanzas repeat the last two
lines of the ninth stanza. What effect does the repetition, and the
fact that the last two stanzas are different in form from all the
other stanzas, have?

WRITING ASSIGNMENTS

1. What arguments could you propose to agree with Angelou that
"we are more alike . . . /than we are unalike"? What arguments
can you find that would oppose that view? Which set of arguments
do you find more convincing and why?

2. Write a rhyming poem on the theme of nationality or identity.

3. In this poem, Angelou refers to names (Jane and Mary Jane),
personality and appearance (variety of skin tones, mirror twins),
ethnicity, and nationality, and so touches on many of the themes
in this book. Do you think this poem is a fitting conclusion to a
book of readings on identity? Why or why not?

Making Connections: Nationality

1. Discuss the connections and conflicts among race, ethnic affiliation, family ties, and nationality as they contribute to your own identity. Use the selections in this unit and your own experience to inform your writing. Begin thinking about the topic by considering the following questions: What are your associations with nationality? Would you ever change your nationality? Have you ever changed it? Why? What feelings does such a change cause? Who should be allowed to adopt a new nationality? Who shouldn't? Should the rights of nationality ever be taken away? What about the homeless, the poor, and illegal aliens—what about their rights to get an education, health care, unemployment and welfare benefits, and protection of the law?

2. Discuss the images that have been used to describe the diversity in America—melting pot, salad bowl, bouillabaisse, rainbow, mosaic—and relate them to the concepts of assimilation, two-way acculturation, and the maintenance of cultural pluralism. What are the advantages of each image, and what problems does each concept cause? You might find it interesting to read Israel Zangwill's 1909 play *The Melting-Pot*.

3. Do library research to find out about the experiences of immigrants when they came to North America in large numbers from 1880 to 1904. What caused them the most problems? What caused them joy? What were their attitudes to their new nation?

4. With reference to the selections in this unit and other essays in this book, discuss Perry Miller's statement that "being an American is not something to be inherited so much as something to be achieved." Do you agree with this statement? What ramifications does it have, and what conclusions does it lead to?

5. Collect examples of aspects of popular culture that make reference to what it means to be an American, for example, advertisements, magazine articles, photographs, songs, radio

and TV programs, and films, and describe and analyze what you find. Does any composite picture emerge?

6. Interview someone who immigrated to North America within the last twenty years and tell that person's story. Describe the reasons for immigration, expectations, and experiences.

7. Examine four history books used in public high schools, two in use today and two that were used more than ten years ago. How are all or some of the following covered:

the "discovery" of America by Christopher Columbus

the Puritans

the 1830 Indian Relocation Act

"The Trail of Tears"

the Harlem Renaissance

the internment of Japanese Americans during World War II after the United States declared war against Japan

Plessy v. Ferguson

Brown v. the Board of Education of Topeka, Kansas

the struggle against racial segregation and for civil rights

the relationship between Puerto Rico and the U.S. mainland

the border between Mexico and the United States

migrant farm workers

illegal aliens

8. Look at six pictures by Andy Warhol (in museums, galleries, art books, slides, electronic media, or catalogs) and describe what view of America they depict and what they imply about what it means to be American.

9. Make connections between the essays in this unit that refer to the American character and the American Dream, for example, those by Reed, Skoratowicz, and Warhol. What views do the authors express? What are the similarities and differences in the views expressed in the various selections? How do they contrast with the picture portrayed by Sanchez?

10. Reflect on the views of attachment to place presented by Lamb, Least Heat Moon, and Sanchez, and discuss how you view the links between place, nationality, and identity.

11. The first unit of this book collected readings related to names. Several of the authors in this last unit have changed their names: Ishmael Reed, Andy Warhol, William Least Heat Moon, and Maya Angelou. Write about these name changes in relation to the perspectives on names and nationality presented in the first and last units of this book.

Acknowledgments

Pages 312–313 Comer, James P. "Adoption and Identity." *Parents,* January 1992: 116. Used by permission of the author.

Pages 302–304 Didion, Joan. "On Going Home." *Slouching Towards Bethlehem.* New York: Delta, 1968. 164–68. Copyright © 1968 by Joan Didion. Reprinted by permission of Farrar, Straus & Giroux, Inc.

Pages 177–181 Epstein, Steven. "Gay Politics, Ethnic Identity: The Limits of Social Constructionism." *Socialist Review* 17 (93/94) 1987: 9–13 and endnotes. Used by permission.

Pages 124–133 Erdrich, Louise. "The Red Convertible." *Love Medicine.* New York: Harper, 1993. 181–93. From *Love Medicine,* new and expanded version, by Louise Erdrich. Copyright © 1984, 1993 by Louise Erdrich. Reprinted by permission of Henry Holt & Co., Inc.

Pages 35–38 Ferraro, Susan. "Name Dropper." *New York Times Magazine,* 2 May 1993: 18, 20. Copyright © 1993 by The New York Times Company. Reprinted by permission.

Pages 389–390 Gates, Henry Louis, Jr. "It's Not Just Anglo-Saxon." *New York Times,* 4 May 1991: sec. A, 23. Copyright © 1991 by The New York Times Company. Reprinted by permission.

Pages 20–27 Gilyard, Keith. "Keith and Raymond." *Voices of the Self: A Study of Language Competence.* Detroit: Wayne State University Press, 1991. 42–43, 44–47, 51–53. Reprinted from *Voices of the Self: A Study of Language Competence* by Keith Gilyard by permission of the Wayne State University Press and the author.

Pages 429–433 Goldman, Ari L. "Buddhism." *The Search for God at Harvard.* New York: Ballantine, 1992: 89–96. Copyright © 1991 by Ari L. Goldman. Reprinted by permission of Times Books, a division of Random House, Inc.

Pages 426–428 Goodman, Ellen. "Religion in the Textbooks." *Making Sense.* New York: Atlantic Monthly Press, 1989. 228–29. Copyright © 1986 by The Washington Post Company. Used by permission of Grove/Atlantic, Inc.

Pages 242–248 Gordon, David J. "Wrestling with the Angel: A Memoir." Copyright © 1993 by David J. Gordon. Used by permission.

Pages 144–153 Gould, Lois. "X.": *A Fabulous Child's Story.* Daughters, 1978. Copyright © 1978 by Lois Gould. Reprinted by permission.

Pages 409–416 Gould, Stephen Jay. "Evolution as Fact and Theory." *Hen's Teeth and Horse's Toes.* New York: Norton, 1983. 253–62. Copyright © 1983 by Stephen Jay Gould. Reprinted with permission.

Pages 250–266 Graham, Lawrence Otis. "Invisible Man." *New York,* 17 August 1992: 26–34. Copyright © 1992 by Lawrence Otis Graham. All rights reserved. Reprinted with the permission of the author and *New York* Magazine.

Pages 493–496 Heat Moon, William Least. "Swamp Guinea's Fish Lodge." *Blue Highways: A Journey into America.* New York: Fawcett Crest/Ballantine, 1982. 78–80. Copyright © 1982 by William Least Heat Moon. By permission of Little, Brown and Company.

Pages 172–176 Heilbrun, Carolyn G. "George Sand." *Writing a Woman's Life.* New York: Ballantine, 1988. 33–38. Copyright © 1988 by Carolyn G. Heilbrun. Reprinted by permission of W.W. Norton & Company, Inc.

Pages 64–65   Hogan, Linda. "Song for My Name." *Calling Myself Home.* Greenfield Center, NY: Greenfield Review Press, 1978. 32. "Song for My Name" appears in *Red Clay Poems & Stories, 1991,* The Greenfield Review Press.

Pages 277–289   Honig, Lucy. "English as a Second Language." *Prize Stories 1992: The O. Henry Awards.* Ed. William Abrahams. New York: Anchor Doubleday, 1992. 60–74.

Pages 79–87   hooks, bell. "Straightening Our Hair." *Z Magazine* (September 1988): XX. Reprinted with permission from the author.

Pages 395–396   Hughes, Langston. "Theme for English B." "Montage of a Dream Deferred," in *Selected Poems of Langston Hughes.* New York: Vintage/Random House, 1959. 247–48. Copyright © 1995 by the Estate of Langston Hughes. Reprinted by permission of Alfred A. Knopf Inc.

Pages 355–360   Jackson, Shirley. "Charles." *The Lottery.* New York: Farrar, Straus, 1949. 91–96. Copyright © 1948, 1949 by Shirley Jackson. Copyright renewed © 1976, 1977 by Laurence Hyman, Barry Hyman, Mrs. Sarah Webster and Mrs. Joanne Schnurer. Reprinted by permission of Farrar, Straus & Giroux, Inc.

Pages 213–225   Jeffries, Dexter. "Who I Am." *Present Tense* 15 (July-August 1988): 49–53. Copyright © 1988 by Dexter Jeffries. Reprinted by permission.

Pages 206–212   Jones, Lisa. "Mama's White." *Village Voice,* 18 May 1993: 31–32.

Pages 195–196   Jong, Erica. "Woman Enough." *Becoming Light.* New York: Harper Perennial, 1991. 312–13. Copyright © 1961, 1962, 1971, 1973, 1975, 1977, 1979, 1981, 1983, 1987, 1991 by Erica Mann Jong. Reprinted by permission of HarperCollins Publishers, Inc.

Pages 392–394   Kagan, Donald. "Western Values Are Central." *New York Times,* 4 May 1991: sec. A, 23. Copyright © 1991 by The New York Times Company. Reprinted by permission.

Pages 162–166   Kanner, Bernice. "Big Boys Don't Cry: Returning the Macho Message." *New York,* 21 May 1990: 20–21. Reprinted with permission from the author.

Pages 40–50   Kim, Richard E. *Lost Names: Scenes from a Korean Boyhood.* New York: Praeger, 1970. 98–110, 115.

Pages 98–106   Kriegel, Leonard. "Summer Dreams." *Sewanee Review* 99 (Spring 1991): 202–11. Copyright © 1991 by Leonard Kriegel. Reprinted with the permission of the editor and the author.

Pages 489–492   Lamb, David. *A Sense of Place: Listening to Americans.* New York: Times Books/Random House, 1993. 3–8. Copyright © 1993 by David Lamb. Reprinted by permission of Times Books, a division of Random House, Inc.

Pages 135–136   Lorde, Audre. "Hanging Fire." *Norton Anthology of Modern Poetry,* 2nd ed. Ed. Richard Ellman and Robert O'Clair. New York: Norton, 1988. 1432–33. From *The Black Unicorn* by Audre Lorde. Copyright © 1978 by Audre Lorde. Reprinted by permission of W.W. Norton & Company, Inc.

Pages 167–170   Mahoney, Rosemary. "What Are You?" *New York Times,* 17 March 1993, sec. A, 21. Copyright © 1993 by The New York Times Company. Reprinted by permission.

Pages 470–475 Miner, Horace. "Body Ritual Among the Nacirema." *The American Anthropologist* 56, 3 (1956): 503–7. Reproduced by permission of the American Anthropological Association. Not for sale or further reproduction.

Pages 290–293 Morales, Aurora Levins. "Class Poem." *Getting Home Alive*. Ed. Aurora Levins Morales and Rosario Morales. Ithaca, N.Y.: Firebrand Books. 45–47. Copyright © 1986 by Aurora Levins Morales. Used with permission from Firebrand Books, Ithaca, NY.

Pages 32–34 Morrow, Lance. "The Strange Burden of a Name." *Time*, 8 March 1993: 76. Copyright © 1993 Time Inc. Reprinted by permission.

Pages 62–64 *New York Times*. 2 letters. 18 November 1992. Copyright © 1993 by The New York Times Company. Reprinted by permission. Letters reprinted by permission of Hector Velez Guadalupe and I.K. Sundiata.

Page 15 Offutt, Chris. Paragraph from *The Same River Twice*. New York: Simon and Schuster, 1993. 149.

Pages 5–11 Ornstein, Robert. Adapted from *Multimind*. Boston: Houghton Mifflin, 1986. 7–9, 141–53. Copyright © 1986 by Robert Ornstein. Reprinted by arrangement with the Virginia Barber Literary Agency. All rights reserved.

Pages 227–240 Phipps, Lang. "Confessions of a Young WASP." *New York*, 2 September 1991: 24–31. Copyright © 1991 by Lang Phipps. Reprinted by permission.

Pages 405–407 Quindlen, Anna. "I Am a Catholic." *New York Times*, 18 June 1986. Also appears in *Living Out Loud*. New York: Random House, 1988. 177–80. Copyright © 1986 by The New York Times Company. Reprinted by permission.

Pages 107–110 Raimes, Emily. "Making Old Friends." *New York Woman* (Dec./Jan. 1989): 86, 89. Reprinted by permission of the author.

Pages 273–275 Raya, Anna Lisa. "It's Hard Enough Being Me." *Columbia College Today* 20, 1 (Winter/Spring 1994): 48. Copyright © 1994 by Anna Lisa Raya. Reprinted by permission.

Pages 480–485 Reed, Ishmael. "America: The Multinational Society." *Writin' Is Fightin'*. New York: Atheneum, 1990. 51–56. Copyright © 1990 by Ishmael Reed. Reprinted by permission of the author.

Pages 361–364 Rodriguez, Richard. "School and Home: Public and Private Identity." *Hunger of Memory*. Boston: David Godine, 1981. 11–12, 26–28. Copyright © 1982 by Richard Rodriguez. Reprinted by persmission of David R. Godine, Publisher.

Pages 370–376 Rose, Mike. "Tracking." *Lives on the Boundary: the Struggles and Achievements of America's Underprepared*. New York: Free Press, 1989: 24–30. Reprinted with permission of The Free Press, an imprint of Simon & Schuster Inc. Copyright © 1989 by Mike Rose.

Pages 116–122 Sacks, Oliver. "A Matter of Identity." *The Man Who Mistook His Wife for a Hat*. New York: Summit, 1985. 103–10. Copyright © 1970, 1981, 1983, 1984, 1985 by Oliver Sacks. Reprinted with the permission of Simon & Schuster, Inc.

National Review, Inc., 150 East 35th Street, New York, NY 10016. Reprinted by permission.

Pages 89–96 Walker, Alice. "Beauty: When the Other Dancer Is the Self." *In Search of Our Mothers' Gardens: Womanist Prose.* New York: Harcourt Brace Jovanovich, 1983. 361–70. Copyright © 1983 by Alice Walker, reprinted by permission of Harcourt Brace & Company.

Pages 486–487 Warhol, Andy. "What's Great About This Country." *The Philosophy of Andy Warhol: From A to B and Back Again.* New York: Harcourt Brace Jovanovich, 1975: 100–101. Copyright © 1975 by Andy Warhol. Reprinted by permission of Harcourt Brace & Company.

Pages 51–57 Waters, Mary C. "Names and Choice of Ancestry." *Ethnic Options: Choosing Identities in America.* Berkeley: University of California Press, 1990. 67–72. Reprinted by permission of the University of California Press and the author.

Pages 306–310 Wolff, Geoffrey. "Memories of My Father." *The Duke of Deception: Memories of My Father.* New York: Random House, 1979. 6–11. Copyright © 1979 by Geoffrey Wolff. Reprinted by permission of Random House, Inc.

Index